Buddhist Logic and Epistemology

Buddhist Logic and Epistemology

Studies in the Buddhist Analysis of Inference and Language

Edited by

Bimal Krishna Matilal
All Souls College, Oxford, U.K.

and

Robert D. Evans
University of Chicago, Chicago, Ill., U.S.A.

PRINTWORLD
Publishers of Indian Traditions

Cataloging in Publication Data — DK
[Courtesy: D.K. Agencies (P) Ltd. <docinfo@dkagencies.com>]

Buddhist logic and epistemology : studies in the Buddhist analysis of inference and language / edited by Bimal Krishna Matilal and Robert D. Evans.

p. cm.

Reprint. Originally published: Dordrecht : Kluwer Academic Publishers, 1986. (Studies of classical India ; v. 7)

Includes bibliogrpahical references and index.

ISBN: 9788124606384

1. Buddhist logic — Congresses. 2. Knowledge, Theory of (Buddhism) — Congresses. I. Matilal, Bimal Krishna. II. Evans, Robert D., 1953-

DDC 181.043 23

ISBN 13: 978-81-246-0638-4 **ISBN 10: 81-246-0638-2**

First Published in The Netherlands in 1986
Republished in India in 2012
with due permission and copyright release from D. Reidel Publishing Company, Dordrecht, Holland

Published and printed by:
D.K. Printworld (P) Ltd.
Regd. Office: 'Vedasri', F-395, Sudarshan Park
(Metro Station: Ramesh Nagar)
New Delhi-110 015
Phones: (011) 2545 3975; 2546 6019; *Fax*: (011) 2546 5926
E-mail: indology@dkprintworld.com
Website: www.dkprintworld.com

In memory of

Arnold Kunst

Preface

For the first time in recent history, seventeen scholars from all over the world (India, Japan, Europe, the United Kingdom, Canada and the United States) collaborated here to produce a volume containing an in-depth study of Buddhist logical theory in the background of Buddhist epistemology. The Tibetan tradition identifies this important chapter in the history of Buddhist philosophy as the *pramāṇa* school. It owes its origin to the writings of the great Buddhist master, Diṅnāga (*circa* CE 480-540), whose influence was to spread far beyond India, as well as to his celebrated interpreter of seventh century CE, Dharmakīrti, whose texts presented the standard version of the school for the later Buddhist and non-Buddhist authors for a long time.

The history of Buddhist and Indian logical and epistemological theories constitutes an interesting study not only for the Buddhist scholars but also for philosophers as well as historians of philosophy in general. Each author of this anthology combines historical and philological scholarship with philosophical acumen and linguistic insight. Each of them uses original textual (Tibetan or Sanskirt) material to resolve logical issues and philosophical questions. Attention has been focused upon two crucial philosophical concepts: *trairūpya* (the "triple" character of evidence) and *apoha* (meaning as "exclusion"). Broadly, the issues are concerned with the problems of inductive logic and the problem of meaning and universals. Besides, some authors address themselves to the general question: why and in what sense does logical theory become relevant to Buddhism, especially to the philosophical soteriology such as Mādhyamika?

Almost all the essays presented here were part of a seminar at Oxford organized by Bimal K. Matilal under the auspices of the International Association for Buddhist Studies in August 1982. Only two papers were written for the conference but not officially presented because the authors were unable to attend.

The Editors would like to thank Dr. Mark Siderits for preparing the index for this volume.

Contents

1

Buddhist Logic and Epistemology

Bimal Krishna Matilal

WHAT is called Buddhist logic and Epistemology here centres around two crucial concepts: *trairūpya* (the "triple-character" of inferential sign from which we derive inferential knowledge) and *apoha* (word-meaning as "exclusion" of other possibilities). The "triple-character" doctrine was formulated some time before Diṅnāga, but Diṅnāga articulated it and developed it in a systematic manner so as to influence the later logical theories.

Diṅnāga's theory of inference may briefly be stated as follows: When we infer some fact or item or characteristic belonging to some object on the basis of our knowledge of some other characteristic belonging to the same object the second characteristic (variously called *liṅga* or *hetu*, "inferential sign" or "indicator-reason") must have the "triple-character." The first characteristic is called the "inferable" (*sādhya*) or the fact to be proven or the characteristic to be established as belonging to the object in question. The object in question is called the *pakṣa*, which is sometimes translated as the subject of the inferred conclusion. For the sake of convenience, I shall call it the OBJECT or the *intended* OBJECT (using capital letters to distinguish it from the ordinary uses of "object"). Similarly, I shall call the "inferable" the intended or *provable* characteristic and the "indicator-reason" the obvious or *evidential* characteristic. A similar OBJECT can be defined in this context as an example or an object to which the intended characteristic is known to belong, and a dissimilar OBJECT may accordingly be defined as an object where the intended characteristic obviously does not belong. Now, the "triple-character" of the evidential characteristic (of the "evidence") is this:

1. The evidential characteristic must belong to the intended OBJECT.

2. It must belong to (at least) one similar OBJECT.

3. It must not belong to any dissimilar OBJECT.

The *apoha* or "exclusion" theory of meaning can be briefly understood as follows: Words or utterances of words behave as inferential signs in that they present to the hearer the knowledge of their meaning by *excluding* any dissimilar OBJECT where the intended meaning does not belong. More particularly, utterance of such common nouns as "cow" or "water" present to the hearer a knowledge of their meaning, a cow or water, not through any objective universal such as cowhood or waterhood, but through the exclusion of complement classes of non-cows or non-water. In modern terminology, we may say that according to the Buddhist logic by such general terms we do not assert genuine predicates of a thing, and that rather we DENY the supposition of all contrary predicates. "This is a cow" does not assert the cowhood of the subject; it denies that anything contrary to cowhood can be predicated of the subject. Properties contrary to cowhood are horsehood, elephanthood, treehood, etc. and those compatible with cowhood are animalhood, thinghood, having a colour and a shape, having motion, etc. The expression "cow" presents the object or the particular *meant* by it by denying only the contrary ones, but not the compatible ones.

In the above I have given a very rough characterization of the two doctrines. For several centuries, the Buddhist logicians disputed among themselves about the correct formulation of these two doctrines as well as their implication for Buddhist epistemology and ontology. In this introductory essay, I shall deal with a few problems connected with the correct formulation of the "triple character" and in the second part I shall show how the last component of the "triple- character" paved the way for the development of the *apoha* theory and in what sense the *apoha* was a Buddhist substitute for the objective universals of the realists, like the Naiyāyikas. In the third part, I shall present some documentation for my account by providing certain verses in translations from Dharmakīrti's *Pramāṇavārttika*. In the fourth part I shall very briefly deal with the Mādhyamika attitude towards the logical method called Buddhist Nyāya. In particular I shall try to analyse what Nāgārjuna said about the style of philosophizing that is embodied in the so-called logical or Nyāya method.

Generally speaking, we come to know something or some fact through direct apprehension or we may know it indirectly through our knowledge of something else. The direct apprehension arises often through our senses, such as an awareness of blue through the visual faculty. We are also directly aware of our "inner" episodes, such as pain or an awareness of pain. But our fund of knowledge is enriched more than ever by indirect knowledge, knowledge that we derive from knowing other things. If knowledge of one thing leads to the knowledge of another, we can call the second knowledge an episode of knowing through a sign or an indicator or "evidence."

On the basis of above consideration, the Buddhist view of knowledge denotes two kinds of knowledge — perceptual and non-perceptual. Both are understood to be the episodes of awareness that arise in us. There is however, no ownership of such episodes in the Buddhist theory, for a "person" is nothing but an "aggregate" constituted by such episodes and much else besides. Each awareness-episode is a discrete member of some awareness-series or the other. Hence we can say that each awareness-episode belongs to a particular awareness-series. (An awareness-series is only a continuous sequence of distinct awareness-episodes, which are connected causally in some relevant sense — the relevant sense being such that the latter is *dependent* upon the former for its "origination"). Hence only in a figurative language could we say that an awareness arises in a "person" or that a "person" owns the awareness.

In order to be a knowledge-episode, a cognitive awareness must be certain. This element of certainty is shared by both kinds of knowledge — perceptual and non-perceptual. There are however two ways of ensuring this certainty, the *direct* way and the *indirect* way. "Ensuring certainty" implies removing all doubts, i.e. all possibilities of error. It is argued that error creeps in as we let our mind, our fancy (imagination = *vikalpa*), take over. Hence the *direct* way to ensure certainty is to prevent the play of fancy before it sets in. Prevention is much better than cure. This is possible only when the pure sensory awareness presents the datum (we call it the "percept") untainted by any imaginative construction (or any play of fancy). This is therefore the first kind of knowledge, according to Diṅnāga : sensation or sense-perception. Each such sense-perception perceives also itself. Therefore, each perceptual event, according to Diṅnāga, has the following structure : [percept-perception (percept) — (self-) perception]. Each percept is a unique particular. Perception yields knowledge because the unique particular shines here in its own glory, uncoloured by any play of fancy, by any operation of the mind. This is the much-coveted epistemologist's foundation. For Diṅnāga, it is not simply a foundation; it is in fact knowledge *par excellence.*

There is however an *indirect* way of ensuring certainty, according to Diṅnāga. This is not a preventive measure as before, but a curative measure. The play of fancy is allowed to set in, but all possibilities of error are gradually removed. A doubt is transformed into a certainty when the grounds for doubt are all removed or destroyed. This can happen either through the employment of an inferential sign or the "indicator reason" (*liṅga*), or through a proper linguistic sign, an expression, a word (*śabda*). In both cases we would be dealing with a general notion of sign. It is through the route of a sign that we are led finally to the object, to the particular. Since we are not directly "sensorily" confronted with the object, we cannot take the direct route. We cannot prevent the operation of the mind before its play of fancy sets in. We in fact let our fancy play, and then use it to reach the required certainty. For example, inference yields knowledge when it is based upon adequate evidence. An evidence is adequate when it not only suggests that something may be the case but also excludes the possibility of the case's being otherwise. When an evidence is simply suggestive, we have a guess-work. When it goes further on to remove supposition of other possibilities, we have an inference.

How does a sign lead to the knowledge of the signified object? It would be highly uninteresting if we say that there will be a particular sign for each particular object, so that by seeing the sign we would know that the object is there. Seeing my friend's car parked outside, I know that my friend is in. But it is more interesting and non-trivial when we can talk about a general sign or a general feature shared by a number of particular objects. In the above case, we have to see not only the sign, but also, at least once, both the sign and the signified object together in order to learn that it is the sign of that object. In the latter case, we connect a general sign with a general concept under which several particular objects fall. In fact, the general aspect of the sign is connected with the general aspect of the objects concerned. Seeing, or obtaining, a particular sign, we consider its general aspect and from the general aspect of the sign we are led to the knowledge of the general aspect of the OBJECT. Our mind, our "imaginative" or constructive faculty, will take us this far. But if the connection between the general aspects is the *right* one (in the manner to be described below), then our knowledge of one general aspect will remove all rival possibilities or chances of all errors and therefore lead us to the certainty that there is a particular object there, an object that falls under that general concept.

What is a sign? Diṅnāga said that any object or characteristic can be the sign for a second object or characteristic, provided: (1) it has been observed to be with the second characteristic at least once, and (2) no example of the "contrary possibility" has been observed or cited. A contrary possibility would be a case where an instance of the sign is present but not the characteristic signified by it. The first condition could be called the "suggestion of the possibility," while the second the "exclusion of the (supposed) contrary possibility." Our knowledge of the sign will yield knowledge of the signified, provided certainty is reached through this dual procedure: the possibility is suggested yielding an "uncertain" awareness and then contrary possibilities are excluded yielding certainty.

Diṅnāga used the above theory of sign and the signified to show how, apart from sensory perception, inference and linguistic utterance yield knowledge in an *indirect* way. A body of smoke is observed with a body of fire suggesting the possibility of one being the sign for the other. This means that sighting of a fire or a body of smoke may lead to the arising of doubt : perhaps, there is also smoke (or fire, as the case may be) there. In such cases, the two conditions of the "triple conditioned" *hetu* or the inferential sign are fulfilled, according to Diṅnāga. Hence only a dubious awareness can be generated as a result. For certainty, we need the third condition called *vipakṣa-vyāvṛtti* or, in our language, the "exclusion of the supposed contrary possibilities." This needs an awareness about the absence of any example ("counter-example"), a case where the sign is present but the signifiable object is not. Now this also determines which one of the two, fire or smoke, in the previous example, could be the inferential sign or the indicator-reason and which one would be the signified object, the inferable characteristic. Examples of fire without smoke are easily available, but none of smoke without a fire. Hence, our sighting of a body of smoke suggesting the possibility of a fire makes it certain by excluding any contrary possibility, viz. that of there being smoke even when there is no fire.

The above way of putting matters as far as inference is concerned would raise problems for logicians; but with Diṅnāga, the epistemologist, this would be unproblematic. For the logicians, the inference of fire from smoke would be bound to arise from the relation that we have pinpointed as "exclusion of the contrary possibilities" (or, "absence of a counter-example"). But, some would argue, the above way of putting matters would be psychologizing logic. For logic, it does not really matter how a person argues or arrives at an inferential conclusion (by first noticing the suggestion of the possibility and thereby entertaining a doubt and then arriving at a certainty). It would be enough to say that *A* is a logical sign of *B*, provided *A* is such that no case of *A* is a case of non-*B*, or, what comes to the same thing, that every *A* is *B*. The only assumption needed here would be that there are *A*s and *B*s. In this way, it will be argued, logic can be freed from the fault of psychologism.

While I fully approve of the way logic is to be done, or is being done today without reference to psychological or epistemological implication, I would like to maintain that the above way of psychologizing logic is not a totally objectionable procedure. For, we are not interested here in the particular way a person infers or derives his conclusions, but rather in the general "impersonal" conditions or factors that give rise to knowledge-episodes and other awareness-episodes. Besides, each knowledge-episode is identified by virtue of what is "contained" in it or "grasped" by it, and not by virtue of its ownership. And what is contained in such knowledge is derived from what is expressed or expressible by a corresponding utterance or linguistic expression. Logic which seems to avoid psychologism deals, nevertheless, with sentences, utterances, statements or propositions. To be sure, utterances are no better than episodes (similar to our knowledge-episodes), and propositions are no worse than abstract entities. The Indian/Buddhist analysis of inference (*anumāna*) is admittedly a "causal" analysis in this way, but it is also a "logical" analysis, for the additional claim is that it is a part of the concept of inference (*anumāna*) that an inference-token is caused by the awareness-tokens of the sort already described.

Conceding in this way the charge of psychologizing logic (psychologism is not always a crime), we may return to Diṅnāga, the epistemologist. One of the traditional problems, that persisted for a long time in the history of Indian logic, is the following. Of the so-called triple-character of the inferential sign, the *hetu*, the indicator-reason: (1) the indicator-reason is to be present in the *intended* OBJECT; (2) it is to be present in a similar OBJECT; and (3) it is to be absent from any dissimilar OBJECT. However, it seems that not all three are jointly necessary. Even if 2 is not interpreted as "it is to be present in all similar OBJECTS," it seems clear that 1 and 3 together would be sufficient to make the indicator-reason adequate to generate a sound inference. This apparently falsifies Diṅnāga's insistence upon the necessity of 2 along with 1 and 3 as constituting the required sufficient condition of the indicator-reason or inferential sign.

I have already said that part of our problem arises as soon as we switch from epistemology to logic. In epistemology, our problem is to find how certainty is to be attached to an awareness-episode, when the said *direct* route to certainty, direct perception disallowing the "mind" or the play of fancy to operate, is not available. It is to be observed that an awareness-episode may very well be true or fact-corresponding, even when it lacks the required certainty. For it lacks certainty when and only when proper evidence or argument cannot be given. But this does not affect the fact of its being true. The epistemological enterprise is to supply the required evidence or argument, so that without such evidence we may not attach the required certainty to a false awareness. (For very often we feel sure even of our false awareness.) Thus, if the proper evidence or argument can be adduced, we can eliminate *false* psychological certainty, and arrive at what we may now call "logical" certainty. Psychological certainty is simply subjective, while logical certainty is both psychological and supported by evidence or reason. (This is however an extension of the term "logical"as it is used in today's philosophical discourse. But this use is not entirely counter-intuitive.)

In inference, knowledge of the indicator-reason or the inferential characteristic *A* characterizing the intended OBJECT leads to a knowledge of the inferable characteristic *B*. First, we have to grant that the knowledge of *A* characterizing the same intended OBJECT or OBJECTS must be certain if it has to yield certainty in our awareness of *B* characterizing the same intended OBJECT. The situation is this: certainty of *A* characterizing the particular intended OBJECT coupled with some additional information will yield certainty of *B* characterizing the same intended OBJECT. This additional information comes from our previous knowledge. We usually call this process induction. An assumption is made; if a rule or pattern emerges from previous knowledge or examined cases we may hold it true also for the unexamined case under consideration. Therefore, if previous knowledge yields that the contrary possibilities (possibilities of there being *A* without there being *B*) are absent, we may hold the same to be true in the unexamined case or cases under consideration. In this way, the indicator-reason *A* will fulfil the third and the first condition of a proper sign and hence we may reach the required certainty. But Diṅnāga insisted that something more is needed as the additional information from previous knowledge in order to lead us to the required certainty: condition 2. In other words, exclusion of contrary possibilities is not enough. Information about an actual case of co-occurrence of *A* and *B* in a place, or an example is to be supplied from previous knowledge in order to ensure the required certainty. Why? Is it not enough to know that there cannot be absence of *B* in the present place, i.e. the case under consideration (i.e. the intended OBJECT), for there is *A*? What, in other words, did Diṅnāga have in mind when he insisted that the second condition is necessary.

A tentative answer is the following. We find it easier to collect from previous knowledge some information about a co-occurrence of *A* with *B* than the information about the exclusion of the contrary possibilities. Hence we can imagine that the citation of a case of co-occurrence would bring us nearer to certainty. That is to say, a doubt whether there is *B* or not would be brought within the range of possibility. Next, the exclusion of contrary possibilities would assign the required certainty. This answer seems plausible if we regard Diṅnāga as being concerned here only with psychology of inference, and not with logic. But I would now argue that this answer is wrong, for Diṅnāga cited definite examples where such gradual steps, viz. doubt — possibility — certainty, have not been marked separately. This leads us to the consideration of those particular examples where contrary possibilities are eliminated but it is not possible to obtain examples of co-occurrence from previous knowledge. For in such cases, *A* is such that it could be and is present only in the given places, i.e. the intended OBJECTS. In other words, *A* is a unique mark or characteristic of the *pakṣa*, the unexamined but intended OBJECT. I shall now deal with illustrations to make the issue clear.

Imagine the following dialogue:

M — Rāma was born at midnight on 31 January 1970, at a town called Dee (and he was the only child born there at the moment).

N — Oh! Then Rāma must be a happy man.

M — Why?

N — I have never seen a man born on that date in that town to be unhappy.

M — But, have you seen such a man to be happy?

Is the last question a stupid one? If not, then we might have resolved a problem that is faced by any modern interpreter of Diṅnāga's theory of inference based upon what he called the "triple-character" *hetu*. For rewrite the above as:

M — *a* has *A*.

N — Oh! Then *a* has *B*.

M — Why?

N — I have never seen something having *A* but not having *B*.

M — But, have you seen something having *A* along with *B*?

I shall explain that here *M* may be simply insisting, as Diṅnāga did, that all the three characters of the *trairūpya* doctrine are jointly needed to give the sufficient condition for an adequate *hetu* or inferential characteristic. This example, however, is purely fictitious. Let us now discuss examples which Diṅnāga cited.

The fifth type of inference in Diṅnāga's *Hetucakra* (scheme of nine model inferences of which only two are sound and the other two are decisively incorrect and unsound and the remaining five are inconclusive and undecidable) is :

Sound is imperishable because it is audible.

This is called the uniquely inconclusive one (*asādhāraṇa*). To underline the problem involved let us consider another example:

P1. Sound has impermanence, for it has soundhood (or audibility).

It does not seem counter-intuitive to say that soundhood or being sound (a noise) cannot be the logical mark or basis for inferring impermanence. If, however, we reformulate the argument as given below, and as is the practice of most modern writers on the history of Indian logic, it seems logically impeccable.

P2. Whatever is a sound or is audible is impermanent. This is audible (a sound). *Ergo*, this is impermanent.

I submit that P2 cannot be a proper reformulation of P1. For P1 does not want to show, as P2 wrongly assumes, that a particular case is a case of sound (an audible object) and therefore it is impermanent. Rather, it tries to show that all cases of sound are impermanent, for they are simply cases of sound. I shall therefore dismiss P2 as a reformulation of P1, and consider only P1 instead. It should also be noted, in the light of my previous comments, that the proposition "Sound is impermanent" may very well be true or the awareness that sound is impermanent may be fact-corresponding, but Diṅnāga's claim here is simply that it lacks the required logical certainty (in the sense defined earlier).

We can now face the question of justifying this claim. If the contrary possibility of something being a sound and not being impermanent has been excluded by the information available from previous knowledge (i.e. by available information), why can't we decide that sound (all cases of sound) is impermanent? Here we reach the crux of the matter. We have to remember that all cases of sound are not (at least, in principle) part of the available information. They lie out-side the domain which is constituted by available information. We are only certain of one more thing: sounds are sounds, or have soundhood, (or have audibility). This is an a priori certainty. But this does not guarantee that cases (instances) of sound are the kind of things of which such properties as impermanence and permanence are predicable. It could be that sounds are neither. Such a guarantee is available only if we could cite a case, independently of the present situation, where both the indicator-reason and the inferable characteristic are together, and thereby show that the present case is similar to such a case. This is, therefore, part of the justification for Diṅnāga for not being totally satisfied with the exclusion of contrary possibilities (*vipakṣasattva*), and this is why he insisted upon the citation of a similar case or a similar OBJECT, (*sapakṣasattva=sādharmyadṛṣṭānta*). P1 may accordingly be declared as inconclusive or uncertain. It is therefore not a deductively valid argument (as P2 is). It is uncertain because it is quite a different sort of argument, whose certainty is not determinable. From the available information, we may deny the possibility of sound's being imperishable, but we may also deny in the same way the contrary possibility of sound's being perishable, for no further evidence is available (unless we can take an actual sound-token into consideration and regard its perishability as part of our body of information) to tilt the balance in favour of either of these two.

The above discussion raises many fundamental philosophical and logical issues — issues connected with induction, with the meaning of negation, logical negation and contraposition, contraries and contradictories, possibility and certainty. I do not wish to enter into these issues here while I admit that they are all relevant questions. Briefly, I would note a couple of points. Among other things, the above justification assumes that lack of togetherness of *A* with non-*B*s does not ensure togetherness of *A* with *B*. As Richard Hayes has rightly stated (see his paper below), while "Every *A* is *B*" may presuppose (as it does in the interpretation of the Aristotelian syllogistic) that there are *A*s, "No *A* is non-*B*" may not, in the present theory, presuppose that there is at least one *A* which is also *B*.

It may be noted here that part of the problem is connected with the confirmation of induction. For Diṅnāga insisted (in the account of the second type of inference noted in his *Hetucakra*) that to confirm that all products are perishable or impermanent we need not only a perishable product, such as a pot, as a positively supporting example, but also a non-perishable non-product, such as the sky, as a negatively supporting example (cf. *vaidharmyadṛṣṭānta*). The puzzle here is reminiscent of C. G. Hempel's puzzle in a similar context, viz. confirmation of an induction.[1] Just as each black raven tends to confirm that all ravens are black so each green leaf, being a non-block non-raven, should confirm that all non-black things are non-ravens (which is equivalent to saying that all ravens are black).

For Diṅnāga however, one can propose the following resolution of the puzzle. Taking some liberty with the notion of negation and contraposition, one may say that for Diṅnāga while "All ravens are black" implies "All non-black things are non-ravens," it is not equivalent to the latter. In other words, the latter may not imply the former. For suppose all black ravens are destroyed from the face of the earth. It will still be true that all non-black things are non-ravens, for there will be green leaves, etc. to certify it, but "All ravens are black" need not be held true at least under one interpretation of such a universal proposition. (For there are no ravens to confirm it!) This also means that in Diṅnāga's system we will have to assume that only universal affirmative propositions carry existential presupposition.

If we view matters in this way, we can find an explanation why Diṅnāga insisted that both a *positive* and a *negative* example are needed to confirm the required inference: sound is perishable because it is a product. It seems to explain also why in the above example, P1, it is claimed that because of the lack of a positive example to confirm that each audible fact is perishable, the inference (certainty of the conclusion) is not decidable. We may notice that Diṅnāga did supply the so-called negative example in each of the three cases in his *Hetucakra* to confirm the assertion "No non-*B* is *A*."

---

1. Carl Gustav Hempel, *Aspects of Scientific Explanation and Other Essays* (New York: Free Press, 1965), p. 15.

But why this stricture upon "All audibles are perishable"? Why can it not be implied by "All non-perishable things are non-audible?" One may think that we need to be sure that there are audible things before we can assert that all audibles are perishable. But this will not do. For if we admit the first character of the "triple-character" of the reason we have to allow that there are audible things, for we have admitted that sounds or noises are audible. Hence the previous consideration for disallowing equivalence between "All audibles are perishable" and "All non-perishable things are non-audible" does not arise in the context of the given inference. Then why this insistence? An answer to this puzzle is not easily forthcoming from the tradition of the Buddhist logicians after Diṅnāga.

A tentative suggestion may be given. Suppose that "audible" and "perishable" have only their contraries in such formulations as "inaudible" and "non-perishable." This means that there may be things which are neither audible nor inaudible. The "audible-inaudible" predication applies to the domain of only percepts: colour and shape, sound, smell, taste and touch. Further, suppose that the domain of perishable-imperishable things may not lie wholly within the domain of audible-inaudible things. In this case it would be possible that some imperishable things (or even a perishable thing) could be neither audible or inaudible! It is not always counterintuitive to say that non-perishable things such as the sky or the soul are very different sorts of things to which neither audibility nor inaudibility will apply. In this case it may be trivially true (allowing some ambiguity in the notion of negation) that no non-perishable things are audible. But confirmation of this trivial truth will not remove the said doubt whether an audible thing is perishable or not. For it may be neither! Such a dubious possibility is removed only if we can cite an example which is both audible and perishable (or imperishable, as the case may be). If we believe that a particular instance of sound is both audible and perishable then citing such a supporting example we can decide that sound is perishable. This way of citing an example from the domain of the *pakṣa* (which should ideally remain in the twilight zone of doubt until the inference is concluded) to support the *vyāpti* relation is called the *antarvyāptisamarthana.* This was a later development in the post-Diṅnāga period.[2]

The above defence of Diṅnāga is admittedly very weak. But Diṅnāga the epistemologist, was concerned with both the certainty over all possible doubt and the confirmation of induction. Since he claims that the "negative" example is not enough and a "positive" example is needed for the required certainty, he must deny that "All ravens are black" is in any way implied by "All non-black things are non-ravens." This denial forces us to search for a possible situation which may not have been eliminated. Suppose "non-black" in my dictionary means white. It will still be true that all non-black things are non-ravens, which may be confirmed by a white crane. Further suppose that I have never seen a raven and that I imagine that they are neither black nor white, they are *grey.* Only an actual black raven can remove my doubt in this case. The oddity implicit in such a consideration is not any more serious than the oddity in assuming that a green leaf confirms the rule "All ravens are black," or even in claiming that certain predicates are projectible in the sense of N. Goodman,[3] while the complements of such predicates need not be so.[4]

I have tried to show that there is a deep philosophical problem that is implied by a rather odd claim by Diṅnāga: "a positive example" is still necessary even when there is a

2. See Kamaleswar Bhattacharya, "Some Thoughts on *Antarvyāpti, Bahirvyāpti,* and *Trairūpya,*" this volume.

3. N. Goodman, *Fact, Fiction and Forecast* (Cambridge, Mass.: Harvard University Press, 1955), pp. 156-60.

4. See W.V. Quine, "Natural Kinds," in S.P. Schwartz, *Naming, Necessity, and Natural Kinds* (Ithaca: Cornell University Press, 1977), p. 156.

negatively supporting example. It is obvious from Diṅnāga's writing that he was never comfortable with such so-called "negative" example (where no "positive" example is available for citation). What I have stated here is, I think, compatible with what S. Katsura has recently argued.[5] Katsura cites two passages from Diṅnāga (*PSV*(K) 149b3-5, 150b5) where it is clearly said that a "negative" example may be unnecessary if the *vyāpti* "invariance" relation is supported by a "positive" example and if the two examples are "well known" either would be sufficient for they imply each other. I interpret that these comments of Diṅnāga are concerned with the cases that are called *anvaya-vyatirekin* (in Nyāya), i.e. cases where both (a "positive" and a "negative") examples are available (*prasiddha* "well known") but not both of them may be cited in the argument-schema. In other words, these comments do not concern the "limiting" cases where a "negative" example is cited simply because no positive example is even available (cf. *vyatirekin* or *kevala-vyatirekin* and the *asādhāraṇa* in the *Hetucakra*). The *asādhāraṇa* or "uniquely inconclusive" evidence (no. 5 in the *Hetucakra*) is such a limiting case. For Diṅnāga, both the *asādhāraṇa* and the *vyatirekin* (which is claimed to be correct by Nyāya) are equally inconclusive for similar reasons (absence of a citable positive example to support the induction).

2

In the above I have been mainly concerned with the exact significance of the so-called second character of the "triple-character" of the indicator-reason or the inferential sign. Many post-Diṅnāga writers found this to be redundant from a logical point of view, and it was generally admitted that the first character (which transpires as *pakṣadharmatā* in the Nyāya system) along with the third (which becomes another description of the *vyāpti* relation) would be sufficient to yield correct inferential

5. S. Katsura, "Diṅnāga on Trairūpya," *Journal of Indian and Buddhist Studies* 32 (1984).

knowledge. In this section, I shall concentrate upon the third character in order to show how Diṅnāga extended his theory of inference to include also his theory about how to derive knowledge from language or words and this gave rise to the celebrated Buddhist doctrine of *apoha*, or exclusion of rival possibilities, as an explication for universals. The general sign, whether inferential or linguistic, leads us to the knowledge of the signifiable object provided it is (empirically) established that the former is excluded from whatever excludes the latter, the signifiable object.

Perception yields knowledge of the particulars. Knowledge from the sign, i.e. from inference and language, is always about the general. We cannot know the particulars in this way. From my knowledge of the inferential sign, a body of smoke, there arises my knowledge of fire in that place (the *pakṣa*), i.e. my knowledge that the place excludes connection with non-fire. Our non-perceptual knowledge based upon the sign cannot be more definite than this sort of general connection. We cannot, for example, know what particular fire-body is there in the place from simply seeing the smoke that is there, but we can only ascertain that the hill (the place) is, at least, not without fire (i.e. it is not the case that the hill lacks fire; cf. *ayoga-vyavaccheda*). Similarly, from the word "fire" (i.e. the utterance of the word "fire") the hearer has a knowledge of the object referred to only in some general way. The hearer becomes aware that the object referred to is not something that is non-fire. The sign "fire" (the word) certifies simply the lack of connection of the intended object with non-fire. Just as the knowledge of smoke (the inferential sign) leads to our knowing that the hill lacks the connection with some fire-body, knowledge of the word "fire" leads to our knowing the object of reference as excluded from non-fire. Just as from smoke we cannot know what particular fire-body is there, from the word "fire" too we cannot know a particular fire-body but only that something excludes non-fire.

If by the meaning (*artha*) of a word we understand what the hearer knows from hearing the utterance of it then "fire" can be said to MEAN "exclusion of non-fire" or "what excludes non-fire."

After underlining the similarity between both the ways an inferential sign and a linguistic sign yield knowledge of the *signified*, Diṅnāga argued that this would be a reasonable course to take in order to dispense with the objective universals of the Naiyāyikas (or at least a large number of such universals) as ontological entities, distinct from the particulars. It is easy, for example, to assume that because common names, i.e. kind-names and material-names, are applied to different and distinct particulars, we must posit some common or shared character, shared by the group of particulars to which they are applied. Realists like the Naiyāyikas regard these shared characters (kind-properties or fundamental class-properties), at least some of them, to be not only real but also distinct from the individuals that instantiate them. This has traditionally been understood as the problem of universals. For if we assume, as the Naiyāyikas do, that a shared character such as "cowhood" or "firehood" is a distinct reality locatable or manifested in a particular then we are further required to assume a suitable relation that would make manifestation of one reality in another possible. In other words, there should be a relation which will make it possible for one reality, cowhood, to be located in another, a cow. The Naiyāyikas' answer is that there is such a relation, *samavāya*, which we translate, in the absence of a better word in English, by "inherence." This relation combines real universals with particulars. This raises many intricate questions. For example, how can a real entity be shared by many real and distinct entities, and still be one and the same? How can one and the same entity be present in many disconnected and different spatio-temporal locations? What happens to such an entity if and when all its particular manifestations are extinct? Whenever a new set of similar entities (artefacts) are manufactured, do we thereby create new (objective) universals? And so on and so forth.

In simple language, the familiar problem of universals arises in this way. We would generally say that there are cows, and pots, there is water, fire, gold and so on. In effect this means that there are distinct (identifiable) individuals (in this world) to which we apply the term "cow" or "fire." We need a philosophical explanation to answer the obvious question: what warrants us (i.e. becomes the *nimitta* for us) to apply such terms the way we do apply such terms, to different individuals? Words, to use the modern style, either denote or designate objects, yes. But is there any basis, causal or otherwise, which we can call the *nimitta*, for such designation or denotation? What accounts for the use of the same term to designate different particulars? For if there is none, language-learning would be for the most part an unexplained mystery.

Some philosophers would like to treat the above question as only a rhetorical question, the answer to which is obvious. For it will be claimed that there is some *unity* among the disparate entities denoted by a term, the unity that provides the *nimitta*, i.e. that accounts for the application of the term in question. This *unity* may not be regarded as an ontologically real entity distinct from each individual that has it. If such *nimitta*s or "bases," i.e. the purported unities, are observable criteria (as happens in most cases), then the problem is easily resolved. King Daśaratha had three wives, and hence these three individuals shared the feature, being married to Daśaratha, by which we may only refer back to the three observable events of marriage. But, for most of our basic terms such a device is not at all available. To sustain the claim that the purported unities in such cases are distinct realities has been one of the hardest problems in philosophy. And yet one has nagging doubt as to whether the full-fledged nominalistic programme can succeed. In fact, it seems more tolerable if one can maintain that the so-called abstract universals, those unities, are neither full-blown realities, as the Naiyāyikas and some other realists would like to have them, nor totally dispensable concepts. In this matter, the Buddhist of the Diṅnāga-Dharmakīrti school seems to suggest a way out. This is called the *apoha* doctrine. It is regarded as an epistemological resolution of an ontological problem. The point is the following. We need not accept universals as real and distinct entities merely on the basis of the familiar argument that has been sketched here, unless of course there are other compelling reasons to believe in such entities. Our ability to use the same term to denote different individuals presupposes our knowledge or awareness of sameness or similarity or some shared feature in those individuals. This shared feature may simply be our agreement about what these individuals are not, or what kinds of terms cannot be applied to them. "This is a cow" denies simply such predicates as cannot be predicated of the object in question. True, we talk here in terms of a broader indefinite class on each occasion. The cow is said to be excluded from the class of non-cows, and the white lotus from both the class of non-white and that of non-lotus.[6] But such classes (the so-called complement classes) are constructible each time with the help of the particular linguistic sign (the word) we use on each occasion. They are arguably less substantial and less objective than the *positive* classes such as the class of cows or the class of lotuses or the class of blue things. For in the latter cases, there is a tendency in us to believe further that there are objective class-properties shared by, and locatable in, the members of such classes. If these objective class-properties are explained in terms of some other realities that we do concede, well and good. In our previous example, "being married to King Daśaratha" did not present any problem. Similarly we can, for example, say that the university studentship is only a convenient way of talking about a bundle of particular

---

6. On this point, see my *Logical and Ethical Issues of Religious Belief* (Calcutta: University of Calcutta, 1982), pp. 91-112.

facts, admission of each person in university as a student. But in some cases the so-called objective property tends to be a unitary abstract property, a full-blown real universal and thereby invites all the other problems that go along with it. In the case of *constructed* class of non-cows, the search for a common property as an objective class-property is less demanding, for it is clear from the beginning that we cannot find any objective property (except the trivial one, non-cowness) to be shared equally by horses, cats and tables. The programme for finding such a common property is, so to say, "shot" from the beginning. We may note that the trivial property, the lack of non-cowness or denotability by "cow," is constructible on each occasion and hence it is a "conditional" or conceptual property.

If the above argument is sound, then we have captured at least part of the Buddhist philosophical motivation for developing the *apoha* doctrine as a viable alternative to the doctrine of real universals. It is also true that in constructing the so-called "negative" classes, we implicitly depend upon the notion of some "positive" class-property. For how can one talk about the class of non-cows without having the notion of the class of cows? (In modern terminology we call the class of non-cows the "complement" class in order to underline this dependence upon the initial class of cows.) This is, in substance, part of the criticism of Kumārila and Uddyotakara against the Buddhists.

A tentative answer is the following. We can formulate or construct the class of non-cows as the class of those entities where the term "cow" is *not* applicable. True, the word "cow" itself is a universal. But we do not have to accept any objective universal such as cowhood over and above the word "cow." (This coincides with the Nominalist's intuition that words are the only universals that we may have to concede. This is also partly Bhartṛhari's intuition about universals when he talks about word-universal (*śabda-jāti*) and object-universal (*artha-jāti*) and makes the latter only a projection of the former. (But this will take us beyond the scope of this introductory essay).[7] We can actually define our "negative" class as one constructible on the occasion of the use of each substantial word in terms of the word itself. Once this is done, a search for the common unitary class property (a real one) is not warranted any more, unless there is some other compelling reason. This is not pure nominalism, for word-universals are admitted.

There may be another alternative answer, which may not amount to a very different sort of consideration. Each non-perceptual awareness of a cow (which follows, and is inextricably confused with, the pure sensory perception of a cow-particular) has a common "cow-appearance" (*go-pratibhāsa*). We may treat this as the shared feature of the all distinct events of our non-perceptual awareness of cows. This would be similar to a *type* of which each awareness-event (of a cow) would be *token*. Now the class of non-cows can be redefined as the class of non-cow-appearance, which may then be explained as the class of items that are not connected with the awareness-events having cow-appearance. Now the origin of this cow-appearance or appearance of the cow-form (distinct from the appearance of the object, the particular, in the perceptual awareness) belonging to the non-perceptual awareness, can be traced to our desire to conceptualize and verbalize, i.e. to sort out distinct awareness-events and make them communicable. This becomes possible due to the availability of the concept "cow" and the word "cow." In this consideration also we move closer to the Bhartṛhari thesis about language, according to which words and concepts are implicitly and inextricably mixed up so much so that a concept is nothing but an implicit speech-potential, a not-yet-spoken word.

This cow-appearance or cow-form is no part of the objective reality which we sensorily perceive but it is supposed or

7. See also Radhika Herzberger, "*Apoha and Śiṁśapāvṛkṣa*," this volume.

imagined to be there. Hence it is less substantial than such an objective universal as cowhood, which it is meant to replace. This suggested paraphrase of "cowhood" by "denial of or exclusion of non-cow predication" may be regarded as philosophic reparsing. [We can take this paraphrase to be somewhat like the "paraphrasis" in Jeremy Bentham's theory of fiction. As W.V. Quine has noted, this is a method which enables a philosopher, when he is confronted with some term that is convenient but ontologically embarrassing, to continue to enjoy the services of the term while disclaiming its denotation.[8]] Diṅnāga's motivation in explaining cowhood as exclusion of non-cows was not very far behind. For indeed Dharmakīrti found the real universals of Nyāya ontologically embarrassing and suggested that they can be conveniently explained away by using the notion of "exclusion" and "otherness." Again, this is not pure nominalism.

It is true that the so-called non-perceptual awareness of a cow is sequentially connected with the sensory perception of a particular. But, for the Buddhists, this is a contingent connection, the latter awareness being contingent upon our desire, purpose, inclination, etc. as has already been emphasized. The same thing for example, can be called a doorstopper, a brick, an artefact, a work of art, or a murder instrument, depending upon the motivation of the speaker. The cow-appearance, or the cow-form, the common factor, becomes part of the latter "non-perceptual" awareness only when our perception becomes contaminated by some such motivation or other and thereby becomes impregnated with conceptions and latent speech-potentials. If we are motivated to obtain milk we call it a cow, if we are motivated otherwise we call it a beast, and if we are motivated, for example, to protect our flower-beds we may call it a nuisance.

---

8. W.V. Quine, *Theories and Things* (Cambridge: Harvard University Press, 1981), pp. 68-69.

Word-application or concept-application is an important part of our mental faculty. It is called by Diṅnāga (and others) *vikalpa* or *kalpanā*, "imagination," "conceptual construction," "imaginative construction." This is a means for identifying and distinguishing the percept or the "representation" of the object in perception. This distinguishing activity is performed with the help of words (or concepts, if one wishes). Conception, for the Buddhist, is a negative act. It is the exclusion or rejection of the imagined or supposed possibilities. Concept-application should thereby be reinterpreted as rejection of contrary concepts, and word-application similarly as rejection of contrary words. Non-contrary words need not be excluded. Therefore we can apply "cow" and "white" to what we call a white cow, "fire" and "hot" or "fire" and "substance" likewise to a fire-body. For these are not contrary pairs. Application of words makes us presuppose contrary possibilities only in order to reject them later. We may apply "a product" to remove the doubt whether the thing under consideration is a non-product or not, and we may apply "impermanent" to the same thing in order to eliminate the possibility of its being permanent. Hence the two terms "a product" and "impermanent" are not synonymous in spite of their being applied to the same object or objects. In fact, true synonymity is a hard thing to achieve in this theory. Two words can be synonymous not because there is some common objective universal which they mean, but because they may serve to exclude the same contrary possibilities (see *Tattvasaṁgraha* of Śāntarakṣita, verses 1032-33).

Dharmakīrti and his followers developed a theory of dual object for each awareness, perceptual or non-perceptual. One is what is directly grasped and called the "apprehensible" (*grāhya*) and the other is what is ascertained through the first and is called the "determinable" (*adhyavaṣeya*). In a perceptual awareness the apprehensible object is the datum or the particular whereas the determinable object is such a concept as cowhood, and therefore we pass the verbal judgement "It is a cow." In a non-perceptual (inferential or linguistic) awareness the apprehensible object is the concept cowhood, and the "determinable" is a particular. In the awareness arising from the utterance of the word "cow" what we apprehend is cowhood or cow-appearance or cow-form and what we *determine* through it is the (external) object "out there" whereupon we superimpose the cow-appearance or cowhood.

This cow-appearance or cowhood is to be interpreted as exclusion of non-cows. Thus in the so-called perceptual judgement "It is a cow" we determine that it is not a non-cow or that it excludes our non-cow supposition. In the inference or in the knowledge from the linguistic sign "cow," we like-wise apprehend (directly) the exclusion of non-cows, which is then attributed or superimposed (cf. *āropa*) upon the "determinable" object, the external thing, which we *determine* as excluding our non-cow supposition. In other words, hearing the word "cow" we not only apprehend cowhood but also determine an external object as being excluded from non-cows and such determination in its turn prompts us to act, i.e. to proceed to get hold of the cow-particular which will give us milk, etc. This answers the question about how are we prompted to act from simply a word-generated knowledge of the phony universal.

To sum up, it must be admitted that the Buddhist substitute *anyāpoha* (exclusion of the other), has a clear advantage over the Naiyāyikas' objective universal such as cowhood. Since "exclusion" is not construed as a separate reality, we need not raise the question of how it is related to what by its own nature excludes others. Exclusion of non-cows is a shared feature of all cows and therefore can very well be the "basis" for the application of the general term "cow." It is not absolutely clear whether talking in terms of the "exclusion" class, that of non-cows, has any clear advantage over our talking about the class of cows, i.e. the positive class. It is however clear that formation of the "exclusion" class, that of non-cows, is ad hoc and dependent upon the occasion of each use of the general term. It is more clearly an artificially formed class without any illusion about any underlying common property (a positive one) to be shared by its members. Furthermore, there is the denial rather than assertion of the membership of this artificially formulated class in the final analysis of the use of such general terms. It seems to me that this device satisfactorily explains the use of the general terms at least without necessarily assuming objective universals. But whether or not we usually learn the use of such terms in this way is, however, another matter. Diṅnāga has said:

> The theory that the meaning (*artha*) of a word is exclusion of other "meanings" (*artha*) is correct because there is an excess of advantage (*guṇa*) in this view. For the characters of the objective universal, e.g. being a unity it is manifested fully in many (distinct things), can apply to "exclusion" since such exclusions are also nondistinct (a unity) in each case, and they do not have to vanish (being supportless) when the objects (individuals) vanish, and they are manifested fully in many.
>
> — Quoted by Kamalaśīla, under verse 1000, p. 389

Notions such as "exclusion," "otherness," or "similarity" are not however dispensable even in this theory.

It may be noted here that the Naiyāyikas would also maintain that not all general terms would need objective universals as the "basis" for their application. The term "chef" for example can be applied to different persons and the so-called basis for such application can be easily identified as similar objective particulars in each case, training in the culinary art, the action of cooking, etc. Objective universals are posited sometimes to account for natural kinds, water, cows, etc. Sometimes it helps to explain causal connection (cf. *kāraṇatāvacchedaka*, and *kāryatāvacchedaka* in Navya-Nyāya) such as one between seedhood and sprouthood (to explain that from each seed comes out some sprout or other). Sometimes admission of objective universals helps scientific taxonomy. Besides, objective universals are posited when we reach certain fundamental concepts such as substance, quality and action. Objective universals can be treated as "unredeemed notes" as Quine has called them: "the theory that would clear up the unanalyzed underlying similarity notion in such cases is still to come."[9] In Quine's view, they remain disreputable and practically indispensable and when they become respectable being explained by some scientific theory they turn in principle superfluous.

3

What I have argued here to throw some light upon the *apoha* and the *trairūpya* doctrine, seems to receive the required support from Dharmakīrti in his *Pramāṇavārttika, Svārthānumāna,* to which we must now turn:

> Verse 18. If (mere) non-observation proves absence then why (it was claimed by Diṅnāga that) the "inductive" evidence could be non-conclusive? Even a "negative" evidence could be a (proper) inferential sign. And the interpretation of *asiddhi* (as given by Diṅnāga) should not have been given.

Note : An "inductive" evidence is one where the characteristic to be cited as evidence is not (simply) observed to be present where the inferable characteristic is not present. There is thus agreement only in absence. Dharmakīrti explained and refuted inferences based upon such inconclusive "inductive" evidence in the same chapter, verses 14, 15. Three arguments are given here to show that the "positive" example is necessary in Diṅnāga's system (i.e. to show why induction based upon mere non-observation is not enough):

(a) Diṅnāga attacked the *Nyāyasūtra*'s *śeṣavat* type of inference as inconclusive. According to one interpretation, it is an inference based upon an induction which is supported

9. Quine, "Natural Kinds," p. 174.

simply by absence of counter-example, i.e. supported only by the citation of examples where both the sign and the signified are *observed to be absent.* (See Vātsyāyana under *Nyāyasūtra* 1.1.5.) For mere non-observation cannot remove the doubt about the possibility of a counter-example. It may be that the sign is such that it would be absent also from those cases where the supposed inferable characteristic (*sādhya*) is present.

(b) According to Diṅnāga, a "negative" evidence is not conclusive. An inferential sign is a "negative" evidence if we try to prove that something is *B* because it is *A* on the basis of a "negative" premise: All that is not *B* is not *A*. We might have inductive support for this "negative" premise for indeed we can find instances (supporting examples) which are both not *B* and not *A*, but we cannot have inductive support for the "positive" (contraposed) premise; Each *A* is *B*. In other words, if we do not know and cannot cite an instance (supporting example) which is both *A* and *B*, our evidence is inconclusive. To illustrate, consider the old Nyāya inference: Living bodies have souls, for they have life. The Buddhist may concede (the premise) that whatever lacks a soul lacks life, supported by a pot which lacks both. But this cannot warrant the (contraposed) premise that whatever has life has a soul, unless of course we know (prior to the inference) and can cite an instance which has both life and soul. This shows Diṅnāga's stricture on contraposition. From the "positive" we may infer the "negative," but from the "negative" we may not infer the "positive."

(c) If mere non-observation proved absence, then Diṅnāga did not have to explain different types of "unestablished" sign, one of which is the case where the purported sign's presence in the *vipakṣa* is only doubtful, but not observed.

Verse 19: (Further) even the "unique" sign (*viśeṣa= asādhāraṇa*) would be appropriate to exclude both (the "signifiable" property and its absence, permanence and impermanence) based on (simple) non-observation. If such exclusion of both (presence and absence) is contradicted by other evidence (absence and presence being incompatible), then it is shown that non-observation does not prove absence.

Note: A "unique" sign is one which is the unique characteristic of the *pakṣa* (the intended OBJECT, where the inferable characteristic is not yet known to be present). It does not characterize anything else. For example, sound is a permanent entity because it has soundhood. Now absence of soundhood is found to be associated with both permanence and its absence, e.g. the sky and a pot. Hence if simple non-observation were enough, soundhood could prove the existence of both permanence and impermanence in sound. If it is argued that it is contradictory to say that something is both permanent and impermanent then it proves a fortiori that the "unique" inferential sign is in this way inconclusive. In my opinion, this leaves open to the possibility of sound being neither. And since such a possibility, although a remote one, is not blocked (excluded) by the "unique" sign, it is said to be inconclusive by Diṅnāga. Karṇagomin gives a slightly different interpretation. Further Dharmakīrti notes:

Verse 26: Therefore in the citation of the "negative" example, the existence of its substratum (*āśraya*) need not be taken into account (seriously), for the "contra-positive" (the fact of the absence of the signifiable in the absence of the sign) is understood even from the statement that if one (the signifiable) is absent the other (the sign) is also absent.[10]

10. The translation by Mookerjee and Nagasaki is misleading here. See Dharmakīrti, *The Pramāṇavārttikam*, tr. S. Mookerjee and H. Nagasaki (Patna: Nava Nalanda, 1964).

Note: The point here seems to be that if "Each *A* is *B*" is true and supported by some "positive" example, then "All non-*B*s are non-*A*s" may be taken to be true although we may lack a *real* example which is both non-*A* and non-*B* to support it. This seems to be a volte face about the contra-positive: If "Each *A* is B" is true, "All non-*B*s are non-*A*s" is true, but if the latter is true, the former may not be so! For the former presupposes that there are *A*s, but the latter need not presuppose that there are non-*B*s!

> Verse 27: An example announces the co-presence of the sign and the signifiable for (only) those who have not comprehended their natural relation; for those who have comprehended it, only the sign should be adduced (to prove the signifiable, and no example will be needed).

Note: This seems to be a pragmatic solution of the problem, and it perhaps changes the original intention of Diṅnāga. Dharmakīrti argues that citation of an example to certify the natural invariance between the sign and the signifiable may not be essential for the system of Diṅnāga. For otherwise why did he not take the "negative" example at all seriously? To be sure, he cited the sky as the substratum of both lack of being a product and lack of impermanence, but this makes the sky (a so-called permanent entity) a non-existent entity by the same token, for nothing is permanent as far as the Buddhists are concerned. The sky is a "nominal" example, not a real one. It is cited only for those who have not yet understood the real natural invariance relation.

Dharmakīrti concludes that there must be *natural* concomitance or "invariance" (*svabhāva-pratibandha*) between the sign and the signifiable in order that one can be the *appropriate* sign of the other. See his *Svavr̥tti* under verse 25 in the same context. In other words, simple observation and non-observation of "positive" and "negative" examples will not be enough. Dharmakīrti thinks that Diṅnāga apparently intended such a natural invariance to be there between the sign and the signifiable although he articulated it in terms of the citation of "positive" and "negative" examples. We may take this interpretation of Dharmakīrti with a grain of salt! In Diṅnāga, I believe, very often the problem of induction is not sharply distinguished from a separate issue, that of an actual inference based upon the "invariance relation," which is inductively comprehended.

Let us now see briefly what Dharmakīrti had to say about this natural concomitance between the appropriate inferential sign and the inferable or the signified. An adequate sign is either "natural" or "causal." A "natural" sign is one, which is non-distinguishable from the "nature" of the signified. A "causal" sign is one whose nature it is to be *caused* by the signified. In both cases there should be "natural invariance." It seems clear here that Dharmakīrti here was moving away from the notion of the purely empirical determination of the "invariance" relation between the inferential sign and the signified, a notion that we may ascribe to Diṅnāga. For Dharmakīrti, such an invariance must be a *necessary* relation, being based upon either a "natural" connection or a "causal" connection. The natural connection is one where the two items are ontologically indistinguishable (cf. *abheda*) but epistemologically distinguishable: being impermanent and being a product, being a tree and being a beech tree. The "causal" connection is one, where the two items are both ontologically distinguishable (cf. *bheda*) and still such that one is the natural outcome of the other: smoke and fire. Regarding the "natural" sign Dharmakīrti insists (see his *Svavṛtti* under verse 27) that whatever generates a particular as a product generates it by the same token as an impermanent entity. The two properties are only two sides of the same coin.

In an earlier paper I had described the "natural" connection as based upon an analytical proposition. This was inaccurate, as some (e.g. E. Steinkellner) have pointed out. This cannot be strictly described as analytical. However, I still believe that

Dharmakīrti, probably unlike Diṅnāga, wanted a sort of *necessary* connection to obtain between the sign and the signified, obviously in order to avoid the contingencies of an inductive generalization based purely upon observation. This is underlined by his doctrine of "natural invariance" and in particular by what he called the "natural" connection. The naturalness lies here in its being *necessary*, i.e. in its opposite's being impossible. Let me quote:

> Verse 39: With regard to the natural sign, there is its invariance with the signified, for if the signified is not present the sign by virtue of its non-difference (from the signified) will not be present either.

Dharmakīrti's argument to establish this "natural" connection is somewhat a priori and involves modalities. This does not mean that we do not in practice establish such a connection by looking at experience or by "empirical" examples. In general we do establish the said connection in this way but that is because we are in general (in Dharmakīrti's language) *a-viduṣaḥ,* those who have not comprehended the natural connection. For those who have so comprehended, the examples would be useless. I take this to mean that the so-called "natural" connection is actually a *necessary* connection, ontologically based, although it need be neither a priori nor analytic. If analyticity is regarded as a linguistic notion we need not connect it with the present issue. It may be said that the natural invariance between being a product and being impermanent (expressed as "All products are necessarily impermanent") is a necessary proposition which we know posteriori. In this way, our position is not incompatible with at least some modern account of necessity.

Dharmakīrti has said: Verse 39, *Svavṛtti:*

> The being (*bhāva*) that follows the very existence (*bhāva*) of a thing is called its own-nature (or essence). That itself is its real being. How can it exist (*bhavati*) having discarded its own self? Therefore

whatever is a product is also impermanent, for there is no (real) difference.

(Objection): But then the statement of the sign will be only a part of the statement of the provable thesis, the sign and the signified being the same? (Answer:) This is not a fault.

Dharmakīrti continues in verses 40, 41 and 42:

Since all things (beings=*bhāvas*) are naturally established in their own-nature and thereby differentiated from similar and dissimilar things, different class-properties, which supply the basis for the differentiation of a group of things from other things, are imagined to be anchored in the particulars. Therefore the exclusive nature (*viśeṣa*) that is understood in terms of one feature (*dharma*) cannot be understood in terms of other features. Thus the sign and the signified are differently understood (in spite of their essential non-difference).

4

I wish to conclude this introduction with a reference to another topic that is connected with the general theme "Buddhist Logic" in an indirect way. This is the Mādhyamika attitude towards logic. Briefly stated, the attitude is one of ambivalence. I shall concentrate here on Nāgārjuna, as the original thinker of the school. The dilemma was obvious. Nāgārjuna was one of the finest philosophers of India. In ancient India, philosophy meant argument and evidence in favour of some thesis or position, something or other, as well as refutation with argument and evidence of the rival positions. To be sure, philosophical method was ingrained in what was called the Nyāya method. Since the Buddhist logic of Diṅnāga and Dharmakīrti did not develop before Nāgārjuna, by "philosophic method" one used to understand at that time the Nyāya method as it was adumbrated in the *Nyāyasūtras*. Roughly, the "short" form of Nyāya was that there should be the statement of a position (called *pratijñā*) which should then be supported by reason or evidence (and examples to strengthen the evidence and so on). This will be reinforced by refutation of the counterposition with reason, evidence and so on.

Nāgārjuna accepted this philosophical method on the one hand; being a philosopher at that age he had no real choice. His dilemma, on the other hand was that as a Mādhyamika Buddhist he was convinced that this method was fundamentally flawed and hence this style of philosophizing cannot lead to the truth which is supposed to be its goal. By using arguments which can be variously interpreted as destructive dilemmas, *reductio ad absurdum*, and so on, Nāgārjuna wanted to show that the so-called Nyāya method is defenceless against proving a contradiction and letting in paradoxes. In particular, Nāgārjuna showed that there is this untenable contradiction between our a priori certainty that every being has its own-being (own-nature) and the empirical evidence that every being is dependently originating (in order to become), and one is therefore driven to the conclusion that every being is empty, i.e. empty of its own-being or own-essence or own-nature, for otherwise it could not have been dependently originating. This also reveals that Nāgārjuna did not flout the verdict of empirical evidence (and in this he shared the attitude of his fellow philosophers who used the Nyāya method) but rejected the metaphysical presuppositions of others. But now it seems to generate another paradox. If everything is empty of its own-being, this very fact cannot be *stated* as a thesis. For this statement itself would be *empty* and thereby defeat its purpose,

> (Objection:) If everything lacks own being, your statement, which (also) lacks its own-being, cannot refute the own-being (of everything).
>
> (Reply:) If my statement does not arise either from a combination of causes and conditions or in some other way, then surely EMPTINESS is proven since things have no own-being.
>
> — *Vigrahavsyāvartanī*, Introduction or *vṛtti* to verse 29

I have argued elsewhere that the resolution of the paradox in this way is similar to Jean Buridan's way of resolving similar paradoxes (as it was once explained by A.N. Prior).[11] Briefly the point is this. If God decreed that no one makes a negative statement then it would be true that no statement is negative but nobody then would be able to state that truth. Hence even if Nāgārjuna's statement does not arise at all, it would be or still could be the case that everything is empty (nothing has its own-being) but then no philosophical discourse would be possible about such a truth. Nāgārjuna brings his point into sharp relief by the following:

> If I had stated any thesis, I would be at fault. But since I have not stated any thesis, I am not at fault.
>
> — *Vigrahavyāvartanī*, verse 29

I wish to emphasize here an exegetical point which has often been missed by modern interpreters. The word *pratijñā* is a technical term. It means, strictly speaking, the statement of a position or a thesis, rather than a position itself. In the *Nyāyasūtra* (1.1.33), *pratijñā* is taken to be part (literally a "member" *avayava*) of a verbalized statement of an inference. It is one of the five *avayava*s, according to the Nyāya school. It is defined as the statement (*vacana*) which states what is to be proven (*sādhya-nirdeśa*). Hence, when Nāgārjuna says *nāsti mama pratijñā* he obviously means that he has no *stated* thesis of his own and therefore he should not be faulted. This fits squarely with the attempted resolution of the paradox that I have referred to above. It may be that everything lacks its own-being or essence, that is to say, everthing is empty, but this cannot be *stated* as a thesis. For a thesis that lacks essence or own-being is unstatable.

This brings me to the second point, which I have only briefly discussed elsewhere. Some scholars have disagreed and hence I

11. See my *The Logical Illumination of Indian Mysticism* (Oxford : Clarendon Press, 1977).

wish to clarify. There was a much older tradition of philosophical debate (codified in the *Nyāyasūtras* and elsewhere) in India, which recognized three varieties of such acceptable debate : *vāda, jalpa,* and *vitaṇḍā*. The first variety is what establishes a position (an acceptable hypothesis or a truth) and refutes the rivals by using proper reason and adequate evidence. The second variety is something like a verbal fight where winning the debate becomes more important than the employment of proper reason and adequate evidence. It is similar to the principle that is expressed as "Nothing is unfair in love and war." The third kind is what refutes the rival positions but does not establish any position of its own. I said earlier that Nāgārjuna and Śrīharṣa would probably endorse such a debate and presumably their style of philosophical argumentation could be called *vitaṇḍā*. But unfortunately the word *vitaṇḍā* has been associated over the ages with a despicable form of verbal wrangling. (Even some interpreters have translated *vitaṇḍā* as "wrangling.") However, this is certainly misleading. It is true that *vitaṇḍā* could be a verbal wrangling when, let us say, some slimy character tries to destroy the rivals in a debate by fair or foul means but at the same time he himself, escapes unscathed (for he claims that he has no position to defend). In fact, even Vātsyāyana understood *vitaṇḍā* somewhat in this way. But looking at the traditional history of Indian philosophy and being acquainted with the writings of such respectable philosophers as Nāgārjuna and Śrīharṣa, I would beg to differ from the view that *vitaṇḍā* can simply be a verbal wrangling. In fact, with such philosophers as Nāgārjuna and Śrīharṣa and Jayarāśi on the scene, it gradually dawned upon the tradition that the so-called "negative" type of debate or *vitaṇḍā* need not always be a despicable verbal wrangling. For one can respectfully refute the rival positions (perhaps all of them) with proper reason and adequate evidence and then claim that his own position cannot be stated in the strictest sense of the term. To use a modern jargon, one can say that the said position can only be *shown*, not *said*. This simply means that a debater who endorses the third variety of debate (which is described in *Nyāyasūtra* 1.2.3) simply as one where the counterposition is not *established*), can follow either the model of the first variety of debate, i.e. *vāda*, or that of the second variety, i.e. *jalpa*. An obnoxious person may resort to the second model but a respectable philosopher with integrity will, to all intents and purposes, resort to the first model. The *Nyāyasūtra* text itself is ambiguous here, for it uses the pronoun "*saḥ* (=that)" which can alternatively refer to both *jalpa* and *vāda*. Awareness of this point is reflected in the tradition itself. For later in the history of Nyāya, Sanātanī, a Prauḍa Gauḍa Naiyāyika (as Udayana calls him in his *Tātparya-Pariśuddhi*), classified debate as follows:[12]

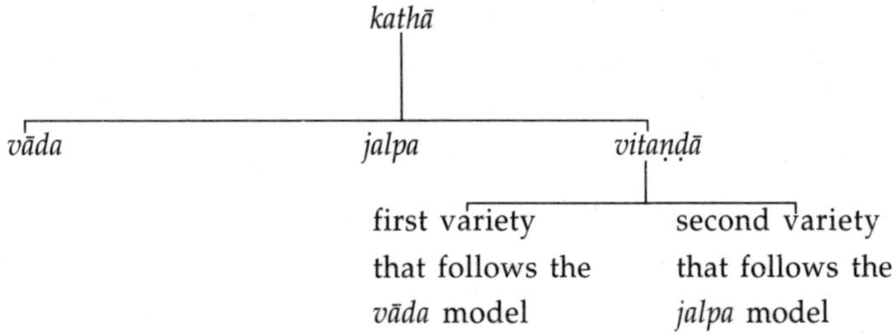

From the above it should be clear that later Naiyāyikas (at least some of them) did recognize that a *vitaṇḍā* can be an adorable form of philosophical debate if the participant follows the *vāda* model. Hence, if I describe Nāgārjuna as a philosopher following this variety of debate, it does not seem to be very far from the truth. The calumny that is usually associated with *vitaṇḍā* in the age-old tradition need not attach to the first variety which is modelled after *vāda*. This is also compatible with Nāgārjuna's having a position of his own and his simultaneous claim that such a position is not statable.

How are we then to understand the utterance of Nāgārjuna such as "everything is empty of its own-being because everything

12. See also my *Nyāya-Vaiśeṣika* (Wiesbaden: Otto Harrassowitz, 1977).

is dependently (contingently) originating?" I suggest that the answer comes from Nāgārjuna himself. Such utterance of his is itself empty! Utterances of this type do not assert or state anything! This is what I have called before the problem of non-assertion. If the utterance does not assert anything it cannot be part of a debate. I think Nāgārjuna would concede this point gladly : while everything else, he says, would be part of a "make-belief" debate, such utterances would not. Hence he is not involved in any paradox: "I have no fault." Only *prajñā* or mystical insight will SHOW that everything is empty of its own-being or empty of its own substantiality or essence but this cannot be stated or SAID or proven. I think this will answer some of the misgivings voiced by some modern scholars about my description of Nāgārjuna's debate as a *vitaṇḍā.*

The development of the Buddhist Nyāya, the logical method in Buddhism as found in the Diṅnāga-Dharmakīrti school, was entirely a reaction against the rather sceptical tendency of the Mādhyamikas — a point that has been made by many modern scholars. I wish to understand it as a *natural* reaction. For the sceptical non-assertion of Nāgārjuna implicitly indicated that reality can never be positively characterized but it can be experienced. The Buddhist logicians supplanted this sceptical non-assertion by a positive assertion: realities of our direct perceptual experience are inexpressible, and so is the ultimate truth. This may not have been clearly asserted by Diṅnāga, but Dharmakīrti asserted it in no uncertain terms. This is even corroborated by the later development in Buddhism where, for example, Śāntarakṣita could easily combine his Svātantrika Mādhyamika philosophy with the "practical" Yogācāra logical method.

2

An Interpretation of Anyāpoha in Diṅnāga's General Theory of Inference[1]

Richard P. Hayes

THE *apoha* theory as found in Diṅnāga's *Pramāṇasamuccaya* is presented both as a general observation about the inferential process and as a special observation about the meanings of linguistic expressions. The aspect of the theory that has received the greater amount of attention, in the hands of both classical and modern scholars, is the special application of the doctrine to linguistic expressions. Relatively little attention has been paid to the fact that in Diṅnāga's presentation of the relation between linguistic expressions and the knowledge that such expressions convey, the linguistic expression is regarded as but one type of sign. Accordingly, the contention that linguistic expressions

1. The preparation of this paper was made possible by a research grant from the National Endowment of the Humanities, an agency of the United States Federal Government. I wish to thank Mr Brendan S. Gillon and Prof. Hans G. Herzberger for making very helpful criticisms of earlier drafts of the paper, and I also gratefully acknowledge that a number of improvements in the present form of the paper were precipitated by comments made by other participants in the panel on Buddhist logic at the fifth conference of the International Association of Buddhist Studies held at Oxford University on 17 August 1982, where a much briefer version of the paper was presented. In particular, comments by Prof. D.D. Daye, Dr S. Katsura, Prof. D.S. Ruegg and Dr M. Siderits caused me to reconsider several key issues involved in the interpretation of Diṅnāga's logic.

convey knowledge of a particular type of relation known as *apoha,* the nature of which relation will be discussed below, is for Diṅnāga merely a special case of the more general contention that every sign conveys knowledge of the *apoha* relation.[2] What I wish to explore in this paper is the significance of the *apoha* doctrine in Diṅnāga's overall theory of inference or *svārthānumāna.*

Svārthānumāna may be seen as a process of comparing the relations of each of two classes of individuals to a third class of individuals with the aim of discovering the relation that the first two classes have to one another.[3] To state the matter in the

2. The fifth chapter of Diṅnāga's *Pramāṇasamuccaya* opens with the following verse:

   na pramāṇāntaraṁ śābdam anumānāt tathā hi tat ।
   kṛtakatvādivat svārtham anyāpohena bhāṣate ।।

   Verbal communication is not different from inference as a means of acquiring knowledge. For it names its object in a way similar to (an inferential indicator such as) the property of having been created (which indicates its object, namely the property of being transitory), by a process of precluding the (indicated property's) complement (namely, the loci of the property of being permanent).

3. A very similar statement appears in Morris R. Cohen and Ernest Nagel, *An Introduction to Logic* (New York: Harcourt Brace Jovanovich, 1962), p. 77, where it is said that a syllogistic inference may be interpreted as "a comparison of the relations between each of two terms and a third, in order to discover the relations of the two terms to each other." While it seems to me undeniable that the general problem to be solved by the traditional European syllogism and by the Indian inference is the same, it is equally clear that the methods employed by the European and Indian traditions differ in detail. The importance of these differences, and the specific question of whether or not the differences are so great as to render it inaccurate to call Diṅnāga's reasoning scheme a type of syllogism or even a type of formal logic, is a matter of considerable controversy into which I shall not enter in this paper. I shall, however, freely employ some concepts from both traditional European logic and from Boole-Venn logic in discussing Diṅnāga's theory of inference in the hope that so employing them will do more to elucidate than to obscure the issues at hand.

terminology familiar to students of Indian logic, *svārthānumāna* consists in the comparison of the relations that (a) the *pakṣa* class and (b) the class of *sādhyadharma*-possessors have to (c) the class of *hetu*-possessors, this comparison being done towards the goal of discovering the relation of the *pakṣa* class to the class of the *sādhyadharma*-possessors.[4]

The task of describing the procedure outlined by Diṅnāga in determining the relations between classes is somewhat complicated by the consideration that Diṅnāga's theory of inference seems to have undergone subtle but important changes between the early part of his career, during which he devised his celebrated *Hetucakra*, and the latter part of his career, during which he compiled the *Pramāṇasamuccaya*, the text that contains all his extant discussions of *apoha*. Thus in what follows I shall attempt to isolate these two stages in the development of Diṅnāga's expression of the features required of a successful inferential mark or indicator.

The Hetucakra Phase

We have seen that *svārthānumāna* involves comparing the relations that obtain between pairs of classes. A study of the structure of the *Hetucakra* suggests that Diṅnāga saw as his first task to describe the process by which we can arrive at a judgement of whether one class contains another, whether the two classes overlap, or

4. Here the term *pakṣa* designates any given set of individuals that are collectively cast in the role of being the subject under investigation. This set may be construed as having a plurality of members or as having a single individual member, depending on the specific inference at hand. *Sādhyadharma* designates a specified problematic property, that is, a property about which the reasoner wishes to know whether it occurs in (or is possessed by) each individual in the set of individuals that are the subject of investigation. *Hetu*, *liṅga*, and *sādhyadharma* are interchangeable terms that designate a specified property tentatively regarded as evidence for the problematic property's being possessed by each individual in the subject of investigation.

whether the two classes are disjoint.[5] The first step in arriving at such a judgement is to examine each individual within a given domain of individuals and to determine for each individual whether or not it is a member of each of the two classes the relation between which we are trying to ascertain. In the *Hetucakra* the two classes being compared are the class of *hetu*-possessors and the class of *sādhyadharma*-possessors. The domain of individuals within which these two classes are compared may be seen as a limited sample of the universe of all individuals, the sample being limited in the sense that it excludes all individuals of the *pakṣa* class. In the discussions that follow, I shall call this set of observed individuals that excludes individuals in the *pakṣa* class the *induction domain*. In comparing the relation of the class *H* (*hetu*-possessors) to the class *S* (*sādhyadharma*-possessors) within the induction domain, we find that each individual occupies exactly one of four subdomains or compartments of the induction domain. The four compartments are as follows:

(1) the set of individuals that belong to both *H* and *S*,

(2) the set of individuals that do not belong to *H* but do belong to *S*,

---

5. One class *contains* a second in case every member of the second is a member of the first. Two classes *overlap* in case there are individuals that belong to both, individuals that belong to the first but not to the second and individuals that belong to the second but not to the first. Two classes are *disjoint* in case they have no members in common. In Diṅnāga's writing we find no terms that exactly correspond to the relations of containment, overlapping and disjunction described here. Diṅnāga tends to talk not about classes themselves but rather of the properties that are the intensions of classes. The relations he talks about between properties are: (a) *vyāpti*, (b) *vyabhicāra* and (c) *virodha*. Two properties are in a *vyāpti* relation in case the extension of the first contains the extension of the second. One property is in a *vyabhicāra* relation with a second in case part of the extension of the second is a proper subset of the extension of the first. And two properties are in a *virodha* relation in case their extensions are disjoint.

(3) the set of individuals that belong to H but do not belong to S,

(4) the set of individuals that belong neither to H nor to S.

In the following set of discussions I shall represent these compartments through a notation employed by John Venn[6] as follows:

(N1) HS

(N2) $\bar{H}S$

(N3) $H\bar{S}$

(N4) $\bar{H}\bar{S}$

These four compartments of the induction domain may also be represented by Venn diagrams, which I shall also be employing throughout the following discussions.

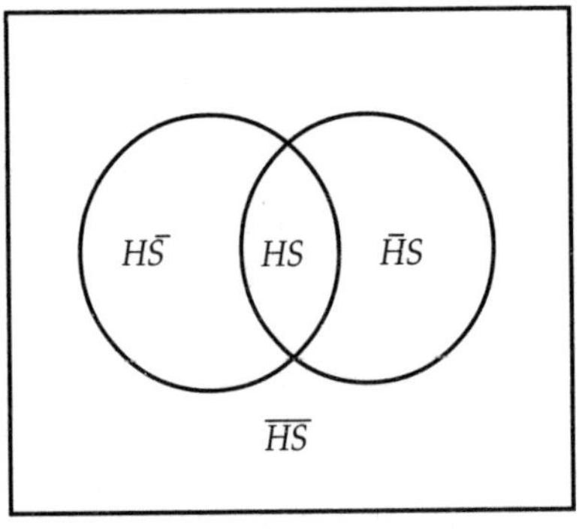

Once we have examined each individual in the induction domain and determined which of the four compartments it

6. John Venn, *Symbolic Logic*, 2nd rev. edn. originally published in 1894, rept. (New York: Burt Franklin, 1971). See especially chapters two, four, and five. In this system of notation the juxtaposition of two or more symbols representing classes indicates the intersection of the classes in question; a bar over a letter indicates the complement of the class for which the letter stands. Thus HS stands for the class that is the intersection of the class of *hetu*-possessors and the class of *sādhyadharma*-non-possessors, which latter is the complement of the class of *sādhyadharma*-possessors.

occupies, we may then examine each compartment and determine for it whether individuals occupy it or whether it remains empty. Theoretically speaking, since there are four compartments each of which is either occupied or empty, there are $2^4=16$ possible distributions of individuals in the four compartments of the induction domain. Of those sixteen, Diṅnāga considers nine in his *Hetucakra*.[7] The sixteen possible distributions may be seen in the table below. The numbers followed by the sign "*" indicate those distributions that Diṅnāga does not consider. In general, in the following discussion the fact that a class or compartment A is not empty will be expressed by the notation "$A>0$," to be read "(The class) A has (more than zero) members." And the fact that a class or compartment is empty will be expressed by "$A=0$," to be read "A has zero members." In the following chart, however, in order to ease reading a non-empty class will be indicated by "+" and an empty class by "0."

7. The so-called examples given in the *Hetucakra* are always given in the following order: an individual that occupies H or an individual that occupies $\bar{H}S$ or both. In the Tibetan translation this (pair of) example(s) is followed by the phrase *bzhin dang*, after which is named either an individual that occupies HS or an individual that occupies $\bar{H}S$ or both. This latter (pair of) example(s) is then followed in Tibetan by the phrase *bzhin no*. This suggests that the original Sanskrit formula was something like the following:

$(HS+\bar{H}S)$-*vat*; $(H\bar{S}+H\bar{S})$-*vat ca*

where "+" indicates a *dvandva* compounding of the words in question; this compound is then suffixed by the *taddhita-pratyaya VATi* (*Pāṇini-Sūtra* 5.1.115). Thus the example or pair of examples showing that S is occupied always precedes and is set off from the example or pair of examples showing that S is occupied; and within a pair an example of H always precedes an example of $\bar{H}$.

	HS	$\bar{H}S$	$H\bar{S}$	HS
1	+	0	+	0
2	+	0	0	+
3	+	0	+	+
4*	+	0	0	0
5	0	+	+	0
6	0	+	0	+
7	0	+	+	+
8*	0	+	0	0
9	+	+	+	0
10	+	+	0	+
11	+	+	+	+
12*	+	+	0	0
13*	0	0	+	0
14*	0	0	0	+
15*	0	0	+	+
16*	0	0	0	0

An examination of the seven theoretically possible distributions that Diṅnāga does not consider shows that he eliminates from the *Hetucakra* all distributions in which either both HS and $\bar{H}S$ are empty (13, 14, 15, 16) or both $H\bar{S}$ and $\bar{H}\bar{S}$ are empty (4, 8, 12, 16). In other words, he eliminates every case in which the induction domain is devoid of either any individual that belongs to S or any individual that does not belong to S. As we shall see in greater detail below, the class of individuals of the induction domain that belong to S is called the *sapakṣa*, and the class of individuals in the induction domain that do not belong to S (i.e. do belong to S) is called the *vipakṣa*. Thus, Diṅnāga considers in the *Hetucakra* only those cases in which each the *sapakṣa* and the *vipakṣa* is occupied by at least one individual.

In illustrating each of the nine distributions of individuals in compartments remaining in the *Hetucakra*, Diṅnāga picks for each distribution one *hetu* that is among the properties known to belong to every individual in the class of sounds, and he picks one *sādhyadharma*, a property whose occurrence in every sound is in question. The induction domain in all cases considered in the *Hetucakra* is, of course, the set of all individuals that are not sounds. The first step undertaken is to see for each of the four compartments mentioned above whether there exists in the induction domain an individual that occupies it. The results of this first step may be seen in the following table. If an individual is found in the induction domain that occupies one of the four

	HS	$\bar{H}S$	$H\bar{S}$	$\bar{H}\bar{S}$
1 *s*=eternal *h*=knowable	ETHER	ø	A POT	ø
2 *s*=transitory *h*=created	A POT	ø	ø	ETHER
3 *s*=man-made *h*=transitory	A POT	ø	LIGHTING	ETHER
4 *s*=eternal *h*=created	ø	ETHER	A POT	ø
5 *s*=eternal *h*=audible	ø	ETHER	ø	A POT
6 *s*=eternal *h*=man-made	ø	ETHER	A POT	LIGHTN-ING
7 *s*=nature* *h*=transitory	LIGHTING	ETHER	A POT	ø
8 *s*=transitory *h*=man-made	A POT	LIGHTN-ING	ø	ETHER
9 *s*=eternal *h*=formless+	ETHER	AN ATOM	ACTION	A POT

* *natural* is to be understood in the sense of not man-made

\+ formless is to be understood in the sense of non-corporeal

compartments, its name is recorded. If no individual is found to occupy a given compartment, the absence of an example is indicated by the symbol "ø."

Once this tabulation of examples — individuals representative of the four possible compartments of the induction domain — has been carried out, our next step is to see whether, on the basis of our knowledge, which of the four compartments of the induction domain are occupied and which are empty, we can arrive at any general propositions regarding the relation of the class of *hetu*-possessors to the class of *sādhyadharma*-possessors. It will be convenient at this point to introduce two further technical terms that are used for variables of classes and two technical terms applied to relations between those classes. It will be remembered that the induction domain is the complement of the *pakṣa* class and so maybe represented by the symbol P. The induction domain is itself divided into two mutually exclusive classes, namely the class of all individuals that are *sādhyadharma*-possessors, which class is traditionally termed the *sapakṣa* and which we shall represent by the symbol $\bar{P}S$, and the class of all individuals that are *sādhyadharma*-non-possessors, which class is traditionally termed the *vipakṣa* and which we shall represent by the symbol PS.[8] Special names are also given to two kinds of relations that can occur between the class of *hetu*-possessors and either the *sapakṣa* or the *vipakṣa*. An *anvaya* relation holds between the *hetu* and the *sādhyadharma* just in case there exists at least one individual in the induction domain that is a *hetu*-possessor and is also a member of the *sapakṣa* class. But a *vyatireka* relation holds between the *hetu* class and the *sādhyadharma* class just in case there exists no individual that is a member of both the class of *hetu*-possessors and the *vipakṣa*. We may symbolize these two relations as follows:

8. Diṅnāga actually seems to have used the term *asapakṣa* instead of *vipakṣa*, but I shall employ the better known terminology used by the later Buddhist logicians.

anvaya $\bar{P}HS>0$

vyatireka $\bar{P}HS=0$

It is important to realize that as Diṅnāga uses the technical terms *anvaya* and *vyatireka* at this stage of his development, the terms refer to relations that are logically independent. That is, if one of the relations is known to hold, it is still impossible to infer immediately whether or not the other holds, and if one fails, it is equally impossible to infer immediately whether or not the other holds. As we shall see below, post-Diṅnāga Indian logicians usually use the term *anvaya* to name a relation that is identical to that named by *vyatireka,* and this later usage of the terms came to be the standard for Buddhist logicians from Dharmakīrti onwards. But, at least in the *Hetucakra* period, Diṅnāga's understanding of the terms is more in line with the grammarians' usage, namely to refer to the two relations symbolized above.[9]

Let me now consider the problem of how we can move from knowledge of which compartments of the induction domain are occupied and which are empty to the formulation of a universal affirmative proposition regarding *hetu*-possessors and *sādhyadharma*-possessors. Before going any further, I must make it clear that as I use the term "universal affirmative proposition" in the following discussions I mean a proposition of the form "Every *A* is *B*" in which it is understood that the subject term *A* names a class that is non-empty. In this respect it differs from a proposition that states a *vyatireka* relation as described above. The propositional form that best captures a state of affairs in which a *vyatireka* relation holds between classes *A* and *B* is the obverse of a universal affirmative, that is, a proposition of the form "No *A* is non-*B*." I take it that when the class *A* has no members, this latter proposition is true, for it simply says that

9. See George Cardona, "*Anvaya* and *Vyatireka* in Indian Grammar," *Adyar Library Bulletin*, 31-32 (1967-68): 313-52.

there exists no member of the class *A* that is non-*B*. Thus if the class *A* has members, then "Every *A* is *B*" and "No *A* is non-*B*" are logically equivalent. But if *A* has no members, then I shall regard "No *A* is *B*" and "No *A* is non-*B*" as true, while I shall take "Every *A* is *B*" to be indeterminate in truth-value.[10] Diṅnāga's views on the conditions necessary to warrant asserting a universal proposition (whether or not he was actually aware of having any views at all on such a matter) would rest upon the intuition that we are not likely to believe that one property always occurs with a second property unless the two following circumstances obtain: (a) there is some precedent of the two properties' actually occurring together, and (b) there is no reason to deny that the first always occurs with the second. The *anvaya* relation between a class *H* and a class *S* serves to justify our entertaining the possibility that every (member of) *H* is (a member of) *S*, although it is of course not a sufficient ground for asserting that every *H* is *S*. If, however, there is also a *vyatireka* relation between *H* and *S*, then there is no reason to deny that every *H* is *S*. If the *anvaya* relation fails to hold while the *vyatireka* relation holds, then we have no warrant to assert a universal affirmative proposition. The instance that Diṅnāga gives of *anvaya* failing while *vyatireka* holds is the case in which the property of being audible is under review as a tentative *hetu* for any *sādhyadharma* for the *pakṣa* class of sounds. If the *pakṣa* is the class of sounds, the induction domain is the class of non-sounds; but the property of being audible fails to occur at all in this induction domain, for only sounds are audible. Hence, the *anvaya* relation between audibility and the *sādhyadharma* fails to hold, so we have no justification to believe

10. See John Venn, *Symbolic Logic*, chapters six and seven, or Cohen and Nagel, *Introduction to Logic*, 41 ff. for discussions of the implicit existential import in the traditional universal affirmative proposition and the lack of implicit existential import in the Boolean counterpart thereof. In this paper I shall always use the term "universal affirmative" in its pre-Boolean sense.

that every *H* is *S* nor to deny that no *H* is *S*; but the *vyatireka* relation does hold in this case, because it is not the case that some audible non-sound is *S*, and so we have no justification either to deny that every *H* is *S* nor to believe that every *H* is non-*S*. But if there is no reason either to affirm or deny either the universal affirmative or its contrary, we must simply suspend judgement altogether on the relation between this *hetu* and other properties.

Let us now return our attention to examples given in the *Hetucakra*. It will be observed that for each of the nine *Hetucakra* positions the presence or absence of an example allows us to assign a truth-value to each of four particular propositions of the form "some *H* is *S*," "some non-*H* is *S*," "some *H* is non-*S*" and "some non-*H* is non-*S*." If we now pay heed to just the values assigned to propositions of the form "some *H* is ....," we find the nine *Hetucakra* positions can be divided into four distinct categories according as the *anvaya* and *vyatireka* relations hold or fail to hold. This division can be seen in the following table. In the table *Ihs* reads "some *H* is *S*;" *Ehs* reads "no *H* is *S*;" *Ahs* reads "every *H* is *S*;" *nh* reads "non-*H*;" "*N*...." reads "It is not the case that ......"

Category	*Ihs*	*Anvaya*	*Ihns*	*Vyatireka*	*NIhs* *Ehs*	*NIhns* *Ehns*	obverse of *Ehs* *Ahns*	*Ehns* *Ahs*	*Hetucakra* Positions
I	T	holds	F	holds	F	T	F	T	2, 8
II	T	holds	T	fails	F	F	F	F	1, 3, 7, 9
III	F	fails	T	fails	T	F	T	F	4, 6
IV	F	fails	F	holds	T	T	?	?	5

The results of the above examination of the *Hetucakra* positions were generalized in the second and third conditions stated in Diṅnāga's earlier version of the *trirūpa-hetu* doctrine. In these two conditions Diṅnāga states in effect that in order to derive a universal proposition of the form "every *hetu*-possessor in the induction domain is a *sādhyadharma*-possessor," it must be observed that (a) there are *hetu*-possessors in the domain, and (b) there are no *hetu*-possessors that are *sādhyadharma*-non-possessors. The first condition in the *trirūpa-hetu* formulation specifies that the *hetu* must belong to every member of the *pakṣa* class. Although Diṅnāga does not specify how it is that we are to arrive at this conclusion, I think we can safely assume that a procedure parallel to the one described above in determining that every *hetu*-possessor in the induction domain is a *sādhyadharma*-possessor is to be followed in determining that every member of the *pakṣa* class is a *hetu*-possessor. That is, we must determine (a) that the *pakṣa* class is not empty and (b) that there are no individuals in the *pakṣa* class that are *hetu*-non-possessors. When both these conditions are determined to obtain, the first requirement of the *trirūpa-hetu* is fulfilled; this requirement is traditionally called *pakṣadharmatā*. Using our notation we may symbolize the three conditions as described in the earlier phase of Diṅnāga's career as follows:

pakṣadharmatā	$PH>0$ and $P\bar{H}=0$
anvaya	$\bar{P}HS>0$
vyatireka	$\bar{P}H\bar{S}=0$

Let us now assume that we have conducted our investigation of individuals in the induction domain and of individuals in the *pakṣa* domain for some set of properties and that our investigations have shown that (a) every *hetu*-possessor in the induction domain is a *sādhyadharma*-possessor and (b) every member of the *pakṣa* class is a *hetu*-possessor. Is this knowledge sufficient to compel us to conclude that every member of the *pakṣa* class is a *sādhyadharma*-possessor? To this question it is clear that we must give a negative reply. To see why this is so, consider diagram two.

In diagram 2A, eight compartments have been numbered. Compartments 1 and 2 represent part of what we have been calling the induction domain, the remainder of the induction

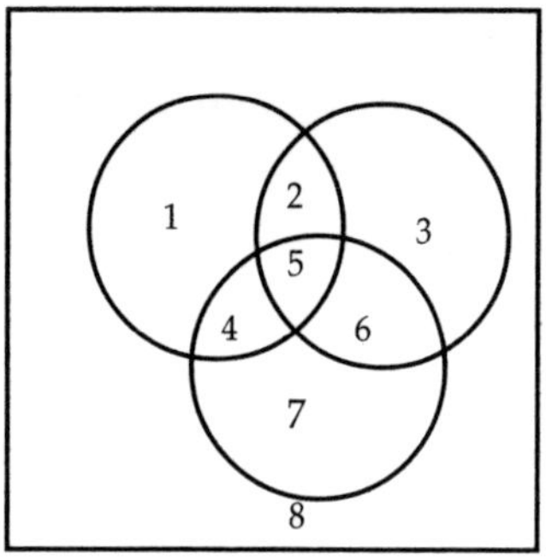

1. $\bar{P}H\bar{S}$
2. PHS
3. $\bar{P}HS$
4. PHS
5. PHS
6. PHS
7. PHS
8. $\bar{P}HS$

2A

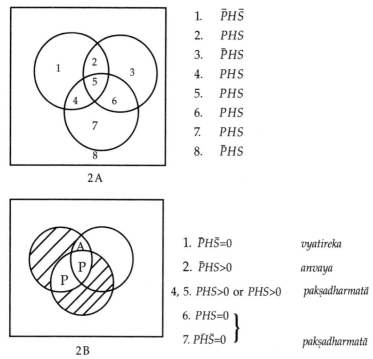

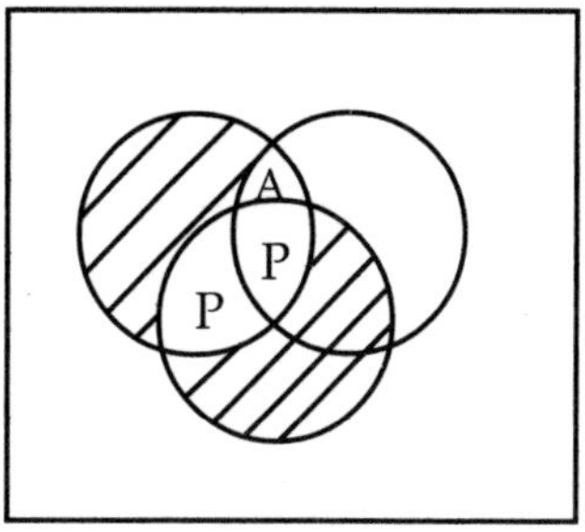

1. $\bar{P}H\bar{S}=0$	*vyatireka*
2. $\bar{P}HS>0$	*anvaya*
4, 5. $PHS>0$ or $PHS>0$	*pakṣadharmatā*
6. $PHS=0$ } 7. $P\bar{H}\bar{S}=0$ }	*pakṣadharmatā*

2B

domain being represented by compartments 3 and 8. Compartments 4, 5, 6 and 7 taken together constitute the *pakṣa* class. Supposing now that we have determined that every *P* is *H* and that therefore *trirūpa-hetu* condition one is fulfilled, we can represent this on the diagram by shading in compartments 6 and 7 to show that they are empty and by placing the symbol *P* in regions 4 and 5 to show that at least one individual occupies at least one of those two compartments. Let us now suppose that we have determined that there is no *hetu*-possessor in the induction domain outside the class S, which we indicate by shading in compartment 1. Let us finally suppose that the *anvaya* relation holds in the induction domain, which we indicate by the symbol *A* in compartment 2. The resulting diagram (diagram 2B) indicates in which regions it is possible, given that all the *trirūpa-hetu* conditions are fulfilled, for members of the *pakṣa* class to occur. They may occur in any part of the *pakṣa* circle that is not shaded in, namely in compartments 4 or 5. As can be seen, it is possible that some *P* may be *S*, for compartment 4 is not shaded. Thus, fulfilment of the *trirūpa-hetu* conditions alone do not warrant belief in the proposition "every *P* is *S*."

What is needed in order to warrant belief in the conclusion "every *P* is *S*" is fulfilment of the aforementioned *trirūpa-hetu* conditions plus the granting of one further assumption. The problem we face now is to determine the exact nature that this further assumption is to take. Its general content is clear enough: we are to assume that the same relations that have been found to hold between the *hetu* class and the *sādhyadharma* class in the induction domain will also be found to hold outside the induction domain or, in other words, in the *pakṣa* domain. But in arriving at the exact content of this assumption we must take into consideration one further set of data, namely, the types of argument that Diṅnāga labelled successful and the types that he labelled unsuccessful and his explanations for his decisions. As we saw above, the nine types of argument considered in the *Hetucakra* can be divided into four categories according as the *anvaya* and *vyatireka* relations hold or fail to hold. Let us now examine these four categories in greater detail.

Category I contains two arguments, the second and eighth considered in the *Hetucakra*, in which the *anvaya* and the *vyatireka* relations both hold. The arguments, as Diṅnāga gives them are as follows:

> (*HC*2) Sound is transitory. Because it is created. Consider a pot (created and transitory) and consider ether (not created and not transitory). Present in all similar cases, (i.e. in all transitory things in the induction domain) and absent in dissimilar cases (i.e., in non-transitory things in the induction domain), the *hetu* (i.e. the property of being created) is good.

> (*HC*8) Sound is transitory. Because it is man-made. Consider a pot (man-made and transitory) and lightning (not man-made but

transitory), and consider ether (not man-made and not transitory). Both (present and absent) in similar cases (i.e., present in some transitory things and absent in other transitory things in the induction domain) and absent in dissimilar cases, the *hetu* is good.

A look at the diagrammatic representation of these two arguments shows that the arguments will be successful provided that we make the following assumption: if *vyatireka* holds in the induction domain, then it holds in the *pakṣa* domain. That is, if *PHS*=0 then *PHS*=0.

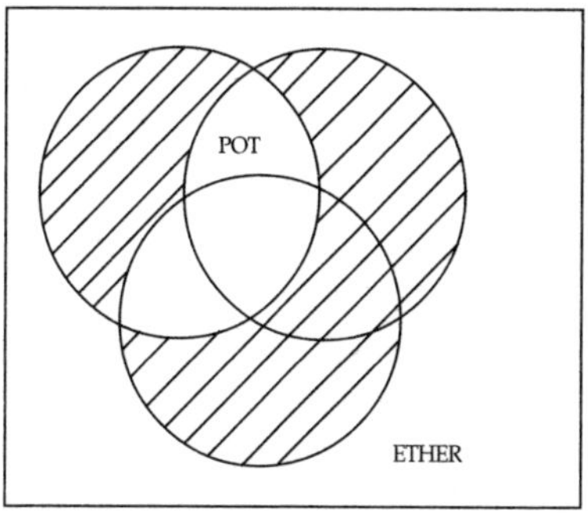

*HC*2 *trirūpa* conditions filled

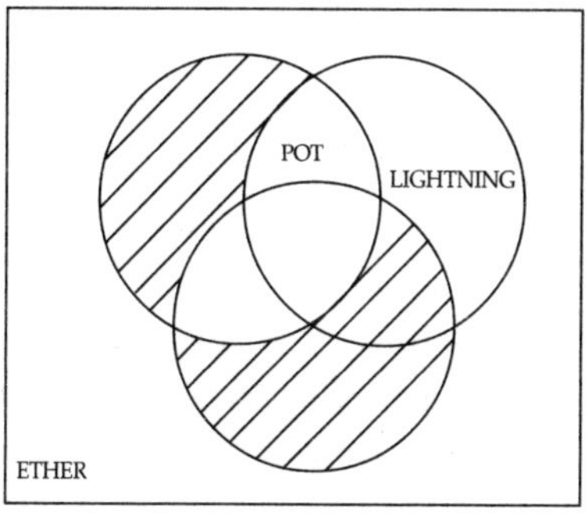

*HC*8 *trirūpa* conditions filled

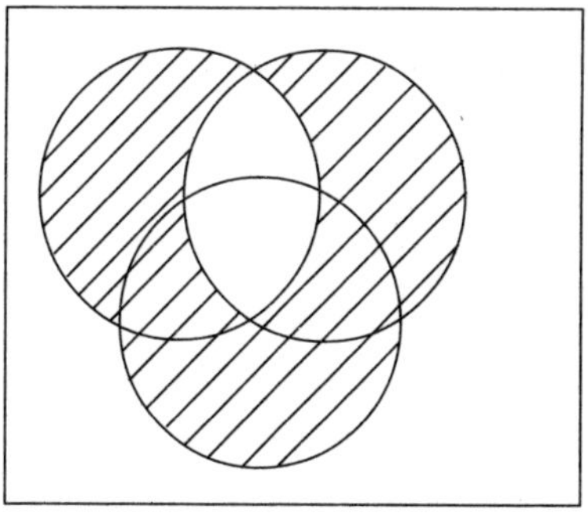
*HC*2 with added assumption

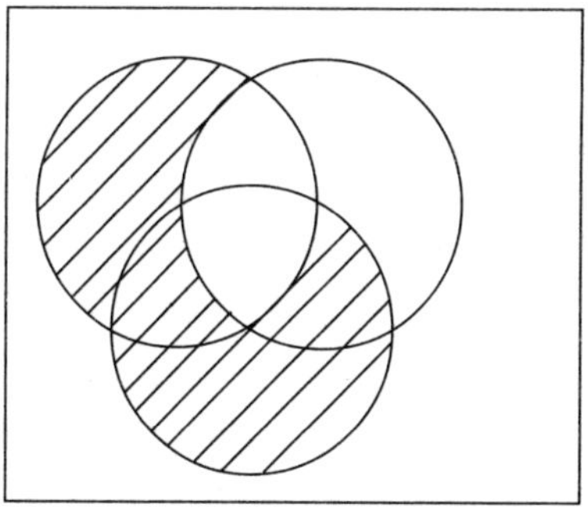
*HC*8 with added assumption

Category II contains four arguments in which *anvaya* holds and *vyatireka* fails. The four arguments as given by Diṅnāga go as follows:

(*HC*1) Sound is eternal. Because it is knowable. Consider ether (knowable and eternal) and consider a pot (knowable and not eternal). Present in all similar cases and present in all dissimilar cases, the *hetu* is inconclusive.

(*HC*3) Sound is man-made. Because it is transitory. Consider a pot (transitory and man-made), and consider lightning (transitory and not man-made) and ether (not transitory and not man-made). Present in all similar cases and both (present and absent) in dissimilar cases, the *hetu* is inconclusive.

(*HC*7) Sound is natural. Because it is transitory. Consider lightning (transitory and natural) and ether (not transitory but natural), and consider a pot (transitory but not natural). Both (present and absent) in similar cases and present in all dissimilar cases, the *hetu* is inconclusive.

(*HC*9) Sound is eternal. Because it is formless. Consider ether (formless and eternal) and an atom (not formless but eternal), and consider action (formless and not eternal) and a pot (not formless and not eternal). Both (present and absent) in similar cases and both (present and absent) in dissimilar cases, the *hetu* is inconclusive.

A look at the diagrams for these four arguments shows that in none of these four cases are the compartments $\bar{P}HS$ and $\bar{P}H\bar{S}$ empty. But if neither of these compartments is empty, then we have no justification to assume that their counterparts outside the induction domain, i.e. PHS and $PH\bar{S}$, are empty either. In fact, if the same relations hold in the *pakṣa* domain as in the induction domain between the classes H and S, it is natural to assume that some members of the *pakṣa* class will be *sādhyadharma*-possessors and some will be *sādhyadharma*-non-possessors. Thus, in all four cases the profferred *hetu* fails to warrant the conclusion that every P is S.

Category III contains two arguments in which both *anvaya* and *vyatireka* fail in the induction domain. Diṅnāga presents these arguments as follows:

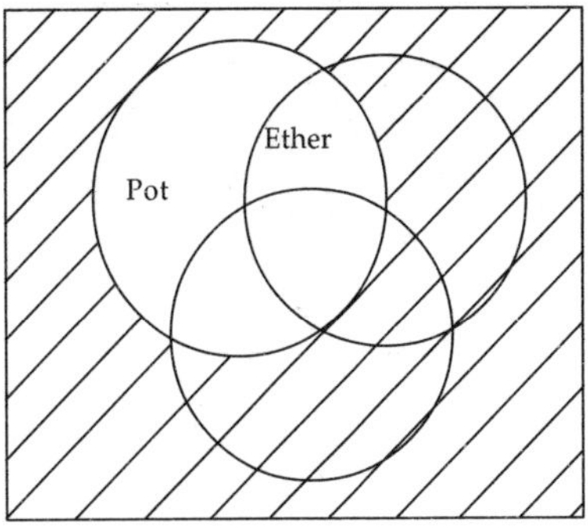

*HC*1

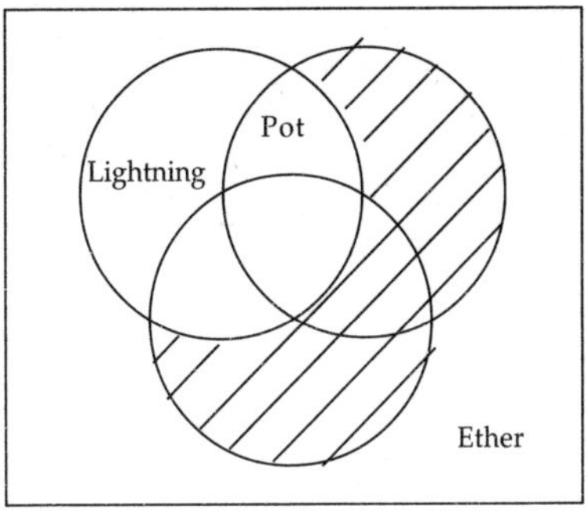

*HC*3

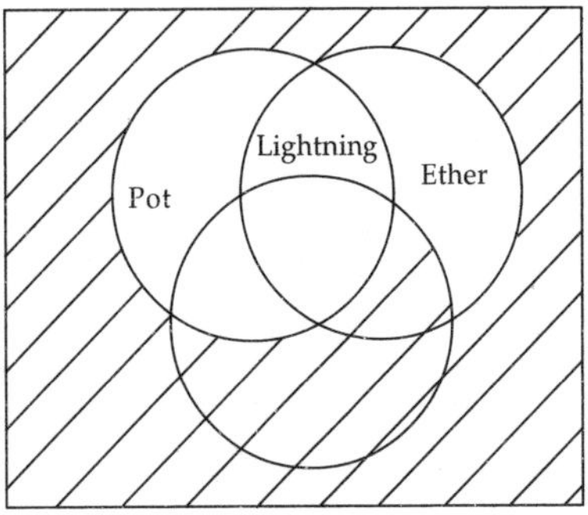

*HC*7

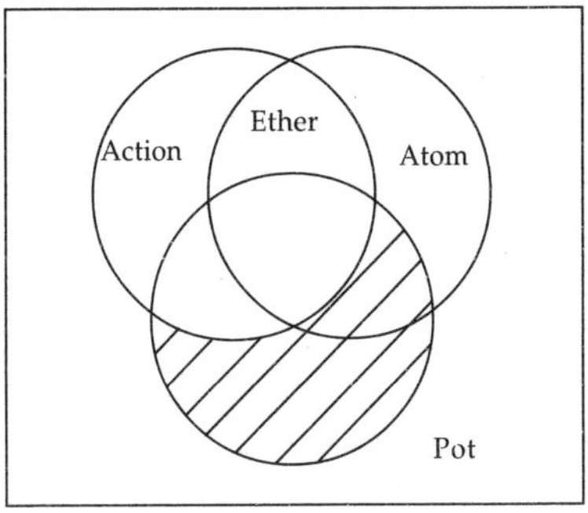

*HC*9

(*HC*4) Sound is eternal. Because it is created. Consider ether (not created but eternal), and consider a pot (created but not eternal). Absent in similar cases and present in all dissimilar cases, the *hetu* is incompatible (with the stated conclusion).

(*HC*6) Sound is eternal. Because it is man-made. Consider ether (not man-made but eternal), and consider a pot (man-made but not eternal) and lightning (not man-made and not eternal). Absent in similar cases and both (present and absent) in dissimilar cases, the *hetu* is incompatible (with the stated conclusion).

As the diagrams for these arguments show, the *hetu*s will succeed in proving the negation of the desired conclusion provided that we make the following assumption: if *anvaya* fails in the induction domain, then it fails in the *pakṣa* domain.That is, if $\bar{P}HS$=0 then *PHS*=0.

Category IV contains only the fifth argument considered in the *Hetucakra*. Diṅnāga presents this argument as follows:

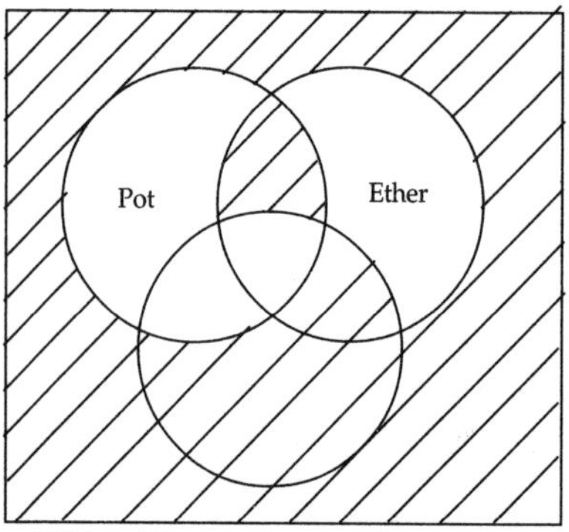

*HC*4 without assumption

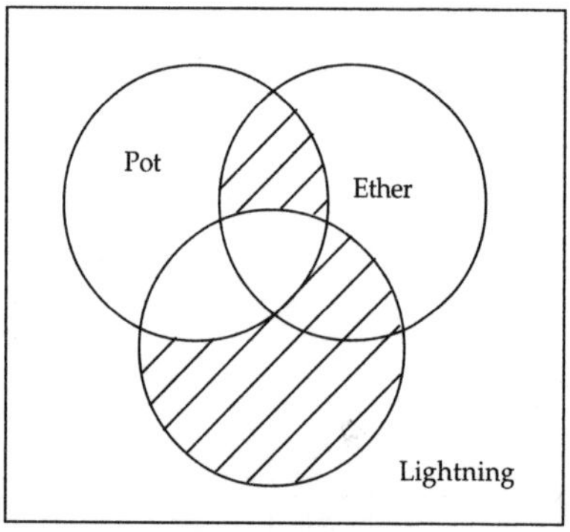

*HC*6 without assumption

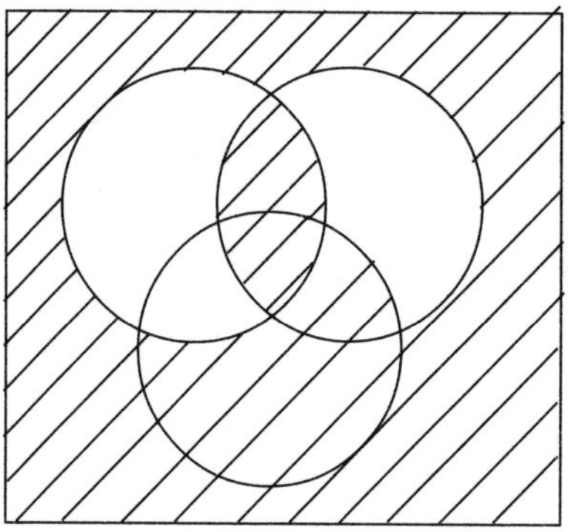
*HC*4 with assumption

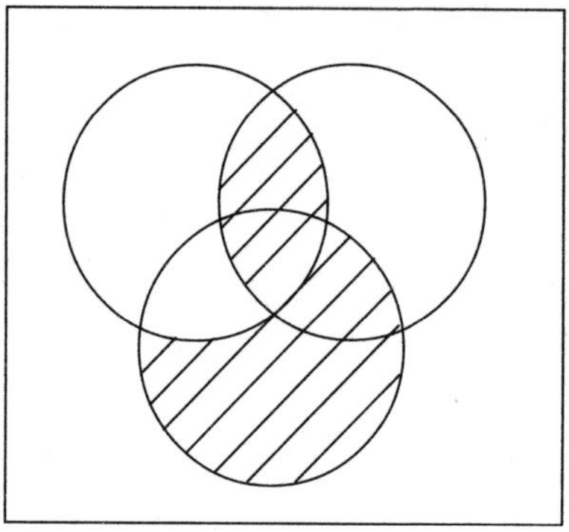
*HC*6 with assumption

(*HC*5) Sound is eternal. Because it is audible. Consider ether (not audible but eternal), and consider a pot (not audible and not eternal). Absent in similar cases and absent in dissimilar cases, the *hetu* is unique (to sound).

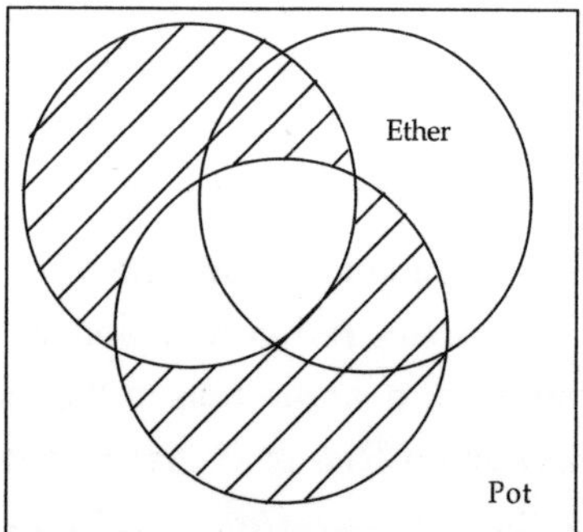

*HC*5

We saw above in studying the arguments of categories I and III that we were to make the assumption that whichever compartment of the *hetu* class is empty in the induction domain, its counterpart in the *pakṣa* class is also empty. That is, if *PHS*=0 then *PHS*=0, and if *PHS*=0 then *PHS*=0. Thus, at first blush it might seem reasonable to make a similar assumption for *HC*5, in which case we might assume that both *PHS* and *PHS* are empty. The result of following out this assumption, however, would be to render the *pakṣa* domain entirely empty. But if the *pakṣa* class is entirely empty, then the first condition of the *trirūpa-hetu* cannot be fulfilled. Thus, if the first condition of the *trirūpa-hetu* is fulfilled, we cannot assume that both *PHS* and *PHS* are empty. It is possible, given that *pakṣadharmatā* and *vyatireka* hold while *anvaya* fails, that either both *PHS* and PH$\bar{S}$ are occupied or that only one of them is occupied; it is not possible on the given evidence to conclude anything more than that at least one of the two compartments must be occupied. And so Diṅnāga's conclusion is that arguments appealing to *hetu*s having characteristics such as those described in *HC*5 are inconclusive, just as arguments appealing to *hetu*s having characteristics such as those described in *HC*1, 3, 7 and 9.

Diṅnāga's *Hetucakra* is a very spare presentation, consisting only of nine arguments and an indication of whether the arguments are good or not and a brief account of what makes them successful or unsuccessful. There is no explicit account of what procedure one is to go through in determining whether or not an argument is good. Nevertheless, one can reconstruct a definite procedure, a series of steps, that one might go through in order to arrive at the results presented in the *Hetucakra*. It seems fairly clear that in asssessing the success of an argument that claims that all members of the *pakṣa* class possess a given indicated property because all members of the *pakṣa* class possess a given indicator property (*hetu*), one is to go through the following steps in the order indicated:

Step One: Examine the members of the *pakṣa* class and ascertain whether the *hetu* is present in each and every member. If it turns out that $PH>0$ and $PH=0$, go on to step two. If not, declare the *hetu* inadequate to yield the stated conclusion.

Step Two: Examine the members of the induction domain and ascertain whether *anvaya* holds ($\bar{P}HS>0$) and whether *vyatireka* holds ($\bar{P}HS=0$). If both hold or if both fail, go on to step three. If only one holds, declare the *hetu* inadequate to yield the stated conclusion.

Step Three: Assume that the counterpart of whichever compartment of the *hetu* class is empty in the induction domain is also empty in the *pakṣa* domain.

After going through the third of these steps, one will be in a position to make a reasonable judgement that every member of the *pakṣa* class is a *sādhyadharma*-possessor or that every member of the *pakṣa* class is a *sādhyadharma*-non-possessor. It is preferable to say that these judgements are reasonable rather than certain, since they rest upon an inductive assumption, i.e. the assumption that the relations that obtain between the classes H and S in a domain of $\bar{P}$ of observed individuals also obtain between those classes in a domain of unobserved individuals, viz. the class P.

By going through the above three steps, we can write out a "proof." Suppose we have carried out the required investigations of individuals in the *pakṣa* and in the induction domain and have found that all three conditions of the *trirūpa-hetu* are met. We are then in a position to record the results of these investigations and the conclusions drawn from them in the following seven steps:

1. $PH>0$ by	observation	(*pakṣadharmatā*)
2. $P\bar{H}=0$ by	observation	
3. $\bar{P}HS>0$	by observation	(*anvaya*)
4. $PH\bar{S}=0$	by observation	(*vyatireka*)

5. $PH\bar{S}=0$ assumption warranted by 3 and 4

6. $H\bar{S}=0$ 4, 5

7. $P\bar{S}=0$ 2, 6

It will be observed that neither the *anvaya* relation (3) nor the *vyatireka* relation (4) plays a direct role in arriving at the conclusion (7). Rather, their function is to work together to warrant the assumption (5) that, taken in conjunction with the *vyatireka* relation, yields the premise (6) that allows us to derive the conclusion. It will also be observed that none of the above seven steps corresponds exactly to the major premise, minor premise and conclusion of the Barbara syllogism known to European logic. We can, however, very easily derive the components of a Barbara from these seven steps. A Barbara consists of three universal affirmative propositions of the form "every *A* is *B*," which it will be recalled is to be interpreted "there are *A*s and no *A* is non-*B*." The major premise of the Barbara reads, using Indian terminology, "every *H* is *S*." This can be derived from (1), which says "there are individuals in the *pakṣa* class that possess the *hetu*," and from (6), which says "no *hetu*-possessor is a *sādhyadharma*-non-possessor." Similarly, we can derive the Barbara minor premise, "every *P* is *H*" from (1) and (2); and we can derive the conclusion, "every *P* is *S*" from (1) and (7).

There is one further observation that we can make about the above proof namely, the form of the conclusion in the seventh step. The conclusion as stated says that every member of the *pakṣa* class is excluded (*apoha*) from the complement (*anya*) of the class of *sādhyadharma*-possessors. The nature of the *anyāpoha* relation in Diṅnāga's theory of inference is, then, just the exclusion of the *pakṣa*'s members' non-possession of the *sādhyadharma*. A question that now arises is this: does the fact that the *pakṣa*'s members' non-possession of the *sādhyadharma* is excluded imply that the *pakṣa*'s members do possess the *sādhyadharma*? Since the propositional form that most literally captures the *anyāpoha* relation is "no *P* is non-*S*," and since this proposition carries with it no commitment that the *pakṣa* class has members nor that the class of *sādhyadharma*-possessors has members, it is generally held that the *anyāpoha* relation is entirely negative — or, as I would prefer to say, hypothetical — in character. In other words, it is held that the *anyāpoha* relation warrants our saying only "if there are *P*s, then every *P* is *S*," but not "there are *P*s and no *P* is non-*S*." Given, however, that the statement of the *anyāpoha* relation can be derived in Diṅnāga's set-up only from a set of statements of which the first states explicitly that the *pakṣa* class is not empty, there is no need to limit ourselves to the purely hypothetical form of the conclusion mentioned above; the *anyāpoha* relation derived in the way we have seen in the above seven-step proof cannot fail to have positive implications.

THE PRAMĀṆASAMUCCAYA PHASE

At the outset of this paper the claim was made that Diṅnāga's theory of inference seems to have undergone a change between the early and final stages of his career. In the final part of this paper I wish to deal with those apparent changes rather briefly without going into the full implications of the modifications introduced in the *Pramāṇasamuccaya* formulation of the *trirūpa-hetu* doctrine. Let me begin by simply quoting what Diṅnāga actually says. The second chapter of the *Pramāṇasamuccaya* opens with this statement:[11]

> The inferential process is of two kinds: that which is for one's own sake and that which is for the sake of other people. Of those, inference for one's own sake consists in discerning an object through an indicator (*liṅga*) that has three characteristics.

11. In these translations of passages from the *Pramāṇasamuccaya*, the portions in italics indicate the verse portions of the original text, while the portions in ordinary typeface indicate his own prose *vṛtti*.

Referring later at *PS* (II.5cd) to this opening passage, Diṅnāga continues thus:

> The phrase "through an indicator that has three characteristics"must now be explained. (A successful indicator must be) present in the object of inference (*anumeye sadbhāvaḥ*) and in what is similar to it (*atha tattulye sadbhāvaḥ*) and absent when (what is similar to the object of inference is) absent (*nāstitā 'sati*). The object of inference is a property-locus (*dharmin*) qualified by a property (*dharmaviśiṣṭa*). By discerning, either through sensation or through inference, (the indicator) in that (property-locus), one later establishes its existence generally either in some or in all loci of the same class. Why do we say that? Because there is a restriction that (the indicator) occurs only in what is similar (i.e. that it does not occur in what is not similar); there is no restriction that it only occurs (i.e. that it does not fail to occur in whatever is similar). In that case it would appear that nothing is gained by saying that the indicator is absent in the absence (of what is similar to the object of inference). This (latter statement) makes the point that (the indicator), being absent when (what is similar to the object of inference is) absent, is not present in what is other than or what is incompatible with (the object of inference).

It appears to me that, on the most natural interpretation of the passage just quoted, conditions two and three of the *trirūpa-hetu* — the conditions describing *anvaya* and *vyatireka* — are to be formulated in a different way from the way in which they were formulated in the *Hetucakra* discussion. For according to this passage we are to understand the statement of the *anvaya* relation as being a statement that says two things: (a) the *hetu* does occur "generally" with possessors of the *sādhyadharma*, as opposed to being restricted to occurring with *pakṣa*-member *sādhyadharma*-possessors, and so *PHS*>0, and (b) the *hetu* occurs only with the *sādhyadharma*, which means that it does not occur without the *sādhyadharma*, in things outside the *pakṣa* class, and so *PHS̄*=0. In other words, the reformulated *anvaya* clause alone says all that was said by the *anvaya* and *vyatireka* clauses together in the *Hetucakra* formulation of the *trirūpa-hetu*. This raises the question, anticipated by Diṅnāga himself, of what point there is in repeating the *vyatireka* clause separately, for it appears now to be redundant. Diṅnāga's answer to this question is not entirely clear, but two possible interpretations suggest themselves. First, it could be that the *vyatireka* clause is indeed redundant and does no more than repeat part of what is intended by the reformulated *anvaya* clause. Second, it could be that the *vyatireka* clause adds one new piece of information by saying "no *hetu* anywhere (whether in the *pakṣa* class or outside it) occurs without the *sādhyadharma*." To see this difference let us diagram the reformulated *anvaya* clause and the two alternative interpretations of the *vyatireka* clause.

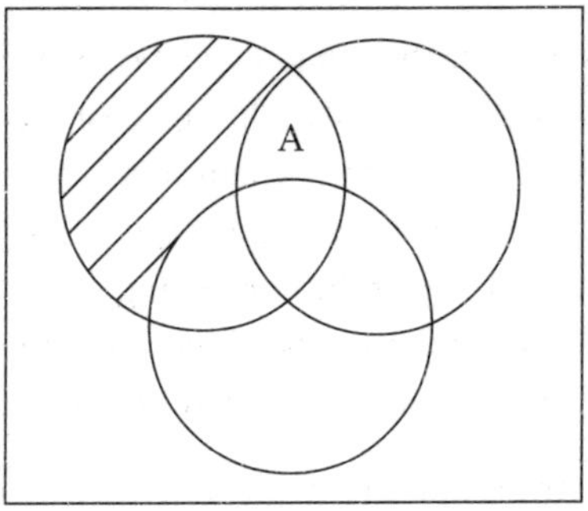

Reformulated *anvaya*

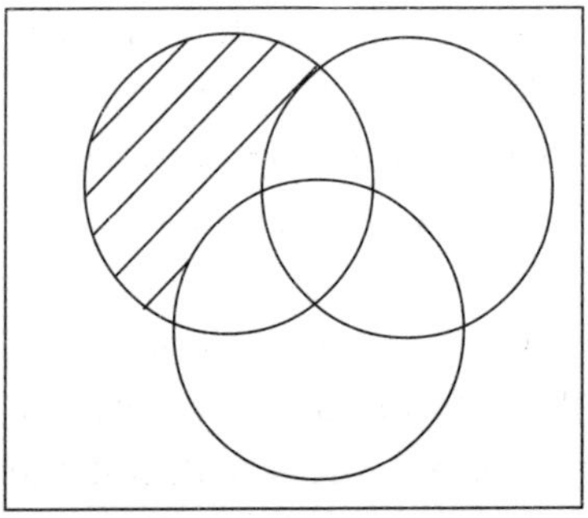

Reformulated *vyatireka*, 1st interpretation $\bar{P}HS=0$

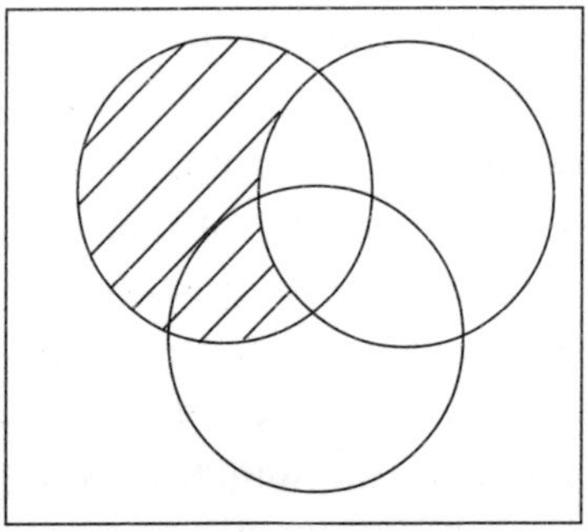

Reformulated *vyatireka*, 2nd interpretation $H\bar{S}=0$

Adopting the second interpretation of the *vyatireka* clause, whereby it specifies that $HS=0$, has as a consequence that the *anvaya* clause becomes altogether superfluous, for it is possible to derive a conclusion from *pakṣadharmatā* and *vyatireka* alone.

1. $PH>0$ 2. $PH=0$	*pakṣadharmatā*
3. $HS=0$	*vyatireka*
4. $PS=0$	*anyāpoha*

Moreover, we can derive this conclusion without any intervening assumption about relations in the induction domain corresponding to relations in the *pakṣa* domain. There is, however, one serious obstacle in the way of our attributing this interpretation to Diṅnāga, which is that further on in the *Pramāṇasamuccaya*[12] he still insists that the following argument is not conclusive: "Sound is transitory because it is audible."[13] It is
∴ Diṅnāga's claim that the *hetu*, the property of being audible, does not compel us to accept that every sound has the *sādhyadharma*, the property of being transitory. Why? Now what we should expect to find him saying is something equivalent to the observation that although the argument is formally valid (for $PH=0$, $HS=0$, $PS=0$ is a valid form), it is unsound, i.e. one of the premises is false. And since "no sound is inaudible" is true by

12. See *PS* II.7. This passage is translated and commented upon in my article "Diṅnāga's Views on Reasoning (*svārthānumāna*)," *Journal of Indian Philosophy* 8 (1980): 254.

13. It is interesting to note that in the *Hetucakra* the argument went "sound is eternal (*nitya*), because it is audible," while here it goes "Sound is transitory (*anitya*), because it is audible." In these two examples the same evidence is advanced to support two contradictory conclusions — a sure sign that something is very wrong with the evidence. The *Pramāṇasamuccaya* example of this faulty argument is perhaps more effective pedagogically in that it shows how an argument may have a conclusion that is true but inconsequent of the facts adduced to support it.

definition (a sound being for Diṅnāga that which one is aware of hearing), we should expect that the false premise is "no audible thing is non-transitory." And we should expect this premise to be false on the grounds that there are audible things, namely sounds, that are non-transitory. In short, we should expect Diṅnāga to say that the *hetu* under discussion is inconclusive for the reason that it does not fulfil the *vyatireka* condition, which by our second interpretation is to be understood as saying that $H\bar{S}=0$. But this is not what Diṅnāga in fact says. For according to him the *hetu* is inconclusive because it fails to fulfil the *anvaya* condition. And so, it would appear, the *anvaya* relation is not superfluous after all, for it still appears in Diṅnāga's mind to be necessary in order to eliminate arguments like that given in *HC*5 in which the *hetu* class is coextensive with the *pakṣa* class. In the final analysis I think we must reject the second of the two aforementioned possible interpretations of the *vyatireka* clause as stated in the *Pramāṇasamuccaya.*

Does rejection of the second of the two above interpretations of *vyatireka* compel us to accept that *anvaya* and *vyatireka* are nearly coextensive, differing only to the extent that a universal affirmative proposition and its obverse differ? If so, why does Diṅnāga still claim that both conditions are necessary and that arguments in which only one is fulfilled are incompetent? In an attempt to answer that question, a consideration of the specific argument forms discussed by Diṅnāga in the *Pramāṇasamuccaya,* along with a study of his reasons for declaring some forms "good" and others not, leads me to believe that in the final analysis he intends the *trirūpa-hetu* conditions be interpreted in the *Pramāṇasamuccaya* exactly as they were interpreted in the *Hetucakra*. The apparent modifications introduced in the notions of *anvaya* and *vyatireka,* if my hunch is correct, turn out to be *only* apparent. One can hardly deny, however, that subsequent generations of Buddhist logicians, beginning with Dharmakīrti, took this appearance at face value and did clearly reformulate the *anvaya* and *vyatireka* clauses of the *trirūpa-hetu* with the effect of rendering one of them redundant. The problems entailed by this reformulation have already occasioned much discussion, and I have nothing to add on the matter here.[14]

14. The following articles all present interpretations of the *trirūpa-hetu* as formulated by the early Buddhist logicians. H.N. Randle, *Indian Logic in the Early Schools* (London: Oxford University Press, 1930), pp. 180-89; Th. Stcherbatsky, *Buddhist Logic*, 2 vols. (Leningrad: Izdatel's stov Akademii Nauk SSSR, 1930-32), 1: 242-45, 2: 51-58; R.S.Y. Chi, *Buddhist Formal Logic* (London: The Royal Asiatic Society of Great Britain and Ireland, 1969), pp. xi-xlii; J.F. Staal, "Contraposition in Indian Logic," *Logic, Methodology and Philosophy of Science: Proceedings of the 1960 International Congress* (Stanford: 1962), pp. 634-49; Karl H. Potter, ed. *Encyclopedia of Indian Philosophies: Indian Metaphysics and Epistemology* (Princeton, New Jersey: Princeton University Press, 1977), pp. 191-95; Brendan S. Gillon and Martha Lile Love, "Indian Logic Revisited: Nyāyapraveśa Reviewed," *Journal of Indian Philosophy*, vol. 8 (1980): 349-84. Several of the above works present interpretations that differ in detail from the one I have presented in the present paper. In fact, I am alone in taking *vyatireka* as PHS=0 rather than HS=0, this latter formulation having enjoyed universal acceptance until now. While the latter formulation is correct for all the post-Diṅnāgas that I know of, I believe it will not work for Diṅnāga.

3

Three Systems of Buddhist Logic

Hans G. Herzberger

1. Introduction

A CHARACTERISTIC problem for historians of logic is that the rules to be found in many texts tend to strike the contemporary reader as somehow awry. In certain respects the rules may seem too weak, and in other respects needlessly strong. In this paper I will examine three reconstructions of Diṅnāga's logic which exemplify several aspects of this problem. The main system under consideration certifies some logically unsound arguments, and in this sense its rules seem to be "too weak." Of the two alternative systems under consideration, the rules of one seem to be "almost sufficient" for logical soundness, and the rules of the other seem to be "oversufficient." Each of them in its own way cuts against the grain of familiar logical standards.

From the standpoint of philosophical exegesis, there are various ways of accommodating this situation, some of which are well known from the history of Western logic. One favourite method for dealing with the problem of insufficiency is to look for tacit assumptions or presuppositions that limit the domain of application for the rules to cases within which they give acceptable results. This has been done for Aristotelian logic with some success by J. Lukasiewicz and his followers; and has to some extent been tried for Buddhist logic by Richard Chi and some others.[1]

1. Jan Lukasiewicz, *Aristotle's Syllogistic from the Standpoint of Modern Formal Logic* (Oxford: Clarendon Press, 1951); R.S.Y. Chi, *Buddhist Formal*

The ultimate test in all cases is not whether the posited assumptions are plausible to us, but whether they fit the text and help to make sense of it. Probably the author was not putting forward a formal system or following any paradigm of modern formal logic. In dealing with the systems under consideration here, a determined effort will be made to keep the author's standards (codified here by conditions of "goodness") separate from modern canons of logical validity. It is useful to compare them, and this will be done. But I believe it is most important to be wary of prejudging the question of whether or not the author was aiming for a codification of logical validity or soundness in any received sense. One has to puzzle out the author's standards and try to locate them within some larger philosophical enterprise. This is especially important in connection with the oversufficiency problem, for it may emerge that goodness according to the author's standards is a motley notion made up of some parts of logical validity, some parts of soundness and some parts of other things. Here it seems to me that we are still pretty much groping in the dark so far as Buddhist logic is concerned — the most elementary questions about this subject remain unsettled and quite controversial. One almost gets the impression that there may be as many different systems of Buddhist logic as there are scholars writing on the subject.

Part I of this paper will examine a logical system *HD* derived from Diṅnāga's *Hetucakra* by Richard Hayes in his paper for this conference (to be cited below as *ADT*).[2] Part II will be devoted to variations on this system, with a brief sketch of two alternative systems *HD*1 and *HD*2 which are designed to serve as objects of comparison with *HD*.

→ *Logic*, Part I (London: Royal Asiatic Society of Great Britain and Ireland, 1969).

2. Richard Hayes, "An Interpretation of Anyāpoha in Diṅnāga's General Theory of Inference," this volume.

I

In *ADT*, Dr Hayes reconstructs from Diṅnāga's *Hetucakra* a miniature logic of classes with a distinctive inductive slant. It is safe to say that some questions of textual interpretation must be raised about this reconstruction. However, I propose initially to accept Dr Hayes' reading of the text as given, and to examine from a logical point of view the system of inference he attributes to Diṅnāga. I view this as a preliminary to exegetical criticism. My aim will be to formulate certain key features of this system so they can be firmly grasped and to some extent evaluated, and I will undertake to do this with a minimum of formal apparatus.

I propose to focus rather sharply on a certain "inductive assumption" [*IA*] which seems to me especially problematic. The role assigned to *IA* is to bridge a gap between premises and conclusion:

> What is needed in order to warrant a belief in the conclusion "Every *P* is *S*" is fulfilment of the aforementioned *trirūpa-hetu* conditions plus the granting of one further assumption. The problem we now face is to determine the exact nature that this further assumption is to take.[3]

From a purely formal standpoint, it is easy to verify that *IA* as formulated does indeed bridge the gap. There is no question that *IA* is sufficiently strong to play the role of a logical bridge. The problem is rather that *IA* is much too strong. It is neither strictly true nor even highly probable; nor are there any obvious qualifications that could be imposed upon its application to render it inductively sound. So, in the end this will bring us back to the question of textual intrepretation. If Diṅnāga was indeed committed to *IA*, on what grounds could he have held it to be a reliable assumption? Or is there some other reading of the text which would release Diṅnāga from this apparently unsupportable burden of *IA*?

---

3. Richard Hayes, "An Interpretation of Anyāpoha in Diṅnāga's General Theory of Inference," this volume, p. 54.

2. The System *HD*

I understand the Hayes-Diṅnāga system [*HD*] to consist of a certain pattern of argument involving three principal terms (*pakṣa, hetu, sādhya*) and certain conditions relating those terms to one another.[4] Some of the conditions are explicitly if somewhat gnomically formulated in the *trirūpa-hetu*.

At least one additional condition — the inductive assumption — is imposed on what seem to be logical rather than textual grounds; this will be examined in some detail below.

At the heart of any *HD*-argument is a compound statement: *pakṣa* is *sādhya* because it is *hetu*. The triple (*P, H, S*) of terms will be called *good according to HD* (a technical term) if and only if they satisfy all the *trirūpa-hetu* conditions as interpreted in *ADT*:

pakṣadharmatā:	All *P* are *H*
	Some *P* are *H*
anvaya:	Some *HP* are *S*
vyatireka:	All *HP* are *S*

In these formulations the universal quantifier "all" is to be read as free from existential import. In the notation of *ADT*, the statment "All *X* are *Y*" is to be considered true if and only if $X\bar{Y}=0$. The conclusion of an *HD* argument, according to *ADT* is a universal statement without existential import:

conclusion:All *P* are *S*

On this formulation, the canonical pattern of argument for *HD* has four premises.

An equivalent, more compact format can be obtained by using the strong quantifier "every" of *ADT*. This quantifier carries existential import; the statement "Every *X* is *Y*" is to be considered

4. Following *ADT*, the examples ("similar" and "dissimilar") whose role is to secure the *trirūpahetu* conditions, are left in the background for present purposes.

true if and only if $X\bar{Y}=0$ and also $XY>0$.[5] The two *pakṣadharmatā* conditions can be consolidated into a strong universal statement ("Every *P* is *H*"); the *anvaya* and *vyatireka* conditions can also be consolidated into a single strong universal statement ("Every $H\bar{P}$ is *S*"). This yields a two-premise "consolidated format" for *HD*:

pakṣadharmatā: Every *P* is *H*

anvaya-vyatireka: Every $H\bar{P}$ is *S*

All *P* are *S*

The reader will note that the premises of this argument carry existential import while the conclusion does not. *ADT* considers this asymmetry and remarks that the stronger conclusion "Every *P* is *S*" could also be drawn:

> [T]here is no need to limit ourselves to the purely hypothetical form of the conclusion mentioned above.[6]

I will return to this curious asymmetry in section 8.

The *Hetucakra* considers nine types of examples and sorts them out into several categories: those for which "the *hetu* is good," those for which "the *hetu* is incompatible," and two kinds of argument for which "the *hetu* is inconclusive." I believe that the three main categories are all definable in terms of the technical notion of "goodness." By definition, a triple (*P*, *H*, *S*) of terms is good according to *HD* if and only if they fit together in a canonical argument which satisfies all *trirūpa-hetu* conditions according to the interpretation of those conditions put forward in *HD*. Let any triple (*P*, *H*, *S*) be called *contrary according to HD* if and only if the complementary triple (*P*, *H*,*S*) is good according to *HD*; these correspond to cases in which "the *hetu* is incompatible." All other triples of terms may be called *inconclusive according* to *HD*.

---

5. Richard Hayes, "An Interpretation of Anyāpoha in Diṅnāga's General Theory of Inference," pp. 49-50.

6. Ibid., p. 62.

Under these definitions, the main sorting of examples can be reconstructed from the single major division between good triples and all others.

Some remarks in *ADT* leave room for a slightly narrower definition of goodness:

> [Diṅnāga] considers in the *Hetucakra* only those cases in which each the *sapakṣa* and the *vipakṣa* is occupied by at least one individual.[7]

Now, the fact that Diṅnāga did not consider arguments of certain kinds does not in itself tell us how to evaluate those arguments. The proposed definition of goodness permits some of the unconsidered cases to count as good arguments. Alternatively, one might want to see how the theory would look on the supposition that non-emptiness of *sapakṣa* and *vipakṣa* were necessary conditions for goodness. Nothing in the present paper hinges on this.

3. Formulation of the Inductive Assumption

The problem of "the inductive assumption" arises in *ADT* from the observation that the *trirūpa-hetu* conditions do not seem strong enough to "warrant belief" in the conclusion of the canonical argument form. The notion of warranted belief is taken quite narrowly in *ADT*, so as to require deductive cogency:

> Is this knowledge sufficient to *compel* us to conclude that every member of the *pakṣa* class is a *sādhyadharma*-possessor? To this question it is clear that we must give a negative reply.[8] (emphasis added)

In other words, the canonical pattern of argument is not formally valid. I would like to put this in terms of a comparison between goodness and a certain notion of soundness.

7. Richard Hayes, "An Interpretation of Anyāpoha in Diṅnāga's General Theory of Inference," p. 46.

8. Ibid., pp. 52.

Soundness as used in logical theory requires the truth of both premises and conclusion of an argument. Goodness according to *HD* corresponds exactly to the truth of the "premises." Let a triple (*P, H, S*) of terms be called *sound relative to HD* if and only if it satisfies all *trirūpa-hetu* conditions and in fact all *P* are *S* (*PS*=0). So, a triple is sound relative to *HD* just in case the corresponding canonical argument has true premises and a true conclusion.

The canonical argument pattern would be formally valid just in case, all good triples were sound. But this is not the case as can be seen from counter-examples. Consider the triple (cetacean, mammal, land-dweller). The cetaceans (whales, porpoises, etc.) are aquatic mammals. Every cetacean is a mammal; every non-cetacean mammal is a land-dweller; but it is of course not true that all mammals are land-dwellers. So this triple is one counter-example; several others will be presented in the next section.

Now *ADT* proposes to bridge the gap between goodness and soundness by means of a "further assumption"[9] and engages in a search for its correct formulation by reference to Diṅnāga's treatment of the nine sample argument-types in the *Hetucakra*. It is my impression that Diṅnāga sorts these examples strictly according to the *trirūpa-hetu* conditions. If this is right, then the purely formal problem of *IA* can be treated directly in terms of the notion of goodness based on those conditions. The principal formal test of *IA* will be that the canonical argument pattern should be somehow *valid relative to IA*. So, one might try to set down a condition of adequacy of formulations of *IA*, somewhat along the lines:

> *IA* is to be the weakest principle such that every good triple which satisfies *IA* will be sound.

---

9. Richard Hayes, "An Interpretation of Anyāpoha in Diṅnāga's General Theory of Inference," p. 54.

Now this has to be taken with a grain of salt, for there may be no unique weakest principle of this kind. If one looks at the problem more closely, it is not even clear that a weakest formulation would be a most adequate one. Other considerations such as simplicity and naturalness might compete with weakness. Fortunately we won't have to cope with these problems of fine detail in dealing with the several formulations of *IA* offered by *ADT*, for these all turn out to be mutually equivalent and so they can all be regarded as equal in adequacy. Let us first look at some of the formulations.

An initial rough statement of *IA*:

> Its general content is clear enough. We are to assume that the same relations that have been found to hold between the *hetu* class and the *sādhyadharma* class in the induction domain will also be found to hold outside the induction domain or, in other words, in the *pakṣa* domain.[10]

Several more definite formulations are then offered to test against Diṅnāga's treatment of the nine argument-types:

(1) If *vyatireka* holds in the induction domain, then it holds in the *pakṣa* domain.[11]

(2) If *anvaya* fails in the induction domain, then it fails in the *pakṣa* domain.[12]

(3) The counterpart of whichever compartment of the *hetu* class is empty in the induction domain is also empty in the *pakṣa* domain.[13]

The third is presented as the final and presumably most adequate formulation.

---

10. Richard Hayes, "An Interpretation of Anyāpoha in Diṅnāga's General Theory of Inference," p. 54.

11. Ibid., p. 55.

12. Ibid., p. 57-58.

13. Ibid., p. 60.

My first task will be to show that these are not competing formulations, but are in fact all mutually equivalent. Since the third formulation is plainly equivalent to the conjunction of the first two, it will only be necessary to show the equivalence of (1) with (2). I understand each to be a constraint on all triples of terms; the equivalence comes about because what either principle requires for any triple (*P, H, S*) is exactly the same as what the other principle requires for the complementary triple (*P, H,* $\bar{S}$). The only assumption needed for the equivalence proof is that terms are closed under complementation — that for every possible term *S* there is a complementary term $\bar{S}$ whose extension is the complement of that of *S*.

The "induction domain" of *ADT* is the complement *P* of the *pakṣa*;[14] so the formulations (1) and (2) are respectively equivalent to the propositions that for any triple (*P, H, S*) of terms:

(i) All *HP* are *S* → All *HP* are *S*

(ii) No *HP* are *S* → No *HP* are *S*

Assuming that (i) holds for all triples of terms, consider any arbitrary triple (*X, Y, Z*) which satisfies the antecedent of (ii), so no *XY* are Z. By the interdefinability of "all" and "no" it follows that all *XY* are $\bar{Z}$. By hypothesis the triple (*X, Y, Z*) also satisfies (i). Consequently all *XY* are $\bar{Z}$, so no *XY* are Z. This shows that (ii) holds for all triples of terms on the hypothesis that (i) does. Conversely, assuming that (ii) holds for all triples of terms, consider any arbitrary triple (*X, Y, Z*) which satisfies the antecedent of (i), so all $X\bar{Y}$ are Z. By the interdefinability of "all" and "no" it follows that no $X\bar{Y}$ are $\bar{Z}$. By hypothesis (ii) also holds for the triple (*X, Y,* $\bar{Z}$). Consequently no *XY* are Z, so all *XY* are Z. This shows that (i) holds for all triples of terms on the hypothesis that (ii) does. Therefore (1) and (2) are equivalent.

The equivalence of formulations (1) and (2) in turn shows that all three formulations are equivalent; anyone could be taken

---

14. Richard Hayes, "An Interpretation of Anyāpoha in Diṅnāga's General Theory of Inference," pp. 46-48.

as representative. However, in view of the inductive terminology of *ADT*, I am inclined to favour a fourth — equivalent — formulation over any of these three:

(4) If *vyatireka* holds in the induction domain (all $H\bar{P}$ are S) then it holds without qualification (all HP are S).

This formulation permits us to consider the class $H\bar{P}$ as a "sample" from which to "inductively generalize." *IA* invites us to assume that if all members of the sample $H\bar{P}$ belong to S, then all members of the *hetu* belong to S.

Now, it should be obvious that *IA* in any one of these equivalent formulations is formally adequate according to the suggested criterion. Let an *IA-triple* be any triple of terms, which satisfies condition 4, then it is easy to see that *every good IA triple is sound.*

4. Material Adequacy of the Inductive Assumption

Once a formally adequate version of *IA* has been obtained, the question arises as to its *material* adequacy and finally — most importantly — its *historical* adequacy. These questions are logically independent but each has some bearing on the other in subtle and interesting ways. Even though the question of material adequacy will be foremost in this paper, I will try to draw out some of its historical relevance.

The question of material adequacy is basically the question of whether *IA* is true, or at least in some sense highly probable. According to *ADT* something like probability should perhaps be expected:

> It is preferable to say that these judgements are reasonable rather than certain, since they rest on an inductive assumption.[15]

It should be clear by now that *IA* is not in fact true. Indeed, every counter-example to the validity of the canonical form of

15. Richard Hayes, "An Interpretation of Anyāpoha in Diṅnāga's General Theory of Inference," p. 60.

argument is at the same time a counter-example to the truth of *IA*. Here are a few counter-examples:

*E*1. (cetacean, mammal — land-dweller)

*E*2. (monotreme, mammal — viviparous)

*E*3. (white tiger, tiger — striped)

*E*4. (odd integer, integer — divisible by two)

*E*5. (verb, word — untensed)

The first counter-example has already been discussed. Monotremes are exceptional egg-bearing (oviparous) mammals. White tigers, having no pigment, have no stripes. The example from arithmetic is particularly striking — the exceptions here are as numerous as the positive cases. Finally, verbs may be tensed, but other words are untensed. The general pattern should be abundantly clear. It depends on regularities which have exceptions. Whenever some term extends over all exceptions to a given regularity, a counter- example to *IA* can be constructed. These are quite common in biology, in arithmetic, in grammar, and can be found in many other domains as well. No doubt, some cases of this kind could be found involving pots, sounds and others favourite Buddhist terms. Assuming, for example, that pots are either clay or metal, a counter-example to *IA* might arise with some triple like (metal, pot, fragile).

Accordingly, the inductive assumption is not true; but is it at least in some sense highly probable? One way of testing this claim might be to consider whether *IA* holds for most, if not all, triples or terms. To believe this would be to believe something like the statistical proposition that most samples are representative of any population from which they are drawn. Here "most" has to stretch over all possible samples, not just over those which may be judiciously selected by someone. Let us try to formulate this a little more definitely, by rewriting *IA* with the weaker quantifier "most":

(4*) For most triples (*P, H, S*) of terms: If all *HP* are *S* then all *H* are *S*.

Think of the class *H* as the "population" and its subclass *HP* as a "sample" drawn from it, to test for membership in the class *S*. The only restriction here is the formal one that the sample be describable as the difference *HP* between two describable classes *H* and *P*. But, this is practically no restriction at all. Assuming terms to be closed under complements, they are practically bound to be closed also under such differences, so that any describable subclass of *H* can be made to play the role of "inductive sample" for the purpose of testing *IA*. Let *W* be any such class (that is, assume that all *W* are *H*). Then there will be a way of choosing *P* such that *HP* = *W*; just take *P* to be the difference *HW* between *H* and *W*. Then *HP* = *H(HW)* = *HW* = *W*. So, the "statistical variant" (4*) of *IA* is equivalent to the unacceptable claim that most describable samples are representative of the populations from which they are drawn.

To certify unrestricted inference from sample to population would be tantamount to certifying the general inference from "Some *H* are *S*" to "All *H* are *S*," which is hardly a legitimate form of reasoning. Under special conditions inferences of this kind may be drawn with some probability of success. Those special conditions have to secure in some way that the sample is probably representative of the population — because it is sufficiently comprehensive and varied, because it has been selected by some random process, and so on. It seems hopeless to inductively generalize without considering some factors relevant to representativeness of the sample; and yet this is just what *IA* invites us to do.

5. The Problem of Historical Adequacy

The inductive assumption does not stand up well under examination, and this leaves us with the problem of explaining how or why Diṅnāga might have been committed to it, if he was indeed so committed. Before attempting to answer that question, of course, it is advisable to review the evidence for attributing *IA* to Diṅnāga. If that evidence is weak or ambiguous, it may leave room for alternative readings of the text which might relieve Diṅnāga of some or all of the unsupportable burden of *IA*.

In point of fact, *ADT* does not cite any direct textual evidence for attributing *IA* to Diṅnāga. This would not pose a serious problem if *IA* were a reasonable principle, for then it could be justified as a reasonable interpolation. However, *IA* is notably tenuous. If there were clear direct textual evidence, that might tend to force the attribution, probably to Diṅnāga's discredit as a logician. Suitable indirect evidence might at least help us to understand why Diṅnāga might have been committed to an assumption which seems so unsupportable to us. But textual evidence of neither kind has been forthcoming. At the critical juncture, *ADT* is cautiously tentative in its claims:

> Diṅnāga's *Hetucakra* is a very spare presentation. . . . There is no explicit account of what procedure one is to go through in determining whether or not an argument is good. Nevertheless, one can reconstruct a definite procedure, a series of steps, *that one might go through* in order to arrive at the results presented in the *Hetucakra*.[16] (emphasis added)

Considerations of the previous sections suggest that someone going through those steps would do well to exercise restraint in actually drawing the conclusions those steps lead up to. And one might recommend a similar attitude of restraint in actually attributing the reconstructed procedure to Diṅnāga. Is there any viable alternative reading of the text which could free Diṅnāga from this burden?

II

In the next two sections I would like to consider two variants of the system *HD* with increasingly lighter inductive demands. The

16. Richard Hayes, "An Interpretation of Anyāpoha in Diṅnāga's General Theory of Inference," p. 89.

first variant of *HD* reduces — without altogether eliminating — the weight of the inductive assumption; its canonical argument format, like that of *HD*, falls short of logical validity. The other variant of *HD* transfers the entire inductive burden onto the individual reasoner: by doing this it achieves a canonical format that is deductively valid. In settling the matter of logical cogency, the last system finally throws into sharp relief the problem of logical redundancy. Although this shows up most prominently in the third system, I will suggest that in some form it was there all along in the other systems. I take this as an indicator that goodness of arguments according to Diṅnāga, incorporates some extralogical factors whose role in his system — whichever variant one favours — has yet to be fully worked out.

6. Restricting the Syntax

According to some scholars, the *pakṣa* should be an individual rather than a class.[17] If so, it should be denoted by a singular term, for example by a categorized demonstrative "this *P*."[18] Any such change of syntax would entail no small departure from *HD*; to avoid confusion a new label will be adopted for what will now be regarded as a new system, *HD1*. Apart from the modified syntax and its immediate consequences, other departures from *HD* will be minimized. The canonical format for *HD1* will be:

pakṣadharmatā:	This *P* is *H*
anvaya-vyatireka:	All other *H* are *S*
	This *P* is *S*

where the second premise means: "all *H* apart from this *P* are *S*." The notion of goodness is essentially as before: a triple (this

17. As remarked by Professor D. Seyfort Reugg in the discussion of *ADT* at this conference.

18. The particular form of singular term is not essential for present purposes, although it may assume greater importance elsewhere. Definite descriptions or other forms of singular term could also be used here.

P, H, S) is *good according to HD1* if the three terms in that triple make up a canonical *HD1* argument with true premises.

To assess the goodness of an *HD1* triple, one needs to know the denotation of the *pakṣa* term. In practice, it is convenient to specify this explicitly within the triple of terms, thus: (this number [2], prime number, odd).

Once again, the canonical argument pattern is formally invalid: we have just specified a counter-example. The number 2 is prime, and all other prime numbers are odd, but of course the number 2 is not odd. So not all good *HD1* triples are sound. Nor is it obvious that almost all good *HD1* triples are sound. Counter-examples are plentiful in mathematics. Practically any number has many distinctive features, which set it apart from all other numbers. Therefore, many propositions are true for all numbers but for a single exception. All positive integers apart from one are smaller than their squares; all prime numbers apart from two are odd; all odd primes apart from three are unequal to the sum of all their predecessors; and so on. Arithmetic is a rich source of counter-examples; but it is not the only source. Counter-examples can also be found in practically any domain containing nameable individuals. All members of the solar system — apart from the Sun — are planets; all Presidents of the US — apart from Grover Cleveland — had uninterrupted terms; all wives of Henry VIII — apart from Ann Boleyn — died childless; and so on. With counter-examples so plentiful, it is far from obvious that "almost all" good *HD1* triples are sound.

The system *HD1* is clearly an improvement over *HD* from a logical standpoint. Instead of licensing a blanket inference from "some" to "all," it only has to license inferences from "all but one" to "all." Such inferences still carry inductive risk; but at any rate they are not inductively wild. Inferences of this kind for which *H* extends over a large class, actually constitute a special case of the traditional problem of induction: if a long unbroken string of observed *H* have been *S*, is it reasonable to expect the next *H* to be an *S*? The *HD1* problem adds one extra bit of information — that the next H will also be the last.

Doubts that arise about such inferences are based on rather sophisticated considerations such as the coherence of the generalization *All H are S* with the whole corpus of knowledge. Although some vestiges of the *IA* problem survive the transition from *HD* to *HD1*, I think the modified system could plausibly be attributed to Diṅnāga without raising grave problems of historical explanation.

7. The Distributive Strategy

Part I of this paper treated *IA* as a proposition, whose truth is presupposed by Diṅnāga's logical theory. On this construal, *IA* is a heavy burden for the theory to bear. However, in the absence of compelling historical evidence for this construal, we should be free to consider other more favourable ways of locating inductive ingredients in Diṅnāga's logic. An alternative approach would be to let the individual reasoner assume the responsibility for his or her own "inductive leaps." This "distributive" strategy would have the advantage of exegetical charity — it would not force any individual to embrace *IA* in full strength. Indeed, it would not force any individual to embrace so much as a single counter-example to *IA*.

In pursuit of this strategy, let us consider a second variant system *HD2*, whose canonical format has one additional premise:

pakṣadharmatā:	All *P* are *H*
	Some *P* are *H*
anvaya:	Some $H\bar{P}$ are *S*
vyatireka:	All $H\bar{P}$ are *S*
inductive premise:	All *HP* are *S*
	All *P* are *S*

I have cast this in fully articulated form so that we can more easily focus on the logical role of various parts.

A triple of terms (*P, H, S*) is *good according to HD2* if and only if the corresponding *HD*2 argument has all of its premises true. So, we have built into the conditions of *HD*2-goodness the requirement that the terms of the argument form an *IA* triple — the *HD*2-good triples are exactly the *HD*-good *IA* triples. So, at least this accomplishes the desideratum of somehow restricting the scope of *HD* to those cases for which the problematic *IA* actually holds. All inductive risk is thereby transferred onto the individual reasoner's confirmation of his or her premises. The canonical argument format of *HD2* is formally valid: *all possible HD2-good triples are sound.*

The new canonical format could be partly reconsolidated now, so as to bring it more into line with the second reading of Diṅnāga's "later" theory of inference which is briefly discussed in the final section of *ADT*:

> [I]t could be that the *vyatireka* clause adds one new piece of information by saying "no *hetu* anywhere (whether in the *pakṣa* class or outside it) occurs without the *sādhyadharma*."[19]

Following this interpretation, the "new piece of information" contained in the "inductive premise" of *HD2* could be incorporated into a strengthened *vyatireka* condition, yielding a variant format for *HD*2:

pakṣadharmatā:	All *P* are *H*
	Some *P* are *H*
anvaya:	Some $H\bar{P}$ are *S*
strong *vyatireka*:	All *H* are *S*
	All *P* are *S*

Here the *vyatireka* and inductive premise are jointly replaced by the strong *vyatireka* condition.

19. Richard Hayes, "An Interpretation of Anyāpoha in Diṅnāga's General Theory of Inference," p. 64.

Having finally settled the problem of deductive insufficiency, we immediately confront the opposite problem of deductive oversufficiency. The premises of *HD*2 are strong enough to secure the conclusion, but they are curiously stronger than necessary for this purpose. The two existential premises (*anvaya* and the second *pakṣadharmatā* condition) are deductively redundant in the straightforward sense that removing them would preserve formal validity of the argument pattern. We shall want to consider what this means.

The two existential premises pose somewhat different problems, so it seems best to look at them separately. The second *pakṣadharmatā* condition apparently entered into the system *HD* through a textual interpolation:

> Although Diṅnāga does not specify how it is that we are to arrive at this conclusion, I think we can safely assume that a procedure parallel to the one described above . . . is to be followed in determining that every member of the *pakṣa* class is a *hetu*-possessor.[20]

Thus parity of treatment is accorded to the two premises of the canonical (consolidated) format of *HD*. They are uniformly treated as strong ("every") universal statements, with existential import. If so, however, it is somewhat surprising to find the conclusion being treated as a weak ("any") universal statement, without existential import; and indeed this is the crux of the matter. The second *pakṣadharmatā* condition is deductively redundant in *HD*, *HD1* and *HD2* if and only if the conclusion is construed as a weak ("all") rather than a strong ("every") universal statement.[21] So the oversufficiency of *pakṣadharmatā*

20. Richard Hayes, "An Interpretation of Anyāpoha in Diṅnāga's General Theory of Inference," p. 52.

21. The notion of deductive redundancy is clear enough in application to valid arguments (as in *HD*2) but troublesome to explicate in application to deductively incomplete arguments (as in *HD* and *HD*1). My working criterion is: a premise is deductively redundant →

could be resolved in either of two ways: by strengthening the conclusion (as mooted in *ADT*)[22] so as to require existential import, or by weakening the *pakṣadharmatā* so as not to require it. On this matter one would like to let the texts decide — if they will.

The situation with respect to the *anvaya* condition is rather different. In *ADT*, deductive redundancy of *anvaya* is treated as presenting a "serious obstacle" to attributing the strengthened *vyatireka* — and so in effect *HD2* — to Diṅnāga. Let us review the argument.

8. What is Goodness?

It is clear enough that deductive redundancy is a feature of *HD2* — and, I shall suggest, of *HD1* and *HD* as well. But it is less clear what kind of a *problem* this poses. To me it suggests that goodness according to Diṅnāga involves more than deductive validity and soundness; or at any rate, involves something apart from those purely deductive factors.

In the words of *ADT*, the strengthened *vyatireka* condition seems to render the *anvaya* condition "altogether superfluous," whereas Diṅnāga continued to use that condition for the evaluation of arguments:

→ in an argument if and only if it is removable without loss of validity from every "admissible completion" of that argument. The admissible completions of an argument are certain selected valid expansions of that argument. The notion of admissibility is hard to explicate but is needed in order to disallow certain ways of undercutting the criterion such as the adjoining of conditional premises, inconsistent premises, etc. Having acknowledged the difficulty of formalizing this notion, I appeal to the reader to see that Some *P* are *H* is deductively irrelevant to All *P* are *S*. One must be prepared to make some such judgements on an intuitive basis in any event, in order to be in a position to test proposed explications of deductive redundancy as they come forward.

22. Richard Hayes, "An Interpretation of Anyāpoha in Diṅnāga's General Theory of Inference," pp. 62-63.

> [A]ccording to him the *hetu* is *inconclusive* because it fails to fulfil the *anvaya* condition. And so, it would appear, the *anvaya* relation is not superfluous after all, for it still appears in Diṅnāga's mind to be necessary in order to eliminate arguments like that given in *HC5* in which the *hetu* class is coextensive with the *pakṣa* class.[23]

As I understand this situation, Diṅnāga evaluates as "inconclusive" a type of argument which on the strengthened interpretation is formally valid. Now the argument in question (Sound is transitory because it is audible) is in fact inconclusive in the technical sense — neither the triple (*S*, *A*, *T*) nor the complementary triple (*S*, *A*, *T*) is good according to *HD*2. If this argument is put into canonical format for *HD*2, it will have one false premise (*anvaya*) since there are no audible non- sounds. What this shows so far is that *anvaya*, has a role to play in the evaluation of arguments by Diṅnāga's standards. We can see it to be "superfluous" by purely deductive standards, and the text here shows it to be "not superfluous" for goodness according to Diṅnāga. Two different standards are involved.

If there is a problem here I think it is one of accurately formulating and coming to understand the rationale for what appear to be extra-deductive factors in the criteria of goodness. Diṅnāga deliberately disqualified triples with coextensive *pakṣa* and *hetu* terms; *anvaya* as formulated throughout *ADT* rules out all such cases. But, *anvaya* is common to all the three systems we have considered. One can verify more generally that goodness according to any of the systems *HD*, *HD*1, *HD*2 never permits the *pakṣa* to be coextensive with the *hetu*, nor does it permit the *pakṣa* to be coextensive with the *sādhya*. *Anvaya* as formulated in *ADT*, rules out both forms of coextensivity. And yet these strictures against coextensivity make no purely logical contribution to securing the conclusion. Some valid and even "reasonable" inferences violate them, as in:

23. Richard Hayes, "An Interpretation of Anyāpoha in Diṅnāga's General Theory of Inference," p. 66.

All featherless bipeds are human
All humans are rational

All featherless bipeds are rational

and yet the triple (featherless biped, human, rational) is not good according to *HD*, *HD1*, or *HD2*. Both coextensivity requirements go beyond the demands of pure logic; they make no purely logical contributions to the *anyāpoha* conclusion, nor for that matter would they have any purely logical contributions to make even to the stronger (every *P* is *S*) conclusion.

One more indication that something beyond purely logical demands is in question here is the fact that none of the three systems imposes any coextensivity structure on the (*hetu-sādhya*) pair: there can be arguments which are good according to all three systems and which have coextensive *hetu* and *sādhya*.

There are several unexplained discrepancies here, which might be put to work as signposts towards the extralogical factors operative in Diṅnāga's notion of goodness. But each of them is common to all three systems and so I submit that none of them should count as evidence for one or against another as an interpretation of the *Hetucakra*.

4

Dharmakīrti and His Theory of Inference

Brendan S. Gillon

0. Introduction

What I want to examine is the coherence of Dharmakīrti's basic metaphysics in so far as that metaphysics provides the grounds for his definition and classification of inference. In particular, I shall show that the basic metaphysics, that is, the basic ontology and epistemology, which underlies his definition of inference does not sustain his classification of inference into three types.

In undertaking this task, I proceed from three assumptions. First, I assume that Dharmakīrti believes that some arguments are good and others are bad. Second, I assume that he believes that there are principles on the basis of which good arguments are distinguished from bad ones. And finally, I assume that he believes that such principles are factual (i.e. grounded in the way things are). These assumptions about Dharmakīrti, if not uncontroversial, should be. After all, Dharmakīrti uses a criterion (*trairūpya-hetu*) to distinguish good arguments from bad ones, and the criterion is based on a view of the way things are.

1.0. Basic Ontology and Epistemology

In basic ontology, the world consists of objects and relations.[1] There are two kinds of object, substratum (*dharmin*) and superstratum (*dharma*). A superstratum (*dharma*) bears at least

1. This claim will be modified in the course of the paper, as other facts of the basic ontology require enlargements of it.

one relation to a substratum (*dharmin*). This relation is designated in a variety of ways. For convenience here, I shall use the name given it by Navya-Nyāya, namely, occurrence (*vṛtti*). This relation obtains if and only if a superstratum (*dharma*) is in or on the substratum (*dharmin*). One such relation is inherence (*samavāya*). To see how this relation obtains, suppose that the world includes such objects as blueness (i.e the colour blue) and pots and that if a pot is blue, then blueness occurs in the pot, that is blueness inheres in the pot. The converse of the relation of occurrence is the relation of possession. A substratum (*dharmin*) possesses a superstratum (*dharma*) if and only if the superstratum (*dharma*) occurs in the substratum (*dharmin*). In addition, there is a relation which superstrata (*dharma*) bears to superstrata (*dharma*). This relation can usually be defined in terms of occurrence. Later, this relation comes to be known as pervasion (*vyāpti*), but here it is also known by its converse, concomitance (*anvaya*). One superstratum (*dharma*) is concomitant with another if and only if in whatever substratum (*dharmin*) the former occurs, the latter occurs. The relation is both reflexive and transitive. That is to say, every superstratum (*dharma*) is concomitant with itself; and, if a superstratum (*dharma*) is concomitant with another, and the other with a third, then the first is concomitant with the third.

As a result of these relations, the world embodies a structure. If one superstratum (*dharma*), designated by H (*hetu-dharma*), is concomitant with another S (*sādhyadharma*), and if the former superstratum (*dharma*) occurs in a substratum (*dharmin*), designated by p (*pakṣa*), then superstratum (*dharma*) S occurs in substratum (*dharmin*) p. This structure can be expressed by the following:

Major Premise:	Whatever has H has S
Minor Premise:	p has H
Conclusion:	p has S

Basic epistemology presupposes the ontology just described; but the deployment of the basic epistemology requires the basic ontology to be augmented. The most obvious augmentation of the ontology is the addition of an observer to the world. The observer has a set of beliefs. An observer is said to accept a belief if and only if the belief is a member of the set of beliefs which the observer has. Thus, if an observer has a set of beliefs which includes the belief that the pot is blue and the belief that every oak is a tree, then the observer accepts the belief that the pot is blue and the belief that every oak is a tree. Beliefs about the world are of two kinds: beliefs about which superstrata (*dharma*) are in which substrata (*dharmin*) and beliefs about which superstrata (*dharma*) are concomitant with which superstrata (*dharma*). Beliefs of the first kind can be expressed in the form "Substratum (*dharmin*) *a* has superstratum (*dharma*) *C*," or more succinctly as "*a* has *C*." This belief is illustrated by the first example given above. Beliefs of the second kind can be expressed in the form "Whatever has superstratum (*dharma*) *A* has superstratum (*dharma*) *B*," or more easily as "Whatever has *A* has *B*." The second belief in the set of beliefs given above as example has this form.

Also, if an observer accepts a belief, then he necessarily accepts that the superstrata (*dharma*) of the belief exists, if it is a belief of the second kind, or, he necessarily accepts that both the superstratum (*dharma*) and the substratum (*dharmin*) of the belief exist, if it is a belief of the first kind. So, if an observer accepts that whatever is an oak is a tree, then he accepts that oaks exist (more precisely, that oakness exists) and that trees exist (more precisely, that treeness exists). Similarly, if he accepts that the pot is blue, then he accepts that the pot exists and that blue things exist (more precisely, that blueness exists).

An observer may augment the number of beliefs in the set of his beliefs in two ways, by perception (*pratyakṣa*) or by inference (*anumāna*). In the first way, if an observer perceives that a substratum (*dharmin*), say *a*, has a superstratum (*dharma*), say *C*, then he adds a belief to that effect to his set of beliefs. That is, if an observer perceives that *a* has *C*, then he accepts that *a* has *C*. So, an observer accepts that the pot is blue when he perceives that the pot is blue. In the second way, an observer adds to his set of beliefs a belief wherein what is believed fits the form of the conclusion of the inference-schema, if an observer picks from his set of beliefs wherein what is believed fits the form of the two premises of the inference-schema. In other words, if an observer accepts two beliefs which can be expressed in the form of the premises of the inference-schema, then he accepts the belief which is expressed in the form of the conclusion of the schema. The ontic schema set out above can now be taken over as an epistemic capacity of the observer.

Major Premise:	*A* (whatever has *H* has *S*)
Minor Premise:	*A* (*p* has *H*)
Conclusion:	*A* (*p* has *S*)

(*A* abbreviates the epistemic operator "the observer apprehends that (*a*)").

Note that the acceptability of the conclusion of an inference depends not only on the logical deducibility of the conclusion from the premises but also on the acceptability of the premises.

2.0. Dharmakīrti's Definition and Classification of Inference

Let me now turn to what Dharmakīrti says about the inference-schema. Two points need to be recalled. First, consider what he says about the form of the inference-schema.

pakṣa-dharmaḥ tat-aṁśena vyāptaḥ hetuḥ

> The *hetu* is a superstratum (*dharma*) of the *pakṣa* and it (i.e. the *hetu*) is pervaded by a feature (i.e. another superstratum (*dharma*), that is, the *sādhya*] which is in it (i.e. the *pakṣa*).

Second, consider the criterion (*trairūpya-hetu*) he requires the relation of pervasion (*vyāpti*) to satisfy.

sapakṣe eva sattvam [*hetu-dharmasya*]

The *hetu* is (i.e. occurs) only in *sapakṣa* [i.e. those substrata (*dharmin*) other than the *pakṣa* where the *sādhya* is, i.e. occurs].

asapakṣe asattvam eva [*hetu-dharmasya*]

The *hetu* is not (i.e. does not occur) in any *asapakṣa* [i.e. those substrata (*dharmin*) in which the *sādhya* is not, i.e. does not occur].

Now, observe that the two crucial relations are pervasion (*vyāpti*), a relation between superstrata (*dharma*), and occurrence (*vṛtti*), a relation between a superstratum (*dharma*) and a substratum (*dharmin*). While one might have an intuitive grasp of occurrence (*vṛtti*) in so far as it is exhibited in such paradigm cases as a pot being blue, one does not have any such intuitive grasp of pervasion (*vyāpti*).

2.1. Inference from Subsets (Svabhāva-Anumāna)

In any event, a paradigm example of inference from subsets (*svabhāva-anumāna*) provides a good intuitive grasp of both relations. Consider the following one:

ayam vṛkṣaḥ śiṁśapātvāt

This is a tree because it is a *śiṁpśapā.*

For the ease of thought, let me translate this into a canonical form with the inference-schema set out above.

Major Premise: Whatever has *śiṁśapā-tva* has treeness.

Minor Premise: This has *śiṁśapā-tva.*

Conclusion: This has treeness.

In this particular inference, the relation of occurrence (*vṛtti*) is the relation which treeness (*vṛkṣa-tva*), say, bears to a tree (*vṛkṣa*). This relation is more specifically referred to as the relation of inherence (*samavāya*), the relation which a superstratum (*dharma*) bears to its possessors, that is, each of its substrata (*dharmin*). In general, it is assumed that a superstratum (*dharma*) either does or does not inhere in a substratum (*dharmin*) and that it does not both inhere and not in a substratum (*dharmin*). It follows from this that each superstratum (*dharma*) determines a set of substrata (*dharmin*), namely, the set of substrata (*dharmin*) in which the superstratum (*dharma*) inheres. So, for every inference which fits the form of the inference-schema and in which the relation of occurrence (*vṛtti*) is taken to be the relation of inherence (*samavāya*), the relation of pervasion (*vyāpti*), or its equivalent converse, the relation of concomitance (*anvaya*), can be reduced to the relation of being a superset, or its equivalent converse, the relation of being a subset (*svabhāva*) respectively.

2.2. Inference from Effect (*Kāryānumāna*)

Notice that the inference-schema commits one to the same substratum (*dharmin*) being mentioned in both the minor premise and the conclusion. This requires, then, that cause and effect must share the substratum (*dharmin*), when one is inferred from the other. Yet, the notion of cause and effect, at least as used in ordinary language, strains this requirement. Frequently, those things which are connected by cause and effect have different substrata (*dharmin*). Thus, for example, the striking of a match causes a house to burn down. The striking occurs in the match and the burning in the house. Indeed, if the world has only superstrata (*dharma*), substrata (*dharmin*), and the relation of inherence (*samavāya*), then it is hard to see how there are inferences where pervasion (*vyāpti*) is the relation of cause and effect (*kārya-kāraṇa-bhāva*). Consider the following paradigm example of inference from effect (*kāryānumāna*):

Major Premise:	Whatever has smoke has fire.
Minor Premise:	Mt. Meru has smoke.
Conclusion:	Mt. Meru has fire.

Although smoke is thought to be the effect of fire, neither smoke nor fire inhere in Mt. Meru. In fact, neither smoke nor fire are thought to inhere anywhere. Hence, smoke and fire never have a common substratum (*dharmin*). What is needed, then, is some change or addition to the basic ontology. What is done is to introduce the relation of contact (*saṁyoga*) as another form of the relation of occurrence (*vṛtti*). As with the relation of inherence (*samavāya*) so with the relation of contact (*saṁyoga*), it either obtains between two putative relata or it does not, and it does not both obtain and not obtain. As a result, each object determines a set, namely the set of other objects with which it is in contact. Similarly, a set of objects determines a set, namely the set of objects with which some member of the first set is in contact. And so, for every inference whose form is that of the inference-schema and whose relation of occurrence (*vṛtti*) is that of contact (*saṁyoga*), the relation of pervasion (*vyāpti*), or its equivalent converse, the relation of concomitance (*anvaya*), is reducible to the relation of being a superset, or its equivalent converse, the relation of being a subset (*svabhāva*) respectively.

This manoeuvre introduces certain strains into the ontology. Previously, the relation of occurrence (*vṛtti*), in so far as it was taken to be the relation of inherence (*samavāya*), was asymmetrical: if one thing occurs (that is, inheres) in another, then the other does not occur (that is, inhere) in the one. This asymmetry divided the objects of the world into two disjoint kinds, superstrata (*dharma*), intuitively taken to be universals, and substrata (*dharmin*), intuitively taken to be particulars. The relation of contact (*saṁyoga*) is a symmetrical relation: that is, if one object contacts another, then the other contacts the one. The subsumption of the relation of contact (*saṁyoga*) under the relation of occurrence (*vṛtti*) implies that the latter relation is neither asymmetrical nor symmetrical. It also implies that the terms "superstratum" (*dharma*) and "substratum" (*dharmin*) are not terms of material ontology as, say, "universal" and "particular" are, but are terms of formal ontology as, say, "relatum" is. So the division of the material ontology is lost, for now a particular, say a pot, can be both a superstratum (*dharma*) with respect to the ground with which it is in contact and it is a substratum (*dharmin*) with respect to the colour blue (that is, blueness) which inheres in it. The accommodation of the inference from effect (*kāryānumāna*) is at the expense of preserving asymmetry in the relation of occurrence (*vṛtti*). While this change is by no means disastrous, it does insinuate strains into the simpler conceptions.

Let me now draw attention to a crucial point about inference from effect (*kāryānumāna*) which will come up later, and the full and proper discussion of which is not to be taken up by me here. I stated earlier that the relation of pervasion (*vyāpti*) is not symmetrical. The example of inference from subsets (*svabhāvānumāna*) illustrates this: treeness pervades *śiṁśapā-tva*, but *śiṁśapā-tva* does not pervade treeness. The example of inference from effect (*kāryānumāna*) illustrates that the effect (e.g. smoke) pervades its cause (i.e fire). But the question arises, does the cause pervade its effect? The answer to this question is that it does and it does not, depending on how one construes cause. Without going into an elaboration of Dharmakīrti's notion of causation, let me just point out that the effect pervades its "sufficient" cause, that is, when the cause is the minimal set of states of affairs sufficient to bring about its effect and this minimal set has indeed brought about its effect (cf. *kāryānupalabdhi* discussed in the Svārthānumāna Chapter of the *Nyāyabindu*).

2.3. Inference from Non-Apprehension (Anupalabdhy-anumāna)

This form of inference differs in a crucial way from the previous two kinds of inferences. Whereas the two previously discussed inferences depend on facts completely independent of the observer (for the paradigmatic cases, in any event), this form of inference depends crucially upon the state of mind of the observer.

Let me now introduce states of affairs into the ontology. Intuitively, states of affairs are what in the world correspond to, or make true, true propositions. I shall not attempt to give both necessary and sufficient conditions for them, rather I shall only give sufficient conditions. If a substratum (*dharmin*) *a* exists and a superstratum (*dharma*) *P* exists, and superstratum (*dharma*) *P* exists in substratum (*dharmin*) *a*, then *P* being in *a* is a state of affairs and *P* not being in *a* is a state of affairs. The former is a positive one and the latter is a negative one.

The ontology now sustains a distinction between negative and positive states of affairs. What was said earlier about the basic epistemology was confined to remarks about what conditions in the world, when apprehended (*upalabdha*), bring an observer to apprehend something else in the world. It is now necessary to say more about the relation of the observer to what he perceives or infers, the two exclusive modes of apprehension (*upalabdhi*). In particular, we need to know more about the epistemology of the knower. The apprehender (i.e the observer in so far as he apprehends) was viewed earlier as a set of beliefs. Here it is convenient to speak in terms of states of mind or cognitions (*jñāna*) instead of beliefs. And so now the apprehender is viewed as a set of states of mind or cognitions. States of mind can be regarded as resulting from an act, a mental act, namely cognition. The term "cognition" (*jñāna*), as should now be evident, is ambiguous. This ambiguity, known for some time now to lexicographers, is the one between the act and the result of the act which a nominalized verb denotes. It is the same ambiguity which one finds in the mathematician's use of the word "function," either denoting the rule whereby a unique value is associated with some value or set of values, or denoting the associated value. Indeed, one can think of cognition as a function (in both senses): it is that which associates a unique state of mind with a state of affairs, and it is that state of mind which is associated with the state of affairs. The central problem in epistemology can be seen as the problem of defining this function. And Dharmakīrti's treatment of inference from non-apprehension (*anupalabdhy-anumāna*) can be seen as an attempt to address this problem.

What, then, is his notion of inference from non-apprehension (*anupalabdhy-anumāna*)? To begin with, consider one of his paradigm examples of such an inference.

na atra dhūmaḥ upalabdhi-lakṣaṇa-prāptasya anupalabdheḥ

Smoke is not here since it is not apprehended and it is *upalabdhi-lakṣaṇa-prāpta*.

What is crucial here is the proviso of the minor premise, which is left untranslated above. Dharmakīrti explains it as follows:

upalabdhi-lakṣaṇa-prāptiḥ upalambha-pratyayāntara-sakalyam svabhāva-viśeṣaś ca

Upalabdhi-lakṣaṇa-prāpti includes the particular [*svabhāva-viśeṣa*] and all the other causal factors leading to its being perceived.

To see how this conception works, let me turn to an example. Consider an observer perceiving smoke. The state of mind in which the observer is perceiving smoke is the effect of some minimal but sufficient set of states of affairs. Let me denote this set by S and its members by $s_1, \ldots, s_{n+1}$. One state of affairs, which is sure to be a member of this set is the state of affairs, which is the smoke being present (to the observer). Let me call that state of affairs p. The set which results from taking this state of affairs out of S will be denoted by C. *Svabhāva-viśeṣa* denotes p, that is to say, the state of affairs of the smoke being present (to the observer); and *upalambha-pratyayāntara-sakalya* denotes set C. Let me denote the members of C by $c_1, \ldots, c_n$. Then, using these abbreviations, the essential idea can be expressed in the following compact form:

p and c_1 and . . . and c_n cause Ap.

In light of the notion of causation in use here, the following seems true. If some minimal but sufficient set of states of affairs causes an observer to apprehend some state of affairs, and if this minimal but sufficient set obtains, then the observer apprehends the state of affairs. This can be displayed somewhat more perspicuously by the following symbolic representation.

$((p \ \& \ c_1 \&. . . \& \ c_n$ cause $Ap) \ \& \ p \ \& \ c_1. . . \& \ c_n$=>$Ap$.

This is logically equivalent to the following:

$-Ap \ \& \ c_1 \ \& \ . . . \ \& \ c_n \ \& \ ((p \ \& \ c_1 \ \& \ . . . \ \& \ c_n)$ cause $Ap)$ =>$-p$.

In other words, if (1) an observer does not apprehend that *p*, but (2) *p* is a member of a minimal but sufficient set of states of affairs causing the apprehension of *p*, and (3) all members of the set but *p* obtain, then *p* does not obtain.

What the foregoing considerations show is that, to be good, any purported inference from non-apprehension (*anupalabdhy-anumāna*) must ultimately have the following form:

Major Premise: $-A(Pa) \ \& \ c_1 \ \& \ . . . \ \& \ c_N \ \& \ ((Pa \ \& \ c_1 \ \& \ . . . \ \& \ c_N)$ cause $A(Pa))$=> $-Pa$.

Minor Premise: $-A(Pa) \ \& \ c_1 \ \& \ . . . \ \& \ c_N \ \& \ ((Pa \ \& \ c_1 \ \& \ . . . \ \& \ c_N)$ cause $A(Pa))$.

Conclusion: $-Pa$.

And if Dharmakīrti is to have a unified view of inference, then good inferences from non-apprehension (*anupalabdhy-anumāna*) must be adequately specifiable in terms of the (ontic) inference-schema (given above in section 1.0) and construable in the basic metaphysics developed so far. In other words, the form of inference just stated must be reducible to the canonical inference form used to represent the first two types of inferences; and the relation of pervasion (*vyāpti*), at the same time, must, when construed in terms of the basic metaphysics, be reducible to the relation of being a superset.

But not only does Dharmakīrti not do this, there are good reasons to believe it cannot be done in a way consistent with the basic metaphysics so far developed, no matter how it is extended.

To see why, recall that the basic metaphysics, at this point, has only two relations, inherence (*samavāya*) and contact (*saṁyoga*), the former relation obtaining between a universal and a particular and the latter relation obtaining between pairs of particulars. There is no relation between particulars (e.g. a pot) and apprehensions of universals (of particulars) (e.g. apprehensions of blueness in a pot). Moreover, there is no relation between particulars (e.g. a pot) and states of affairs (e.g. the states of affairs which together with a pot's presence to an observer produce an apprehension of its presence). And finally, the notion of causality, implicit in the basic metaphysics for inferences from effect (*kāryānumāna*) is not appropriate to the notion of causality explicitly required for inferences from non-apprehension (*anupalabdhy-anumāna*): the former relation of causality is a relation defined between pairs of particulars (e.g. smoke and fire), the latter notion of causality between sets of states of affairs and a state of affairs (e.g. the minimum but sufficient set of states of affairs, including the presence of a pot and the apprehension of the presence of a pot).

But even if one supposes that the basic metaphysics could be properly supplemented to fill these lacunae, there is an excellent reason to believe that the inference from non-apprehension (*anupalabdhy-anumāna*) will not be reduced to the inference from subsets (*svabhāvānumāna*). The validity of the latter inference is provided by a structure which need only embody set-membership and set-inclusion. The inference from non-apprehension (*anupalabdhy-anumāna*), when formulated by the commentators in terms not using the proviso *upalabdhi-lakṣaṇa-prāpti* is formulated as a counterfactual inference (cf. for example, Dharmottara's discussion of this proviso in Dharmakīrti's Svārthānumāna chapter of his *Nyāyabindu*). Here, one is told that one infers the absence of a pot from the knowledge that one has no such apprehension and from the knowledge that if it were present it would be apprehended. It is known from modern logic that these kinds of inferences, counterfactual ones, are essentially richer than the kinds of inferences seen so far. That is, not only does their logical formulation require a richer language for their adequate expression but their truth requires a world with an essentially richer structure, that is, one in which there are not only particulars and sets of particulars (provided by universals) but also sets of sects of particulars.

There is one interesting sidelight to all this, which should not go unremarked. In this discussion of inference from non-apprehension (*anupalabdhy-anumāna*), it was seen that this inference rested on an unexplicated notion of causality. Just now, it was pointed out that the inference often receives a counterfactual formulation, in particular when the proviso *upalabdhi-lakṣaṇa-prāpti* is being explained by commentators. Recent work in modern philosophy has attempted to define various notions of causality in terms of counterfactuals.[2]

---

2. Cf. John Pollock, *Subjunctive Reasoning* (Dordrecht: D. Reidel Publishing Company, 1976).

5

Some Thoughts on Antarvyāpti, Bahirvyāpti, and Trairūpya

Kamaleswar Bhattacharya

INDIAN logic, whether Brāhmanical, Buddhist or Jaina, considers the *vyāpti,* i.e. the invariable concomitance (literally, "pervasion") between the "reason" (*hetu*) and the "object to be established" (*sādhya*), to be the ground of all inference. However, the logicians are divided on the question of whether this concomitance is external or internal. And these "external" and "internal" concomitances, in turn, have given rise to diverse problems of interpretation among modern scholars. In the present paper I wish to make an attempt to solve some of these problems.

Surendranath Dasgupta, in his famous *History of Indian Philosophy,* thus defines "external concomitance" (*bahirvyāpti*) and "internal concomitance" (*antarvyāpti*):

> The concomitance of smoke with fire is technically called *vyāpti.* When this refers to the concomitance of cases containing smoke with those having fire, it is called *bahirvyāpti;* and when it refers to the conviction of the concomitance of smoke with fire, without any relation to the circumstances under which the concomitance was observed, it is called *antarvyāpti.*[1]

Satkari Mookerjee, in his pioneer work *The Buddhist Philosophy of Universal Flux,* published some fifty years ago but still valuable,

1. Dasgupta (1922), p. 346. Cf. pp. 156-57, about Ratnākaraśānti (see below).

proposed to translate *antarvyāpti* as "intrinsic determination," borrowing the expression from McTaggart.[2] And this interpretation has been adopted by other scholars working under Mookerjee's influence, direct or indirect.

Although these interpretations are not without justification, the primary distinction, as expressed by the ancient logicians, seems to be this: there is *bahirvyāpti* "external concomitance" when this concomitance is apprehended in a corroborative example (*dṛṣṭānta*), whereas there is *antarvyāpti* "internal concomitance" when it is apprehended in the subject (*pakṣa*) of the inference itself.[3]

Dasgupta also writes: "The Buddhists, since they did not admit the notion of generality, etc. preferred *antarvyāpti* view of concomitance to *bahirvyāpti* as a means of inference."[4]

This idea is certainly wrong, as it is only rarely that the Buddhist logicians adopt the *antarvyāpti* theory: apart from a passage of the *Nyāyamañjarī*, where Jayantabhaṭṭa associates this theory with the Buddhists,[5] and the famous *Antarvyāptisamarthana* of Ratnākaraśānti, of which I am going to speak later, we do not possess — so far as I am aware — any clear evidence in this respect.

The origin of this theory of *antarvyāpti* seems to lie elsewhere. Siddhasena Divākara, the Jaina logician, appears to have been the first logician to proclaim it, in his *Nyāyāvatāra*.[6] Siddhasena's

2. Mookerjee (1935/1975), p. 400.

3. Cf. Siddharṣi, *Vivṛtti on Nyāyāvatāra* 20: *antaḥ pakṣamadhye vyāptiḥ sādhanasya sādhyākrāntatvam antarvyāptiḥ. tayaiva sādhyasya gamyasya siddheḥ pratīteḥ bahir vivakṣitadharmiṇo 'nyatra dṛṣṭāntadharmiṇy udāhṛtiḥ vyāptidarśanarūpā vyarthā* . . . Vādidevasūri, *Pramāṇanayatattvālokālaṁkāra* III, 38: *pakṣīkṛta eva viṣaye sādhanasya sādhyena vyāptir antarvyāptiḥ, anyatra tu bahirvyāptiḥ.*

4. Op. cit., p. 346.

5. *Nyāyamañjarī* I, p. 101.

6. *Nyāyāvatāra* 20.

date, unfortunately, has not yet been determined with certainty.[7] Be that as it may, it was the Jainas who upheld the *antarvyāpti* theory most resolutely, and it seems that it was the necessity to establish their philosophic position which led them to invent it, and that it was the same necessity which pushed some Buddhists to adopt it. The Jainas had to establish inferentially their thesis: "All things are composed of many aspects" (*anekāntātmaka*), from the logical reason (*hetu*) "existence" (*sattva*),[8] and the Buddhists had to establish, from the same logical reason, their own: "All things are momentary" (*kṣaṇika*). Now, the theory of *trairūpya* "three characteristics [of the valid reason]" ("existence in the subject," *pakṣe sattvam*, "existence in what is similar to the subject," *sapakṣe sattvam*, and "non-existence in what is dissimilar to the subject," *vipakṣe sattvam*),[9] — a theory which the Buddhist logician Diṅnāga had brought to perfection (but it was not invented by him, as it existed long before him in the Buddhist tradition),[10] and which, clearly, is in favour of the theory of *bahirvyāpti*, since, in accordance with it, the concomitance, positive and negative, between the reason and the object to be established has to be apprehended in external examples, homogeneous and heterogeneous, — was not applicable to these inferences. The reason "existence," according to this theory, would be a fallacious reason, a reason that is inconclusive, being a property peculiar to the subject (all things), with respect to which no extraneous example, either homogeneous (*sapakṣa*) or heterogeneous (*vipakṣa*), is forthcoming — like the sixteenth reason of Uddyotakara.[11] In order that the reason could be valid, one had, therefore, to give up having recourse to the examples and conceive the concomitance as "internal," that is, as one to be apprehended in the subject of the inference itself.

---

7. See Mimaki (1976), n. 192.
8. Cf. Vādidevasūri, *Pramāṇanayatattvālokālaṁkāra* III, 39.
9. This is a crude formulation, enough for our present purpose.
10. Cf. Mimaki (1976), p. 47.
11. Cf. Randle (1930), p. 237.

In this respect, an important problem has arisen concerning the relative chronology of three masters of the Buddhist University of Vikramaśilā, at the end of the tenth and the beginning of the eleventh century. Dr Katsumi Mimaki, in his valuable work *La réfutation bouddhique de la permanence des choses* (*Sthirasiddhidūṣaṇa*) *et la preuve de la momentanéité des choses* (*Kṣaṇabhaṅgasiddhi*), writes:

> Ratnākaraśānti, connu par ailleurs sous le nom de Śānti-pa ou Śānti-pāda, est éléve de Nāropa pour l 'étude du tantrisme et un des maîtres d' Atīśa (982-1054). Nāropa eut aussi pour éléve Jñānaśrīmitra et Atīśa doit également beaucoup à ce dernier. Ratnakīrti a étudié les Sūtra et Tantra sous la direction de Ratnākaraśānti. Donc, pour ce qui est des études tantriques, on peut établir ainsi l'ordre chronologique de ces trois logiciens: Ratnākaraśānti — Jñānaśrīmitra — Ratnakīrti.[12]

The same author states, however:

> En revanche, pour ce qui est des études logiques, l'ordre diffère sensiblement. C'est Jñānaśrīmitra qui a achevé la logique bouddhique de l' époque tardive. Ratnakīrti a développé sous sa direction certaines théories typiques de la logique bouddhique tardive, telles que celles de l' exclusion conceptuelle (*apoha*) et de l' inclusion (*vyāpti*). D'autre part, l' *Antarvyāptisamarthana*, le seul traité logique de Ratnākaraśānti que nous connaissions, prend visiblement en considération la *Kṣaṇabhaṅgasiddhi* de Ratnakīrti. Par conséquent, nous pouvons établir ainsi l'ordre chronologique de la progression des études logiques: Jñānaśrīmitra — Ratnakīrti — Ratnākaraśānti.[13]

Later on, he clearly says, by referring to other authors: "Ratnakīrti est le maître de Ratnākaraśānti pour ce qui est des études de logique."[14]

---

12. Mimaki (1976), p. 3.
13. Ibid.
14. Ibid., p. 54.

It has often been thought, indeed, that Ratnākaraśānti, the author of the *Antarvyāptisamarthana*, was a disciple or, at least, a successor (rather than a predecessor) of Ratnakīrti. Mahāmahopādhyāya Phaṇibhūṣaṇa Tarkavāgīśa, in his great work in Bengali on the *Nyāyadarśana*,[15] thought so, on the basis of a passage of the *Antarvyāptisamarthana*. There, speaking of the example (*dṛṣṭānta*) in a syllogistic argument, Ratnākaraśānti cites the formulation of the concomitance between existence (*sattva*) and momentariness (*kṣaṇikatva*) given by the "Ācārya," and states that the latter employs here the example of the pot (*ghaṭa*) simply to satisfy the demand of the dull people, the intelligent ones not being in need of any such example:

> *tasmād vyasanamātraṁ bahirvyāptigrahaṇe, viśeṣeṇa sattve hetau kevalaṁ jaḍadhiyām eva niyamena dṛṣṭāntasāpekṣaḥ sādhanaprayogaḥ paritoṣāya jāyate, teṣām evānugrahārtham ācāryo dṛṣṭāntam upādatte: yat sat tat kṣaṇikam, yathā ghaṭa iti, paṭumatayas tu naivaṁ dṛṣṭāntam apekṣante*[16]

Exactly the same formulation is found, indeed, in Ratnakīrti's *Kṣaṇabhaṅgasiddhi, Anvayātmikā* and *Vyatirekātmikā*.[17]

It would thus appear that Ratnākaraśānti composed his only logical work, the *Antarvyāptisamarthana*, after Ratnakīrti's *Kṣaṇabhaṅgasiddhi*, and that the chronological order adopted by Dr Mimaki in the second passage quoted above is well grounded.

Dr Mimaki further observes: ". . . il est déjà démontré que Ratnakīrti, bien qu'il se prétende partisan de la théorie de la *bahirvyāpti*, est en fait un partisan de la théorie de l'*antarvyāpti*, et que la théorie de l'*antarvyāpti* que Ratnākaraśānti a complétée avait déjà été préparée dés Ratnakīrti."[18] He refers here[19] to a work in Japanese by Professor Y. Kajiyama. This again is an old

---

15. Tarkavāgīśa (1939), pp. 292-93.
16. *Antarvyāptisamarthana*, p. 112.
17. *Ratnakīrtinibandhāvali*, 67, 83.
18. Op. cit., p. 54.
19. Note 214.

idea, expressed, for the first time it seems, by Satkari Mookerjee,[20] and repeated more than once since then. Mookerjee called Ratnākaraśānti a "worthy disciple" of Ratnakīrti.[21] In accordance with this theory, the word *ācārya* in the passage cited above would refer to no other than Ratnakīrti.[22]

Professor David Seyfort Ruegg, however, has on more than one occasion protested against this way of looking at the question. In his review of A.C. Senape McDermott's book on Ratnakīrti, *An Eleventh-Century Buddhist Logic of "Exists,"* he observes: ". . . it is quite impossible to hold that Ratnākaraśānti was Ratnakīrti's disciple."[23] Furthermore, he considers Ratnakīrti — who was actually following his master Jñānaśrīmitra — as an upholder of the theory of *bahirvyāpti* "external concomitance," and thus to be a "conservative."[24] Taking up the question, recently, in a note devoted to Mimaki's book, he writes:

> But even if it is true that a *typologically* earlier form of the *antarvyāpti* doctrine is to be found in Ratnakīrti's work, chronological considerations appear to make it most unlikely that he was the teacher of Ratnākaraśānti, as Mimaki asserted (p. 54). . . . At all events, contrary to Mimaki's hypothesis (in his note 198), Ratnakīrti has not been explicitly named anywhere in the *Antarvyāptisamarthana*. . . .[25]

Since the question is related to the *sattvānumāna*, that is, the inference of momentariness (*kṣaṇikatva*) from the logical reason "existence" (*sattva*), it seems that, in order to solve this problem, it is necessary to go back to Dharmakīrti, who invented this

20. Op. cit., p. 399.

21. Ibid.

22. Mahāmahopādhyāya Satis Chandra Vidyābhūṣaṇa also considered Ratnākaraśānti to be a disciple of Ratnakīrti. See Vidyābhūṣaṇa (1921/1971), p. 338.

23. Ruegg (1971), pp. 305-06.

24. Ibid., pp. 303 and 306.

25. Ruegg (1982), p. 157.

inference. Professor E. Steinkellner has traced with precision the evolution of this inference in the works of Dharmakīrti.[26] It is intimately connected with the definition, given by Dharmakīrti himself, of existence as "causal efficiency" (*arthakriyāsāmarthya*). Now, the principle on which Ratnākaraśānti based his *antarvyāpti* theory, that of [*sādhya-*] *viparyaye bādhakapramāṇa* "proof that contradicts [the presence of the reason] in the absence [of the object to be established]," — a principle which the Jainas express as *anyathānupapatti* "impossibility otherwise," although they also use the expression *vipakṣe bādhaka*, and even *viparyaye bādhaka-pramāṇa*, — originated neither with [Jñānaśrīmitra] Ratnakīrti nor with Śāntarakṣita-Kamalaśīla,[27] but with Dharmakīrti, who, so far as the existing records in Sanskrit show, enunciated it for the first time, in his works belonging to the later phase of his philosophic career, to establish the concomitance between existence and mometariness.[28] Another concept that Ratnākaraśānti mentions, and which the Jainas mention as well, — although, as we are going to see, it is not exclusively related to the theory of *antarvyāpti* — is that of *sarvopasaṁhāravatī vyāpti* "all-inclusive pervasion." This also originated, so far as the extant

26. Steinkellner (1968).

27. Cf. Mimaki (1976), p. 53.

28. *Hetubindu*, pp. 37 (4*), 67 (19*); *Vādanyāya*, pp. 8 ff. For details see Steinkellner (1968), pp. 372-74. Cf. Frauwallner (1935) [Vācaspatimiśra, *Nyāyavārttikatātparyaṭīkā*, pp. 387 ff.]; Jayantabhaṭṭa, *Nyāyamañjarī* II, pp. 16 ff.; Bhāsarvajña, *Nyāyabhūṣaṇa*, p. 510. The inferential process involved in the establishment of this concomitance — existence (*sattva*), i.e. causal efficiency (*arthakriyāsāmarthya*), is denied of the (presumed) non-momentary entities through "non-perception of the pervader" (*vyāpakānupalabdhi*), i.e. of connection with succession or simultaneity (*kramayaugapadyayoga*) — gave rise to much interesting discussion between the Buddhists and the Naiyāyikas in later times: see Mookerjee (1935/1975), pp. 24 ff.; Mimaki (1976), p. 60; Matilal (1970). Kamalaśīla (*Tattvasaṁgrahapañjikā*, p. 144; cf. Mimaki (1976), p. 61) considers the inference not to be an independent inference but →

records show, not with Jñānaśrīmitra-Ratnakīrti, nor even with Śāntarakṣita-Kamalaśīla, but again, with Dharmakīrti.[29]

This being so, it seems that if anybody among the Buddhist logicians prepared the ground for Ratnākaraśānti's *Antarvyāptisamarthana*, it was no other than Dharmakīrti himself. And though the quotation under the name of Ācārya does not tally exactly with Dharmakīrti's enunciation of the concomitance between existence and momentariness: *yat sat tat sarvaṁ kṣaṇikam, yathā ghaṭādayaḥ*,[30] may it not be supposed that Ratnākaraśānti slightly simplified this formulation by omitting the word *sarvam* and by putting *ghaṭaḥ* in place of *ghaṭādayaḥ*?

If this solution is adopted, then the puzzle we are dealing with vanishes altogether. I am all the more tempted to adopt it because Ratnākaraśānti's view of the example (*dṛṣṭānta*) accords perfectly with that expressed by Dharmakīrti. In the *Pramāṇavārttika*, the latter not only says that in the enunciation of the heterogeneous example (*vaidharmya-dṛṣṭānta*) no concrete instance need be mentioned, as it suffices to state: "In the absence of this, that does not exist"[31] — but he goes so far as to say that

→ only as bringing out the absurdity of the opponent's thesis (*prasaṅgāpādanaṁ paraṁ prati kriyate*).

29. See below.

30. *Hetubindu*, p. 39 (5*). cf. *Vādanyāya*, p. 8.

31. *tasmād vaidharmyadṛṣṭānte neṣṭo 'vaśyam ihāśrayaḥ* |
tadabhāve ca tan neti vacanād api tadgateḥ ||

Pramāṇavārttika I, 26. See also Kamalaśīla, *Tattvasaṁgrahapañjikā*, p. 145. Note that, according to Diṅnāga, "if that [negative instance] does not exist, [it is evident that the predicate] does not reside in it": *Nyāyamukha*, p. 27. Jayantabhaṭṭa (who, against the general trend among the Naiyāyikas, does not admit the existence of a *kevalānvayi-hetu*, i.e. a reason in respect of which there is no heterogeneous example, although, unlike the Buddhists, he does admit the existence of a *kevalavyatireki-hetu*, i.e. a reason in respect of which there is no homogeneous example) endorses this view: . . . *vipakṣa eva nāstīti tadabhāvāt sutarāṁ tatrāvṛttir bhavatīti. na hi sapakṣa iva vipakṣe vṛttir iṣyate yena yatnatas*

→

the example is resorted to only for the sake of the ignorant,[32] and that, for those who know the relations of identity and causality on which is based the concomitance between the reason and the object to be established, the reason alone ought to be stated.[33] This view of Dharmakīrti was found so striking that the verse in question is also quoted by the Ālaṁkārikas Kuntaka[34] and Mahimabhaṭṭa[35] in support of their own arguments. In actual practice, when Dharmakīrti enunciates the "negative concomitance," he does not cite any concrete example: *kṣaṇikatvābhāve sattvābhāvaḥ*.[36] In his enunciation of the "positive concomitance," however, he gives one: *yat sat tat sarvaṁ kṣaṇikam, yathā ghaṭādayaḥ*.[37] This has led Arcaṭa, the commentator on the *Hetubindu*, to state that the mention of the example is designed for reviving the memory of one who has apprehended the concomitance in an object such as a pot (but who has forgotten it), not for establishing the object to be established.[38]

→ *tatsiddhaye yateta*, *Nyāyamañjarī* I, p. 102. (Cakradhara, in his *Nyāyamañjarīgranthibhaṅga* [p. 59], cites in this connection the verse of the *Pramāṇavārttika*.)

32. Cf. Māṇikyanandin, *Parīkṣāmukhasūtra* III, 46; Vādidevasūri, *Pramāṇanayatattvālokālaṁkāra* III, p. 42; Hemacandra, *Pramāṇamīmāṁsā* I, 2, 74, pp. 53-54.

33. *tadbhāvahetubhāvau hi dr̥ṣṭānte tadavedinaḥ ,*
khyāpyete viduṣāṁ vācyo hetur eva hi kevalaḥ ||
— *Pramāṇavārttika* I, 27.

34. *Vakroktijīvita*, p. 8: . . . *dr̥ṣṭāntas tarhi kathaṁ na darśitaḥ? tarkanyāyasyaiva cetasi pratibhāsamānatvāt. tathocyate. . .*

35. *Vyaktiviveka*, p. 12: *atha yadi sarva eva vākyārthaḥ sādhyasādhanabhāvagarbha ity ucyate tad yathā sādhyasādhanayos tatra niyamopādānam tathā dr̥ṣṭāntasyāpi syāt tasyāpi vyāptisādhanapramāṇaviṣayatayāvaśyāpekṣaṇīyatvāt. na, prasiddhasāmarthyasya sādhanasyopādānād eva tad-apekṣāyāḥ pratikṣepāt. tad uktam . . . . .*

36. *Hetubindu*, p. 39 (5*).

37. See above.

38. *yasya sattvakṣaṇikatvayoḥ pratibandhaprasādhakaṁ pramāṇaṁ ghaṭādau* →

What, then, is the position of Dharmakīrti? One thing seems certain: although he adheres to the doctrine of the *trairūpya*, he considerably modifies it. Inference with Dharmakīrti has ceased to be an "affair of examples." Concomitance (*vyāpti*), for him, is a universal law expressed in a universal proposition, without reference to a concrete example.[39]

Arcaṭa, commenting upon the word *sarvam* used in the enunciation of the concomitance cited above, says that by this Dharmakīrti rejects "external concomitance": *atra sarvagra-haṇena cāśeṣaparigrahād bahirvyāpter nirāsaḥ.*[40] Of course, as indicated earlier, Dharmakīrti himself uses the expression *sarvopasaṁhāreṇa* in connection with *vyāptipradarśana.*[41] Here again, Arcaṭa comments: *sarvasmin sādhanadharmavati dharmiṇi na dr̥ṣṭāntadharmiṇy eva sādhyadharmasyopasaṁhāraṇam upasaṁhāro ḍhaukanam. . . .*[42]

But the rejection of *bahirvyāpti* does not necessarily imply the acceptance of *antarvyāpti*. Arcaṭa's remarks[43] seem to recall those of the upholders of the *antarvyāpti* theory. However, Śāntarakṣita, in his commentary on the *Vādanyāya*, observes that by using the word *sarvam* in his enunciation of the concomitance Dharmakīrti states the "all-inclusive" concomitance, and this to indicate that concomitance is neither "internal" nor "external," but something natural between the reason and the object to be established, without any reference to the subject (*pakṣa*) of the inference or something similar to it (*sapakṣa*).[44] In the

---

→ *pravr̥ttaṁ taṁ prati tatra smr̥tisamādhānārthaṁ dr̥ṣṭāntavacanam, na sādhyasiddhyartham: Hetubinduṭīkā*, p. 62. See also Durvekamiśra's remarks: *Āloka*, p. 314. The same idea is expressed in the *Nyāyāvatāra*: see *Nyāyāvatāra* 18 with Siddharṣi's *Vivr̥tti*, p. 65.

39. See also Steinkellner (1967), pp. 104-05 (Notes 11 and 12 to chapter II).

40. *Hetubinduṭīkā*, p. 62.

41. *Hetubindu*, p. 39 (5*).

42. *Hetubinduṭīkā*, p. 62.

43. Ibid., pp. 62-63.

44. *anena sarvopasaṁhāreṇa vyāptipradarśanaṁ kathayati. kimartham?* →

Tattvasaṁgraha, Śāntarakṣita, while criticizing the Jaina theory of *antarvyāpti* (advocated by Pātrasvāmin, according to Kamalaśīla), appeals to the same principle.[45] Indeed, it must be admitted by all — as Vācaspatimiśra observed, coming after Dharmakīrti — that concomitance, whether "internal" or "external," is "all-inclusive"; in other words, whether this concomitance is apprehended in the subject or outside the subject, it must be between the reason in general and the object to be established in general, irrespective of their locus.[46]

Now, if it is admitted that concomitance is "all-inclusive," the question of where it is apprehended, in the subject or outside the subject, becomes immaterial. If no external example exists, why not apprehend it in the subject of the inference itself; or, even if there is one, why at all care for it? But then, the canon of the *trairūpya* falls to the ground, unless it is interpreted the way Ratnākaraśānti interpreted it: this canon only emphasizes concomitance in its two aspects, positive and negative, but is indifferent with respect to the cases where this concomitance is

---

→ *vipratipattinirāsārtham. tathā hi pakṣasapakṣāpekṣayāntarvyāptiḥ bahirvyāptiś ca pradarśyate ity eke vipratipannāḥ. tac ca na yuktam, vastubalāyātatvād vyāpteḥ.* *Vipañcitārthā*, p. 8.

45. *Tattvasaṁgraha* 1389. cf. also ibid., 421, and Kamalaśīla thereon: *yā hi pakṣasapakṣavibhāgam akṛtvā sāmānyena hetor vyāptiḥ pradarśyate sā sarvopasaṁhārā vyāptiḥ.*

46. *antar bahir vā sarvopasaṁhāreṇāvinābhāvo 'vagantavyaḥ*: *Nyāyavārttikatātparyaṭīkā*, p. 29. Cf. also Jayantabhaṭṭa, *Nyāyamañjarī* I, p. 102. — *sarvopasaṁhāravatī hi vyāptiḥ sādhyasiddher aṅgam. tad iyam anapekṣitadharmi-viśeṣaṁ sādhanadharmamātram avalambate. tadyathā yatra dhūmas tatrāgnir iti, na punar yatra mahānase dhūmas tatrāgnir iti*: Ratnākaraśānti, *Antarvyāptisamarthana*, pp. 104-05; *vyāpteḥ sāmānyālambanāyāḥ*: ibid., p. 106 (cf. p. 105). — *na hi sākalyena liṅgasya liṅginā vyāpter asiddhau kvacit kiṁcid anumānaṁ nāma*: Akalaṅka, p. 5, etc.; *vyaktirūpaṁ ca nidarśanaṁ sāmānyena tu vyāptiḥ . . .* : Māṇikyanandin, *Parīkṣāmukhasūtra* III, 40; *vyāptiḥ sarvopasaṁhāreṇa pratīyate:* Anantavīrya, *Parīkṣāmukhalaghuvṛtti* III, 7. Cf. also Mokṣākaragupta, *Tarkabhāṣā*, p. 22: *sādhanaṁ khalu sarvatra sādhyasādhanayoḥ sarvopa-saṁhāreṇa pramāṇena vyāptau siddhāyāṁ sādhyaṁ gamayed iti sarvavādisaṁmatam.*

to be apprehended; so it should be apprehended wherever it is possible to apprehend it.[47] Dharmakīrti's theory ultimately led to this conclusion. However, in practice, he was "conservative" enough not to transgress the limits laid down by the canon of the *trairūpya*. And so were his followers, Śāntarakṣita-Kamalaśīla on the one hand, and Jñānaśrīmitra-Ratnakīrti on the other. So far as I am aware, Dharmakīrti did not envisage the inference: "All things are momentary, because they exist." The subject of his inference is a determined thing, e.g. sound (*śabda*).[48] And similarly, with his followers, the subject of the inference is determined things: "these things" (*ime bhāvāḥ*), or "those things under discussion" (*amī vivādāspadībhūtāḥ padārthāḥ*). The difficulty arising, even here, from the fact that no concrete heterogeneous example is available, given that for the Buddhist logicians nothing non-momentary exists, could be easily avoided, as we have seen,[49] but a homogeneous example at least had to be provided! Now, since concomitance, in its two aspects, positive and negative, is ultimately the same, one aspect implying the other,[50] once the concomitance between existence and momentariness was established in its negative form through the "proof that contradicts [the presence of the reason] in the absence [of the object to be established]," — *kṣaṇikatvābhāve sattvābhāvaḥ* "in the absence of momentariness, there is absence of existence," — one could convert it into the positive form: *yat sat tat sarvaṁ kṣaṇikam* "All that is existent is momentary," and apprehend it in a homogeneous example, e.g. a pot. The case

47. *tasmin sapakṣa eva sattvam asapakṣe cāsattvam eva yathākramam anvayavyatirekau. tau punar yatra tatra vā dharmiṇi grahītavyau yatra śakyau grahītum. Antarvyāpti-samarthana,* p. 112. cf. Jayantabhaṭṭa, *Nyāyamañjarī* II, p. 17.

48. Cf. also *Dharmottara*: Frauwallner (1935); Vācaspatimiśra, *Nyāyavārttikatātparyaṭīkā*, pp. 387 ff.; Śrīdhara, *Nyāyakandalī*, p. 76.

49. See note 31 above.

50. Cf. *Pramāṇavārttika* I, p. 97, 11. 13 ff. See also *kārikā* 28 and the *vṛtti* thereon; *Nyāyamukha*, pp. 43-44.

was different when the subject of the inference was unlimited in extension: "all things." Here two solutions were possible: either one stuck desperately to the theory of *bahirvyāpti*, but then had no choice but to allow one or other of the things which constitute the subject to figure in the capacity of example, being fully aware that it is not one; or one adopted the theory of *antarvyāpti* and apprehended the concomitance in the subject itself, thus doing away with the example.[51]

It might be thought, and it is indeed tempting to think, that Ratnākaraśānti came at the end of the evolution, that he took the leap which his predecessors, from Dharmakīrti to Ratnakīrti, had not dared to take. But the external chronological evidence, as we have seen, is not favourable to this conclusion, and there is nothing in the internal evidence, which compels us to think this way: all that is common between Ratnākaraśānti and [Jñānaśrīmitra-]Ratnakīrti already existed in Dharmakīrti, who was, perhaps, the real source of Ratnākaraśānti.[52]

---

51. *Antarvyāptisamarthana*, p. 113, 11.1-4; p. 114, 11.8 ff. (delete the *daṇḍa* between *hetuḥ* and *sattvādivan*, 11.9-10, and between *syāt* and *dṛṣṭāntaḥ*, 11.11-12). See also Jayantabhaṭṭa, *Nyāyamañjarī* II, p. 19.

52. Ratnākaraśānti only succinctly indicates, at the beginning of the *Antarvyāptisamarthana*, the *vyāpakānupalabdhi* mentioned above, (see n. 28). Jñānaśrīmitra and Ratnakīrti establish both "positive concomitance" and "negative concomitance" for the inference of momentariness from existence: the former through *prasaṅga* and *prasaṅgaviparyaya*, and the latter through *viparyaye bādhakapramāṇa* (see Mimaki (1976), pp. 55 ff.). The former procedure so far as I am aware, is foreign as much to Dharmakīrti as to Ratnākaraśānti. Mookerjee's interpretation of a passage of Ratnakīrti's *Kṣaṇabhaṅgasiddhi Anvayātmikā* (Mookerjee, 1935/1975, p. 399, n. 1; cf. Ratnakīrti : Shāstrī, p. 26; Thakur, p. 70) in the sense of an admission of *antarvyāpti* is wrong. The objection is raised that if through *prasaṅga* and *prasaṅgaviparyaya* momentariness is established in an example, why should it not be established by the same means in the subject as well, and thus, why should one have recourse to a further inference? And Ratnakīrti's reply is : If one has the courage to do it for each individual case, it is possible indeed; but, otherwise, one →

Addenda

Thanks to a gift from Professor Y. Kajiyama, I have just been able to see his annotated translation of Mokṣākaragupta's *Tarkabhāṣā* (*An Introduction to Buddhist Philosophy: An Annotated Translation of the Tarkabhāṣā of Mokṣākaragupta* — *Memoirs of the Faculty of Letters*, Kyoto University, No. 10, 1966). In n. 302 (p. 112) he writes: "Buddhist logicians in general maintain *bahirvyāptivāda*; at the later stage of Buddhist logic Jñānaśrīmitra and Ratnakīrti asserted it in contrast to *antarvyāptivāda* held by Ratnākaraśānti. The former two logicians recognized the necessity of a corroborative example even in the inference of the Buddhist theory of universal momentariness, though they are not so far from Ratnākaraśānti inasmuch as they also rely on *viparyayabādhakapramāṇa* when determining the *vyāpti* between existence and momentariness. . . . " Upon the whole I agree with Professor Kajiyama; although I find no reference, in this work of his, to the fact that the use of the *viparyaye bādhakapramāṇa* goes back to Dharmakīrti.

In the *Citrādvaitaprakāśavāda* (*Ratnakīrtinibandhāvali*, p. 130), Ratnakīrti speaks of *bahirvyāpti* in connection with the *sattvānumāna: tataś ca yathā bahirvyāptipakṣe ghaṭe dṛṣṭāntadharmiṇi viparyayabādhakapramāṇabalāt sattvaṁ kṣaṇikatvaniyatam avadhārya sattvāt pakṣe kṣaṇabhaṅgasiddhiḥ* . . .

Concerning n. 31 see also Shoryu Katsura, "New Sanskrit Fragments of the Pramāṇasamuccaya," *Journal of Indian Philosophy* 3 (1975): 75-76.

→ should first establish the concomitance in a homogeneous example and then proceed to establish momentariness, through the reason "existence," in other cases:. . . *yas tu prativastu tannyāyopanyāsa-prayāsabhīruḥ sa khalv ekatra dharmiṇi yad yadā yajjana-navyavahārayogyaṁ tat tadā taj janayatītyādinyāyena sattvamātram asthairyavyāptam avadhārya sattvād evānyatra kṣaṇikatvam avagacchatīti katham apramatto vaiyarthyam ācakṣīta?*

Bibliography

Akalaṅka, *Akalaṅkagranthatrayam*, ed. Mahendra Kumar Shastri, Ahmedabad-Calcutta 1939 (Siṅghī Jaina Series 12).

Anantavīrya, *Parīkṣāmukhalaghuvṛtti*, ed. Mahāmahopādhyāya Satis

Chandra Vidyābhūṣaṇa, Calcutta: Asiatic Society of Bengal, 1909.

Arcaṭa, *Hetubinduṭīkā: Hetubinduṭīkā of Bhaṭṭa Arcaṭa with the Sub-Commentary entitled Āloka of Durveka Miśra*, ed. Pandit Sukhlalji Sanghavi and Muni Shri Jinavijayaji, Baroda, 1949 (Gaekwad's Oriental Series 113).

Cakradhara, *Nyāyamañjarīgranthibhaṅga*, ed. Nagin J. Shah, Ahmedabad: L. D. Institute of Indology, 1972 (L. D. Series 35).

Dasgupta, Surendranath, *A History of Indian Philosophy* I, Cambridge, 1922.

Dharmakīrti, *Pramāṇavārttika* I (*Svārthānumānaparicched*a): R. Gnoli, *The Pramāṇavārttikam of Dharmakīrti.* The first chapter with the Autocommentary. Text and Critical Notes. Roma, 1960 (Serie Orientale Roma 23).

———, *Hetubindu*: E. Steinkellner, *Dharmakīrti's Hetubinduḥ*. Teil I. Tibetischer Text und rekonstruierter Sanskrit-Text. Wien, 1967 (Österreichische Akademie der Wissenschaften, philosophisch-historische Klasse, Sitzungsberichte, 252. Band, 1. Abhandlung. Veröffentlichungen der Kommission fòr Sprachen und Kulturen Sòd-und Ostasiens, Heft 4).

———, *Vādanyāya*, ed. with the Commentary *Vipañcitārthā* of Śāntarakṣita, by Swami Dwarikadas Shastri, Varanasi, 1972 (Bauddha Bharati Series 8. *Dharmakīrtinibandhāvali* 2).

Diṅnāga, *Nyāyamukha*: G. Tucci, *The Nyāyamukha of Dignāga . . . after Chinese and Tibetan Materials*, Heidelberg, 1930 (Materialien zur Kunde des Buddhismus, 15. Heft).

Durvekamiśra, *Hetubinduṭīkāloka* (*Arcaṭāloka*): see Arcaṭa.

Frauwallner, Erich, "Dharmottaras Kṣaṇabhaṅgasiddhiḥ." *Wiener Zeitschrift fòr die Kunde des Morgenlandes* 42 (1935): 216-58.

Hemacandra, *Pramāṇamīmāṁsā*: *Hemacandra's Pramāṇa-Mīmāṁsā*. Text and translation with Critical Notes by Satkari Mookerjee in collaboration with Nathmal Tatia, Varanasi: Tara Publications, 1970 (Prachya Bharati Series 11) [rpt].

Jayantabhaṭṭa, *Nyāyamañjarī*, ed. Sūryanārāyaṇa Śukla, Benares: Chowkhamba, I: 1936, II: 1934 (Kashi Sanskrit Series 106).

Jñānaśrīmitra, *Jñānaśrīmitranibandhāvali*, ed. Anantalal Thakur, Patna: Kashi Prasad Jayaswal Research Institute, 1959 (Tibetan Sanskrit Works Series 5).

Kamalaśīla, *Tattvasaṁgrahapañjikā*: see Śāntarakṣita, *Tattvasaṁgraha*.

Kuntaka, *Vakroktijīvita*: *The Vakroktijīvita of Kuntaka*, critically ed. with Variants, Introduction and English tr. by K. Krishnamoorthy, Dharwad: Karnatak University, 1977.

Mahimabhaṭṭa, *Vyaktiviveka*: *The Vyaktiviveka of Rājānaka Mahimabhaṭṭa and its Commentary of Rājānaka Ruyyaka*, ed. with Notes by T. Gaṇapati Śāstrī, Trivandrum, 1909 (Trivandrum Sanskrit Series 5).

Māṇikyanandin, *Parīkṣāmukhasūtra*: in Prabhācandra, *Prameyakamalamārtaṇḍa*, ed. Mahendra Kumar Shastri, Bombay: Nirnaya Sagar Press, 1941.

Matilal, B. K., "Reference and Existence in Nyāya and Buddhist Logic." *Journal of Indian Philosophy* 1, No. 1 (1970) : 83-110.

McDermott, A.C. Senape, *An Eleventh-Century Buddhist Logic of "Exists."* Dordrecht: D. Reidel Publishing Company, 1969.

Mimaki, Katsumi, *La réfutation bouddhique de la permanence des choses (Sthirasiddhidūṣaṇa) et la prevue de la momentanéité des choses (Kṣaṇabhaṅgasiddhi)*, Paris, 1976 (Publications de l'Institut de Civilisation indienne 41).

Mokṣākaragupta, *Tarkabhāṣā*, ed. E. Krishnamacharya, Baroda, 1942 (Gaekwad's Oriental Series 94).

Mookerjee, Satkari, *The Buddhist Philosophy of Universal Flux: An Exposition of the Philosophy of Critical Realism as Expounded by the School of Diṅnāga*. Calcutta: University of Calcutta, 1935. Rpt: Delhi: Motilal Banarsidass, 1975.

Randle, H. N., *Indian Logic in the Early Schools. A study of the Nyāyadarśana in Its Relation to the Early Logic of Other Schools.* Oxford: Oxford University Press, 1930.

Ratnākaraśānti, *Antarvyāptisamarthana: Six Buddhist Nyāya Tracts in Sanskrit*, ed. Mahāmahopādhyāya Haraprasād Shāstri, Calcutta: Asiatic Society of Bengal, 1910, 103-14. A fairly good summary of the arguments is to be found in Mokerjee (1935/1975), ch. XXIV. The text is badly printed and needs numerous corrections. A Japanese translation, which also uses the Tibetan, was published by Prof. Y. Kajiyama in 1960: *Bukkyō-shigaku* VIII, 4.

Ratnakīrti, *Ratnakīrtinibandhāvaliḥ*, deciphered and ed. Anantalal Thakur, Patna: Kashi Prasad Jayaswal Research Institute (Tibetan Sanskrit Works Series III), 2nd ed. 1975. Ratnakīrti's *Apohasiddhi and Kṣaṇabhaṅgasiddhi* (*Anvayātmikā and Vyatirekātmikā*) were published by Haraprasād Shāstrī in *Six Buddhist Nyāya Tracts in Sanskrit* (see preceding item).

Ruegg D. Seyfort. "On Ratnakīrti." *Journal of Indian Philosophy* 1, No. 3 (1971): 300-09.

———, "Review of Sāratamā: A *Pañjikā* on the *Aṣṭasāhasrikā Prajñāpāramitā Sūtra*" by Ācārya Ratnākaraśānti, ed. Padmanabh S. Jaini. *Indo-Indian Journal* 24 (1982):156-57.

Śāntarakṣita, *Tattvasaṁgraha*, ed. with the *Pañjikā* of Kamalaśīla, by E. Krishnamacharya, Baroda, 1926 (Gaekwad's Oriental Series 30-31).

———, *Vipañcitārthā*: see Dharmakīrti, *Vādanyāya*.

Siddhasena Divākara, *Nyāyāvatāra*, ed. with the *Vivṛtti of Siddharṣi*, by A.N. Upadhye, Bombay: Jaina Sāhitya Vikāsa Maṇḍala, 1971.

Siddharṣi, *Nyāyāvatāravivṛtti*: see Siddhasena Divākara.

Śrīdhara, *Nyāyakandalī*: *The Bhāṣya of Praśastapāda together with the Nyāyakandalī of Srīdhara*, ed. Vindhyeśvarīprasāda Dvivedin, Benares, 1895 (Vizianagram Sanskrit Series, vol. 4).

Steinkellner, Ernst, *Dharmakīrti's Hetubinduḥ*. Teil II. Übersetzung und Anmerkungen. Wien, 1967 (Österreichische Akademie der Wissenschaften, philosophisch-historische Klasse, Sitzungsberichte, 252. Band, 2. Abhandlung. Veröffentlichungen der Kommission fòr Sprachen und Kulturen Sòd- und Ostasiens, Heft 5).

———, "Die Entwicklung des *Kṣaṇikatvānumānam* bei Dharmakīrti." *Beiträge zur Geistesgeschichte Indiens. Festschrift fòr Erich Frauwallner*. Wien. *Wiener Zeitschrift fòr die Kunde Sòd- und Ostasiens und Archiv fòr Indische Philosophie* 12-13 (1968): 361-77.

Tarkavāgīśa Mahāmahopādhyāya Phaṇibhūṣaṇa, *Nyāyadarśana* (annotated translation, in Bengali, of the *Nyāyasūtras* and of Vātsyāyana's *Bhāṣya*, vol. I, Calcutta: Vaṅgīya-Sāhitya-Pariṣad, 2nd edn., 1939 (Bengali era 1346).

Vācaspatimiśra, *Nyāyavārttikatātparyaṭīkā*, ed. Mahāmahopādhyāya Gaṅgādhara Śāstri Tailaṅga, Benares, 1898 (Vizianagram Sanskrit Series, vol. 13).

Vādidevasūri, *Pramāṇanayatattvālokālaṁkāra*: in *Ratnaprabhasūri's Ratnākarāvatārikā, being a Commentary on Vādi Devasūri's Pramāṇanayatattvāloka, with a Pañjikā by Rājaśekharasūri, a Ṭippaṇa by Pt. Jñānacandra and Gujarati Translation by Muni Shri Malayavijayaji*, ed. Dalsukh Malvania, Ahmedabad: L.D. Institute of Indology, 1965, 1968, 1969 (L. D. Series 6, 16, 24).

Vidyābhūṣaṇa, Mahāmahopādhyāya Satis Chandra, *A History of Indian Logic (Ancient, Medieval and Modern Schools)*. Calcutta: Calcutta University, 1921. Rpt. Delhi: Motilal Banarsidass, 1971.

6

Diṅnāga and Post-Russell Logic

R.S.Y. Chi

THE encyclopaedic work *Principia Mathematica* has won almost universal acceptance as the most systematic and comprehensive treatment of logic of the day. It has been said to be "ranked only with the Theory of Relativity" (R.B. Braithwaite in *The Nation*). In such a thorough study, however, there is the lacking of an overall system and of the treatment of some fundamental concepts.

One very obvious omission is a systematic treatment of constants such as truth functions. Some active members of the class, such as conjunctions, disjunctions and implications, appear in every page of the book, yet there is no indication about whether there should be backbenchers and whether there should be a definite number of such functions.

After the publication of the first edition of the book, new ideas were introduced to fill the gap. In his important article "Introduction to a General Theory of Elementary Propositions."[1] E.L. Post gave the total number of truth functions of order n: ${}_{2}2^{n}$. The number for order 2 should be ${}_{2}2^{2}=16$. As a mathematician, Post did not give a list of all the truth functions, which should belong to the scope of logic and not to that of pure mathematics.

In the same year (1921), L. Wittgenstein listed all sixteen truth functions in his monumental work *Tractatus Logico-Philosophicus.* As

1. E.L. Post, "Introduction to a General Theory of Elementary Propositions," *American Journal of Mathematics* 43 (1921): 163-85.

a philosopher, he did not elaborate the logical technicalities of these functions. Extensive study of these functions was done later by R. Carnap, J. Lukasiewicz and others.

Russell gave his response to the new ideas in his *Introduction to the Second Edition* (1927),[2] in which he adopted Wittgenstein's "Thesis of Extensionality," yet he mentioned nothing about the formal aspect of the listing of sixteen functions, as if it had not existed.

In contrast to his indifference to the listing, in the paragraph immediately following Russell gave an overwhelming praise to the new invention called "Sheffer stroke." He has gone as far as saying:

> It should be stated that a new and very powerful method in mathematical logic has been invented by Dr. H.M. Sheffer. This method, however, would demand a complete re-writing of *Principia Mathematica*. We recommend this task to Dr. Sheffer, since what has so far been published by him is scarcely sufficient to enable us to undertake the necessary reconstruction.[3]

Apparently there were two alternative ways to make logic more systematic, namely creating an organic structure of all functions, and using one function as the primitive concept to define all the rest. Russell selected the second.

Using one function to replace all the rest is not only pointless but also what makes the process impossible. Russell's comment apparently indicated his preference for unity to multiplicity. In the transmission of message of whatever kind, there is a contrary preference, the preference for distinctiveness to uniformity. Using Sheffer stroke to replace all other truth functions in logic is like using "bits" to replace the entire English vocabulary. The bits may be able to preserve the information in all books in all

---

2. A.N. Whitehead and B. Russell, *Principia Mathematica*, 2nd edn. (1927), p. xiv.

3. Ibid., p. xv.

libraries, but it is hard to find a human audience who can comprehend their meaning.

Moreover, the very reason why Russell selected Sheffer stroke is that this function alone, without the company of anything else, even the sign of negation, can be used as a primitive concept to define all other functions. This line of reasoning is fallacious because Russell has confused two different meanings of an ambiguous symbol. The symbol *p* has two utterly different meanings: either the naming of a proposition without truth value, or the assertion of a proposition. There is no assertion sign merely because of abbreviation. When this symbol is used to define a Sheffer stroke, it definitely means the assertion of a proposition, and not just naming of it. Consequently, the Sheffer stroke can be free from the sign of negation; it cannot be free from the sign of assertion, even if it is merely implied. When an unabbreviated symbolism is used, we can see that there is no categorial difference between Sheffer stroke and other truth functions. In other words, Sheffer stroke is not a unique member of the family.

As a philosopher and a scientist, it is not unnatural for Russell to have a desire for simplicity, the "first principle," or "primitive concept." What is wrong is that his primitive concept was wrongly placed. The primitive concept should not be a member of the set of functions, but should go beyond it. Simplicity should be judged by the result of operation; a single primitive concept may not necessarily be simpler than plural primitive concepts.

What can really achieve simplicity is the "tabulation process," in which not one but a few primitive concepts are involved. By the application of proper primitive concepts, numerous theorems in different branches of logic would become parallel or analogous. This would make the book not only more systematic but also a great deal shorter. Post mentioned in his article:

> Further development suggests itself in two directions. On the one hand this general procedure might be extended to other portions

> of *Principia*, and we hope at some future time to present the beginning of such an attempt. . . .[4]

Whether anything has actually been done or not, Post's recommendation is a great deal more feasible and meaningful. Even at a quick glance, the procedure can be instantly applied to the logic of apparent variables (quantificational logic), to the logic of relations and to the logic of classes. At any rate, Post's theory is not limited to elementary propositions.

In all these branches of logic, the total number of functions is exactly $_{2}2^{2} = 16$. The procedure of "tabulation" involves the following steps:

First, the "naming" of two arguments, which can be propositions, either real variables *p* and *q*, or apparent variables *fx* and *gx*, relations *R* and *S*, or classes *a* and *b*.

Secondly, the "recognition" of these arguments, namely: "identity" and "complement." In the case of propositions, identity means the proposition *p* itself, and the complement means its negative proposition but not denial, because at this stage, truth value has not yet been introduced. In the case of classes, identity means the class *a* itself, complement means its complementary class $\bar{a}$.

Thirdly, the "evaluation," in which the concept of "value" has been extended from "truth value" to other kinds of values. In the case of propositions, the values would be "true" and "false." In the case of classes, the values would be non-empty $a \neq 0$, and empty, $a = 0$.

The actual procedure of tabulation, involving repeated operation of product-partition-product, is lengthy. The present author has stated the procedure in detail elsewhere (*Buddhist Formal Logic*, xlix-liii). It will not be repeated here.[5]

---

4. Post, p. 164.
5. R.S.Y. Chi, *Buddhist Formal Logic*, 1969.

What is amazing is that the extension of Post's Theory to the logic of apparent variables or to the logic of classes may not need to be implemented "at some future time," as it had already been done in the past, by Indian logicians thirteen to fifteen centuries ago.

Diṅnāga's *Hetucakraḍamarū* is exceedingly short; it seems to be an outline of a treatise for his pupils to memorize.[6] The treatise does not survive, and this short outline has puzzled scholars throughout the ages. Even in our own century, this work has been described by St. Stasiak as "Mysterious."

I take the work to be an extensional study of propositions. Its aim is to find out the right kind of propositions which can be used as the major premiss of a syllogism to derive a universal affirmative conclusion.

"Syllogism" was an important topic in logic in Diṅnāga's time as well as it was in Aristotle's time, when logic was used as a tool for doctrinal debate. We are more interested in a broader aspect of logic; let us ignore its syllogistic meaning and concentrate our attention on the classification of propositions. Four stanzas are particularly relevant. I give below these stanzas in translation:

Knowable, produced, impermanent (5)
Produced, audible, effort-made,
Impermanent, effort-made and incorporeal,
Are used to prove the properties of being:
permanent, impermanent, effort-made,
Permanent, permanent, permanent,
Non-effort-made, impermanent and permanent. (6)

Space-pot, pot-space, (9)
Pot-lightning-space,
Space-pot, (space-pot), space-pot-lightning,
Lightning-space-pot,

6. R.S.Y. Chi, *Buddhist Formal Logic*, 1969, pp. xi-xii.

Pot-lightning-space,
Space-atom-action-pot. (10)

Not being equipped with symbols, Diṅnāga utilized concrete objects to express his abstract ideas. The stanzas (5) and (6) give nine pairs of properties (a_1, b_1), (a_2, b_2) to (a_9, b_9). The stanzas (9) and (10) give nine sets of concrete objects as examples which possess either one property, i.e ($\bar{a}\bar{b}$) or ($\bar{a}b$), or both properties, i.e (ab), or neither, i.e($\bar{a}\bar{b}$).

Nine pairs of properties:

knowable	permanent
produced	impermanent
impermanent	effort-made
produced	permanent
audible	permanent
effort-made	permanent
impermanent	non-effort-made
effort-made	impermanent
incorporeal	permanent

Nine sets of examples:

space-pot
pot-space
pot-lightning-space
space-pot
space-pot
space-pot-lightning
lightning-space-pot
pot-lightning-space
space-atom-action-pot

What is confusing is that Diṅnāga gave examples when they are existent, but gave nothing when they are not existent. In order to avoid confusion, the description should be made explicit. Let us insert the word "null" to denote the slots where examples do not exist:

space-pot-null-null
pot-null-null-space
pot-lightning-null-space
null-pot-space-null
null-null-space-pot
null-pot-space-lightning
lightning-pot-space-null
pot-null-lightning-space
space-action-atom-pot

In the above, there has been a slight change of order in the two middle examples in order to suit our familiar convention today. Diṅnāga's order is (*ab*, *āb*, *ab̄*, *āb̄*), while our order is (*ab*, *ab*, *ab*, *āb̄*,). The change constitutes only a matter of convention, and there is nothing in substance.

The first pair can be read as the following:

That which is knowable and permanent: yes, such as space

That which is knowable but not permanent: yes, such as a pot

That which is not knowable but permanent: no, no such thing

That which is not knowable and not permanent: no, no such thing.

The nine sets of examples can be written as the following:

ab	*ab*	*āb*	*āb*
space	pot	-	-
pot	-	-	space
pot	lightning	-	space
-	pot	space	-
-	-	space	pot
-	pot	space	lightning
lightningpot	space	-	
pot	-	lightning	space
space	action	atom	space

If we use the symbol "1" to represent "there is at least one thing which possesses the property that," and the symbol "0" to represent "there is nothing which possesses the property that," then the above list will become:

1100

1001

1101

0110

0011

0111

1110

1011

1111

Unlike the classification of propositions in traditional Western logic, Diṅnāga's way provides a system which is non-arbitrary. On account of practical reasons, however, his table is non-arbitrary yet not complete. From the elementary mathematics of permutation, one can easily see that several items are missing. The one who completed the system was not his follower but his Nyāya critic Uddyotakara, who preferred completeness to practicality. The system of sixteen was completed by the addition of the following items:

1000

0001

0010

0000

When the two tables are put together, they will become

1111

1110

1101

1100

1011

1010

1001

1000

0111

0110

0101

0100

0011

0010

0001

0000

This is the earliest "logical tabulation" in history. The table established by Diṅnāga can be called "existential table," which is to be applied to quantificational logic and the logic of classes. It is analogous to the "truth table" in truth-functional logic, which is familiar to every student of logic of our time. The two kinds of tables belong to two different branches of logic and have different meanings, but they have exactly the same structure.

Apparently, Diṅnāga's logic has a particular stress on the extensional relationship between two concepts, which are usually represented by the "middle term" and the "major term" in traditional Western logic. Unlike traditional logic which elaborates "figures" and "moods," Diṅnāga's logic does not go beyond the "Barbara" mood. This process is not restricted to "syllogism" in a formalized debate; it is applicable whenever one uses a clause beginning with the word "because" to give a justification of one's claim.

Of the sixteen functions, four can satisfy the required condition: 1011, 1010, 1001, 1000. The others are either inconclusive or contradictory. Any two concepts in the world, e.g. "democracy" and "freedom," "blue" and "furious," should have relationship belonging to one of the sixteen. An extensional analysis of the relationships would enable us to judge whether a given reason is justified. We are confronting influence peddlers everyday, whether political, doctrinal, religious or commercial, who apply false reasons for their persuasion. An extensional analysis would expose their fallacies immediately.

The process of evolution of logic is somewhat unpredictable. Shortly after Kant had announced "Formal logic was not able to advance a single step (after Aristotle) and is thus to all appearance a closed and complete body of doctrine,"[7] J.D. Gergonne declared that Aristotelian logic had fallen into general discredit during the eighteenth century, "though still taught in some Gothic academies."[8]

Principia Mathematica marks a great step forward: it has been, as mentioned above, "ranked only with the Theory of Relativity." It does not seem, however, to have reached an Einsteinian stage, despite the immense ingenuity in every detail of the book. In the absence of an overall systematization through major laws comparable to Newton's, it can hardly be more mature than Kepler's physics.

When Russell commented "This method, however, would demand a complete re-writing of *Principia Mathematica*," it seemed that he was not unaware of some inadequacy of his book. Apparently he intended to find major laws as breakthroughs to put logic in order; unfortunately his choice was not the right one, and the re-writing was never implemented.

The real counterpart of Newton's Laws is Post's Theory, with Diṅnāga's *Hetucakra* as its *avant-garde*. It would provide us with a "logic of logic," or "meta-logic," by which various factors in logic: the constants (functions), the variables (arguments) and rules of inference, would be introduced in an orderly way. A comprehensive treatment applying Post's Theory has not yet come into existence. The immense volume would make the task formidable.

---

7. I. Kant, *Critique of Pure Reason*, English tr. by N. Kemp Smith, 2nd edn., p. viii.

8. J.D. Gergonne, "Essai de dialectique rationelle," *Annales de Mathèmatiques* 7 (1816-17), English tr. W. and M. Kneale, *The Development of Logic* (1962), p. 350.

7

Metalogical Remarks on the Procrustean Translation of the Buddhist Parārthānumāna into the Anglo-European Predicate Calculus[1]

Douglas Dunsmore Daye

IN this article, I focus on the translation of the Buddhist "logic" into Anglo-European "logics." I make explicit nine assumptions; then I assert twelve (briefly stated) reasons why I believe that the widespread presumptions of the formally deductive qualities of the Buddhist *parārthānumāna* may not be quite what they seem. Last, I focus on what I believe to be a fundamental issue, the deeply buried assumption that the Buddhist schema is an untidy, implicit approximation of some form of *modus ponens*; the latter may be expressed informally as "if *P* then *Q*, and *P*, therefore *Q*."

I. Nine Assumptions

1. Philosophical and religious Buddhism and its various theses have entered the international arena of comparative philosophical dialogue and thus its assumptions and the means of its *pramāṇavāda* style of

---

1. This is a modified version of the paper which I delivered at the Oxford Conference of the International Association for Buddhist Studies, Oxford University, Oxford, England, August, 1982. I expand all of the remarks in this paper in my forthcoming monograph on these topics.

demonstration are open to international critical analysis and comparison.

2. The scope and models of my critical comparative remarks are confined to the history of twentieth- century scholarship of Buddhist logic and the sixth-eighth-century (CE) Sanskrit text and Chinese translation of the *Nyāyapraveśa* and the *Nyāyamukha* the latter surviving only in Chinese.[2]

3. I examine the public, textually-grounded Buddhist (so-called) "inference-schema for others" (*Parārthānumāna* cited hereafter as the *PA*). I shall not examine here any psychological claims about inferring; I shall examine only some problems and virtues inherent in the formalistic translation of the *PA* into some uses of the Anglo-European (cited hereafter as "AE") models of formal logics.

4. The relevant general *models* of AE formal logic, the relative accuracy of which I question with the *PA*, are those models which are exemplified throughout the twentieth century history of Nyāya scholarship. The two models are the fairly simple uses of syllogistic and/or the first order predicate calculus. These AE models have been the target formal languages of the translation of the *PA*. The scope of AE

---

2. Sanskrit editions of the *Nyāyapraveśa* may be found in: A.B. Dhruva, *The Nyāyapraveśa*, Part I (Baroda: Gaekwad's Oriental Series, 1930); H. Ui, *Bukkyo Ronrigaku* (Buddhist Logic), Tokyo, 1944; N.D. Mironov, "*Nyāyapraveśa*, 1, Sanskirt Text, edited and reconstructed," in *T'oung Pao*, Leiden, 1991, pp. 1-24; M. Tachikawa, "A Sixth-century Manual of Indian Logic," *Journal of Indian Philosophy*, 1 (1971): 111-45. A Chinese translation of this text may be found in the *Taishō Shinshū Daizōkyō*, Buddhist *Tripiṭaka*, vol. 32, no. 1630, 11-13. The Tibetan translation has been edited by V. Bhattacharya in the *Nyāyapraveśa*, Part II (Baroda: Gaekwad's Oriental Series, 1927) and in the *Tibetan Tripiṭaka*, Peking edn. rpt., ed. by D.T. Suzuki, Tokyo, 1962, No. 5706, 130, 74-76. The Chinese translation of Diṅnāga's *Nyāyamukha*, is found in the *Taishō*, vol. 32, 1628.

models and formalistic machinery are greater than the scope of AE models and machinery actually used in the twentieth century with the *PA* (see 9 below).

5. I claim that the "inference-schema" of the Indian Buddhist Nyāya, Pramāṇavāda tradition is logical but not formally deductive, given the twentieth century AE models of deductive logic *actually* used by scholars. However, Buddhist logic shares the same "spirit" of all logicians, namely precision, formalism and accuracy, in the sense of generating alleged truth preserving conclusions and subsequent formalistic justifications of its demonstrated claims.

6. I am not arguing for a relativity of formal logics, nor am I arguing for a "relativity of rationality," whatever these phrases might mean to the reader. I am arguing about the usefulness and legitimacy of alternative means of formalistic, mutually exclusive, systematized translations from the Buddhist logic into some modern formal ideal languages *via* the presumed adequacy of the *utilized* twentieth-century AE models.

7. The philosophical value of the Nyāya *PA* is not diminished because it is or is not uncontroversially "deductive"; to the contrary, its differences with AE logics greatly enhance the potential *heuristic* value of its comparative study.

8. First, the deeply buried methodological presupposition of twentieth-century scholarship is that the *PA* was/is an implicit form of *modus ponens* (or an untidy exemplification of the Rule of Detachment) which needed only the tidying hand of the Indologist-cum-logician to make a few (formalistic) adjustments to bring the *PA* round to its implicit form of a (subliminally assumed) legitimate form common to many of the familiar AE models. I examine this presupposition in Section III.

9. Second, what is not appreciated by such translators are the widely divergent forms, metalogical machineries and philosophies of logic, which are evidenced in the AE tradition of logics but which have been ignored or remain unknown to most scholars interested in formalistic translations of the *PA*. This type of ignorance is not unknown in the AE tradition; examples are the relatively recent ignorance of (1) Stoic logic, (2) Peirce's and Frege's independently generated machinery of both quantification, and (3) a complete set of axioms for propositional logic plus (4) Sheffer's rediscovery of this. Finally, the long ignorance of the richness and subtlety of Lesniewski's[3] logic remains an example of non-communication between AE scholars about sophisticated but bewitching fads in formal logic. This AE ignorance stands as a compensating counter-example to the criticism of the Nyāya scholar's narrow focus upon the use of an outmoded form of syllogistic, and since the 1930s, the first order predicate calculus as a formal target language into which to translate the *PA*.

II. A Brief Survey of Twelve Reasons Why the Early Buddhist *PA* is not a Formal Deductive Inference Schema Given the Scope of Twentieth-Century AE Models

1. Only one legitimate emic, non-etic[4] model of the *PA* is offered in these sixth-eighth century texts. Its form is

---

3. I wish to acknowledge with gratitude a reference to Lesniewski given to me at Oxford by Prof. Hans Herzberger of the University of Toronto. This should not be construed that Prof. Herzberger is in agreement with any of my remarks.

4. "Emic: Etic." Simply stated, "emic" refers to a *cluster* of metaphysical descriptions, explanations, justifications, cultural presuppositions, questions, stories, parables, the general "world-view" one *finds within* a religio-philosophical *tradition*; "etic" refers to those (usually new) clusters, which one cannot reasonably expect to find *within* or *arising from* such a tradition. For two examples, no one *can* find, nor does →

invariable: "*Q* because of *P* and if *P* then *Q*, as in *X* and not as in *Y*." The AE form of *modus ponens* "if *P* then *Q* and *P* therefore *Q*" is never found in these texts.

2. There are no emic or internal Nyāya transformation rules for the restructuring of the *PA* into another form such as the true deductive AE form of *modus ponens*. Such examples are lacking in that there are, for example, neither emic equivalents of de Morgan's theorem (at this time of *pramāṇavāda* development) nor of transposition $(P \supset Q) = (Q \supset P)$.
3. The determination of the legitimacy of a *PA* is not determined solely on the basis of its form, although the correct emic form is extremely important, the actual form of the *PA* is never the form of *modus ponens*, *modus tollens*, or of a valid transitive series.
4. The emically correct form of a *PA* is not isomorphic with any AE deductive forms actually utilized in the models of twentieth-century Buddhist Nyāya scholarship.
5. The correct emic form of a *PA* is judged in part, by such meta-rules as emically legitimate models, the *trirūpa-hetu* and/or *hetucakra*, all of which require "metalogical

→ any scholar reasonably *expect* to find either questions or answers regarding the Mahāyāna *bodhisattva's aseity* [*sic.*] in Buddhism; likewise, no one *can* find, nor does any scholar reasonably *expect* to find, either questions or answers regarding the Christian God's karmic dependence upon or being karmically influenced by *karma-vipāka* (the effects of *karma*, moral and/or physical causation, *pratītyasamutpāda*). These two terms "etic" and "emic" have their historical origins in anthropological linguistics, where their uses are capable of greater precision in the linguistic contexts of "phonetics" and "phonemics." Here I use them as an abbreviated device for distinguishing between those clusters of concepts, which are from *within* and from *without* a given tradition of formal logics. Thus "emic" refers to those ideas, etc. found within a tradition and "etic" refers to those ideas, etc. not found within the tradition.

clichés," plus a similar and a dissimilar exemplification (a *sapakṣa* and a *vipakṣa*)[5] the requirements of these exemplifications are incompatible with the models and assumptions of mainline AE formal logicians. (See 10 below.)

6. The *PA* does not have true sentential and/or term variables; it has only the more restricted functions of metalogical clichés, partial analogues to the "middle term" and "major term" of the so-called "classical" AE syllogism. A rough equivalent *PA* metalogical cliché is that of the *pakṣa*, *sādhya*, and the *hetu* ("thesis," "property-to-be-demonstrated" and "justification," respectively).

7. A legitimate *PA* allows various degrees of absent *PA* components; these allowed absent components are a function of the degree of philosophical nimbleness of the recipient of a *PA*.[6] In other words, there are no finite number of components of the *PA* without which the *PA* cannot be judged legitimate in same intersubjective contexts, such as excluding the thesis (*pakṣa*) or

---

5. For the point on variables and "clichés," see my "Metalogical Clichés (Proto-Variables) and Their Restricted Substitution in Sixth Century Buddhist Logic," *The Notre Dame Journal of Formal Logic* 20, no. 3 (July 1979): 549-58. For an exposition of my terminology, the *trirūpa-hetu* (the three forms of the justification property) and the *hetucakra* (The Wheel of Justifier-Reasons), see my "Remarks on Early Buddhist Proto-Formalism (Logic) and Mr. Tachikawa's translation of the *Nyāyapraveśa*," *Journal of Indian Philosophy* 3, nos. 3/4 (1975): 383-98. Translations and expositions about the *hetucakra* may be found in Tucci (see note 7 below). Satis Chandra Vidyābhūṣaṇa, *A History of Indian Logic* (Calcutta: University of Calcutta, 1921), p. 299; R.S.Y. Chi, *Buddhist Formal Logic* (London: Royal Asiatic Society of Great Britain and Ireland, 1969), pp. xi-xlii; the earliest translation from Sanskrit is the Chinese translation found in the Taishō, vol. 32, 1628: 2: A: 20-27, ff.

6. For example, see S. Sanghvi, *Advanced Studies in Indian Logic and Metaphysics* (Calcutta: Indian Studies Past and Present, 1961), pp. 74-75.

sometimes, merely asserting the justification (*hetu*); on the other hand, the AE deductive inference allows of no degrees of absent formal components. The AE models must be explicitly complete and all of the components must be present for the AE inference-schema to be justified as legitimate. Thus there are significant differences in the (largely) implicit expectations of the formalistic completeness of the explicit components between the *PA* and AE models.

8. The *trirūpa-hetu*, as a normative metalogical standard (a necessary condition of emic legitimacy) of the *PA* form, is neither compatible nor isomorphic with any valid AE inference form; the *trirūpa-hetu* describes the concomitance (*vyāpti*) of the property to be demonstrated (*sādhya*) and the property of the justifier (*hetu*) as they are or as they are not found in the exemplifications (*sapakṣa*, *vipakṣa*). In metalogical justifications or analyses, the focus for *PA* legitimacy is *not* upon the conditional warrant (*dṛṣṭānta*). The latter focus, would be a focus if the *PA* could be demonstrated as being formally isomorphic with (say) syllogistic and hence justified by reference to the methodological analogue of the inference form of *modus ponens*, for example, justified by reference to the relations of the major term to the minor and middle terms in, say, BARBARA.

9. The early Buddhist *Hetucakra* (found only in the Chinese translation of the *Nyāyamukha*)[7] is a description of correct and incorrect forms (or implicitly normative models) which require two exemplifications. Note that the AE models of deductive validity neither require nor accept this requirement of an exemplification. (See 10 below.) The legitimacy of the relationships of the *PA* metalogical

7. G. Tucci, *The Nyāyamukha of Dignaga*, Heidelberg, 1930, p. 52; *Taishō*, vol. 32, 3: C: 2-9.

clichés is not determined solely by appeal to empirically falsifiable evidence; in almost all cases, it is semantically warranted. Hence, the *PA*s are necessarily true/analytically true, largely dependent upon the paradigm-restricted *darśana* assumptions.

10. There are no emic transformational rules for changing and/or reversing the general form "*Q because* of *P*" into "*P therefore Q*." If by such a translation move one wishes: (1) to radically restructure the *PA* to an apparent *modus ponens* form, expressed as "[$P \supset Q$ and P] $\supset Q$;" (2) and, anticipate a further change of an alleged "therefore" into "$\supset$," this requires that the "backing" or "data" for the full warrant not to be necessary.[8] However, the emic *trirūpa-hetu* requires the presence of the exemplification (the backing or "data") for its emic metalogical justification. Hence "$\supset$" and the *trirūpa-hetu* are incompatible at the second order of metalogical rules, but are not necessarily incompatible at the first order of alleged AE deductive "inference" schemes. Thus, the transition from the Sanskrit ablative case in the *hetu*, into "therefore," and then into "$\supset$," is metalogically illegitimate.

Comparatively, what we have here are incompatible second order philosophies of logic plus an *assumed* compatibility of the translation of the first order machinery of the *PA* into a first order AE scheme for their mutually incompatible but separate, internally justified legitimacies. In other words, both the first order *PA* and syllogistic machineries appear non-isomorphic, but seem *prima facie* translatable and hence compatible with some tinkering. However, between the second order *PA* and AE philosophies of logic, the rules of emic well-formedness and emic allowable transformations, the metalogical rules of the *PA*

---

8. This complex of points was argued in my "Metalogical Incompatibilities in the Formal Description of Buddhist Logic (*Nyāya*)," *The Notre Dame Journal of Formal Logic*, 18, no. 2 (1977): 221-31.

and the utilized AE models are both non-isomorphic and incompatible. It is this unexamined assumption of both first and second order compatibilities between philosophies of logic concerning exemplifications and full warrants, which has been largely ignored in formalistic translations and discussions of the *PA* and of AE models of formal logics.

III. Is the PA an Implicit Form of Modus Ponens?

Two obvious questions appear. The first question is: why would one wish to restructure the *PA* into a new form which is sufficiently similar to an AE form to then enable the formalistic translator to apply AE formalistic vocabulary and subsequently to (again) translate the newly restructured *PA natural language* form into an ideal language, formalized expression? Here, two translations are present. First, the translation of the natural language PA form into an AE natural language form; the second translation is from the latter into an AE fully formalized ideal language form. The answer to the first question is that by completing these moves, the AE translator has (supposedly) "thus shown" that the *PA* is "compatible with" and/or actually is "formal logic," a happily familiar type of logic and one which is *self-evidently* deductive.

The second question is: why does the translator think he/she is warranted in making these restructurings ? The answer is that almost all the (probably *all*) twentieth century formally oriented scholars of this period of Buddhist Pramāṇa- vāda have assumed that the *PA* is an IMPLICIT *form of modus ponens* and they view their task as to make explicit what is (allegedly) implicit in the natural language sources of these two-staged restructurings.

To focus on one fundamental problem, let us turn our attention to this last point by considering a series of relevant analyses. However, I shall start with a counter-example to this assumption to focus my inquiries.

A COUNTER-ARGUMENT: DIṄNĀGA: I

As a counter-example to the claim that the *PA* is an implicit form of *modus ponens*, consider the counterclaim that the schema below is an "implicit" syllogism. The common, but faulty assumption that for purposes of ideal language translation, the *PA* is an "implicit" AE deductive inference is thus shown by a counterclaim to be a function of the formalistically oriented translator's own metalogical presuppositions about what constitutes "standard form." Witness the following schema named "Diṅnāga I."

1. John has the property of mortality.
2. Because John has the property of manness.
3. Where there is the property of manness, then there is the property of mortality, as in Mao-Tse-Tung and as not in the case of "R2-D2" (the robot of the film *Star Wars*).

The above *PA* is emically legitimate by Nyāya standards, but by AE standards it is neither valid nor in proper deductive form.

It would be well to consider that the *assumption* that the schema above is an "implicit *modus ponens*" remains a function about *what constitutes standard form*. Obviously the schema Diṅnāga I is that of the Nyāya *PA* form rather than the usually anticipated *modus ponens* (=MP), the latter being the assumed target model of AE deductive translations in almost all Nyāya scholarship.

For my first case, let us start very simply. Suppose that a beginning student of formal logic was instructed by means of one of a variety of standard logic textbooks such as *Copi, Kahane,* etc. Such AE sources claim that the standard valid form of simple deductive arguments is that of premises followed by a conclusion, usually marked with the word "therefore" or its semantic equivalent; thus the form is usually symbolized as "$p \supset q$" where the premises are p, and where q is the conclusion. This is independent of both whether the variables refer to terms or propositions and of whether the argument is deductively sound. Thus a student who asserted the conclusion first and the premises last, as in the *PA* invariable form "*q* because of *p*" *would be told that he does not have a formal inference* and would be *criticized* for failing to put the argument into standard form. As previously demonstrated, the form "*q* because of *p*" is the canonical, "standard form" of the *PA*. Hence a *prima facie* case now exists that the *PA* does not possess the form of an AE inference schema.

Since the above *PA* form of "*q* because of *p*" is not self-evidently a valid AE inference form of "*p* therefore *q*," the burden of proof is shifted upon one, who wishes to assert that "*q* because of *p*" is an implicit approximation of some form of MP. (See my third point on the next page.) It is important to note that it is on this level of unreflective simplicity that the translation from the *PA* ("*q* because of *p*") to an assumed deductive inference schema "(if) *p* therefore *q*" has occurred among most (if not all) of the Nyāya scholars, who have utilized the artificial languages of the syllogistic and/or the predicate calculus as a target language for the *PA*. Also I am unable to find any specific discussion of this specific point in the twentieth century scholarly literature.

For my second case, let us examine a sequence of seven clusters of sentences, which constitute premises and proto-arguments, but which may not constitute valid deductive inference schemas.

Four main points need be kept in mind here. First, the *PA* and its Nyāya logical tradition has its own invariable canonical standard form. The questions at issue here are whether it is a criteria for (emic) justification and an implicit MP and if it is, which I deny, whether it *should*, for that reason, be translated into the deductive artificial language of syllogistic or the predicate calculus as a way to demonstrate that assumption.

Second, no cluster of reasons grouped around a "conclusion," (regardless of how potentially close to being isomorphic with MP) can be asserted or justified as a formal deductive inference schema, until one knows that it exhibits a valid standard form or can be re-arranged via suitable transformation rules, into an explicit deductive standard form isomorphic with a valid deductive form such as MP.

Third, let us remember that when I speak of "deductive logic," and/or "formal logic," I am presupposing the models and the range of usages of these terms plus their related concepts as has been used in the twentieth century Nyāya scholarship, clearly, this assumption does not exhaust the full range of possible alternative logic systems nor the various formal machineries for their varied applications to natural language argumentation.

Fourth, to assume that potential formal arguments such as I, II, or III below are *potential* deductive arguments *rather than potential PAs,* is to beg the questions at issue here concerning whether the canonical *PA* is actually a deductive inference schema. Let us examine these questions in more detail.

I. a. All men are mortal

b. Therefore John is mortal

c. John is a man

This is not a formal inference; it remains incomplete, for it still lacks something which explicitly connects John and men, as is found in II.c and II.d.

II. a. All men are mortal

b. Therefore John is mortal

c. John is (a member of the class of) men,

(i.e John is a man)

d. "A man" is a member of the class of "men."

Now the class membership connection, the logical relationships, are largely explicit in II, but II is not a formal valid inference schema. That is, II is not in the standard form of a deductive inference schema. In their present forms, neither I nor II are isomorphic with any deductive pattern of valid inference forms such as *modus monens, modus tollens* or a valid transitive series.

Note that II is not valid inference schema because the sequence of the sentences are not "yet" explicitly connected and it remains a non-valid form; please note that just as the first half of this sentence (prior to the semi-colon) is not a valid inference schema nor a formal argument, *for it is a semi-structured explanation*; likewise, the sequence of the *PA* thesis plus justification, etc. is *formally* incorrect on AE criteria, and not a formally valid deductive schema. It is unacceptable as a deductive inference schema or a *PA*, because it violates the sequential criteria of evidence first and then conclusion-thesis, a non-valid form. Hence, the interpretation of the *PA* as a deductive inference schema is unacceptable for the same formalistic reason. That reason is that neither I nor II are isomorphic with either a valid AE form or the single *PA* canonical form. Let us expand these points.

III. a. John is a man

b. All men are mortal

c. Therefore John is mortal.

This is not a formal inference schema. Of course, it *could* be one, but that remains the question at issue. However, III is what we might wish to call a cluster of sentences which, if re-arranged carefully according to the presupposed guidelines of a simple valid deductive argument schema, III *might* become a valid argument schema. Hence, (1) if such re-arranging of these sentences is done in a way which is truth-preserving for them, (2) if the re-arranging satisfies the previous antecedent (1), and (3) if the re-arranged cluster can be shown to be isomorphic (of the same structural form) with a valid deductive form, which satisfies a rule of deductive validity, *then and only then* shall we be able to assert that III was "implicitly" a valid deductive inference schema, a proto-valid argument. Further, one might wish to assert that the deductive valid relations between the sentential components of III were, of course, implicit. Thus, according to this claim, what is implicit is found in the following:

IV. a. All men are mortal

b. A man is a member of the class of mortals

c. Therefore John is mortal

d. John is a man.

I ask: even if IV.c is tacitly understood, what presuppositions make IV an implicit deductive valid form? The answer is that the valid deductive form of *modus ponens* was the *presupposed model projected* upon IV. Thus, the distinction between implicit *vs.* explicit inference forms can be maintained *only if* we are in agreement about what is presupposed as implicit; a Buddhist logician would claim that the PA canonical form (below) was implicit in IV, but an AE valid inference was not implicit.

Consider the counterclaim, that what was implicit in I, II, III and IV was the following: "John is mortal because he is a man, and a man is a member of the class of mortals and where there is manness there is mortalness." This can easily be viewed as an incomplete *PA*, lacking both exemplifications. Now what is implicit?

Certainly the pattern of an AE valid deductive form is not implicit for the Buddhist logician. Just as the implicit class membership relationship of IV.c (a man being a member of the class of men) must be made explicit in order that IV.a, IV.b, IV.d may possibly be rearranged to exhibit the isomorphic form of an explicit valid deductive inference schema, so may the same collection of sentences in IV be rearranged to exhibit an isomorphic form of a legitimate *PA*. This is done in V below.

What guides one in such rearrangements is the *presupposed* model of either (1) a valid AE deductive inference schema or (2) the model of a legitimate *PA*. Thus the presupposed model of "logic" guides one in accordance with what one has already assumed is "implicit" regarding the logical form of natural language argumentation.

Furthermore, if person *A* claimed that such a valid AE deductive pattern was still implicit in IV, how might *A* wish to argue the claim of person *B* that what was implicit was a standard *PA*? The answer is that *A* has no stronger a case than does *B*.

Thus, the presuppositions about what is "standard form" of either deductive logic or the *PA* are what allows one to claim what is implicit; or further, the presuppositions about the implicit standard form of AE deductive logic begs all the questions at issue regarding what is a "true," explicit inference schema, and whether the *PA* meets those criteria.

To return to a contextual view (Nyāya) of the counterclaim at the beginning of this section, consider what reply *A* might make, if *B* asserted that what was "really implicit" in III and IV is Diṅnāga I:

V. John is mortal

Because John is a man (and)

Where there is manness, there is mortality, as in the case of Mao-Tse-Tung and not in the case of "R2-D2," the robot.

Thus to assert that a deductive inference is implicit in III and IV, is to presuppose an answer to the question of whether the *PA* actually is such an implicit AE *modus ponens* form.

In short, if a cluster of sentences does not exhibit isomorphism with a valid deductive inference schema, it is not an AE inference schema. With V then, this condition is not satisfied and thus V is not a deductive inference schema; it is a *PA*.

Hence, for III to be a deductive inference schema, which it is not, premise III.b should be stated first and III.a be stated second; also the incomplete quantification and extensional relationship of "man" and "men" is not explicit as it is explicit in II. Moreover, what is also not explicit, and needs to be so stated, are the relationships between III.a and III.b, and the relationships between III.b and III.c. These assertoric relations may be expressed as conditional ones as interpreted below in VI and VII. Two more reformulations will illustrate these differences.

VI.		VII.	
	a. If		a. If
	b. All men are mortal		b. All men are mortal
	c. And		c. And
	d. If		d. If
	e. John is a man		e. John is a man
	f. And		f. And
	g. *Therefore*		g. *Then*
	h. John is mortal.		h. John is mortal.

The logical operators of a presupposed deductive model of logic, the connectors of the arguments VI and VII, are now explicit. They are the conditional markers "if," "then," "and" in VII, plus "if," "therefore," "and," in VI. In both VI and VII, the first three relations are of the same object language type; the "therefore" of VI.g and the "then" of VII.g are metalogical markers which connect a-f in both VI and VII; "therefore" explicitly asserts the asymmetrical claim that "h" is to be accepted as warranted by the content and the formal relations of VI.h *via* VII. a-f. Substituting "then" in VII.g for "therefore" in VI.g, renders the whole cluster of VII a conditional argument as in a true Aristotelian syllogism.[9] However, VII.g lacks the metalogical implicit assumption that VII.h is demonstrated as a necessary condition rather than merely conditional; the "therefore" of VI.g expresses this assumption. Thus the conditional argument (VII), with "then" (VII.g) rather than "therefore" of VI.g, is a weaker claim. In VII, the claim is that if b and if e are so, then h is so; however VI asserts a much stronger claim by means of the metalogical operator "therefore" (of VI.g). This is that if VI.b

9. See J. Lukasiewicz, *Aristotle's Syllogistic*, 2nd edn., (Oxford: Oxford University Press, 1957).

and if VI.e are so, therefore, VI.h is so. In a metaphorical sense, the "therefore" stands "outside" the cluster of sentences (as stated in VI.g). The force of the latter connector of "therefore" (not merely "conjunction"), asserts something stronger, a relationship beyond the relations of conjunction (and) of VI.c-f and VII.c and the conditionality of "if," "then." Hence, "therefore" (VI.g) implicitly asserts that (A) that VI.a, d and VII.a, d, g are acceptable by the relevant speech community, and that (B) VI.b and e and VII.b and e are true and, (C) that both A and B (of this sentence) cannot be accepted while rejecting VI.h, and metalogically, (D) that to accept C (of this sentence) is metalogically wrong; this latter point (C) is the central implicit metalogical (normative) rule at issue in this process of justifying a formalized translation of the PA as deductive inference schema.

An AE deductive inference schema satisfies points, A, B, C, and D of the preceding sentence; the form of the PA does not. Thus the PA is not a formal AE deductive inference schema.

On the other hand, the truth of the premises, here VI and VII.a-c, in a deductive argument, when coupled with (to simplify not incautiously) the public recognition that the cluster is isomorphic with a valid inference FORM such as *modus ponens* (or *modus tollens* or a valid transitive series, etc.) jointly constitutes a sufficient condition for the cluster to be called an AE inference schema. This is (1) expressed by "therefore" and (2) by an appeal to which constitutes the means of justifying the truth of VI.h but not of VII.h. This point is replicated in the following threefold cluster:

VIII. 1. a.-c. If all men are mortal and

2. d.-f. If John is a man (i.e II. d. is understood)

3. g.-h. Therefore John is mortal.

Thus, the function of "therefore" which implicitly asserts that the proper AE deductive isomorphism holds has now been sketched; the function of "therefore" and its justification has not been demonstrated or justified for that remains an AE emic inquiry outside of this article.

My point here is that in I, II and III the forms of these three clusters do not permit the satisfaction of one half of the two sufficient clusters for evaluating a cluster as a true inference form such as MP (MT, etc.).

To refresh us, an analogous version of V as a so-called PA (pseudo) "inference" is:

IX. John is mortal:

Because John is a man;

(and) when there is manness there is mortality,

as in the case of Mao-Tse-Tung and not in the case of "R2-D2," the robot.

As is now obvious, neither this form (IX) nor I, II, and III are valid AE deductive forms as noted above.

To claim that I, II, or III are inference schemas or even proto-inference-schemas entails that the proper re-arrangement of their individual premises (1) necessitates an approximation of, say, *modus ponens*, etc.; and to make this claim is to beg the question regarding the legitimate "inference-schemaness" of the *PA* and what a proper rearrangement *should* be. (2) Such a claim excludes the possibility that a canonical *PA* form *could* be the/a possible legitimate logical form of rearrangement from ordinary language.

Now both V and IX are the forms, which a Buddhist logician would require as a "proper" rearrangement of I, II, and III into the canonical form of a Nyāya *PA*; to claim that a valid deductive form is both (1) implicit and thus allows one to assert that I, II, and III are deductive inference schemas, however implicit in their present forms, and (2) that the rearrangement of I, II, and III into the canonical form of a legitimate *PA* is neither implicit nor proper, is simply to beg the question of what constitutes the "proper" form of an inference schema. My following deductively sound argument summarizes the foregoing discussion; it is named "Diṅnāga II."

X. a. All deductive sound inference schemas must (then) exhibit an isomorphism with one valid deductive inference form (and must possess true premises).

b. I, II and III do not exhibit isomorphism with a valid deductive form; the *PA* schemas, as in V and IX, fail to exhibit such valid forms.

Therefore I, II, III, V, and IX are not valid deductive inference schemas (by *Modus Tollens*).

As in V and IX, the "potential" deductive arguments in I, II, and III can, of course, be easily rearranged into the standard canonical *PA* form or can be rearranged into, say, *modus ponens*.

Thus the "potentiality" for a cluster of reasons for a conclusion to be of either an accurate valid deductive inference schema or to be a legitimate canonical *PA* remains a *function* of one's *presuppositions* regarding what is (formally) *potential*. This, in turn, is a function of what system of formal logic one is predisposed to utilize and superimpose upon a cluster of reasons expressed in ordinary language for a given conclusion. Aristotle, Frege and company had their presuppositions; Diṅnāga, Dharmakīrti and company had theirs. The two lineages and their various schemas are neither wholly compatible nor isomorphic. They are, of course, translatable, but it is folly to suppose that one is "implicit" in the other as *grounds* for so translating.

It is most important to note that for an invariably structured natural language claim to be correctly shown as being necessarily true (analytically true) is significantly *different* than showing that it is *implicitly*, a system of deductive logic via the usually presupposed AE models of this century.

What is at issue in these comparative analyses is not that one or the other forms, the *PA* or the AE models, *could* or *should* be used to attempt to convey all the machinery of the other; what is at issue here is an analysis of how they are similar, how they are different, and in what details and metalogical levels they are similar and different from each other. Finally, the crucial issue here is how much of a price we shall pay in distortion, omission and inaccuracy in such translations when we use the formal machinery of AE systems as a target language for the conceptual approximation and formalized translation of the Buddhist *PA*. That "price" will be demonstrated elsewhere.

That these *PA* models are not inductive arguments does seem obvious; that they could be so considered seems equally implausible since, as with the Jaina *pramāṇa* of *tarka* or the *pramāṇa*s of the "Hindu" *āstika* schools (*darśana*s), there seems to be no explicitly quantified, or even a semi-quantified sense of probability relation between the *pakṣa* and the *hetu dṛṣṭānta, sapakṣa* and *vipakṣa*.[10]

However, as all philosophers know, "East and West," the formalized argument represents the tip of the philosophical iceberg after the real business of epistemological and foundational analyses (an analogue of *tarka*) has been brought to a pragmatically justified closure within the respective contexts of each philosophical-metalogical tradition.

While the detailed arguments for my critical remarks will be exemplified in my forthcoming monograph, it remains my hope that these points will kindle a dialogue about the Buddhist Nyāya *PA* which will remain focused upon comparative philosophies of inference and/or natural language argumentation rather than solely upon textual history, Cartesian epistemologies or the implicit but unrewarding superimposition of claims about formalistic parity across different philosophical cultures.

---

10. "Circularity in the Inductive Justification of Formal Arguments (Tarka) in 12th Century Indian Jaina Logic," in *Philosophy East and West*, 29, no. 2 (1979): 177-88, and forthcoming in the Pt. Sukhalalji Memorial Volume, L.D. Institute of Indology, Ahmedabad, India.

8

Dharmakīrti's Definition of "Points of Defeat" (Nigrahasthāna)

Michael Torsten Much

DHARMAKĪRTI defined "points of defeat" (*nigrahasthāna, nigrahādhikaraṇa, parājayasthāna, parājayādhikaraṇa*) in the first part of his *Vādanyāya* (*VN*).[1] Modern descriptions of his definitions are rare and short, and in most cases misleading.

In Vidyābhūṣaṇa's *History of Indian Logic* once two, once twenty-two "points of defeat" are mentioned.[2] Quoting the *śāstraśarīraśloka* of the *VN* Tucci and Vostrikov spoke of two forms.[3] Vostrikov, moreover, attempted a first translation of the programmatic verse and gave a rough outline of the text.[4] Likewise, Anantalal Thakur maintained, that Dharmakīrti "advocated the acceptance of two varieties [of *nigrahasthāna*] only."[5]

---

1. In the second part of the *VN* the "points of defeat" as defined in *NS* Vb are treated one after the other.
2. S. Ch. Vidyabhusana, *A History of Indian Logic* (Calcutta: University of Calcutta, 1921), pp. 137 and 150.
3. G. Tucci, *Pre-Diṅnāga Buddhist Texts on Logic from Chinese Sources.* Baroda, 1929, 12 of notes. A. Vostrikov, "The Nyāyavārttika of Uddyotakara and the Vādanyāya of Dharmakīrti." *Indian Historical Quarterly* 11 (1935): 1-31.
4. Loc. cit. Vostrikov mainly dealt with the second part of the *VN*. A translation of the verse is also found in: S. Mookerjee and N. Tatia, *Hemacandra's Pramāṇa-mīmaṁsā* (Varanasi: Tara Publications, 1970), p. 189.
5. Anantalal Thakur, *Ratnakīrti-nibandhāvaliḥ*, 2nd edn. (Patna: Kashi Prasad Jayaswal Research Institute, 1975), p. 3 of Introduction.

Mahendrakumar Jain was the first to point out at least,[6] that Dharmakīrti was "entangled in various explanations" of *nigrahasthāna*, but Warder, who mentioned the *VN* briefly in his *Outline of Indian Philosophy* as "quite elementary and self-explanatory," again spoke of "only two kinds of defeat situation."[7]

All forms of *nigrahasthāna* as defined by Dharmakīrti were listed for the first time by Esther Solomon in a survey of the first part of the *VN*.[8] This survey however remains dissatisfying, which is not surprising, since the Sanskrit text published by Sāṅkr̥tyāyana in 1935-36, is in such a bad state, that it is almost impossible to work with it.[9]

However, with the help of Śāntarakṣita's commentary, the Tibetan translation and other philological sources, a good text can be constituted and the following interpretation of the *śāstraśarīraśloka* and the importance of the *VN* results from my work towards a critical edition of the text together with an annotated translation.

I

Dharmakīrti's definition of "points of defeat" is condensed in the programmatic verse:

asādhanāṅgavacanam adoṣodbhāvanaṁ dvayoḥ ।
nigrahasthānam anyat tu na yuktam iti neṣyate ॥1॥[10]

A pleasant and meaningful translation of the two crucial terms of this verse is impossible. I therefore offer a literal rendering in

---

6. Mahendrakumar Jain, *Siddhiviniścayaṭīkā of Śrī Anantavīryācārya* [vol. 1], (Benares: 1959), p. 109 f. of Introduction.

7. A.K. Warder, *Outline of Indian Philosophy* (Delhi: 1971), p. 206.

8. E. Solomon, *Indian Dialectics*, vol. 1 (Ahmedabad: 1976) pp. 249-53.

9. As noted already by E. Steinkellner, "Die Entwicklung des kṣaṇikatvānumānam bei Dharmakīrti," *Wiener Zeitschrift fòr die Kunde Sòdasiens* 12-13 (1968/69): 371-77, 375, n. 46.

10. *VN* 2.1-2. References are given to Sāṅkr̥tyāyana's edition; however, texts quoted are in accordance with my forthcoming critical edition.

accordance with the interpretational variations offered by Dharmakīrti:

> The non-means-of-proof-formulation (and) the non-fault-indication are for the two (the proponent and the opponent respectively) a point of defeat. Another (point of defeat), however, is not correct, therefore not accepted.

Since the negation in the compounds *asādhanāṅgavacana* and *adoṣodbhāvana* may refer to *aṅga* or *doṣa* respectively as well as to *vacana* or *udbhāvana* and since the terms *sādhana*, *aṅga* and *vacana* can be understood as having different meanings, two, four, eight or even eleven (depending on the level of counting) "points of defeat" are contained in this verse, not just two, as asserted so often.

The other "points of defeat" mentioned, the wrong ones, which are not accepted, are the *nigrahasthāna* as defined in the *NS*.

The "points of defeat" are divided into two groups: one for the proponent (*vādin*), called *asādhanāṅgavacana*, and one for the opponent (*prativādin*) called *adoṣodbhāvana*.

The compound *asādhanāṅgavacana* is in addition analysed in two ways by changing the construction of the negation: it is analysed as "the non-formulation of a means of proof" (*sādhanāṅgasya avacanam*)[11] and "the formulation of something, which is not a means of proof" (*asādhanāṅgasya vacanam*).[12]

The first interpretation comprises again three possible variations of meaning, thus actually bringing the first three concrete cases of "points of defeat."

Sādhana can be *siddhi*, the resulting inferential cognition[13] or the *trirūpavacanasamudāya* respectively, and *aṅga* can be *trividham*

11. *VN* 12.1

12. *VN* 61.4 f.

13. *Ś* 3.10: *tasya siddhiḥ pratipattiḥ sādhanam*. So not the act of proving, which causes the cognition, is here referred to, as maintained by Solomon, op. cit., 249, and Mookerjee and Tatia, op. cit., 190.

eva liṅgam, or *pakṣadharmādivacana*. In the first case, besides mentioning the maintenance of silence (*tūṣṇīṁbhāva*)[14] for completeness' sake, Dharmakīrti interprets as a "point of defeat" mainly any insufficient usage of the logical forms in terms of his own logical theories.

In this sense a "point of defeat" consists in the non-formulation (*avacana*), i.e. the non-justification (*asamarthana*) of the means (*aṅga*) for the proof, i.e. of that, which brings about (*nirvartaka*) the proof, i.e. the reason (*liṅga*).[15] Śāntarakṣita defines non-justification (*asamarthana*) as "the non-showing of a definite cognition (*niścayāpradarśana*) related to the three aspects (of the reason)."[16] The term is new with Dharmakīrti and is used exclusively in accordance with his logical tenets.

In the case of an essential property (*svabhāva*) the reason has to be justified by producing a *bādhakapramāṇa*, a means of cognition, which does away (*bādhate*) with the probans in the opposite (*viparyaya*) of the probandum.[17] In the case of an effect (*kārya*) the reason must be justified by establishing the causal relation (*kāryakāraṇabhāvaprasādhana*),[18] and in the case of a non-perception by proving the non-perception of something, which meets the requirements for perception (*upalabdhi-lakṣaṇaprāptasyānupalabdhisādhanam*).[19]

---

14. *VN* 3.1-3 (s.n. 15), cf. n. 22.

15. *Ś* 3.14: *tac ca sādhanāṅgam iha niścitatrairūpyam liṅgam ucyate*. *VN* 3.1-3: *iṣṭasyārthasya siddhiḥ sādhanam, tasya nirvartakam aṅgam, tasyāvacanaṁ tasyāṅgasyānuccāraṇaṁ vādino nigrahādhikaraṇam, tad abhyupagamyāpratibhayā tūṣṇīṁbhāvāt sādhanāṅgasyāsamarthanād vā.*

16. *Ś* 3.26.

17. *VN* 6.5-6 *atra vyāptisādhanaṁ viparyaye bādhakapramāṇopa-darśanam.*

18. *VN* 73.3-74.1: *yat kāryaliṅgam kāraṇasya sādhanāyopādīyate, tasya tena saha kāryakāraṇabhāvaprasāḍhanaṁ bhāvā-bhāvasādhanapramāṇābhyām.*

19. *VN* 78.3-4: *anupalabdhāv api pratipattur upalabdhilakṣaṇaprāptasyānupalabdhisādhanaṁ samarthanam.*

Dharmakīrti states explicitly, that it is not enough to use a fit (*samartha*) reason, its fitness (*sāmarthya*) for proof has to be justified, nonj-ustification being a "point of defeat."[20]

The third "point of defeat" is based on understanding *sādhana* as the complete formulation of the logical reason with its three aspects, which is the act by which something is proven to somebody, and *aṅga* as *pakṣadharmavacana* and *sapakṣasattvavacana* or *vipakṣāsattvavacana*. There occurs then a "point of defeat," if even one of such "means of proof" is not formulated.[21]

The non-formulation of both members is again a case of defeating silence (*tūṣṇīṁbhāva*).[22]

The analysis of the compound *asādhanāṅgavacana* into *asādhanāṅgasya vacanam* results in two more "points of defeat."

Based on the understanding of *sādhana* as *trirūpa-hetu vacanasamudāya*[23] and *an-aṅga* as something, which is not a means for that proof, the formulation of a thesis, etc. is a "point of defeat."[24] It comprises: (1) the formulation of a thesis application, conclusion, etc. (*pratijñopanayanigamanādi*)[25] as proposed, e.g. by the Naiyāyika; (2) the formulation of both *anvaya* and *vyatireka*;[26]

---

20. *VN* 12.1-13.2: *tasyāsamarthanaṁ sādhanāṅgavacanaṁ tadvādinaḥ parājayasthānam ārabdhārthāprasādhanāt, vastutaḥ samarthasya hetor upādāne 'pi sāmarthyāpratipādanāt.* cf. also *VN* 77.4-78.2, 60.2-3.

21. *VN* 60.4-67.3: *athavā sādhyate tena pareṣāṁ apratīto 'rtha iti sādhanaṁ trirūpahetuvacanasamudāyaḥ. tasyāṅgaṁ pakṣadharmādivacanam. tasyaikasyāpy avacanam asādhanāṅgavacanam. tad api vādino nigrahasthānam, tadavacane heturūpasyaivāvacanena siddher abhāvāt.*

22. Cf. *Ś* 61.17-18. Silence may appear on two occasions: instead of the proof (*sādhana* in sense of the proving act) and after completion of the proof, instead of *samarthana* (referring to *sādhana* as *siddhi*).

23. *VN* 61. 4 f. *athavā tasyaiva sādhanasya yan nāṅgaṁ . . . tasya . . . upādānaṁ . . . nigrahasthānam.*

24. As above, cf. n. 21.

25. *VN* 61.4-6.

26. *VN* 65.1-3.

(3) the formulation of a thesis,[27] which, according to a certain opinion — possibly Īśvarasena's — is to be used for showing the object of the proof, although not strictly speaking a means of proof; (4) the formulation of fallacious reasons (*hetvābhāsa*);[28] and (5) fallacious examples (*dṛṣṭāntābhāsa*).[29]

The second meaning of *asādhanāṅgasyavacanam* is based on the following interpretation: *sādhanāṅga* is taken as a *bahuvrīhi* and characterizes the object (*artha*), which as the basis of divergence of views (*vivādāśraya*) is the reason for taking up the disputation (*vādaprastāva-hetu*). This object has the proof — understood as resulting cognition — as a constituent part (*aṅga*) or property (*dharma*).[30] That means, that there may be a "point of defeat," if the proposing party brings something into play, which is not the primary aim of the proof. This kind of formulation is specified as digression (*ghoṣaṇa*) and side-remark (*prakṣepa*).[31] These two, however, are a "point of defeat" only if the opponent is not interested in the additional materials drawn into the discussion by the proponent.[32]

These then are the "points of defeat" for the proponent, the "points of defeat" for the opponent number two, again according to different possibilities to construct the negation.

First, the "non-indication of a fault" (*doṣasya anudbhāvanam*)[33] consists in not pointing out the faults of proof (*sādhanadoṣa*), which are deficiency (*nyūnatva*), irrelevance (*asiddhi*), inconclusiveness (*anaikāntikatā*), proving the opposite of what is

27. *VN* 65.4-13.

28. *VN* 66.1-2.

29. *VN* 66.2-5.

30. *VN* 66.6-7: *athavā siddhiḥ sādhanaṁ, tadaṅgaṁ dharmo yasyārthasya vivādāśrayasya vādaprastāvahetoḥ, sa sādhanāṅgaḥ.*

31. *VN* 66.7-9.

32. *VN* 67.1 *jijñāsāyām adoṣaḥ.*

33. *VN* 69.4: *yadā na doṣam udbhāvayati.*

intended to be proved (*viparyayasādhana*) and finally the eighteen faults of example (*dṛṣṭāntadoṣa*).[34]

Second, the "indication of something, which is not a fault" (*adoṣasya udbhāvanam*).[35]

This is of course only a rough survey of the ingenious interpretational art of Dharmakīrti with which he is able to account for no less than eleven individually definable "points of defeat" with the two definitory formulations of the *śāstra-śarīra*-verse. It should be noted finally, that all these "points of defeat" are valid only, when claimed by the opponent, otherwise there is no decision on victory and defeat.[36]

II

The above survey of the "points of defeat" is only one example for some of the results, that can be expected from not only taking Dharmakīrti's *VN* as a serious piece of philosophical literature, but also from carefully studying and analysing it. One of the most intriguing general questions, that might be asked with regard to this text, is probably, why Dharmakīrti wrote a treatise of that kind at all. In order to give you my hypothetical answer to this question a quick survey of the known literature on this special category of dialectics may be useful.

---

34. *VN* 69.6-8. The *sādhanadoṣa* do not correspond entirely to the *nigrahasthāna* for the proponent. To the accusation of *hetvābhāsa* and *dṛṣṭāntābhāsa* a *samarthana* would be the reply. *Nyūnatva* would be the objection against not stating *pakṣadharma*, etc. Not indicating *ghoṣaṇa* and *prakṣepa* is no "point of defeat" for the opponent, since he might be eventually interested, *ghoṣaṇa* and *prakṣepa* then being no point of defeat for the proponent. It remains unclear, why the non-indicating of the use of *pratijñā*, etc. and the use of both, *anvaya* and *vyatireka*, is not explained as a *nigrahasthāna* for the opponent.

35. *VN* 72.1-3. *athavā yo na doṣaḥ sādhanasya tadbhāve 'pi vādinā sādhayitum iṣṭasyārthasya siddher vighātābhāvāt, tasyodbhāvanaṁ prativādino nigrahādhikaraṇaṁ, mithyottarābhidhānāt.*

36. *VN* 70.7-8: *nirākaraṇaṁ hi tasyānyena parājayaḥ, na siddhyabhāvaḥ.*

The oldest definitions of *nigrahasthāna* from the side of the Buddhists are known from the **Upāyahṛdaya* (**Prayogasāra*) and the *Tarkaśāstra*, where much space is devoted to their treatment. From the four chapters of the **Upāyahṛdaya* the second and the third deal with *nigrahasthāna*, the first one deals with dialectics in general and the fourth with wrong refutations (*jāti*); apparently similar to the *Tarkaśāstra*.

Vasubandhu introduced a division of dialectical matters into proof (*sādhana*) and refutation (*dūṣaṇa*) and attempted in his *Vādavidhāna* and *Vādavidhi* to combine this new scheme with the structure of the other dialectical handbooks, anticipating Diṅnāga's *Nyāyamukha*, which treats under "proof" the *avayava* and *avayavābhāsa*, as well as the *pramāṇa* (*pratyakṣa* and *anumāna*) and under "refutation" refutation and *jāti*. This structure was still followed by Śaṅkarasvāmin in the *Nyāyapraveśa*, with the exception that he dropped the treatment of *jāti*.[37]

As far as the material is available, it is still unclear why "points of defeat" were not dealt within the period from Vasubandhu to Śaṅkarasvāmin. Perhaps this was because they were in general use in public disputations (*vāda*) and well known to both Buddhists and Naiyāyika. In the Nyāya-school the explanation of these terms was kept alive, because they were listed in *NS* Vb. No redefinition, however, was attempted in accordance with logical principles, even after Diṅnāga offered his new rules for the *hetu*. Only the *nigrahasthāna* where *hetu*-forms apply were adapted (e.g. *hetvābhāsa*).

The *VN* signifies a crucial change. Dharmakīrti proposed a new meaning of public disputation (*vāda*) in general: there can be no acceptance of *vijigīṣuvāda*, a disputation of people who wish to win.

---

37. Above account follows E. Frauwallner, "Vasubandhu's Vādavidhiḥ." *Wiener Zeitschrift fòr die Kunde Sòd- und Ostasiens* 1 (1957) : 104-46, 706-08.

"[Opponent:] 'Although *chala* is used there is a *vāda*.' [Answer:] No, because righteous people (*sad*) do not teach a *śāstra* in reference to quarrels among bad people (*durjana*)."[38] "Therefore, there is really no so-called 'disputation of those, who want to win' (*vijigīṣuvāda*), which is free from rules."[39] Disputation on the contrary has to serve the investigation of truth (*tattvacintā*): "In investigating truth there is no usage of *chala* whatsoever."[40] Dharmakīrti, moreover, defines victory: "Explanation of truth (*tattva*) for assisting others is victory for the proponent, elimination of false cognition by pointing out an existing fault is victory for opponent."[41]

He correspondingly rejects, that *chala*, etc.[42] may be used at least for the purpose of protecting the truth (*tattvarakṣaṇārtha*) as recommended, e.g. in the *NS*:[43] "[Opponent:] 'For the purpose of protecting the truth righteous people (*sad*) who want to win should, of course, use *chala*, etc.' [Answer:] No. (Rather in addition) it should be said: 'Also by means of fingernails, boxes on the ear, weapons, stocks, setting on fire, etc."[44] This is the way of the wicked (*śaṭha*),[45] As the ones who are jealous of the good fortune of others.[46] The *vāda* of righteous people, who rejoice

---

38. *VN* 71.5-7: *chalavyavahāre 'pi vijigīṣunā vāda iti cet, na, durjanavipratipattyadhikāre satāṁ śāstrāpravṛtteḥ.*

39. *VN* 71.10-11. *tasmān na yogavihitaḥ kaścid vijigīṣuvādo nāma.*

40. *VN* 70.6: *na hi tattvacintāyām kaścic chalavyavahāraḥ.*

41. *VN* 71.20-21: *tasmāt parānugrahāya tattvakhyāpanaṁ vādino vijayaḥ, bhūtodoṣadarśanena mithyāpratipattinivarttanaṁ prativādinaḥ.*

42. *vitaṇḍā* is not mentioned explicitly in the *VN*, but from the definition of victory given above it seems clear that it is also rejected by Dharmakīrti.

43. *NS* IVb 49.

44. *VN* 71.15-16: *tattvarakṣanārthaṁ sadbhir upahartavyam eva chalādi vijigīṣubhir iti cet, na nakhacapeṭaśastraprahārādīpanādibhir apīti vaktavyam.*

45. *VN* 1.5.

46. *Ś* 1.5.

in the welfare of others,[47] follow logical rules (*nyāyānusaraṇa*).[48] And since disputation is an instrument for investigating the truth (*tattvacintā*) the "points of defeat" had to be newly defined and explained according to whether they are organized in terms of logical rules or not.

Abbreviations

VN *Dharmakīrti's Vādanyāya.* With the Commentary of Śāntarakṣita. Edited by R. Sāṅkṛtyāyana. Patna: 1935-36.

Ś Śāntarakṣita's *Vipañcitārthānāma Vādanyāyaṭīkā*, s. *VN*.

NS *Die Nyāyasūtras*. Text Übersetzung, Erlaòterung und Glossar. Von W. Ruben. Leipzig: 1928. Nachdruck Nendeln 1966.

Appendix

Synopsis of the *nigrahasthāna* as defined in the *VN*

1.	*asādhanāṅgavacanam*	3.1-69.2
1.1.	*sādhanāṅgasya avacanam*	3.1-61.3
1.1.1.	*sādhanam=siddhiḥ, aṅgam=trividham eva liṅgam: tūṣṇīṁbhāvaḥ*	3.1-3
1.1.2.	*sādhanam=siddhiḥ, aṅgam=trividham eva liṅgam: asamarthanam*	3.1-60.4
1.1.3.	*sādhanam=trirūpahetuvacanasamudāyaḥ aṅgam=pakṣadharmādivacanam*	60.4-61.3
1.2.	*asādhanāṅgasya vacanam*	61.4-69.2
1.2.1.	*sādhanam=trirūpahetuvacanasamudāyaḥ aṅgam=pratijñopanayanigamanādiḥ*	61.4-66.5
1.2.1.1.	*pratijñādeḥ sādhanavākye upadānam*	61.4-6
1.2.1.2.	*anvayavyatirekayor dvitīyasyāpy abhidhānam*	65.1-3

47. *VN* 142.4.

48. *VN* 71.19.

1.2.1.3.	*vyarthaṁ sādhanavākye pratijñāvacanopādānam*	65.4-13
1.2.1.4.	*hetvābhāsasya vacanam*	66.1-2
1.2.1.5.	*dr̥ṣṭāntabhāsasya vacanam*	66.2-5
1.2.2.	*sādhanam=siddhiḥ, tadaṅgaṁ dharmo yasyārthsya vivadāśrayasya vādaprastāvahetoḥ, sa sādhanāṅgaḥ: ghoṣaṇam, prakṣepaḥ*	66.6-68.11
2.	*adoṣodbhāvanam*	69.3-73.4
2.1.	*prativādī yadā na doṣam udbhāvayati*	69.3-71.21
2.2.	*yo na doṣah sādhanasya . . . tasyodbhāvanam*	72.1-73.4

9

Apoha and Śiṁśapāvṛkṣa

Radhika Herzberger

I

THE Indian philosophical past does not reveal itself in neatly stratified layers, but sometimes, as in an archaeologist's nightmare, artefacts representing varied stages of technological development lie side by side without forming any obvious pattern. D.D. Kosambi, himself a noted archaeologist and historian, acknowledging this very impacted appearance of his Indian material, perceived in this appearance an invitation to reconstruct earlier historical periods on the basis of a hypothesis linking tools of production, artefacts and ideological superstructures.[1] Drawing inspiration from his example, I shall try in the course of this paper to identify the philosophical problems that Diṅnāga's *apoha* doctrines were designed to solve, and to locate the problem so identified within a historical frame of reference; a part of my overall concern will be to articulate the relevant philosophical issues in universally recognizable terms.

The major theories regarding names can be identified as predating Diṅnāga's writings on *apoha*: the first can be traced to Bhartṛhari, a philosophical grammarian belonging to the fifth century CE whose name ancient tradition associated with that of a celebrated poet: the second is attributed to Kātyāyana, a grammarian who belonged to the second or third century BCE

1. Damodar Kosambi, *Myth and Reality* (Bombay: Popular Prakasan, 1962), p. 22.

My attempt in this paper will be to find a place for Diṅnāga's *apoha* doctrines within the tensions arising between Bhartṛhari's and Kātyāyana's theories.

Bhartṛhari's theory is referred to by Diṅnāga in a polemical stanza found in the fifth chapter of the *Pramāṇasamuccaya* (*PS*) in the following way:[2]

> The word which signifies a universal (*jātiśabda*) designates all the individuals which belong to it; the word which signifies an individuals (*bhedaśabda*) is for the sake of restriction (of the scope of the universal) to the context of what is said.
>
> — *vrPS* 5.1: NC.2, p. 607

The theory referred to above by Diṅnāga is developed by Bhartṛhari in the *Jātisamuddeśa* (*JS*), and elsewhere, I have traced the step-by-step emergence of the position.[3] My present concern will be to cite a stanza in which the salient features of Bhartṛhari's thought are set forth. In the very first chapter of the *Vākyapadīya* (*VP*), he says:

---

2. *jātiśabdaḥ svabhedān sarvān evābhidhatte. ukteṣu niyamārthaṁ bhedaśabdah.* Diṅnāga's phrase here *ukteṣu niyamārthaṁ bhedaśabdaḥ* echoes similar phrases used by Bhartṛhari in the *VP*. At least twice (in *JS* 89 and *VP* 2.64), Bhartṛhari illustrated the conception of *bhedaśabda* in the following way. From the Vedic injunction, "You should sacrifice" one arrives at the notion that some substance in general should be sacrificed. This could include rice, sheep and goats. On hearing the additional word "rice" as part of the injunction, the idea of substance in general is specified, and the other substances implied by the injunction, in this case goats and sheep, stand rejected. Thus, the word "rice" (*vrīhi*) is described by Bhartṛhari as the "word repeated for the sake of restriction" (cf. *niyamārthā punaḥ śrutiḥ, VP* 2. 64), because it restricts the scope of the more general word to the one possibility out of the many possibilities suggested by it. Diṅnāga's stanza sums up this view, that a word which in general defines possibilities which the less general word restricts.

3. Radhika Herzberger, "The Development of Logic in Fifth and Sixth Century India" (Ph.D. dissertation, University of Toronto, 1982), pp. 29-78. I have traced the emergence of these ideas through the *JS*, specifically from *JS* 6 to *JS* 13.

> From that (*śabdabrahman*), situated in a family of universals (*ākṛtigotra*), are born a gamut of individuals, which possess (other) transformations, like rain-bearing clouds from the wind.
>
> — *vrVP* 1.1, p. 13.3-4

A rather complex view of meaning relations is presented in the stanza, woven around two images: the founding father of a stable family, extending over many generations, bestowing his essence over future generations; and moisture, which is present in wind and rain, transforming itself into a series of clouds. Both images have in common the idea of a substance persisting through various modifications. The view presented so obstrusely in the stanza can be summed up in the following way:

1. A universal (*ākṛti* or *jāti*) defines the whole class of individuals (*dravya* or *vyakti*) which falls under it.
2. Individuals so defined can in turn be treated as universals, i.e. as defining sub-classes of individuals.
3. The distinction between a word for a universal (*jātiśabda)* and a word for an individual (*bhedaśabda*) ceases to be hard and fast, and depends on the place an element occupies on the scale defined in terms of higher and lower universals.
4. The breakdown of the distinction between what is a universal and what is an individual allows meaning relations to be treated in a hierarchical fashion (see diagram below).
5. Meaning relations can then be viewed extensionally, as a hierarchical ordering of classes and sub-classes.
6. Meaning relations can also be treated intensionally, the lower universal contains the higher universal, and the highest universal is contained in every lower universal.

These abstract conclusions can be justified on the basis of the stanza from the *VP* quoted above: From the highest universal which is the *śabdabrahman*,[4] a gamut of individuals (*vyakti-grāmā*) are born (*jāyate*) or defined.[5] To maintain, as the stanza does, that these individuals are themselves possessed of transformations (*vikārin*) or, as Vṛṣabhadeva puts it, "the wombs of other transformations" (*vikārāntarayonayaḥ*),[6] is to dissolve the sharp distinction between individuals and universals and to replace it with the notion of classes and sub-classes of entities which are both universals or individuals, depending on the point of view taken. Thus in *JS* 11, Bhartṛhari can claim that "Objects of words have functional definitions"; cf. *vyāpāralakṣaṇā . . . padārthāḥ samavasthitāḥ.*

At the heart of the hierarchical analogy hinted at in the genealogical image is an abstract view of meaning relations between names, which can be diagrammed as under:

---

4. My identification of the highest universal (*mahāsattā*) with the *śabdabrahman* is justified on the following grounds. Helārāja, in his comments on *JS* 38 (p. 45.8), describes *sattā* as *brahmātmikā,* his description, in the same chapter of *mahāsattā* as *parabrahma-svabhāva* (p. 41.6) parallels similar descriptions where it is identified with non-dual conception of the *Brahman* (see Helārāja's comments on *JS* 32). Helārāja's comments here that *mahāsattā* is the *anvayirūpā* (the persisting form) repeat Bhartṛhari's description of *śabdabrahman* in for instance *vrVP* 1. 1, pp. 6.1, 7.1. My suggestion here is that *mahāsattā* is the persisting form because as the highest universal it defines the whole universe of discourse, and is part of the analytic content of every nominal (cf. *tām ahus tvalādayah*).

5. The notion that universals define classes of individuals goes back to Kātayāna (*vt.* 43 to *P* 1. 2. 64), where it is maintained that unless the Vedic injunction like "A brāhmaṇa should not be killed" is understood as stated from the point of view of Vājapyāyana that the universal is the meaning of words, it would not have universal force. Patañjali illustrated the point facetiously in the following way. If the injunction were understood as referring to individuals then a man taking care not to kill a particular brāhmaṇa would go about this business killing the rest of them.

6. Vṛṣabhadeva on *vrVP* 1.1, p. 13.

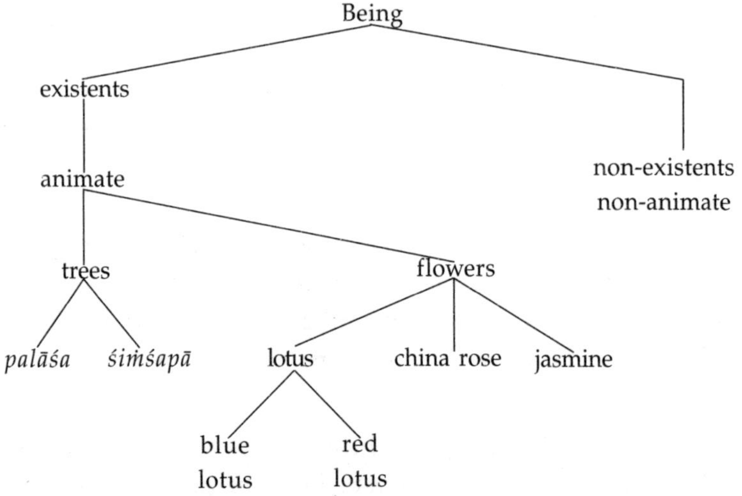

On the basis of this hierarchical arrangement of meaning, Bhartṛhari was able to define two relations: compatible co-inherence (*aviruddhaikārthasamavāya*) and incompatible co inherence (*viruddhaikārthsamavāya*).[7] Borrowing Bhartṛhari's genealogical analogy, let us define, on the basis of the diagram sketched above, the relation "of being a sibling" as one which obtains between individuals who share a common parent; thus "lotus" and "jasmine" are siblings because they share a common

7. These relations are mentioned by Bhartṛhari in *vrVP* 1.15, pp. 52-53, in the following way: "This universal is different from particular universals (such as) being a word. For (the universal) being a word co-inheres compatibly in the same thing with all (particular) universals (such as the universals, being the word for tree and being a word for horse) whose co-inherence in the same thing is incompatible. . . . Just as there is in the pot a compatible co-inherence of (universals such as): being a substance, being earthen, being a pot, so also there is in the word "tree" a compatible co-inherence of particular universals, such as : being a quality, being a word, being the word for tree. (*sā ceyam ākṛtiḥ śabdatvasāmānyaviśeṣād anyā. śabdatvaṁ hi viruddhaikārthasama-vāyinībhir ākṛtibhiḥ sarvābhir aviruddhaikārthasamavāyam . . . yathā hi ghaṭe dravyatva-pṛthivītvaghaṭatvādīnām aviruddhaḥ samavāyas tathā vṛkṣaśabde' pi guṇatvaśabdatvavṛkṣaśabdatvādīnām ākṛtiviśeṣāṇām aviruddhaḥ samavāyaḥ*).

parent in "flower." And the relation of compatible coherence can be defined as the relation which obtains between an individual and all the individuals which lie along the ancestral line, right up to the founding father; thus "lotus" and "flower" and "earth substance" are compatibly co-inherent in "blue lotus" because they lie along its ancestral line.

Bhartṛhari held that a name, on the basis of the universal it expresses,[8] has immediate access to a complex content over which these two relations, compatible co-inherence and incompatible co-inherence, can be defined. I would like to suggest that these relations represent the analytic and the antonymic content of names. To sum up: Bhartṛhari's approach represents a fusion of two ideas, an extensional one and an intensional one. According to the former, universals are viewed as defining classes of individuals which can be arranged in a hierarchical pattern. According to the latter, lower universals are represented as expressing or containing the higher universal.[9] Finally, I would like to bring to the readers' attention the similarity between the view of meaning that I have attributed to Bhartṛhari and the view described in Diṅnāga's polemical stanza (see n. 2).

Having thus rather briefly sketched the outlines of

8. All words, first of all express their own universal (*svā jātiḥ prathamaṃ śabdaiḥ sarvair vābhidhīyate, JS* 6). Through this universal, violating the cardinal principle of the Vaiśeṣikas that universals do not inhere in other universals (see Helārāja on *JS* 11, p. 24. 1-5), a word has access to a network of universals, which inhere in it either compatibly or incompatibly, see n. 7; also R. Herzberger, "The Development of Logic in Fifth and Sixth Century India, " pp. 53-78.

9. The extensional approach, based on the view that universals define all the individuals which fall within their scope, allowed Bhartṛhari to hold that the highest universal (*mahāsattā*) defines or contains the whole universe of discourse (see, for instance, *JS* 33); the intensional approach, based on the view that the lower universal analytically contains the content of higher universals, allowed Bhartṛhari to claim that the occasioning ground of all nominals express the great being (see, for instance, *JS* 34).

Bhartṛhari's conception of names, let us turn our attention to the theory it sought to displace, which was enunciated more than six hundred years before Bhartṛhari by Kātyāyana. In a celebrated aphorism, Kātyāyana defined what came to be known as "the occasioning ground for the use of a word" (*śabdapravṛttinimitta*) as "that quality (*guṇa*) because of whose presence a name is given to a thing." And, he recommended adding the suffixes *tva* and *tal* to the nominal base of the name, in order to articulate its "occasioning ground."[10] From Patañjali's remarks on the aphorism we learn that this "quality," which became the basis of name giving, was conceived of as being sensuous and as properly belonging to the individual or thing which is named.[11] It would seem to follow from this that the object named was conceived of as being external.

The theory has hidden implications of a fairly far-reaching character which I cannot handle within the span of this paper; I will restrict my attention to a rather crucial conclusion which was drawn by grammarians from this aphorism. The quality articulated by the additions of *tva* and *tal* to the nominal base of a name, was believed to be an index to the content of the name on the one hand and to the content of the object named on the other, so that the content of the name, it was held must not "exceed over" (*ati+ric*) the content of this quality.[12] Thus, it was

10. ... *yasya guṇasya bhāvād dravye śabdaniveśas tadabhidhāne tvatalau.* (*vt.* 5 on P. 5.1.119).

11. *MB* to *vt.* 5 on P. 5.1.119 lists the following as *guṇa*s: *śabdasparśarūparasagandhāḥ guṇāh.* That the quality in question must properly belong to the individual which is named is underlined by Patañjali's remark that this relation of belonging must be a matter of cognition (*pratyaya*), and merely of opinion (*abhiprāya*).

12. I have been deeply influenced in this matter by articles of George Cardona, particularly his article "Anvaya and Vyatireka in Indian Grammar," (*Adyar Library Bulletin*, 31-32: 313-52), where the term *vyatireka* and the connected root *ati+ric* are traced through the *MB* and some of the relevant *sūtra*s of Kātyāyana together with Patañjali's →

held, that if a complex name such as *rājapuruṣa* (the king's man) has reference to a more complex content (in this case, the relation of possessor and possessed, which obtains between the king and his man), then the quality (*guṇa*) is described as having been exceeded, but this excess is none the less articulated through a complex quality, which contains reference to a relation; in the present case the quality is *rājapuruṣatvam* (being a king's man).[13]

An implication of the view is that unless a relation is signified by the occasioning ground, names are atomic. Thus all names, except those which are derived by the addition of affixes or are compounds, were believed to be atomic. It was further held that any subsequent relations between these atomic names (and between the individuals they name) are due to the agency of action (or the main verb).[14] Relations between names were thought to emerge only at the sentential level.

→ comments translated; see also George Cardona, "Pāṇini's Kārakas: Agency, Animation and Identity," *Journal of Indian Philosophy* 2 (1974); also n. 13.

13. A widely quoted aphorism which has been traced to Bhartṛhari proclaims that "A relation is signified in compounds, *kṛt* and *taddhita* derivatives." (*samāsakṛttaddhiteṣu saṁbandhābhidhānam*): see Masaaki Hattori, *Dignāga, On Perception, Being the Pratyakṣapariccheda of Dignāga's Pramāṇasamuccaya* (Cambridge: Harvard University Press), n. 1. 28. See also Helārāja on *VP* 3.5.1, P. 194.3-4.

14. My conclusions are based here on a number of assertions made by ancient grammarians, who seem to view relations in general as aspects of *kāraka* relations. These relations can be explored with reference to a passage of Helārāja's, who quotes Patañjali, to explain a certain view of relations between individuals, and by extension, between names. The passage, which I will presently cite, is remarkable in that it treats the material mode, consisting of individuals and action, interchangeably with the formal mode, consisting of verbs and names. The practice which is by no means uniquely Helārāja's, far from being the product of a confusion is, I think, the product of a widely held insistence on treating sense and denotation as co-extensive. Because the meaning of a name never exceeds over (*ati+ric*) the content of the object which is named, the →

If we now consider the assumptions which govern complex formations such as *karmadhāraya* compounds, the implications that

---

→ Sanskrit term *artha* is allowed to stand for both the meaning of a name and for what is denoted by the name. I offer this by way of a suggestion, which requires much more support. Helārāja's passage reads: "Since individuals, which have established natures, lack a mutual relatedness, the relation (literally it) is brought about by action. For action, like a ladder . . . causes a connectedness between individuals. Accordingly it is said in the *Bhāṣya*: 'Qualifications of the base meaning arise, such as the object, the instrument, etc. through action'." (*dravyāṇām hi siddhasvabhāvānām parasparasaṁbandhābhāvāt kriyākṛta eva saḥ kriyā hi niḥśrayaṇīva dravyāṇy upaśleṣayati tathā ca bhāṣyam: prātipadikārthānām kriyākṛtā viśeṣā udbhavanti karma karaṇam ityādi.* Helārāja on *VP* 3.7.156, P. 355.12-15). This passage implicitly presupposes the following premises regarding the *kāraka* relations:

1. The nominative stands for the meaning of the bare stem (see Cardona, "Anvaya and Vyatireka in Indian Grammar," p. 320; *MB* on P. 2.3.46). Names in the nominative are, therefore, unrelated or atomic, unless they happen to be compounds or are derived through the addition of *kṛt* or *taddhita* affixes.
2. *Kāraka* relations such as accusative, instrumental, etc. denote a direct relation with a verb; all inflected names, except those in the genitive are implicitly sentential in character.
3. The genitive alone denotes a relation with two individuals.

However, the genitive is believed to be reducible to one of the *kāraka* relations; it is thought to be derived case presupposing a full-fledged sentence. The matter is explained in the following way. In phrases such as *rājñaḥ puruṣaḥ* (the king's man) the actions such as capturing and buying which originally brought about the relation between the king and the man, are assumed, though unstated. Now this unstated action between the king and the man can be expressed in terms of one of the *kāraka* relations; see *VP* 3.7.156, where Bhartṛhari describes the genitive as "preceded by a *Kriyā-kāraka* (relation) (*kriyākārakapūrvaka*), also Helārāja's remarks on the same stanza, P. 355.2-10 and on *JS* 1.P. 4.14-19. These three unspoken premises serve to substantiate Patañjali's statement, cited by Helārāja in the passage quoted above, that "qualifications of the base meaning arise . . . through action."

I have drawn above, are displayed. These compounds, it is held, are composed of two names, each of which denotes a separate individual (cf. *MB* on *P* 1.2.42: *anekāśrayaṁ ca samānādhikaraṇyam*). And while the constituent names are unrelated, in the compound they are related as qualifier and qualificand, which emerges independently of names at the sentential or compound level, and is, therefore, in excess of the names.[15]

The distance between Kātyāyana's theory and the one that I have attributed previously to Bhartṛhari is very great; according to Kātyāyana, a name is given to a single spatio-temporal entity on the basis of a quality; according to Bhartṛhari, a name given to classes of actual and ideal objects on the basis of universals which belong in names.[16] And while for Kātyāyana names, unless they are derived or compounded, are not related to other names, Bhartṛhari's theory embeds even non-derived names within a network of relations: thus for Bhartṛhari the *śiṁśapā* has compatible co-inherence with *vṛkṣa* and incompatible co-inherence with *palāśa*.[17]

The pre-Bhartṛhari treatment of *śiṁśapāvṛkṣa* is as follows. It is treated as a *karmadhāraya* compound composed of two names both of which denote a substance or individual (*dravyavācin*). The compound signifies the qualifier-qualificand relation (*viśeṣaṇaviśeṣyabhāva*), and refers to a single individual. And while *śiṁśapā* occupies the first place in the compound and is always the qualifier, *vṛkṣa* occupies the second place and is always the qualified; the ordering of the names in the compound is,

---

15. See *MB* on P. 2.3.46; Cardona, "Anvaya and Vyatireka in Indian Grammar," pp. 318-19 outlines the main argument and translates the relevant passages.

16. The idea that language has reference to a realm of ideal objects is systematically developed through the *SS*; from *SS* 42-48, various puzzles connected with negation and motion are solved with the help of the ideal object hypothesis.

17. See n. 7 and diagram.

therefore, invariably fixed.[18] As a general rule the ordering of names in a *karmadhāraya* compound is not always fixed; and why the ordering of names was fixed in some compounds and not fixed in others — for instance the form *khañjakubja* is not less acceptable than the form *kubjakhañja* — was a matter of interest to Patañjali.[19]

Patañjali's answer to the query, "why is the form *śiṁśapāvṛkṣa* acceptable and the form *vṛkṣaśiṁśapā* not?" is too cryptic to concern us here. Let us turn our attention instead to the elaborations of Patañjali's commentator Kaiyyaṭa, who wrote his commentary on the *Mahābhāṣya* (*MB*) more than ten centuries after it was written. According to Kaiyyaṭa's gloss, the name *vṛkṣaḥ* is always the qualificand and will inevitably occupy the position which is second, because it has the larger extension (*mahāviṣaya*) and is the pervader (*vyāpaka*) on the other hand, the same *śiṁśapā* is always the qualifier (*viśeṣya*) because it has the smaller extension (*svalpaviṣaya*) and, by implication, the pervaded. It will therefore, invariably occupy the first place in the compound.[20]

---

18. That both constituent names in the compound *śiṁśapāvṛkṣa* designate individuals (*dravyavācin*) is suggested by the following remarks of Patañjali and by Kaiyyaṭa's gloss: "How are these two words, which are both principal, simultaneously attached to the same thing: the tree is a *śiṁśapā*?" (*kathaṁ tarhīmau dvau pradhānaśabdāv ekasminn arthe yugapad avarudhyete vṛkṣaḥ śiṃśapeti?*) (*MB* on P. 2.1. 57). Kaiyyaṭa's gloss on the above is as follows: "The question arises because both are genus words, expressive of individuals (*dravyavācin*), principal, (and) neither is adjectival." (*dvayor api jātiśabdatvād dravyavācitvāt pradhānatvān nāsty anyatarasya viśeṣaṇatvam iti*) (*Pradīpa* on *MB* on P. 2.1.57). That each of the names in the compound is expressive of a distinct individual is also suggested by Bhartṛhari, see n. 21.

19. See *MB* on *vt.* 2 on P. 2.1.57.

20. Patañjali's comments are found under *MB* to *vt.* 2 to P. 2.1.57. Kaiyyaṭa's gloss reads as follows:

    Because treeness is the pervader, has the large(r) extension, and is alone perceived first from a distance, it is the qualified. Being a →

The following historically relevant issues now serve to put Kaiyyaṭa's explanation within a proper historical and philosophical framework:

1. Kaiyyaṭa's solution to the *śiṁśapāvṛkṣa* problem was anticipated by Diṅnāga, who in the early part of the sixth century CE was the first to propose a solution to Patañjali's query on the basis of an extensional analysis of names, i.e. on the basis of the inclusion of classes. However, he had insisted that *apoha* was an indispensible part of this solution.[21]

→ *śiṁśapā* on the other hand has a smaller extension, is grasped later and functions like a quality, it is only the qualifier. (*Pradīpa* on *MB* to *vt.* 2 to P. 2.1.57: *vṛkṣatvasya vyāpakatvān mahāviṣayatvād dūrāt prathamatas tasyaivopalambhād viśeṣyatvam eva. śiṁśapātvam tu svalpaviṣayatvāt paścād grahaṇāc ca śuklādiguṇakalpatvād viśeṣaṇam eva*).

21. "In the absence of a pervasion there is no assignment to a single substratum (of two names)" (*na . . . asatyām vyāptau sāmānādhikaraṇyam*). (*vrPS*. 5. 4: *NC* 2, p. 607). Diṅnāga's solution to the problem posed by Patañjali regarding the position of the names in a *karmadhāraya* compound is as follows:

Even though the universal (*vṛkṣa*) is distinct, it is conveyed by the individual (*śiṁśapā*), which is non-deviant (with respect to *vṛkṣa*).

The qualifier-qualificandness located in each is not the same. (*anekam api sāmānyaṁ bhedenāvyabhicāriṇā, upāttam na tayos tulyā viśeṣaṇaviśeṣyatā.*) (*PS* 5.27: *NC* 2, p. 638).

The stanza is explained by Jinendrabuddhi in the following way:

"Tree" expects a delimitation through deviance of *śiṁśapā*, therefore the qualifier-qualificand relation exists (in "tree"); *śiṁśapā*, on the other hand, does not expect toward the universal of tree a non-deviance; therefore, there is none (located in *śiṁśapā*). Of two deviant qualifiers, on the other hand, the qualifier-qualificand relation is the same, as for instance in the two (expressions) "blue" and "lotus" (in the compound blue-lotus). (*vṛkṣaḥ śiṁśapādivyabhicāravyavacchedaṁ apekṣata ity asti viśeṣaṇaviśeṣyabhāvaḥ, śiṁśapā tu vṛkṣasāmānyāvyabhicāraṁ nāpekṣata iti nāsti. vyabhicāriṇor viśeṣaṇayos tu viśeṣaṇaviśeṣyabhāvas tulyo yathā nīlotpalayoḥ*). (*NC* 2, p. 639).

2. Bhartṛhari, despite the conceptual tools at his disposal, which included an analysis of names on the basis of their extension, had failed to underpin an analysis of the *śiṁśapāvṛkṣa* type of compound in the manner suggested by Kaiyyaṭa. Instead, he had cast the whole issue of the qualifier-qualificand relation within an epistemological context, suggesting that the whole task of building the qualifier-qualificand relation on the basis of the constituent names was wrong headed. He had proposed instead that the relation be considered as given a priori, part of the innate nature of the inner instrument (*antaḥkaraṇa*).[22] And even when he had produced a defence of the traditional approach of building the

→ The distance between Kaiyyaṭa's statement, that *vṛkṣa* is invariably the qualificand and *śiṁśapā* the qualifier because the former has the larger extension and is the pervader, and Diṅnāga's statement, that the relation of qualifier and qualificand as it belongs to *vṛkṣa* and *śiṁśapā* is not the same since the latter conveys the former through non-deviance, and by implication, the former conveys the latter only deviantly, is not one of substance. Both positions assume the same fundamental structure: that the class of individuals which are trees is larger than and includes within it the class of individuals which are *śiṁśapā*. It is because all *śiṁśapā* are trees, that the idea of *śiṁśapā* conveys the idea of trees non-deviantly. And it is because not all trees are *śiṁśapā* that the idea of trees can convey the idea of *śiṁśapā* only deviantly. Diṅnāga's view that in cases like *nīlotpala* (blue-lotus), where the relation between the two elements in the compound is one of simple overlap, either element can be the qualifier so that the ordering of the elements is not fixed, has partial sanction in *vt.* 1 to *P* 2.1.57.

22. The actual phrase *mahāviṣaya* occurs in *vrVP*. 1.24-26, P. 76.1 and is glossed by Vṛṣabhadeva in the following way: "A universal has the larger scope because it is included in all the individuals (which fall within its range)" (*sarvavyaktyanugatatvāj jātir mahāviṣayā*) (p. 76); see also diagram which makes this structure assumed by Bhartṛhari transparent.

relation out of its constituent names, the solution did not carry over to compounds of the *śiṁśapāvṛkṣa* type.[23]

---

23. Bhartṛhari presented his exposition of the traditional view of *karmadhāraya* compounds between *VS* 9-20, but restricted his solution to the *kṛṣṇatila* type of *karmadhāraya*, where the first member is an adjectival name (*guṇaśabda*), while the second is a genus name (*jātiśabda*). He held that the name *kṛṣṇaḥ* by virtue of its syntactic form, being an adjectival name, has the capacity to combine with a genus name and occupy the initial position in the compound, as the qualifier. The genus name *tilaḥ* has, by virtue of its syntactic form, the capacity to combine with an adjectival name and to occupy the latter position in a compound, as the qualificand. Genus names are closer to individuals because, unlike adjectival names, they are never used as qualifiers: in Sanskrit it is perfectly acceptable to say *paṭasya śuklaḥ* (the white of cloth), but unacceptable when the adjectival name is replaced by a genus name; the form *śābaleyasya gauḥ* (the cow of spotty) is ruled out of court. See *VS* 24-26, also *VS* 12-15 translated below; Helārāja's remarks on these stanzas; S.D. Joshi, *Patañjali's Vyākaraṇamahābhāṣya Karmadhārayānikā* (Poona: University of Poona, 1971), p. 32. In *VS* 12-15, Bhartṛhari addresses the matter of the kinds of presuppositions that constrain an exposition of *karmadhāraya* compounds, and he has in mind the question posed by Patañjali regarding the ordering of the names in the compound and the assertion of Kātyāyana that the qualifier-qualificand relation is in excess of the names, emergent at the sentential level. (*MB* on P. 2.1.57 and *vt.* 2 to P. 2.3.46.) Additional restraints on the exposition include the requirement that the names denote distinct individuals and that the compound also denotes yet another individual, at which stage one of the names becomes the qualifier and the other the qualificand. Bhartṛhari tries to get around these difficult constraints by casting the matter in an epistemological context and by appealing to an appearance-reality distinction: "An individual nature is separately resorted to as a result of distinctions arising out of association with a quality (*guṇa*); a second individual is, as it were, grasped as a result of distinctions arising out of association with a generic feature" (*dravyātmā guṇasaṁsargabhedād āśrīyate pṛthak jātisaṁbandhabhedāc ca dvitīya iva gṛhyate*) (*VS* 12). The union of these two unrelated states is, as it were: "A third stage of the individuals, one in which the two (other states) mingle" (*dravyāvasthā tṛtīyā yasyāṁ saṁsṛjyate dvayam*) (*JS* 14).

Finally, it is asserted that the object so divided is internal, and a creation of the understanding: →

These historical issues begin to fit into a framework only when we observe that Kaiyyaṭa's explanation of why the form *śiṁśapāvṛkṣa* is unacceptable, violates a very basic constraint imposed by grammarians on the analysis of the qualifier-qualificand relation, which is at the heart of the *karmadhāraya* compound. The qualifier-qualificand relation, according to this view, arises only at the level of sentences, and, therefore, in some very real sense exceeds over the content of its constituent names.[24] Now Kaiyyaṭa's analysis by allowing that the extension of *vṛkṣa* is larger than and includes the extension of *śiṁśapā*, allows the qualifier-qualificand relation at the level of names. This traditional pattern of analysis is reinforced by Bhart ṛhari when he insisted

→ The understanding separates the one into the many, and (out of the many) arrives at the one. It is the stages of the understanding which are being divided; for the understanding is the creator of objects. (*budhyaikaṁ bhidyate bhinnam ekatvam copagacchati. buddyāvasthā vibhajyante sā hyarthasya vidhāyikā*) (*JS* 15).

The whole attempt at building the qualifier-qualificand relation out of parts is parodied several stanzas later: "Some declare that integration of meaning takes place when, on the basis of the qualifier (a qualification is placed) in the qualified and when its being (i.e. in the qualification imposed by the qualifier) is exceeded over, the qualifier is again withdrawn" (*viśeṣaṇād viśeṣye 'rthe tadbhāvābhyuccaye sati punaś ca pratisaṁhāre vṛttim eke pracakṣate*) (*VS* 92-93). In *VS* 92-93 it is further iterated that the qualifier-qualificand relation is given in terms of the non-constructed ideal object, an object which is implicitly sentential. The drift of Bhartṛhari's thought, as I have traced it above, shows a dissatisfaction with the view that the qualifier-qualificand relation is built out of its constituent names.

24. The problem whether the elements in a *karmadhāraya* compound are semantically related goes back to a *sūtra* of Kātyāyana's, where it is raised in connection with the general requirements on compounds, that there is *sāmarthya* (compatibility) between the constituent elements. In *vt.* 21 to P. 2.1.1 it is conceded that if the analysis is in terms of Vyāḍi's view that what is meant by a word is an individual (*dravya*) then there will be no semantic compatibility between the elements of a *karmadhāraya* compound. (cf. *yadi dravyaṁ padārthaḥ, na bhavati tadā sāmarthyam*, *MB* on *vt.* 21 to P. 2.1.1).

that the constituent universals, which are the occasioning grounds for the use of the names, be unconnected (*sāmānyānām asaṁbandha*),[25] and is preserved in the stock phrase used to define co-referentiality by Kaiyyaṭa himself: "The assignment to a single substratum of names, the occasioning ground for whose use is distinct, is termed co-referentiality" (*bhinnapravṛttinimittaprayuktasyānekasya śabdasyaikasminnarthe vṛttiḥ samānādhikaraṇyam ucyate*).[26] The constraints imposed by the tradition on the analysis of the qualifier-qualificand relation also explains Bhartṛhari's complex attitude to the problem. Kaiyyaṭa's solution adopts only a part of Diṅnāga's, and thereby violates traditional constraints. In what follows I will argue that Diṅnāga's *apoha* doctrine when combined with the extensional analysis of names he proposed does produce a solution to Patañjali's query regarding the ordering of names in the *śiṁśapāvṛkṣa* type of compound, without violating the constraint on the analysis, that the qualifier-qualificand relation is a sentential affair, but that names are atomic.

II

In the previous section I contrasted two views regarding names. According to the first, which I have traced to the writings of Bhartṛhari, names are given to classes of individuals on the basis of a universal belonging to the name (see n. 10). According to the second, names are given to spatio-temporal individuals on the basis of a quality belonging to the individual. The first is a theory of indirect naming while the second is a theory of direct naming.

I then went on to show that the contrary ideals within the two theories were brought to a point of crisis in Kaiyyaṭa's analysis of *śiṁśapāvṛkṣa*. In the present section, I shall try to suggest that Diṅnāga's *apoha* was meant to break the tension between the two theories, and then go on to offer a reconstruction of *apoha* which accords with this suggestion.

25. *VS* in *VP*.

26. See *Pradīpa* on *MB* on *vt*. 2 to P. 1.2.42.

The following stanza can be viewed as a direct challenge to Bhartṛhari's doctrines:[27]

> Even though a word has multifarious properties, it conveys the object by means of that (quality or property) alone which does not exceed over (*ati+vṛt*) its object; not by means of qualities, etc. which belong to words. — *PS* 5.13:*NC*.2, p. 630

Bhartṛhari is here challenged on two scores: the basis of name-giving is a quality or property (*guṇa* or *dharma*) which belongs in the object which is named, not in the name, and this basis of name-giving does not exceed over what is given in the object.

Apoha is the centre around which Diṅnāga's approach to these problems is coordinated. And *apoha*, which I will translate simply as exclusion, presupposes a complex structure, which includes a definite analysis of names and demonstratives, and a peculiar kind of negation operator. It has moreover distinct historical links with Bhartṛhari's *VP*, which I will very briefly touch upon. My main concern will be to expose the logical structure of the various elements which compose this doctrine.

Let us take as our point of departure Bhartṛhari's theory of names according to which names, on the basis of the universal they express, designate classes of individuals, both actual and ideal; the word "cow" defines a class of cows which includes *śābaleya*, *bāhuleya* and the *kāmadhenu*. Let us next assume that which designates classes of individuals on the basis of a universal can only designate a plurality of individuals; the function of designating singular individuals belongs to demonstratives which designate their objects directly, without the intervention of universals.[28] Given these assumptions, Diṅnāga's *apoha* doctrine at base consists of a pair of singular sentences:

---

27. *anekadharmā śabdo 'pi yenārthaṁ nātivartate pratyāyayati tenaiva na tu śabdaguṇādibhiḥ.*

28. This view has a firm standing in Bhartṛhari's text:

    There are those who say, even when the (perceptual) object is undifferentiated, the object of the word is indeed differentiated. →

This has *H*

This has nonnon *H*

→ For a word applies when capacity, though it belongs to the sphere of a single (undifferentiated perceptual) object, is grasped through a delimitation as, "This is a staff." The demonstrative names that very object (which is grasped) through its visual form; it does not do so by way of a relation with a staff universal, which is also being grasped (on the basis of the word "staff"); because the demonstrative lacks the capacity to name (its bearer, the staff) through a relation with the staff-universal. (*apara aha-yady api vastu na bhinnaṁ śabdārthas tu bhinnaḥ* (.) *śabdo hy ekavastuviṣayānām api śaktīnām avaccedenopagrahe vartate tadyathā ayaṁ daṇḍa iti* (.) *pratyakṣarūpatayā tadeva vastu sarvanāmnābhidhīyate, nopalabhyamānenāpi daṇḍajātiyogena daṇḍajātiyogābhidhāne tasyāsāmarthyaṁ sarvanāmnaḥ*) (*vrVP* 1.69, P. 131.4-6, 132.1).

This passage from Bhartṛhari is conceptually connected with the following of Diṅnāga's where transformation of a perceptual form into a conceptual one is described.

"This has this genus (name)" or "This has this substance (name)" thus having necessarily grasped two elements (*arthadvayam*) a relation is accordingly imagined (between them). Thereafter, it is grasped either by elision of the possessive suffix *-mat* or by an ascribed identity. And since the qualifier becomes established through memory, its existence is possible only in knowledge belonging to mind (rather than to the senses). (*idam asya sāmānyaṁ dravyādi vā 'avaśyam ity arthadvayaṁ gṛhītvā tathā saṁbandhaḥ kalpyate. tato matublopād abhedopacārād vā gṛhyate. tac ca viśeṣaṇaṁ smṛtyopasthitatvād manobuddhāyupapadyate*) (The text is in accordance with Muni Jambūvijaya's reconstruction from the original Tibetan in *Vai. S*, P. 170.11-12; cf. also Hattori, *Dignāga on Perception*, pp. 143-44.

I would like to draw the readers' attention to the following points in the two passages cited above:

1. Both Diṅnāga and Bhartṛhari above hold that the object as it is grasped by language is differentiated into two: a demonstrative plus a nominal.
2. Diṅnāga states and Bhartṛhari implies that the nominal signifies the object via the intervention of the mind and by implication of universals.

→

The sentences are composed of the following elements: a demonstrative of space/time, a name, a doubly negated version of the same name, and a relation between the demonstrative and the name; the relation is signified by the genitive. And it represents inclusion, of an individual in a class.

Let us now divide the content of a name into two segments and label the first segment the denotative content (in Sanskrit it can be called the *dravyavācyāṁśa*) and the second the connotative content (*jātivācyāṁśa*). In the first compartment let us place all those individuals which are designated by the name on the basis of the universal it expresses, and in the latter compartment let us place the universal itself. The two segments can be represented in the following way:

1. *H* = (*H*bearers) + (*H*ness), where *H* is a name.

Let us now define an operation which elides the content of the first segment, the one which contains the *H*bearers. Let us then label the operation single *apoha* negation, thus:

1.1. non*H* = (*O*) + (non*H*ness).

Let us perform the operation twice and call it double *apoha* negation:

1.2. nonnon*H* = (*O*) + (nonnon*H*ness).

Now given the nonnon*H*ness is equivalent to *H*ness, the effect of the joint operation is to elide the denotative content of names while keeping the connotative content secure.[29]

→ 3. Bhartṛhari states and Diṅnāga implies that the demonstrative lacks the capacity to signify its object via the intervention of a universal — it therefore signifies its object directly.

4. Diṅnāga's statement that "having necessarily grasped two elements a relation is accordingly imagined," corresponds to my reconstructed basic *apoha* sentence: "this is *H*" (where *H* is a name). I have interpreted the relation as inclusion, of an individual in a class.

29. Cf. Hans Herzberger, "Double Negation in Buddhist Logic," *Journal of Indian Philosophy* 3 (1975): 3-16.

This slight venture into abstraction makes clear that two operations underpin the *apoha* doctrine: a negation procedure and an elision procedure. While a name defines classes of ideal and actual objects, the same name when subjected to the *apoha* operation negates the complementary class and elides reference to the denotative content of the name. Thus, at the level of the basic *apoha* sentence the contrast can be stated in the following way. The positive sentence (This has *H*) states that an individual in space/time denoted by the demonstrative is a member of a class of individuals denoted by the name on the basis of its universal. The basic *apoha* sentence (this has nonnon*H*) describes the same individual in space/time as having a universal, which is denoted by the name. Apart from the basic sentences, names merely denote universals when subjected to the *apoha* operations. They are, in other words, non-denoting expressions.

Let us now move on to the more complex level represented by the compound *śiṁśapāvṛkṣa*. According to Bhartṛhari's analysis of names, *vṛkṣa* is related to *śiṁśapā* through compatible co-inherence (see n. 7). Also, according to a form of analysis he embraced, the class of individuals defined by *vṛkṣa* includes the class of individuals defined by *śiṁśapā*. Now if this relation, which exists between the names, is made the basis of the qualifier-qualificand relation, then the relation would emerge at the level of names, which would then violate a very basic principle articulated by Kātyāyana that the relation emerges at the sentential level and is in excess of the names (see n. 12). This is why Bhartṛhari, despite the structure at his disposal, dealt with the qualifier-qualificand relation and the compound based on that relation, the *karmadhāraya* compound, in a very complex manner and in a spirit not found in the earlier writers.

Diṅnāga's solution of the *śiṁśapāvṛkṣa* problem is two-pronged. The first prong consists of a pair of basic sentences: "This has *vṛkṣa*" and "This has *śiṁśapā*." Now these two basic sentences translate into: "This has (*V*bearers) + (*V*ness)" and

"This has (*S*bearers)+(*S*ness)," where *V* and *S* stand for the names *vṛkṣa* and *śiṁśapā* respectively. Now the qualifier-qualificand relation will be obtained between *V* and *S* in either of two cases: (i) if the extension of either *V* or *S* includes the extension of the other or (ii) if the extensions of *V* and *S* overlap. And the ordering of names and, by extension, which name is the qualifier and which is the qualified depends on whether the relation between the names is of the former sort or of the latter sort. If the relation is of the former sort, as it is between *V* and *S*, in *śiṁśapāvṛkṣa*, then the ordering of the names will be fixed; the one with the larger extension will always become the qualified and occupy the second place in the compound. If, on the other hand, the relation is of the latter sort and the two names are merely related by overlap, then the ordering of the names in the compound will not be fixed; either will be able to be the qualifier and occupy the initial position in the compound, this is the case, according to Diṅnāga in compounds like *nīlotpala*.[30]

The qualifier-qualificand relation is not given a priori, as part of the structure of the understanding, as it is in Bhartṛhari's system,[31] but is learnt through experience and constructed out of names, by a method the cornerstone of which is observation (*darśana*).[32]

---

30. See n. 21.

31. See *VS* 91-93; also n. 23.

32. Diṅnāga held that the relation between a word and its object can be correctly taught. And in opposition to Dharmakīrti, he held that observation (*darśana*) was sufficient to establish the truth of a pervasion. Even in those cases where the class of objects has an infinite number of members and it is not possible to inspect each instant, Diṅnāga held that it was still possible to establish the truth of a sentence merely by the failure to observe the existence of counter or deviant instances. Thus:

    Agreement in presence and absence alone is the means in denoting the object of names. And agreement in presence and absence consists in residence and non-residence in the similar instance class and the dissimilar instance class (respectively). There, existence in the entire similar instance class is not explicable for sometimes when there is →

A non-designating name or one subjected to the *apoha* operation, as we have seen, strips the name of its denotative content: The basic sentence, "This has *H*" becomes "This has nonnon*H*" which in effect transforms the structure "This has (*H*bearers)+(*H*ness)" to "This has (*O*)+(*H*ness)." The second prong of the theory consists in the *apoha*-phase, and is as follows. The name, stripped of its denotative content becomes atomic (*kevala*, cf. *vrPS* 5.36: *NC*.2, p. 729) or unrelated to other names. This is so essentially because relations of inclusion and overlap exist only between individuals, not between universals; so once the reference to individuals is deleted through the *apoha* operation, relations of inclusion and overlap also cease. They revive only when the name acquires denotation. Being atomic, names are like untethered crows, free to alight on a single pole, which is the object in space/time indicated by a demonstrative (cf. *vrPS* 5.14: *NC*.2, p. 630). By themselves names are not capable of indicating the object which is singular. Thus a cardinal requirement of Kātyāyana's that the qualifier-qualificand relation arises at the sentential level is fulfilled. The theory can be summed up in terms of a sequential presentation:

1. nonnon*H* = Hness, a mere name expresses a universal.
2. "This has nonnon*H*," the name is assigned to an individual.
3. "This has *H*," the name designates classes of individuals and an individual designated by the demonstrative is declared to be a member of that class.

→ an infinity of objects, it is impossible to explain (the relation with respect to) all of them. In the case of the dissimilar instance class, on the other hand, merely on the basis of non-observation (of deviant examples), knowledge of non-residence (of the Reason in the absence of that which is to be established) is possible. (*anvayavyatirekau hi śabdārthābhidhāne dvāraṁ. tau ca tulyātulyayor vṛttyavṛtti. tatra tulye nāvaśyaṁ sarvatra vṛttir ākhyeyā, kvacid ānantye 'rthasyākhyānāsaṁbhavāt. atulye tu saty apy ānantye śakyam adarśanamātreṇāvṛtter ākhyānam*) (*vrPS* 5.34: *NC* 2, p. 650).

4. The possibility of two names becoming related as qualifier and qualificand in a *karmadhāraya* compound arises when the demonstratives in two basic sentences name the same individuals and there is the relation of overlap between the individuals designated by the names.[33]

At the beginning of this section I had quoted *PS* 5.13, in which Diṅnāga claimed that the name "conveys the object by means of that (quality or property) which does not exceed over (*ati+vr̥t*) its object, not by means of qualities, etc. which belong to words." The stanza raises a fundamental question: what is the ontological status of the quality on the basis of which names are given to individuals? Is it, for Diṅnāga, as it was for Bhartr̥hari a universal belonging in names (see *JS* 6, n. 8) or is it, as Patañjali's remarks suggest (see n. 11) a quality which is sensuous? The evidence in the stanza seems to suggest that Diṅnāga stood with the earlier grammarian on this issue; in fact, the stanza emphatically states that the name does not convey its object "by means of qualities, etc. which belong to words" (see n. 7, in which a passage is cited from Bhartr̥hari describing the complexity of words).

In order to suggest how Diṅnāga implemented this conviction regarding the ontological status as the basis on which names are given, we have to restore to the word *apoha* the original sense it had in Bhartr̥hari's *VP*.

My sources for Bhartr̥hari's conception of *apoha* are *JS* 98 and *VS* 102-03. In these stanzas *apoha* is described primarily as an act of abstraction that leaves a residual unity (*ekatva*); by abstracting away unique features which belong to an instance

33. "Due to (their) to-be-excluded individuals different meanings are incapable of comprehending their own objects (i.e sub-classes). Because, in one place, they bring about the same effect, they have the qualifier-qualificand relation" (*apohyabhedād bhinnārthāḥ svārthabhedagatau jaḍāḥ ekatrābhinnakāryatvād viśeṣaṇaviśeṣyakāḥ*) (*PS* 5.14: *NC* 2, p. 630)

of white, an awareness of whiteness in general is produced.[34] By incorporating this notion of *apoha* as an additional layer of his *apoha* doctrines there may be a way of showing how the basis of name-giving could for Diṅnāga be sensuous. If the basis of name-giving is identified with this residual unity which emerges as a result of abstracting away the unique features of spatio/temporal instances of whiteness, then Diṅnāga's ground for name-giving has the same ontological status as Patañjali's; both belong to the temporal realm. Then the universal associated, with a name is no longer "in excess" (*avi+vṛt*) of the object; *H*ness names a property, which has unity (*ekatva*, cf. *crPS*. 5.36: *NC*.2, p. 729: *jātidharmās caikatvānityatvapratyeka-parisamāptilakṣaṇā atraiva vyavatiṣṭhante*).

To sum up: the *apoha* doctrine of Diṅnāga is a complex built out of the three separate operations of abstraction, deletion and negation. The threefold operation functions on a threefold content associated with names: a name-associated spatio-temporal content, which is abstracted of its unique features and left with a residual unity (*ekatva*) a name-associated denotative content, which stands deleted; and finally the connotative complement associated with a name, the universal, whose complement is negated.

These operations which compose Diṅnāga's *apoha* doctrine make sense within a historical framework introduced by Kātyāyana's and Bhartṛhari's views on names. I have argued in the course of this paper that the ideals which inform Kātyāyana's analysis of names are violated by Bhartṛhari's analysis; and that Diṅnāga's *apoha* operations, taking as their point of depature Bhartṛhari's analysis of names, restore to this analysis the ideals embodied in Kātyāyana's analysis.

---

34. "The idea of unity is achieved in a single act by excluding distinctions among entities which have distinct natures, (the idea of) similarity is achieved through repeated acts of exclusion." (*sakṛtpravṛttāu ekatvam āvṛttau sadṛśātmatām bhinnātmikānāṁ vyaktīnāṁ bhedāpohāt prapadyate*) (*JS* 98).

→

My reconstruction of Diṅnāga's *apoha* is a hypothesis, correct only if it is shown to fit the details of his text, a difficult task which I have attempted elsewhere.[35] Here my efforts have been directed to showing that the reconstruction has a certain plausibility. By placing my reconstruction of Diṅnāga's *apoha* within a framework of genuine historical problems, and by producing some textual evidence in its support, I have argued for the plausibility of my hypothesis. I would like to end this paper with a plea: that Dharmakīrti's text should not be the criteria according to which the truth of my hypothesis is tested. It is entirely possible that philosophically speaking Dharmakīrti's system is radically different from Diṅnāga's despite the fact that they were both Buddhists.

Abbreviations

JS	*Jātisamuddeśa*, see Iyer, Subramania: 1963.
MB	*Mahābhāṣya*, see Kielhorn, Lorenz.
NC.1	*Dvādaśāraṁ Nayacakram*, part 1, see Jambuvijaya, Muni: 1966.
NC.2	*Dvādaśāraṁ Nayacakram*, part 2, see Jambuvijaya, Muni: 1977.
P	Pāṇini.
Pradīpa	For references of Pradīpa see Vedavrat, Acarya.
PS	*Pramāṇasamuccaya*.
SS	*Saṁbandhasamuddeśa*.
VP.1	*Vākyapadīya*, First Kāṇḍa, see Iyer, Subramania: 1966.

→ "Just as the bearer of colour is conceptually grasped by means of a form whose particular aspects are not grasped — indeed the distinguishing features of white, etc. cannot be grasped — so also because of the function of only part of the universal (brought about) by means of exclusion of differences (the idea of number) applies. Or, the idea of number is of that sort because of abandonment of distinctions." (*bhedānām vā parityāgāt saṁkhyātmā sa tathāvidhaḥ vyāpārāj jātibhāgasya bhedāpohena vartate. agṛhī- taviśeṣeṇa yathā rūpeṇa rūpavān prakhyāyate na śuklādi bhedarūpas tu gṛhyate.*) (*VS* 102-03)

35. See Radhika Herzberger, "The Development of Logic in Fifth and Sixth Century India," chapter 3.

VP.2	*Vākyapadīya*, Second Kāṇḍa, see Rau, Wilhelm: 1977.
VP.3	*Vākyapadīya*, Third Kāṇḍa, see Iyer, Subramania: 1963 and 1973.
Vai.S	*Vaiśeṣika-sūtra*, see Jambuvijaya, Muni: 1961.
vr	*Vṛtti.*
VS	*Vṛttisamuddeśa*, see Iyer, Subramania: 1973.

Bibliography

Cardona, George, "Anvaya and Vyatireka in Indian Grammar," *Adyar Library Bulletin* 31-32 (1967-68): 313-52.

———, "Pāṇini's Kārakas: Agency, Animation and Identity," *Journal of Indian Philosophy* 2, no. 3/4 (1974): 231-306.

———, *Pāṇini, A Survey of Research*, The Hague: Mouton, 1976.

Carudev, Shastri, *Vyākaraṇa-Candrodaya*, 5 vols, Delhi: Motilal Banarsidass, 1969-73.

Gnoli, Raniero, *The Pramāṇavārttikam of Dharmakīrti*, the First Chapter with the Autocommentary, Text and Critical Notes, Insttuto Roma: Italilano Per II Medio ed Extremo Oriente, 1958.

Hattori, Masaaki, "Fragments from Pramāṇasamuccaya," *Journal of Buddhist Studies* 3, no. 1 (1958).

———, *Dignāga, On Perception, Being the Pratyakṣa Pariccheda of Dignāga's Pramāṇasamuccaya*, Cambridge: Harvard University Press, 1968.

———, "Praśastapāda and Dignāga." *Wiener Zeitschrift fòr die Kunde des Morgenlandes* 16 (1972): 169-80.

———, "Apoha and Pratibhā." *in Sanskrit and Indian Studies, Essays in Honour of Daniel H.H. Ingalls*, ed. M. Nagatomi et al. Dodrecht: D. Reidel Publishing Company, 1980, pp. 61-73.

Hayes, Richard, "Dignāga's Views on Reasoning (Svārthānumāna)," *journal of Indian Philosophy* 8 (1980): 219-77.

Herzberger, Hans, "Double Negation in Buddhist Logic," *Journal of Indian Philosophy* 3, no. 1/2 (1975): 3-16.

Herzberger, H. and R. "Bhartṛhari's Paradox," *Journal of Indian Philosophy* 9, no. 1 (1981): 1-17.

Herzberger, R., "The Development of Logic in Fifth and Sixth Century India," unpublished dissertation, University of Toronto, 1982.

Iyer, Subramania (ed.), (*VP* 3), *Vākyapadīya of Bhartṛhari with the Commentaries of Helārāja kāṇḍa* III, part I. Poona: Deccan College, 1963.

———, *The Vākyapadīya of Bhartṛhari with the Vṛtti*, chapter I; translation. Poona: Deccan College, 1965.

———, (*VP* 1), *The Vākyapadīya of Bhartṛhari with the Commentaries, Vṛtti and Paddhati of Vṛṣabhedeva*, Poona: Deccan College, 1966.

———, *Bhartṛhari: A Study of the Vākyapadīya in the Light of Ancient Commentaries*, Poona: Deccan College, 1969.

———, *The Vākyapadīya of Bhartṛhari*, chapter III, part I; English tr., Poona: Deccan College, 1971.

——— (ed.), (*VP* 3), *Vakyāpadīya of Bhartṛhari, with the Prakīrṇaprakāśa of Helārāja, kāṇḍa* III, part II, Poona: Deccan College, 1973.

———, *The Vākyapadīya of Bhartṛhari, kāṇḍa* II, English tr., with Exegetical Notes. Delhi: Motilal Banarsidass, 1977.

Jambuvijaya, Muni, (*Vai. S*) *Vaiśeṣikasūtra of Kaṇāda with the Commentary of Candrānanda*, Gaekwad's Oriental Series No. 136. Baroda: Oriental Institute, 1961.

———, (*NC* 1) *Dvādaśāraṁ Nayacakram of Ācārya Śrī Mallavādi Kṣamāśramaṇa*.Part-I, Sri Atmanand Jain Granthamala Series, no. 92. Bhavanagar: 1966.

———, (*NC* 2) *Dvādaśāraṁ Nayacakram of Ācārya Śrī Mallavāḍi Kṣamaśramaṇa*, Sri Atmanand Jain Granthamala Series, no. 94. Bhavanagar : 1976.

Joshi, S.D., *The Sphoṭanirṇaya of Kauṇḍabhatta*. edited with introduction, and critical and exegitical notes, Poona: University of Poona, 1967.

———, *Patañjali's Vyākaraṇamahābhāṣya Karmadhārayāhnikā* (P. 2.1.51-2.1.71), edited with translation and explanatory notes, Poona: University of Poona, 1971.

Katsura, Shoryu, "New Sanskrit Fragments of the *Pramāṇasamuccaya*," *Journal of Indian Philosophy* 3, no. 1/3 (1975): 67-78.

Kitagawa, Hidenori, "A note on the Methodology in the Study of Indian Logic," *Journal of Buddhist Studies* 8, no. 1 (1960).

———, "A Study of a Short Philosophical Treatise Ascribed to Dignāga," (an abridged English translation of the *Upādāyaprajñaptiprakaraṇa* of *Dignāga*), *Sino-Indian Studies* 5, nos. 3/4 (1965).

Kosambi, Damodar, *Myth and Reality*, Bombay: Popular Prakashan, 1962.

———, *The Culture and Civilization of India in Historical Outline*, New Delhi: Vikas, 1970.

Kielhorn, Lorenz Franz, (*MB*) *The Vyākaraṇa-Mahābhāṣya of Patañjali*, 3 vols. 3rd edn. Revised and furnished with additional readings, reference and selected notes by K.V. Abhyankar, Poona: 1962-72.

———, "Notes of the Mahābhāṣya"; 7. "Some Devices of Indian Grammarians." *Indian Antiquarian* 16 (1887): 178-284.

Manavalli, Gangadhar Shastri (ed.), *Vākyapadīya, A Treatise of the Philosophy of Sanskrit Grammar by Bhartṛhari, with the Commentary of Puṇyarāja*, Benaras: 1887.

Matilal, Bimal Krishna, *Epistemology, Logic, and Grammar in Indian Philosophical Analysis*, The Hague: Mouton, 1971.

Mīmāṁsaka, Yudhiṣṭhira, *Patañjalimuni-viracitam Mahābhāṣyam*, vols. 2-3, with exposition and translation in Hindi, Sonepat, Haryana.

Rau, Wilhelm, (*VP* 2) *Bhartṛhari's Vākyapadīya, die Mūlakārikā nach den Handschriften Herausgeben und mit einem Pada-Index Versehen*, Deutsche Morgenlandische Gesellschaft, 1977.

Shastri, Kapila Deva. "Bhartṛhari's Discussion of Sāmānādhikaraṇya," *Adyar Library Bulletin* 28, no. 1/2 (1964): 41-54.

Shaw, J.L., "Negation and the Buddhist Theory of Meaning," *Journal of Indian Philosophy* 6, no. 1 (1978): 59-77.

Tucci, Giuseppe, *The Nyāyamukha of Dignāga*, being the oldest Buddhist Text of Logic after Chinese and Tibetan material. Materialen zur Kunde des Buddhismus, 15 Heft, Heidelberg: 1930.

Vedavrat, Acarya, (*Pradīpa*) *Vyākaraṇa-Mahābhāṣyam*, vols. 1-5, *śrikaiyyaṭakṛtapradīpena nāgojibhaṭṭakṛtena bhāṣyapradīpoddyotena ca vibhūṣitam*, Haryana-Sāhitya-Samsthānam, Rohtak, 1962.

10

Jñānaśrīmitra on Apoha[1]

Shoryu Katsura

SINCE Dr Satkari Mookerjee wrote *The Buddhist Philosophy of Universal Flux* (Calcutta, 1935), it seems to have been generally accepted that there are three distinct stages in the development of the *apoha* theory, represented by: (1) the Negativists like Diṅnāga and Dharmakīrti, (2) the Positivists like Śāntarakṣita and Kamalaśīla, and (3) the Synthetists like Jñānaśrīmitra and Ratnakīrti.[2] Now that we have a better knowledge of those Buddhist logicians, it seems to be the time to give a second thought to the hypothesis of Dr Mookerjee.

After reading through Jñānaśrīmitra's *Apohaprakaraṇa*,[3] I had an impression that there was nothing radically new about his theory of *apoha* in comparison with Dharmakīrti's. As a matter of fact, Jñānaśrīmitra quotes extensively from the works of Dharmakīrti in order to justify his understanding of the *apoha* theory.[4] When

---

1. Many thanks are due to my student and colleague, Mr. Hideyo Ogawa, who generously supplied me with his own excellent studies of Jñānaśrīmitra's *Apohaprakaraṇa*.

2. Mookerjee, p. 132; cf. Kajiyama, p. 125, fn. 338.

3. *JNA*, pp. 201-32.

4. The following verses and passages of Dharmakīrti are quoted by Jñānaśrīmitra in his *Apohaprakaraṇa*: *PV* I.54, 57, 71cd, 84ab, 96ab, 123a, 124ab, 125d, 129-30, 132cd-33a, 162, 164cd, 169, 185, 205abc, II.8ab, III.13bc, 147cd, 149cd, 164ab, 165abc, 172, 220d, 235, IV. 262; *PVSV*, p. 2.19 (=*NB* II.18), 92.23-93.1; *PVin* I.15, II. 1cd Comm.; *HB*, p.3*. 14-15, 25*.9, 26*.23-24. Other notable quotations are: *PVBh* v.3 and *ŚV ākṛti* v.10.

examined very closely, most of his arguments stem from Dharmakīrti at least in germ. Therefore, I do not believe that Jñānaśrīmitra actually brought a new phase in the theory of *apoha*. It seems to me that Jñānaśrīmitra merely rearranged and systematized the arguments of Dharmakīrti by defending him from the charges of the Naiyāyikas and the Mīmāṁsakas and by criticizing what he considers the wrong interpretations of Dharmottara.[5] Although Jñānaśrīmitra does not criticize Śāntarakṣita and Kamalaśīla by name, he seems to do so implicitly by insisting upon the simultaneous understanding of both affirmation and negation in verbal or inferential knowledge as I shall discuss later. In this sense, we may be able to hold the distinction between the second and the third stage of the *apoha* theory supposed by Dr Mookerjee.

Further, if we look into the works of Diṅnāga and Dharmakīrti, it is rather difficult to regard them as pure Negativists. A fragment of Diṅnāga quoted by Dharmakīrti, "A portion of the real object is known through the exclusion of the other objects; a linguistic item (*śabda*) expresses the object qualified by the negation of the other objects,"[6] even shows a close affinity to the Synthetist theory. Thus, Dr Mookerjee's hypothesis that there are three stages of the *apoha* theory, despite its attractive outlook, must be considered to be rather simplistic and possibly misleading.

---

5. Jñānaśrīmitra refers to and attacks Trilocana (*JNA* pp. 205, 216, 221), Vācaspatimiśra (pp. 204, 206, 210, 211, 215, 216), Bhūṣaṇakāra (pp. 214, 215, 223), the Kaumārilas (p. 212), and Dharmottara (pp. 205, 228, 229). It is to be noted that Dharmottara with his *nirākāravāda* appears to be one of the main Buddhist logicians to be criticized by Jñānaśrīmitra who supports *sākāravāda*: see A. Thakur's Introduction to *JNA*, p. 28.

6. *PVSV*, pp. 62.26-63.1: *ayam arthāntaravyāvṛttyā tasya vastunaḥ kaścid bhāgo gamyate, śabdo ' rthāntaranivṛttiviśiṣṭān eva bhāvān āha*, the latter half is identified as *PSV* and *PSV*.36d.

Now, the rigorous studies of Buddhist logicians by the Vienna school of Professor Frauwallner and his disciples have gradually revealed various facets of the development of Buddhist theories of epistemology and logic. Thanks to their concerted efforts, we now know the following: Diṅnāga first got the idea of *anyāpoha* (exclusion of the others) while working on the essence of the inference. He then applied it to verbal knowledge (*śābda*), and came to believe that *anyāpoha* was the common function of both inferential and verbal knowledge; therefore, he could include verbal knowledge under the category of inference.[7] While Diṅnāga devoted most of his discussion of *apoha* to the analysis of the object of verbal knowledge or the meaning of the word, Dharmakīrti freely applied the principle of *anyāpoha* to the various problems related to conceptual knowledge (*vikalpa*), such as the object, the essence, the origin, and the function of conceptual knowledge. Thus, to Dharmakīrti, the *apoha* theory was not merely the theory of meaning, but *Problem des Begriffs* as named by Professor Vetter.[8] The fact that Dharmakīrti applies the principle of *anyāpoha* beautifully to the theory of causation in the *Hetubindu*[9] indicates that it is a sort of "working hypothesis,"[10] which is equally applicable to many problems of ontology, epistemology and logic.

With these words, I just wanted to point out that Dharmakīrti as usual marked an important new step in the development of the *apoha* theory and that he and Diṅnāga should not be treated just alike. I believe that it was Dharmakīrti who discussed the theory of *apoha* in the greatest detail, that his successors could not cover all the details of his theory, and that it was most likely

7. Frauwallner (1959), pp. 100-04.

8. Vetter, p. 41; Frauwallner (1935).

9. *HB*, pp. 9*.13-10*.4.

10. I would like to thank Professor Steinkellner, who suggested to me the idea of "working hypothesis" in our personal conversation in May, 1980, in Vienna.

that his difficult and complicated theory had been misunderstood even by the Buddhist logicians — perhaps, Śāntarakṣita was one of them. In any case, Jñānaśrīmitra, too, could not deal with all the topics of *apoha* discussed by Dharmakīrti, but he seems to have tried to reconstruct what he considers the essence of Dharmakīrti's theory of *apoha*.

Now, I would like to proceed to present the contents of Jñānaśrīmitra's *Apohaprakaraṇa*, so that I shall be able to clarify what is his contribution to the *apoha* theory. The *Apohaprakaraṇa* begins with the following verse that presents the content and the aim of the treatise:

> The theorem that *apoha* is revealed by a linguistic item (*śabda*) or an inferential mark (*liṅga*) is proven in order to demonstrate that everything is ineffable (*avācya*).[11]

Now, opponents object to the *apoha* theory by pointing out that it is contradicted by our actual experience (*anubhava-bādhita*). According to them, when we know a fire through a linguistic item (namely, the word "fire") or an inferential mark (namely, smoke), we do not experience it in the negative form, such that non-fire is not absent, but in the positive form, such that there is a fire at a certain spot. Therefore, they insist that what is known by a linguistic item or an inferential mark is not *apoha* (exclusion/negation) but some external reality (*bāhya-vidhi*).[12]

To this objection, Jñānaśrīmitra boldly replies that the above theorem that *apoha* is revealed by a linguistic item or an inferential mark is a mere theoretical assumption (*vyavasthāmātra*) and it does not express the truth of reality (*vastutattva*).[13] Now, what he

---

11. *JNA*, p. 201.3-4 (K.1): *apohaḥ śadbaliṅgābhyām prakāśyata iti sthitiḥ* | *sādhyate sarvadharmāṇām avācyatvaprasiddhaye* | | cf. *PVSV*, p. 25.27-28: *vyāvacchedaḥ śabdaliṅgābhyām pratipadyate.*

12. *JNA*, pp. 201.9-202.22.

13. Ibid., p. 202.22-23: *sthitir iti vyavasthāmātram etat* | *mukhyatayāpohaḥ śabdāder viṣaya iti nedam vastutattvam ity arthaḥ* |

regards as the truth of reality is presented in the following verse:

> By the linguistic item, an object (either external or mental) is communicated primarily and *apoha* is known as its attribute (*guṇa*); one object (i.e. an external particular object or *svalakṣaṇa*) may be postulated as designatum (*vācya*) from the point of view of "determination" (*adhyāsa*) and the other (i.e. a mental image or *buddhy-ākāra*) from the point of view of "appearance" (*bhāsa*); nothing (, however, should be postulated as designatum) in truth (*tattvataḥ*).[14]

It beautifully summarizes Jñānaśrīmitra's theory of *apoha* and the rest of the treatise is devoted to the exposition of this verse.[15]

---

14. Ibid., p. 203.1-4 (k.2): *śabdais tāvan mukhyam ākhyāyate 'rthas tatrāpohas tadguṇatvena gamyaḥ* ǀ *arthaś cāiko 'dhyāsato bhāsate* (read to) *anyaḥ sthāpyo vācyas tattvato nāiva kaścit* ǀ ǀ

15. A brief synopsis of Jñānaśrīmitra's *Apohaprakaraṇa* is as follows:

0.	The content and the aim of the treatise (K.I.)	*JN*A 201.3-8
1.	Objections	201.9-202.22
2.	Answers	202.22-232.11
2.1	*Vastutattva* (K.2)	202.22-203.5
2.11	Exposition of K.2a	203.6-9
2.12	Exposition of K.2b	203.9-208.5
2.13	Exposition of K.2c-d$_1$	208.5-230.8
2.131	Rejection of *svalakṣaṇa* as the object of verbal/inferential knowledge	208.5-220.1
2.132	Rejection of *sāmānya* as the object of verbal/inferential knowledge	220.2-225.11
2.133	An external object is the object of verbal/inferential knowledge from the point of view of "determination"; so is a mental image from the point of view of "appearance."	225.12-230.8
2.14	Exposition of K.2d$_2$	230.8-232.4
2.15	Summing up	232.5-11

→

The first *pāda* of the verse, "By the linguistic item, an object is communicated primarily," is an answer to the preceding objection that the *apoha* theory is contradicted by our experience. Jñānaśrīmitra does not consider a philosophical theory to be able to stand against experience. He accepts that, upon hearing a word or seeing an inferential mark, there arises conceptual knowledge of an affirmative nature.[16]

Now, this does not mean that Jñānaśrīmitra completely surrendered himself to the opponents. In the second *pāda* he qualifies his position: "and *apoha* is known as its attribute (*guṇa*)." At first, Jñānaśrīmitra seems to regard a positive object as the primary object of both verbal and inferential knowledge and *apoha* as the secondary object. However, this is not the case at all. The real position of Jñānaśrīmitra is that, upon hearing a word, say "cow," we understand both a positive object (namely, that which is excluded from non-cows or *agavāpoḍha*) and negation (namely, exclusion of non-cows or *agavāpoha* at the same time, for the positive object and *apoha* are inseparably related to each other and one has no supremacy over the other.[17]

→ 3. Closing verses 232.12-19

It may be worth quoting 2.15 Summing-up portion (*JNA*, 232.5-11): *tad evaṁ katham apohaḥ śabdavācya iti praśne tadguṇatvena yathoktārthenety uttaram* ।
atha buddhyākāraḥ svalakṣaṇam upādhayo vā kasmān na vācyā iti praśnaḥ, tad adhyavasāyasya pratibhāsasya ubhayasya cābhāvād iti krameṇa visarjanāni ।
yadā tu śabdaiḥ kiṁ vācyam iti anuyogaḥ, tadā pratibhāsād athādhyavasāyāt yad vā tattvata iti vikalpya, vikalpasthe (*read stho*) *'nyāpoḍhākāraḥ, anyāpoḍhasvalakṣaṇam, na kiñcid iti prativacanāni krameṇaivety uktam bhavati* ।
tasmāt śabdaliṅgayor apohaviṣayatāsthitiprasādhanaṁ sarvadharmāvācyatvapratipādanaparam iti prathamaślokārthopasaṁhāraḥ ।।
Jñānaśrīmitra mentions three other works of his own in the *Apohaprakaraṇa:* namely, *Kṣaṇabhaṅgādhyāya* (*JNA,* pp. 215, 224). *Vyāpticarcā* (p. 216) and *Sākārasiddhi* (p. 228)

16. *JNA,* p. 203.6-7.
17. Ibid., pp. 203.9-208.5.

Although Jñānaśrīmitra does not refer to Śāntarakṣita and Kamalaśīla on this occasion, his adherence to the simultaneous understanding of a positive object and *apoha* seems to suggest his challenge to their theory of *apoha*. For, they consider that the primary object of a linguistic item is a positive mental image (*buddhi-pratibimba*), and both a particular object (*svalakṣaṇa*) and pure negation (*prasajya-pratiṣedha*), e.g. "this cow is not non-cow," are regarded as the secondary object understood only by implication.[18]

Now, Jñānaśrīmitra's idea of the simultaneous understanding of affirmation and negation is not necessarily unique to him, for a similar idea is already found in the *Hetubindu* of Dharmakīrti.[19] While discussing *anupalabdhi* (non-perception), Dharmakīrti identifies non-perception of *x* with perception of things other than *x*, for instance, non-perception of a pot means perception of a bare spot. Further, he applies it to conceptual knowledge and identifies "discernment" of *x* (*tatpariccheda*) with exclusion of things other than *x* (*anya-vyavaccheda*). Thus, the discernment of water is nothing but the exclusion of things other than water, such as a fire and so on. The fact that Jñānaśrīmitra himself quotes a passage from this portion of the *Hetubindu*[20] indicates that the idea of the simultaneous understanding of a positive object and *apoha* has its root in Dharmakīrti's discussion of *anupalabdhi* in the *Hetubindu*.

In the next one *pāda* and a half, Jñānaśrīmitra explains what he regards as the positive object of verbal or inferential knowledge: "one object (i.e. an external particular object) may be postulated as designatum from the point of view of 'determination' and the other (i.e. a mental image) from the point of view of 'appearance.'" Before explaining this passage,

18. *TS* and *TSP* vv. 1002-12.
19. *anupalabdhi* section of *HB* (pp. 21*. 20-28*.3), esp. pp. 24*. 24-25*. 10, 26*.5-27.13.
20. *JNA*, p. 205 quotes *HB*, p. 26*.23-24: *tat paricchinatti tato* (or *tad-*) *anyad vyavacchinatti.*

he points out that neither a particular object (*svalakṣaṇa*) nor a universal (*sāmānya*) can be the direct object of verbal knowledge.[21] The universal is not the object of verbal knowledge, for it cannot be proven either by perception or by inference to be external reality as maintained by the Naiyāyikas and the Mīmāṁsakas — for the Buddhists, of course, the universal is a mere mental construct designated as *anyāpoha*.

Though several arguments are put forward by Jñānaśrīmitra against the opinion that a particular object is the direct object of verbal knowledge, the most important and convincing one is as follows. An external particular object, such as a pot, is not the object of verbal knowledge, for it cannot be predicated by both "existence" and "non-existence," while the object of verbal knowledge and conceptual knowledge in general should be common to both existence and non-existence (*bhāvābhāvasādhāraṇa*) because, in practice, we can say both "The pot is existent" and "The pot is non-existent." However, with reference to the real pot, we should not be able to say that it is non-existent.[22] This argument also stems from Dharmakīrti.[23] Dharmottara utilized it in a skilful and systematic way in his *Apohaprakaraṇa*.[24] Then he was severely criticized by Vācaspatimiśra,[25] who in turn was criticized by Jñānaśrīmitra in this context.

Jñānaśrīmitra proceeds to the interpretation of the third *pāda*. First of all, he distinguishes two usages of the word "object" (*viṣaya*). Namely, something is called an "object" from the point of view of "determination" (*adhyavasāya*) or from the point of view of "appearance" (*pratibhāsa*).[26] An external particular object

21. *JNA*, pp. 208.5-220.1, 220.2-225.11.
22. *JNA*, pp. 211.1-213.9; for detail, see Ogawa.
23. *PV* IV.223-236 (=*PVin* II.14-27).
24. Frauwallner (1937), p. 244.10 ff.; see Akamatsu.
25. E.g. *NVTT*, pp. 681.11 ff.
26. *JNA*, p. 225.17: *dvidhā viṣayavyavahāraḥ, pratibhāsād adhyavasāyāc ca*.

(*svalakṣaṇa*) can be assumed to be the object of conceptual knowledge from the point of view of "determination," though it does not appear in conceptual knowledge because it is grasped only by perception.[27]

Now, "determination" or *adhyavasāya* is a rather difficult concept and Jñānaśrīmitra discusses it at length. In short, *adhyavasāya* is the capacity or function of conceptual knowledge (*vikalpa*) to determine an object, so that it can induce the knower to a practical activity (*vyavahāra* or *pravṛtti*) towards that object, even if it is not directly grasped by perception.[28] For instance, a mere perception of water, which is by the Buddhist definition devoid of conceptual construction (*kalpanāpoḍha*), has no power to determine that this is water, so that it may prompt the perceiver to an action; only when the perception is followed by some conceptual knowledge, which determines that this is water and nothing else, does the perceiver proceed to an action towards that water, either to drink it or to avoid it.[29] In any case, *adhyavasāya* is that determination or determinative power of conceptual knowledge. Of course, verbal or inferential knowledge, being conceptual in nature, never lacks *adhyavasāya* and always yields a practical activity.

Since we look not for imaginary water but for real water, the object of our practical activity is always the real object which is capable of fulfilling a human purpose (*arthakriyā-samartha*).[30] Therefore, the object of "determination" (*adhyavasāya*), too,

---

27. Ibid., p. 225.17-18: *tad iha pratibhāsābhāve 'pi parāpoḍhasva lakṣaṇasyādhyavasāyamātreṇa viṣayatvam uktam.*

28. Ibid., p. 226.2: *adhyavasāyas tv agṛhīte 'pi pravartanayogyatānimittaḥ,* cf. *RNA,* 137.9-10:*samanantarapratyayabalāyātasvapratibhāsaviśeṣave danamātrād agṛhīte 'pi paratra pravṛttyakṣepo' dhyavasayaḷn.*

29. Such conceptual knowledge is called "perceptual judgement" by Stcherbatsky, pp. 204 ff., and it will be discussed in detail in my forthcoming paper "On Perceptual Judgement."

30. For the concept of *arthakriyā*, see Nagatomi and Mikogami.

should be an external and real object. In this sense, a particular object (*svalakṣaṇa*) is assumed to be the object of conceptual knowledge from the point of view of "determination."

On the other hand, a mental image (*buddhyākāra*) of conceptual knowledge can be assumed to be the object of that knowledge from the point of view of "appearance" (*prati-bhāsa*).[31] According to the Buddhist logicians, every instance of knowledge, whether perceptual or conceptual, is endowed with its own image; in other words, they hold the *sākārajñānavāda*.[32] An image of conceptual knowledge, though it does not truly represent the actual particular object, can be regarded as the object of that knowledge in the sense that it appears in that knowledge. This mental image is the Buddhist version of "universal" (*sāmānya*) which is characterized by *anyāpoha*, though it may be regarded as "particular" (*svalakṣaṇa*) so long as it is self-cognized (*svasaṁvedya*).[33]

Thus, roughly speaking, an external particular object (*svalakṣaṇa*) is the indirect object to be determined and acted upon by conceptual knowledge, and a mental image (which is *sāmānya-lakṣaṇa*) is the direct object to be grasped by conceptual knowledge. The idea of the direct object (*grāhya*) and the indirect object (*adhyavaseya*) goes back to Dharmottara,[34] but the central conception of *adhyavasāya* is, as noted by Jñānaśrīmitra himself, already found in the often-quoted phrase of the *Pramāṇaviniścaya*,

31. *JNA*, p. 228.18-18: *śabdādijanyāyāṁ buddhāv ākāramātrasya pratibhāsanāt sa eva viṣaya ucyate.*

32. For *sākārajñānavāda*, see Kajiyama, pp. 61-63.

33. *PV*, III.9cd-10; Tosaki, p. 70.

34. *NBT*, p. 71.1-4: *dvividho hi viṣayaḥ pramāṇasya — grāhyaś ca yadākāram utpadyate, prāpaṇīyaś ca yam adhyavasyati, anyo hi grāhyo anyaś cādhyavaseyaḥ,*

pratyakṣasya hi kṣaṇa eko grāhyaḥ, adhyavaseyas tu pratyakṣabalotpannena niścayena saṁtāna eva, santāna eva ca pratyakṣasya prāpaṇiyaḥ, kṣaṇasya prāpayitum aśakyatvāt ,

Chapter II namely "*svapratibhāse 'narthe 'rthādhyavasāyena pravr̥tter . . .* "[35] and again a few passages of the *Hetubindu*.[36]

It is now clear that Jñānaśrīmitra postulates the two types of positive objects of conceptual knowledge. For example, upon hearing the word "cow," we have a mental image of a cow in general, which takes the form of something excluded from non-cows (*vikalpastha-agavāpoḍhākāra*), but the object of our practical activity induced by that verbal knowledge — in other words, the object of our determination — is a particular and real object which is characterized by being excluded from non-cows (*agavāpoḍha-svalakṣaṇa*).[37] As I mentioned earlier, those two types of the positive objects are at the same time inseparably connected with negation or *anyāpoha*.

The above, however, is not the ultimate position of Jñānaśrīmitra. He states in the last *pāda* of the above-quoted verse: "nothing (however, should be postulated as designatum) in truth." In his own interpretation of the last *pāda*,[38] Jñānaśrīmitra uses the idea of the two truths in order to justify his position. Namely, according to the conventional truth, both a particular object and a mental image can be postulated as the object of conceptual knowledge; but, according to the higher truth, nothing should be regarded as the object of conceptual knowledge; a particular object cannot be the object of conceptual knowledge because it does not appear in that knowledge, and a mental image cannot be the object of conceptual knowledge because it is not the object of determination. In other words, the twofold object of Jñānaśrīmitra's *apoha* theory is a mere theoretical postulation, and the truth is that everything is ineffable. In this way, he reaches the goal of his treatise mentioned in the introductory verse.[39]

---

35. *PVin*, II, p. 2*. 8-9 quoted in *JNA*, p. 227. 23.
36. *HB*, pp. 3*.14-16, 25*.6-10, 17-19.
37. *JNA*, p. 232.6-9 quoted in Note 15 above.
38. Ibid., pp. 230.8-232.4.
39. Ibid., p. 232.10-11 quoted in Note 15 above.

It may look a little strange to find the ineffability doctrine as the final result of the *apoha* theory, but Jñānaśrīmitra tries to substantiate his claim by quoting Dharmakīrti's conclusion in the *apoha* section of the *Pramāṇavārttika-Svavṛtti:* "Therefore, it is proven that all linguistic items and conceptual knowledge take negation (*viveka*) as their object."[40] Jñānaśrīmitra argues that, just as the sentence "There is absence of *x*" (*abhāvo bhavati*) means "There is no existence of *x*" (*bhāvo na bhavati*), the sentence "*apoha* (or negation) is the designatum" (*apohasya vācyatā*) means negation of anything being designated (*vācyatāyā evāpohaḥ*).[41] As a matter of fact, Jñānaśrīmitra's conclusion should be regarded as the most orthodox approach towards the problem of language and reality among the Buddhist philosophers since Nāgārjuna.[42]

So far I have tried to present the contents of Jñānaśrīmitra's *Apohaprakaraṇa.* It is time to point out what is his original contribution to the *apoha* theory. As I repeatedly mentioned, Jñānaśrīmitra established his theory of *apoha* fully depending upon Dharmakīrti. Yet, the idea of simultaneous understanding of both a positive object and negation seems to be utilized by Jñānaśrīmitra for the first time to clarify the object of verbal and inferential knowledge; the concept of "determination" (*adhyavasāya*) is examined in detail, defined clearly, and used efficiently for the purpose of linking conceptual knowledge with external reality, and the ineffability doctrine set as the final goal of the *apoha* theory seems to be quite unique to Jñānaśrīmitra. Regarding the final point, Ratnakīrti, who composed his *Apohasiddhi* mostly by extracting relevant passages from his teacher's *Apohaprakaraṇa,* shows a slight difference of emphasis, for Ratnakīrti's conclusion centres upon his famous phrase that

---

40. *PVSV,* pp. 92.23-93.1: *tasmāt siddham etat sarve śabdā vivekaviṣayā vikalpāś ca,* quoted in *JNA,* p. 231.21-22.

41. *JNA,* p. 232.2-3: *yathā abhāvo bhavatīti bhāvo na bhavatīty evārthah, tathā apohasya vācyateti vācyatāyā evāpoha ity arthaḥ.*

42. E.g. *MMK,* XVIII. 7,9, XXV.24.

the object of a linguistic item is the positive object qualified by *anyāpoha* (*anyāpoha-viśiṣṭa-vidhi*).[43]

References

Akamatsu, A., "Developments in the Apoha Theory after Dharmakīrti — in the Case of Dharmottara" (in Japanese), *Journal of Indian and Buddhist Studies*, 28-1 (1979): 43-45.

Frauwallner, E., "Beiträge zur Apohalehre, I. Dharmakīrti, Zusammenfassung." *Wiener Zeitschrift fòr die Kunde des Morgenlandes* 40 (1935): 93-102.

Frauwallner, E., "Beiträge zur Apohalehre, II. Dharmottara," *Wiener Zeitschrift fòr die Kunde des Morgenlandes* 44 (1937): 233-87.

Frauwallner, E., "Dignāga, sein Werk und sein Entwicklung," *Wiener Zeitschrift fòr die Kund Sòd - und Ostasiens* 3 (1959): 83-164.

HB: *Hetubindu* of Dharmakīrti. Steinkellner, E., *Dharmakīrti's Hetubinduḥ*, Wien: Österreichische Akademie der Wissenschaften, Sitzungsberichte 252, Band 1, 1967.

JNA: *Jñānaśrīmitranibandhāvalī*, Ed. A. Thakur, Patna: Kashi Prasad Jayaswal Research Institute, 1959.

Kajiyama, Y., *An Introduction to Buddhist Philosophy, Memoirs of the Faculty of Letters, Kyoto University*, No. 10, Kyoto University: 1966.

Mikogami, E., "Some Remarks on the Concept of Arthakriyā," *Journal of Indian Philosophy* 7 (1979): 79-94.

MMK: *Mūlamadhyamakakārikā* of Nāgārjuna, L. de La Valle Poussin, *Mūlamadhyamakakārikas (Mādhyamikasūtras) de Nāgārjuna*. St. Petersburg: Impr. de l' Academie Impériale des sciences, 1913.

Mookerjee, S., *The Buddhist Philosophy of Universal Flux*, Calcutta: University of Calcutta, 1935, rept : New Delhi: Motilal Banarsidass, 1975.

Nagatomi, M., "Arthakriyā," *Adyar Library Bulletin* 31/32 (1967-68): 52-72.

NB: *Nyāyabindu of Dharmakīrti*, ed. with NBT and *Dharmottarapradīpa* by D. Malvania, Patna: 1955.

NBT: *Nyāyabinduṭīkā* of Dharmottara.

NVTT: *Nyāyavārttikatātparyaṭīkā of Vācaspatimiśra in Nyāyadarśana*. Calcutta Sanskrit Series, Nos. 18, 29, Calcutta: 1936-44.

---

43. *RNA*, p. 59.5: *anyāpohaviśiṣṭo vidhiḥ śabdānām arthaḥ*.

Ogawa, H., "Concept Theory of Jñānaśrīmitra" (in Japanese), *Tetsugaku* 33 (1981): 67-80.

PS: *Pramāṇasamuccaya* of Diṅnāga.

PSV: *Pramāṇasamuccayavṛtti of Dignāga*: Chapter V, ed. with *PS* and Jinendrabuddhi's *Ṭīkā* by M. Hattori, *Memoirs of the Faculty of Letters*, Kyoto University, 21.

PV: *Pramāṇavārttika of Dharmakīrti*, ed. Y. Miyasaka, *Acta Indoligica* 2 (1971-72) — I do not follow his Chapter order but Frauwallner's (*Festschrift Weller*, Leipzig, 1954).

PVin: *Pramāṇaviniścaya* of Dharmakīrti, *Dharmakīrti's Pramāṇaviniścayaḥ*. Chapter 1 ed. and tr. by T. Vetter, Wien: Österreichische Akademie der Wissenschaften (Sitzungsberichte 250, no. 3), 1966. Chapter 2 by E. Steinkellner (Sitzungsberichte 287, no. 4), 1973; (Sitzungsberichte 358), 1979.

PVBh: *Pramāṇavārttikabhāṣya of Prajñākaragupta*, ed. R. Sāṅkṛtyāyana, Patna: 1953.

PVSV: *Pramāṇavārttika-Svavṛtti of Dharmakīrti*, ed. R. Gnoli, Roma: 1960.

RNA: *Ratnakīrtinibandhāvali*, ed. by A. Thakur, 2nd edn. Patna: Kashi Prasad Jayaswal Research Institute, 1975.

Stcherbatsky, Th., *Buddhist Logic*, vol. I, New York: Dover Publications, 1962.

ŚV: *Ślokavārttika of Kumārila*, ed. S. Dvārikādāsaśāstrī, Varanasi: 1978.

Tosaki, H., *A Study of Buddhist Epistemology*, vol. I (in Japanese). An annotated translation of *PV* III.1-319. Tokyo: 1976.

TS: *Tattvasaṁgraha of Śāntarakṣita*, ed. with *TSP* by S. Dvārikādāsaśāstrī. Varanasi: Bauddhabhāratī, 1968.

TSP: *Tattvasaṁgraha-Pañjikā* of Kamalaśīla.

Vetter, T., *Erkenntnisprobleme bei Dharmakīrti*, Wien: H. BÖlaus Nachf., Kommissionsverlag der Österreichischen Akademie der Wissenschaften, 1964.

11

Apoha Theory and Pre-Diṅnāga Views on Sentence-Meaning

K. Kunjunni Raja

THE *apoha*-theory of Buddhist logic and epistemology is generally considered to have been first promulgated by Diṅnāga (*c.* CE 480–540).[1] The fifth chapter of his *Pramāṇasamuccaya* contains the earliest available exposition of the theory. Detailed discussions of the *apoha* theory are found in later works like the *Pramāṇavārttika* of Dharmakīrti (*c.* CE 600-60) first introduced to the world of modern scholars by Professor E. Frauwallner.[2] In my book on *Indian Theories of Meaning,* I had made a suggestion that the *apoha* theory of meaning was foreshadowed in earlier pre-Diṅnāga literature, though not in its developed form.[3] Professor Masaaki Hattori has shown clearly that Diṅnāga's *apoha* theory was greatly influenced by Bhartṛhari who was an elder contemporary of his. In the present paper an attempt is made to clarify my position and correlate the *apoha* theory to the theory

1. T. Stcherbatsky, *Buddhist Logic*, vol. 2 (New York: Dover Publications, 1961), p. 404; Masaaki Hattori, "Apoha and Pratibhā," in *Sanskrit and Indian Studies*, ed. Masatoshi Nagatomi, et al. (Dodrecht: D. Reidel Publishing Company, 1980), pp. 61-73.
2. E. Frauwallner, "Beiträge zur Apohalehre, I. Dharmakīrti, Zusammenfassung," *Wiener Zeitschrift för die Kunde des Morgenlandes* 40 (1935): 93-102.
3. K. Kunjunni Raja, *Indian Theories of Meaning* (Madras: Adyar Library and Research Centre, 1963).

of sentence-meaning ascribed to the pre-Kātyāyana philosopher of language, Vyāḍi (*c.* 300 BCE).[4]

Diṅnāga did not accept the reality of word-meanings, but considered that words deal directly with conceptual images or *vikalpa*s which are purely subjective constructions of the mind, and therefore there can be no direct connection between words and external objects. The function of a word in a sentence is similar to the function of an inferential mark (*liṅga*) in the process of inference, and it indicates its object through the exclusion of other things.[5] The Buddhist logicians do not accept the reality of a positive entity called the universal (*jāti* or *sāmānya*). The objective world is a series of momentary particulars (*svalakṣaṇa*s) in a flux of time, like the still pictures of a cinema, none of which can have a direct relation to the world; the apparent identity of the image is produced by the identical efficiency of the momentary particular.[6] The relation of cause and effect is between the word and the concept (*vikalpa*).[7]

It is generally held that "Diṅnāga was primarily concerned with the meaning of a word when he formulated the *apoha* theory." Professor Hattori says, "Regarding the meaning of a sentence, he simply accepted Bhartr̥hari's doctrine, without

4. See B.K. Matilal, *Epistemology, Logic and Grammar in Indian Philosophical Analysis* (The Hague: Mouton and company, 1971), pp. 112-22, for a modern reconstruction of Vyāḍi's theory of meaning.

5. *na pramāṇāntaram śabdam anumānāt tathā hi tat*
kr̥takatvādivat svārtham anyāpohena bhāṣate.
— Quoted by Hattori, loc. cit.

6. Dharmakīrti, quoted by Vācaspati in *Nyāyavārttikatātparyaṭīkā*, p. 486.
ekapratyavamarśasya hetutvād dhīr abhedinī
ekadhīhetubhāvena vyaktīnām apy abhinnatā.
The sensation of sameness, is produced by a repeated series of the same perception, and the sameness of particulars is the consequence of the fact that they produce the same sensation.

7. Diṅnāga, Quoted by Stcherbatsky, *Buddhist Logic*, vol. 2, p. 405n.
vikalpayonayaḥ śabdā vikalpāḥ śabdayonayaḥ.

discussing the problem how the meaning of a simple word is related to the meaning of the sentence."[8] It is true that Diṅnāga followed the basic theory of Bhartṛhari that the sentence has to be taken as the real unit of discourse, the words being only unreal abstracts obtained from the analysis of the sentence and that the sentence-meaning is also an integral unit, being of the nature of *pratibhā*, an intuitive flash of insight. The word-meanings are unreal concepts extracted from the sentence meaning. The word and its isolated meaning have no direct relation to the external reality, however helpful they are in learning the language. Diṅnāga's words are quite explicit.[9]

apoddhāre padasyāyam vākyād artho vivecitaḥ
vākyārthaḥ pratibhākhyo 'yam tenādāvupajāyate

> The individual meaning of the word is abstracted from the sentence through analysis; for first arises the sentence-meaning which is of the nature of an intuition.

From the practical point of view, however, Diṅnāga must have accepted the individual words and their isolated meanings, even as Bhartṛhari did, and tried to extend the *apoha* theory to the sentence as well. The *vyāvahārika* level or the *saṁvṛtisatya* level is accepted by the early Buddhist thinker Nāgārjuna as a necessary stepping stone to reach the *pāramāthika* level.[10] Even

---

8. Hattori, loc. cit., p. 66:

   In consonance with Bhartṛhari, he [Diṅnāga] maintained the indivisibility of a sentence, and admitted that the utterance of a sentence immediately produced *pratibhā* in the mind of the listener. It might therefore be assumed that Diṅnāga attributed to the sentence the faculty of expressing its meaning directly, not indirectly through the exclusion of other meanings.

9. *Pramāṇasamuccaya* V.46 quoted in *Tattvasaṁgrahapañjikā*, p. 365 (quoted by Hattori, loc. cit.).

10. *vyavahāram anāśritya paramārtho no deśyate*
    paramārtham anāgamya nirrvāṇam nādhigamyate
    — *Mūlamadhyamakakārikā*, chapter 24, verse 10.

though detailed discussions about the implications of the *apoha* theory on sentence-meaning are not found in the available works of Diṅnāga, it may be assumed from external sources like the early Jaina work, *Prameyakamalamārttaṇḍa* and later Buddhist works on *apoha* like Ratnakīrti's *Apohasiddhi* that Diṅnāga carried out the negative approach to meaning even in the case of sentences.

In the *Prameyakamalamārttaṇḍa* it is pointed out[11] that according to Diṅnāga in an expression like "the blue lotus," the term "blue" is used to exclude all lotuses that are not blue and the term "lotus" is used to exclude all blue things other than lotuses. Thus the expression signifies the exclusion of the non-blue and the non-lotus. In the *Apohasiddhi*, Ratnakīrti says[12] that in a sentence every word denotes a negation. Thus in the sentence "This road leads to Śrughna" the word "this" excludes all roads other than the one indicated, "road" excludes "footpaths, etc." "leads to" shows that it is not a blind path and "Śrughna" excludes all other places.

This view of *apoha* theory as applied to the sentence is strikingly similar to the theory of Vyāḍi, author of the *Saṁgraha*, who is earlier than Kātyāyana, author of the *Vārttikas* (*c.* fourth century BCE).

Vyāḍi who held that the meaning of a word is *dravya* or the particular,[13] seems to have explained that the function of a word

---

11. *dignāgena viśeṣaṇa-viśeṣyabhāvasamarthanārtham nīlotpalādi-śabdā arthāntaranivṛttiviśiṣṭān arthān āhuḥ ity uktam.* p. 126 b.

12. P. 5 f. Also D. Sharma, *The Differentiation Theory of Meaning in Indian Logic* (The Hague: Mouton & Company, 1969), p. 58.

    eṣa panthāḥ śrughnam upatiṣṭhate ity atrāpi apoho gamyata eva; apra-kṛta-pathāntarāpekṣayā eṣa eva; śrughnapratyanīkāniṣṭasthānāpekṣayā śrughnam eva, araṇyamārgavad vicchedābhāvād upatiṣṭhata eva; sārthadūtādivyavacchedena panthā eveti.

13. Kātyāyana's *Vārttika* on Pāṇini, 1.2.64 -*dravyābhidhānam vyāḍiḥ*. Also *Helārāja* on *VP* III.1.2 *vyāḍimate tu sarvaśabdānām dravyam arthaḥ, tasyaiva sākṣātkriyāsamanvayopapatteḥ*. B.K. Matilal, op. cit., pp. 106-09. Again, Hetārāja ibid.

→

in a sentence is to distinguish the thing it means from all similar possible things. Thus a "cow" means not so much "what is characterized by cowness, as what is distinguished from a non-cow like a horse, etc." Therefore in the case of a phrase "the white cow," the word "white" does not indicate the connection of whiteness with the cow, but denies all colours other than whiteness to it. Similarly, the term "cow" in the phrase means only the exclusion of all white things other than cow.[14] Kumārilabhaṭṭa says[15] that according to this view the import of a sentence is *bheda* or the mutual exclusion of the word-meanings. Pārthasārathimiśra explains it as follows.[16]

> According to those who hold that a word points to the particulars, since the first word itself denotes cows of all colours, namely white, black and so forth, there will be tautology if the second word, though it does not cease to indicate the connection (of the cow) with "whiteness" is understood as intended to signify it. It should accordingly be explained as negatively qualifying the cow in question or as denying all other colours to it. Hence the import of the sentence is stated to be "exclusion."

Patañjali also explains the theory while dealing with the meaning of the term *sāmarthya* which is given by Pāṇini as a condition that should exist between the members of a compound. He says that according to some the term means either *saṁsarga* (mutual

---

→ *vyāḍimate bhedo vākyārthaḥ, padavācyānām dravyāṇām dravyāntaranivṛttitātparyeṇābhidheyatvāt*

14. For a somewhat clear exposition of this point of Diṅnāga about the interpretation of the combination "*nīlam utpalam* (=blue lotus)" see B.K. Matilal, *Logical and Ethical Issues of Religious Belief* (Calcutta: University of Calcutta, 1982), p. 92-110.

15. Kumārilabhaṭṭa, *Tantravārttika*, pp. 447.

    bhedo nāma padārthānām vyavacchedaḥ parasparam . . . vyaktipadārthapakṣe sarvavyaktīnām gavādipadenaivopāttatvāt viṣayaśabdaiḥ śuklādibhiḥ kṛṣṇādivyavacchedamātram vaktavyam.

16. *Ślokavārttika* (Benares edn.), p. 854. See also M. Hiriyanna, "Vyāḍi and Vājapyāyana," *Indian Historical Quarterly* 14 (1938): 265.

association) or *bheda* (exclusion). Regarding *bheda* he says with reference to the compound word *rājapuruṣaḥ:*

> Here when the term *rājñaḥ* is mentioned all that form his property are apprehended and on the mention of the term *puruṣaḥ* all those who form his masters have a chance to be understood. But if the sentence *rājapuruṣamānaya* is uttered the word *rājan* eliminates all other masters of *puruṣa* and the word *puruṣa* eliminates all other possessions of *rājan*. If after both meanings have been restricted by each other, the words abandon part of their meanings, let it be. Never can *puruṣa* who has no connection with *rājan* be fetched.[17]

Though Patañjali is dealing with the compound word, the argument applies to the sentence as well.

Thus it is clear that the theory of sentence-meaning ascribed to Vyāḍi by early grammarians and Mīmāṁsakas is almost identical with the view on sentence-meaning according to the *apoha* theory as explained by later Buddhist writers.

Even though Diṅnāga held, like Bhartṛhari, that the sentence-meaning is of the nature of *pratibhā,* an intuitive flash of insight, he too must have held the restrictive role of word-meanings in the making of the sentence-meaning at the pragmatic and analytical level. This is corroborated by the reference to Diṅnāga's view given in the *Prameyakamala- mārttaṇḍa*, mentioned earlier.

---

17. *Mahābhāṣya* on Pāṇini II.1.1.

bhedasaṁsargau vā sāmarthyam iha rājña ity ukte sarvam svam prasaktam, puruṣa ity ukte sarvaḥ svāmī prasaktaḥ . . . ihedānīm rājapuruṣam añaya ity ukte rājā puruṣam nirvartayaty anyebhyaḥ svāmibhyaḥ, puruṣo'pi rājānam anyebhyaḥ svebhyaḥ. evam etasminnubhayato vyavacchinne yadi svārthaṁ jahāti, kāmam jahātu na jātucit puruṣa mātrasyānayanaṁ bhaviṣyati.

12

Was Śāntarakṣita a "Positivist?"

Mark Siderits

EARLY in *Apohasiddhi*[1] Ratnakīrti states, "What is held by the positivist — that there being the cognition, 'the cow is not other than itself,' exclusion is apprehended by a consequent apperception — and what is held by the negativist — that there being the cognition of the exclusion of the other, what is excluded from the other is apprehended indirectly — that is not right" (*AS* 3.8-12). Modern scholarship has tended to identify Śāntarakṣita as the positivist (*vidhivādin*) and Diṅnāga as the negativist (*prastiṣedhavādin*) had in mind by Ratnakīrti.[2] I shall here be concerned with only the first identification. What I wish to ascertain is whether there is any sense in which it is accurate to contrast the theories of Śāntarakṣita and Ratnakīrti as "positivist" and "neither positivist nor negativist" respectively.

Ratnakīrti's own view is that the meaning of a word is a positive entity qualified by the exclusion of the others (*AS* 3.6-8). In this respect his position resembles that of such Naiyāyikas as Jayanta, who holds that the meaning of a word is the

1. Ratnakīrti, *Apohasiddhi* (*AS*), in *Six Buddhist Nyāya Tracts*, ed. Hara Prasad Shastri, Bibliotheca Indica (Calcutta, 1910). Subsequent citations will be given in the text in parentheses.

2. Cf. Satkari Mookerjee, *The Buddhist Philosophy of Universal Flux* (Calcutta: University of Calcutta, 1935), p. 132; also Raja Ram Dravid, *The Problem of Universals in Indian Philosophy* (Delhi: Motilal Banarsidass, 1972), p. 306.

individual qualified by a universal (*jātiviśiṣṭavyakti*).[3] Ratnakīrti and Jayanta disagree, of course, on the nature of the qualifier: Where Jayanta puts a real universal, Ratnakīrti posits a mental fiction which is negative in function. But they agree on the point that the meaning of a word can be neither the particular which is ordinarily the referent of a token of the word, nor that general character which is shared in by the members of the word's extension. When one uses the word "cow," one generally intends to refer to a particular cow, but this can only be achieved by making use of the class character of the cow. Thus, the meaning of the word must be the particular as qualified by this class character.

Ratnakīrti does not, however, fault previous formulations of the *apoha* theory on the point of focusing exclusively on either the particular or the general element in word meaning. As we have seen, he characterizes both positivist and negativist as making room for both aspects of meaning in their theories. (In the context of Ratnakīrti's discussion of the *apoha* theory, the positive element in word meaning is the particular, the negative element is the class character.) What he objects to, rather, is the predominance which these theories give to one or another of these elements. The positivist is said to hold that verbal comprehension brings about cognition of the positive aspect of meaning directly, the negative aspect indirectly and only by implication. His criticism is this: "We do not find a succession of (stages of) grasping. No one ever, having first grasped something positive, goes on to cognize an exclusion by inference" (*AS* 3.13-14). Thus he takes the positivist to be making a certain claim about the psychology of linguistic cognition, namely that by means of such cognition one is made immediately aware of the particular, and becomes aware of the negative or excluding element of meaning only subsequently, indirectly, and by performing a certain inference. Let us see if this is a proper characterization of Śāntarakṣita's position.

---

3. Jayantabhaṭṭa, *Nyāyamañjarī*, Kashi Sanskrit Series 106 (1936), pp. 297-98.

Śāntarakṣita tells us that what is directly expressed by a word is the representation (*pratibhāsa*) which is caused, in one familiar with the relevant linguistic convention, by an utterance of the word.[4] The occurrence of this representation is also caused by the perception of any of those external particulars (*svalakṣaṇa*) which constitute the (indirect) extension of the word, and in fact it is regularly mistaken for these.[5] What a word primarily

---

4. *Tattvasaṁgraha* (*TS*) of *Ācārya Śāntarakṣita with the Commentary "Pañjikā"* (*TSP*) of *Śrī Kamalaśīla*, ed. Dwarikadas Shastri (Varanasi, 1968), v. 1010. Subsequent citations to *TS* will be given, by verse number, in parentheses in the text.

5. *TSP*, p. 393. Subsequent citations of *TSP* will be given, by page number, in the text.

   Diṅnāga claims in *Pramāṇasamuccaya* that the object of perception is the *svalakṣaṇa*, the object of inference (and thus of verbal cognition as well) is the *sāmānyalakṣaṇa*. The *svalakṣaṇa* is said to be momentary, unique, causally efficacious, and real, while the *sāmānyalakṣaṇa* is permanent, shared by many particulars, non-efficacious, and fictive. A good deal of confusion is engendered by attempting to fit Śāntarakṣita's account of word meaning into this framework. It is true that Kamalaśīla quotes with approval Diṅnāga's remark that the *anyāpoha* possesses all the properties of the realist's universal (*TSP*, p. 389). This suggests that we may identify as the *sāmānyalakṣaṇa* whatever Śāntarakṣita identifies as the *anyāpoha*. But such a strategy will not work, since for Śāntarakṣita there is no entity, real or fictive, that may be called the *anyāpoha*. One source of difficulty here is that Diṅnāga seems to have followed Bhartṛhari in claiming that the meaning of a word is the universal or class character, whereas Śāntarakṣita, like Ratnakīrti, holds that the meaning of a word is a particular qualified by the universal or class character. It is far from clear how we might prise apart the particular and universal elements in Śāntarakṣita's account so as to get something we might call the *sāmānyalakṣaṇa*. We are told that the *pratibhāsa* is a representation of the external particular which is ordinarily referred to through the use of a token of a word. Moreover, the *pratibhāsa* is itself a *svalakṣaṇa*, at least when considered as part of the mental stream of an individual. This might be taken to show that everything else in Śāntarakṣita's account besides the *pratibhāsa* can be thought of as the *sāmānyalakṣaṇa*. But as we shall see in more detail below, it is the →

expresses, then, is a mental content which is taken for the object referred to by the word.

This representation is also characterized as a type of exclusion, however, namely a nominally bound exclusion (*paryudāsāpoha*). We are told that it is so characterized principally because of its difference from the images which are caused by the cognition of other words (*TS, TSP,* p. 391). Here the analogy of the anti-febrile plants is helpful: Just as the various plants *abhayā, dhātṛ,* etc. though mutually distinct, are each capable upon ingestion of combating fever, so the black cow, brindled cow, etc. though mutually distinct, are each capable of causing images which differ from those caused by sheep, goats, etc. It is important to note that Śāntarakṣita does not state that the images caused by different cows resemble one another. Each simply differs from those images, which are caused by words other than "cow." The exclusion class of the image caused by the black cow does not include the image caused by the brindled cow.

While the mental image represents the primary force of a word, there is also a secondary meaning which is implied by the force of a word, namely a verbally bound exclusion (*prasajyapratiṣedhāpoha*). Kamalaśīla explains this as follows: "The self-nature of that which is the 'itself' of the image of the cow, etc. is not the 'itself' of the other, the image of the horse, etc." (*TS, TSP,* p. 393). This is to be considered the secondary meaning of a word because it occurs to one only after the image is cognized. Thus Kamalaśīla replies in the following way to the objection that one word cannot have two results:

> If it were intended that there is directly and simultaneously a double result of one word — a positive as well as a negative cognition — that would be contradictory. When, however, the view is that, as

→ distinctive causal capacity of the *pratibhāsa* to exclude other *pratibhāsas* which serves as the basis for determining the class character of the particular. Thus particular and universal elements appear to be inextricably bound up with each other in this account.

with "not eating during the day," the one result is obtained directly, the other by implication, then there is no contradiction.

— *TSP*, p. 395

The sentence, "Fat Devadatta does not eat during the day," is understood directly to express a certain state of affairs, namely that fat Devadatta does not eat during the day. When one has understood that the sentence expresses this state of affairs, one may then go on to work out the implication that Devadatta eats at night. By the same token, Kamalaśīla claims, when one understands a word one first cognizes a certain image, and only subsequently cognizes that this is not the image associated with various other words.

Is, then, Ratnakīrti's characterization of the positivist position an accurate depiction of Śāntarakṣita's formulation of the *apoha* theory? It will be recalled that Ratnakīrti faults the positivist for supposing that linguistic cognition involves two distinct stages of apprehension. The passage just quoted suggests that this is indeed Śāntarakṣita's view of linguistic cognition. Ratnakīrti also describes the positivist as holding that the first stage of linguistic cognition involves the apprehension of something positive, while the second stage involves the apprehension of something negative. Here we are on somewhat more slippery terrain. For Ratnakīrti, the positivist element in linguistic cognition is the apprehension of the particular which is ordinarily denoted by the use of a token of a term (*AS* 6.11-12). Now it is true that for Śāntarakṣita what one first apprehends in linguistic cognition is that representation which is mistaken for the external particular. But this representation is also characterized as a type of nominally bound exclusion; one cognizes the image caused by "cow" as different from the images caused by "horse," etc. If one is aware of this aspect of the image in the first stage of linguistic cognition, it would seem wrong to speak of this stage of linguistic cognition as apprehending only the positive.

Yet we have already seen that Kamalaśīla describes the first stage of such cognition as positive. And in another passage (*TSP*, p. 392) he uses the claim that this first stage is the apprehension of a mental image to reply to the objection (*TS* 909-10) that what is manifested in linguistic cognition is not mere negation. Śāntarakṣita's account of the primary force of a word, Kamalaśīla argues, shows that the apohist position is not that linguistic meaning is merely negative. The difficulty here is that Śāntarakṣita and Ratnakīrti mean different things by "positive" and "negative." For Ratnakīrti the positive is the particular real denoted by a token of a term, the negative is the exclusion which qualifies the particular. For Śāntarakṣita, however, "positive" and "negative" are, at least in this context, psychological terms. Not only the image which does duty for the particular, but the exclusion which qualifies it as well, may be thought of as psychologically positive in that the apprehension of either is more nearly like the apprehension of a paradigmatically positive entity, such as a pot, than it is like the apprehension of a paradigmatically negative entity, such as the absence of Devadatta from the house.

That the mental image is psychologically positive in this sense should be obvious, but the case of the exclusion which qualifies it, requires comment. This is a nominally bound exclusion, that is, its linguistic representation is best achieved by prefixing a negative particle to a noun or adjective. Thus in the case of "cow" the image is qualified by an exclusion which may be represented as "non-(image produced by words other than 'cow')." It is generally held that the primary force of nominally bound negation is positive, its negative aspect playing only a subsidiary role. This may best be understood in terms of the notion of commitment to the existence of properties. When we characterize an action as impolite, we are not simply refusing to attribute the property of being polite to the action. Rather, we are attributing to the action a quality which is opposed to that of being polite; we may say that "impolite" is a sort of linguistic "poseur." The term thus involves commitment to the existence of a property which qualifies the class of actions to which it is applied. And so it is that "impolite" comes to be thought of as the name of a property every bit as real, as directly cognizable, as the quality of being white. By the same token, the exclusion which qualifies the image produced by a word is apprehended not as the absence of a property which qualifies other images, but rather as a property which is distinctive of that image, its own form. It is this which makes the cognition of this exclusion psychologically positive.

It would appear, then, that it is in the main accurate to speak of Śāntarakṣita as a positivist. For he does employ the notion that there are two stages of linguistic cognition, the first positive, the second negative. Only "in the main," however, since his first stage is positive in the psychological sense, not in Ratnakīrti's sense of being the cognition of a particular as opposed to the cognition of a negative qualifier. And this qualification should alert us to an important point about the present dispute. That Śāntarakṣita intends his two stages to be thought of as positive and negative in the psychological sense shows that his two-stage account is meant as a way of squaring a formal theory with our pre-critical intuitions about the psychology of linguistic cognition. The heart of the theory, I want to suggest, lies elsewhere than in the story of succeeding cognitions. In this case it is at best unhelpful, and possibly misleading, to follow Ratnakīrti's classification.

This claim requires elucidation and defence. In what follows, I shall attempt to provide both. In the first place, it is worth remarking that Śāntarakṣita's two-stage account is offered in response to the objection that the apohist thesis contradicts experience. This raises an interesting question: What sort of experience is there which could contradict a theory of meaning? The answer is to be found in Kamalaśīla's explication of the objection.

> The idea produced by a word is perceived as functioning just by determining something of the form of a real. And that is not a part of linguistic meaning which is not manifested in linguistic cognition.
> — *TSP*, p. 359

What the objector seems to be claiming is that we can introspect that mental content which arises when we apprehend a word, and moreover, that when we do so we find that this mental content is the representation of a positive entity like a pot or the quality of being white, not the representation of something negative like the absence of Devadatta. For my own part, I must confess that I am not sure this is correct; but perhaps this is because my intuitions have been corrupted by engaging in philosophy. What I am sure of is that the second claim of the objection — that intuitions of this sort are decisive for the theory of meaning — is false. Introspection is simply not an appropriate tool for the construction of an account of linguistic meaning. It is generally recognized that the evidence of introspection is coloured by the theory one holds. If one begins the task of constructing a theory of meaning by attempting to introspect those mental states associated with verbal apprehension, one's intuitions will be coloured by one's naïve semantic theory. And naïve semantics is a bad theory. If one asks the cowherd what the word "cow" means, he will amost invariably reply that the meaning is just those things to which the word refers, namely particular cows. If we start with introspection, the Sāṁkhyans will have the last word on the problem of meaning.

Oddly enough it is Ratnakīrti who comes closest to an explicit recognition of this problem. In reviewing the difficulties faced by previous formulations of the *apoha* theory, he considers the objection that one would not ordinarily describe what one was aware of when one understood the meaning of a word as negative in nature (the making manifest of a mere denial). A possible reply to this objection is that while one does not report, "I perceive negation," still there is a negative element in verbal cognition and in that negation is a qualifier of that entity which is excluded (*AS* 1.15). The situation here is compared to that faced by the Naiyāyika, who must agree that one does not ordinarily report apprehension of a universal in describing one's linguistic cognition. This does not by itself rule out the Naiyāyika's claim that universals are involved in word meaning, however, since we still require an account of how a word may be correctly applied to a potentially infinite number of particulars; thus it may well be that the individual referents of the various tokens of a term are all qualified by a common form, and that this is part of the meaning of the term (*AS* 2.1). To this suggestion, Ratnakīrti has the opponent reply that such an approach is of no avail to the *apohavādin*, since it is clear that a horse does not figure in the meaning of the word "cow" (*AS* 2.6-11). This reply is opposite, since the proposal under consideration is that the meaning of the word "cow" is those things which are not cows as qualified by negation. What is important about this exchange is that the counsels of our pre-critical intuitions have been shown to be of less importance than certain more formal constraints on a theory of meaning.

What constraints are these, that is, what is it that a theory of word meaning should accomplish? Diṅnāga took the task of such a theory to be the construction of a satisfactory account of the manner in which words bring about apprehension of sentence meaning,[6] and Śāntarakṣita follows Diṅnāga in this.[7] One important component of this programme is the provision of an adequate account of our use of class terms in sentences,

---

6. On this point cf. Masaaki Hattori, "*Apoha and Pratibhā*," in *Sanskrit and Indian Studies: Essays in Honour of Daniel H.H. Ingalls*, ed. M. Nagatomi et al. (Dordrecht: D. Reidel Publishing Company, 1980), pp. 61-73.

7. I discuss Śāntarakṣita's account of the relation between word meaning and sentence meaning in "Word Meaning, Sentence Meaning, and Apoha," in *Journal of Indian Philosophy* 13, no. 2 (June 1985): 133-51.

and this is the problem to which Ratnakīrti devotes his greatest efforts. But the basic problem remains the explanation of our ability to understand and act in conformity with novel sentences. Now in this task it is clear that, other things being equal, the theory which employs the more plausible psychological model enjoys a distinct advantage over its competitors. For instance, a model which required that humans have infinite memory capacity would obviously be defective. A semantic theory must not be confused with this model, however. A semantic theory is itself just a formal representation of those computations which mediate between verbal input and behavioural output. And the elements employed in this representation need have no status whatever in our ontology. A psychological model of a semantic theory provides an account of how human beings might actually carry out the required computations. This suggests that the model must have some degree of psychological reality, that it be conceivable that it is actually instantiated in the causal capacities of the human mind, if the model is to have any degree of plausibility. But just as the symbols employed in a formal representation of linguistic meaning need not be construed as referring to any elements in our ontology, so the psychological characteristics of those mental states or events involved in the causal processes posited by the model are irrelevant to the model itself. What matters is just that the causal processes function in the right way, that they issue in the sort of behaviour we expect from the input.

It is for this reason that introspective reports concerning the "feel" of linguistic cognition can play no role in the construction of a semantic theory. This is not to say that such reports can play no role in the evaluation of such a theory, however. The ideally complete psychological theory would provide an explanation of all mental phenomena — including those cases in which the results of introspection disagree with the theory itself. The psychological model of a semantic theory is not meant to be an ideally complete psychological theory; its scope is restricted to those mental phenomena connected with linguistic cognition. It is none the less desirable that the model provides some explanation of those areas where it diverges from the evidence of introspection. Other things being equal, the theory which can explain more of its counter-intuitive features is to be preferred. Such considerations can hardly be decisive on their own, however. What count most are such features as the theory's predictive power, economy, and elegance, along with the compatibility of its psychological model with what we know about human mental capacities.

Let us now see how Śāntarakṣita's and Ratnakīrti's theories fare under this interpretation of their project. The formal theories of word meaning which they provide appear to be essentially equivalent, and can be represented as follows. Associated with each term t is some one particular p_c. Then with p ranging over the domain D of particulars, the meaning of a term t is $\hat{p}$ $(\sim\text{-}p_c p)$ (read: p such that it is not non-p_c; for reasons to be noted below, the expression $\text{-}p_c$ names a predicate). The ~- function yields a pseudo-predicate when it takes particulars as arguments. This function may be analysed in terms of the two types of negation of which it is composed — verbally bound (*prasajya-pratiṣedha*) and nominally bound (*paryudāsa*). For each p in the domain D, $\text{-}p$ yields an ordered pair of sets, $<S_1, S_2>$ with S_1 the extension of $\text{-}p$ and S_2 the anti-extension of $\text{-}p$ (i.e., $S_1 \; U \; S_2$ is a proper subset of D; cf. choice negation). For each p_i, S_2 is a set with just one member, namely p_i. Application of verbally bound negation to this pair yields a pseudo-predicate whose extension S_3 is the complement of S_1 (i.e., $S_1 \; U \; S_3 = D$; cf. exclusion negation). We call this a pseudo-predicate because its extension has been determined in such a way as to avoid commitment to the existence of any characteristic or set of characteristics common to the members of S_3.

Śāntarakṣita provides the following psychological model of the theory. The variable p ranges over *pratibhāsa*s or mental images.

A mental image may be caused by an external particular (*svalakṣaṇa*); the external particular is the object of perceptual cognition, but it can also give rise to a mental representation which is the direct object of linguistic or inferential cognition. Such an image may also be caused in another fashion, however, namely through cognition of the appropriate word once the conventions governing the use of that word have been learned. Given that both external particulars and mental images are absolutely unique and devoid of resemblance relations, one wonders how such conventions could be learned in the case of class terms. Consider the term "cow," and suppose its extension to consist of images p_1,......., p_i, each of these images being the sort of representation that would be caused were one in the right type of cognitive relation to what is commonly called a cow. Now an image, say p_1, manifests itself to consciousness in such a way as to be incompatible with or exclude the occurrence of a certain set of images which might otherwise occur, say the set (p_{i+1}, ..., p_k). (Here $D = (p_1, ..., p_k)$. Assume that the particular *pratibhāsa* p_c associated with the term "cow" is p_1. This association comes about through p_1 having been the representation produced on the occasion of learning the term.[8] Now $-p_1 = <(p_{i+1}, ..., p_k) , (p_1)>$. But it was noted above that the nominally bound negation of an image yields a qualifier which is apprehended not as the absence of a property which qualifies other images, but as a qualifier which is distinctive of that image itself, its own form. This means that the extension of $-p_1$ is determined by a predicate which qualifies just p_1, not the set (p_{i+1}, ...,p_k). The point may be made in the following way: To say that a given image has the causal capacity to exclude a certain set of images is to commit oneself to the existence of some property, but this property should be thought of as just a dispositional property of the given

8. We are here assuming that learning comes about through ostension, but only for the sake of simplifying our account. In fact, Śāntarakṣita, as an *anvitābhidhānavādin*, would deny that one ordinarily learns new terms by ostension.

particular image, not as a property which characterizes the various images in the set of excluded images. For the overall strategy to work, we need some way of determining the set (p_{i+1} ,....., p_k); the present point is that this may be done without commitment to the existence of a real property which is common to the members of this set.

Verbally bound negation is to be interpreted as absolute rejection of a set of images as a qualifier of a given image without commitment to the existence of some alternative qualifier as qualifying the given image. Thus to say of some representation p that it satisfies not non-p_1 is just to deny that it is a member of the set (p_{i+1}, ..., p_k). But given that verbally bound negation functions like exclusion negation, this also means that the image in question must belong to the set (p_1....,p_i). Thus the expression -p_1 is a way of characterizing all those representations which belong to the (direct) extension of the term "cow," a way which does not make use of the notion of a real property of cowness.

How, then, does one respond to the command, "Fetch a cow?" Having learned the relevant convention for "cow," one knows that the word refers to anything which satisfies the pseudo-predicate -p_1. Now when we stand in the right cognitive relation to a real cow-particular (i.e. a cow-*svalakṣaṇa*), this causes the occurrence of a representation which satisfies the pseudo-predicate, since each cow-representation is endowed with the causal capacity to exclude the set of images (p_{i+1},.....p_k). Thus we can recognize any representation from the set (p_2,......p_i) as belonging to the (direct) extension of "cow" simply by noting that the recollected image p_1 (which in effect serves as a paradigm) does not exclude that representation. It is worth pointing out that this version of the *apoha* theory differs significantly from Dharmakīrti's. According to the latter's account, we pick out the correct image from among those presented to consciousness by means of a real resemblance relation between that image and a paradigm. On the present theory, on the other hand, real resemblance relations are replaced by the machinery of twofold negation.

With one exception to be noted below, Ratnakīrti does not appear to have provided an explicit formulation of his psychological model. Virtually all of his remarks about the psychology of linguistic apprehension fall under the heading of what I would call accommodations to conflicting intuitions. Since all of these remarks are consonant with the model just sketched, however, it seems fair to take his silence to mean that he accepts it, at least in the main.

Let us now see how Śāntarakṣita tries to answer objections to the *apoha* theory based on pre-critical intuitions about linguistic cognition. I have already claimed that his two-stage account should be taken as just such an attempt. The opponent argues that the object of linguistic cognition feels psychologically positive, and takes this to refute the apohist thesis. Śāntarakṣita replies that what one is first aware of in such cognition, namely the image as qualified by its difference from certain other images, is psychologically positive. The psychologically negative element in linguistic cognition, the exclusion of those other images as a characterization of the given image, is cognized only subsequently and by implication. In fact, Śāntarakṣita seems committed, on independent grounds, to the position that the causal processes involved in cognition of word meaning are not amenable to introspection;[9] thus it would be surprising if he were claiming that these processes can be known to occur in a certain order. I take this rather as the suggestion that the opponent go back and look again at the testimony of introspection. To be sure, what comes to mind first when one reflects on the psychology of linguistic apprehension is some positive content. But subsequent reflection discloses a negative

9. Cf. my "More things in Heaven and Earth," *Journal of Indian Philosophy*, 10 (1982): 205-06. This point is also discussed in "Word Meaning, Sentence Meaning, and Apoha."

element as well: One seems to have become aware of this positive content by virtue of having excluded certain other positive contents. In other words, I am suggesting that the presumptive apprehension which Kamalaśīla describes at *TSP* p. 395 is not part of the psychological model of the theory, but is rather intended as showing a way of obtaining more accurate introspective data concerning the psychological feel of word apprehension. Of course, if I am correct in saying that Śāntarakṣita distrusts the testimony of introspection, then such data cannot be used directly to support the theory. There is, however, a well-known sense in which our intuitions can be used if not to support a theory then at least to motivate it. I think that Śāntarakṣita is here seeking more balanced intuitions about linguistic cognition in order to simply show that the *apoha* theory is not as counter-intuitive as it seems at the first blush.

Ratnakīrti would seem to place more confidence in the ability of introspection to capture the nature of linguistic cognition. Thus as we have already seen, he takes as a decisive objection to Śāntarakṣita's theory the fact that we are not ordinarily aware of two distinct stages of cognition of word meaning. This leads him to propose that the particular and its qualifier are apprehended simultaneously (*AS* 6.8; strictly speaking this claim would seem to belong to his psychological model). But now consider how he seeks to counter the intuition that one is not aware of excluding anything when one apprehends the positive content of linguistic cognition. He argues that in the cognition of a blue lotus the qualifier "blue" operates not by causing the manifestation of a representation of blue but by bringing it about that the manifestation of blue is not excluded from one's mental representations. By the same token, when as a result of linguistic apprehension one cognizes a particular cow, one simultaneously apprehends its qualifier the exclusion of non-cow, not in the form of the performance of an exclusion of non-cow, but rather by way of not excluding the manifestation of the exclusion of non-cow (*AS* 3.19-4.3). That is, to say that one is aware of the exclusion of non-cow and at the same time one is aware of the particular cow, is not to say one is aware at that time of performing the exclusion of non-cow; it means merely that one among a number of possible qualifiers of the particular remains before one's mind at that time, namely the mental representation of such an exclusion. Ratnakīrti is making two distinct points here: that an act of exclusion — viz. the exclusion of qualifiers other than not non-cow — can occur while our attention is focused elsewhere and thus prove invisible to introspection; and that the mental representation of an exclusion is not itself the performance of a mental act of exclusion.

This suggests that Ratnakīrti shares Śāntarakṣita's reluctance to place much weight on the evidence of introspection in formulating and criticizing semantic theories. A difficulty for this interpretation arises, however, out of his discussion of a point of logic. It is objected that the exclusion of the other and what is excluded from the other could not be cognized simultaneously, since they are contradictory. He replies that a contradiction is brought about not by absence of the other (which is what we find in linguistic cognition) but by absence of the entity itself. He argues that qualifier and qualified are not in fact distinct, since they have the same locus, like the (cognition of) the ground and the absence of a pot (*AS* 5.13-16). It is a doctrine of Yogācāra-Sautrāntika epistemology that absences are not perceived but inferred: one perceives the ground, realizes that if a pot were on the ground then it would have been perceived, and infers that a pot is not on the ground.[10] Is Ratnakīrti not here saying that we can confirm by introspection one element of his psychological model, namely its requirement that we are able simultaneously to cognize a positive entity and its negative qualifier?

In fact, he is not, for if this were his intention then the example would backfire. One cannot be said to perceive the

10. Jayanta provides a good discussion of the Buddhist position on non-perception at *Nyāyamañjarī*, pp. 54 ff.

ground and infer the absence of the pot simultaneously; these are distinct mental acts, and must occur at distinct times. In fact, his point here must be that one can stand in some cognitive relation to both a positive entity and a negative entity at the same time. When one is aware of the absence of a pot, one is simultaneously related in some epistemically significant way to the substratum of this absence, the ground. Of course, one is not aware of being so related to the ground when one is cognizing the absence. But this simply confirms our suspicion that introspection cannot tells us all there is to know about the psychology of cognition. In fact, introspection can be positively misleading here, for there is a sense in which what one is really aware of, when one cognizes the absence of the pot, is the ground; introspection tells us the object is negative when it is actually positive.

What emerges from this is the suggestion that we view Ratnakīrti's claim about the simultaneity of the two aspects of linguistic cognition in a different light. In particular it suggests we should not see him as asserting that we are at one moment of such cognition fully aware, in a way which is open to introspection, of both the particular and the exclusion which is its qualifier. His claim is rather that whenever we are fully aware of one aspect, we are also epistemically related (by way of some causal relation) to the other. The causal processes responsible for linguistic cognition are such that full awareness of either element could not be achieved unless both elements had been employed in the computation of the meaning of the term. With respect to these processes it makes no sense to speak of "before" and "after."

If all this is correct, however, one wonders why Ratnakīrti takes such strong exception to Śāntarakṣita's theory, for there seems to be little that divides them. I suspect that Ratnakīrti has simply mistaken the intent of the latter's two-stage account, taking it as a part of the psychological model which is meant to be verifiable by introspection. If that were the actual status of this account, Ratnakīrti would be justified in rejecting it. I argued that it should instead be seen as an attempt to school our intuitions so that these might motivate the theory proper. Ratnakīrti engages in the same task when he analyses the sentence, "This path leads to Śrughna." He points out that "leads," for instance, contributes the sense, "precisely leads, without a break such as is found in forest paths." He concludes that words produce apprehension of something positive in a form qualified by an exclusion (*AS* 6.1-4). Of course, the considerations he brings forth prove no such thing. They simply help us acquire a new intuition about word meaning, one that makes the *apoha* theory seem somewhat less counter-intuitive. In fact, this attempt at schooling our intuitions dovetails rather nicely with Śāntarakṣita's. What Ratnakīrti gives us are instances where our first intuition is that meaning is apprehended as something positive, but where subsequent reflection suggests the presence of a differentiative element as well. It must be admitted, though, that Ratnakīrti's efforts in this direction are much less likely to be misunderstood than Śāntarakṣita's.

In sum, Śāntarakṣita and Ratnakīrti share essentially the same formal theory, psychological model, and methodological principles. One can view Śāntarakṣita as a positivist only if one takes his two-stage account as part of the psychological model of his theory. I have argued that to do so is to view that account outside its proper context, namely as a reply to an objection based on pre-critical intuitions. If I am correct in this, then Śāntarakṣita is not a positivist. Even if I am wrong on this point, however, it is still singularly unhelpful to employ Ratnakīrti's classification, given how little separates the two theories.[11]

---

11. An earlier version of this paper was delivered to the Seminar on Buddhist Logic and Epistemology held under the auspices of the IABS at Oxford University on 17-18 August 1982. I wish to thank the following individuals for helpful comments and criticisms: Douglas Daye, Harry Deutsch, Brendan Gillon, Richard Hayes, Hans Herzberger, Radhika Herzberger, Katsura Shoryu and B.K. Matilal.

13

Identity and Referential Opacity in Tibetan Buddhist Apoha Theory

Tom Tillemans

My purpose in this paper is threefold: to show that the problem of referential opacity in modern intensional logics also plays an important role in Buddhist logic; to sketch out the Buddhist's attempted solution to this problem and, in passing, compare the Buddhist position with that of a conservative logician such as W.V. Quine; to provide guidelines as to which parts of Tibetan Buddhist logic will inevitably require an intensional interpretation. The main Buddhist sources to be used in this enterprise are the *Pramāṇavārttika* and *svavr̥tti* as interpreted by rGyal-tshab-rje in *rNam 'grel thar lam gsal byed.* Various logic texts of Phur-bu-lcog byams-pa rgya-mtsho will also be used.

A. Referential Opacity

The term "referential opacity" comes from Quine,[1] although the modern version of the problem can be said to have originated with Russell's notion of "propositional attitudes" and Frege's problem of sense and reference.

Quine accepts Leibniz's law of substitutivity: "given a true statement of identity, one of its two terms may be substituted for the other in any other true statement and the result will be true."[2] For him, failure to accept this fundamental logical law is

1. Quine (1953b); Linsky (1971), p. 20.

2. Ibid., p. 17.

tantamount to not knowing what sort of entities one is talking about. None the less, seemingly paradoxical cases do arise:

1. Cicero = Tully.

   "Cicero" contains six letters.

   Therefore, Tully contains six letters.[3]

2. Hegel believed that the number of planets = five.

   The number of planets = nine.

   Therefore, Hegel believed that five = nine.[4]

3. Necessarily, nine = nine.

   The number of planets = nine.

   Therefore, necessarily, the number of planets = nine.

(1) is easily dispensed with as an illegitimate application of substitutivity, confusing Cicero with his names "Cicero" and "Tully." (2) and (3) pose much greater problems if we are committed to Leibniz's law. Since Quine and most other modern logicians are so committed, (2) and (3) must also be diagnosed as illegitimate applications of this law. Here is Quine's line of attack. He argues that the key names in the first premise of (2) and (3) do not occur *purely referentially:* "the statement depends not only on the object but on the form of the name. For it is clear that whatever can be affirmed about the object remains true when we refer to the object by any other name."[5] Quotation contexts, epistemic contexts, such as ". . . believes that . . . , " ". . . knows that . . . ," and modal contexts, such as "Necessarily. . . ," "Possibly . . .," can all be said to be referentially opaque: when a statement *S* is embedded in such a context, the otherwise referring names of *S* can cease to refer. Now there have been many different

3. Quine (1953b); Linsky (1971), p. 20.

4. Kaplan (1969).

5. Quine (1953b), p. 18.

Western approaches to this problem. We can mention the trans-formational grammar approach of Heringer, Hintikka's use of the modal logic notion of possible worlds to provide a semantics for belief contexts,[6] Alonzo Church's formalization of Frege's logic of sense and reference,[7] Ruth Barcan Marcus and Gail Stine's use of the substitution interpretation of quantification,[8] David Kaplan's use of Church's denotation function and the notion of a "vivid name" to be able to quantify into opaque contexts,[9] and so on. (The reader can appreciate that it is impossible to prepare a resumé of these different approaches here.) But for our purposes we only need to mention a few elements from this mass of Western philosophical logic:

a. The problem becomes more acute when we introduce quantification and try to quantify into opaque contexts.[10]

4. $(\exists x)$ (Hegel believes that x = nine)

What is the value of x? Is it the number of planets, i.e. nine? But although Hegel surely believed that nine = nine, didn't he also believe that the number of planets = five? (I make no claims to historical accuracy!)

b. Suppose we follow the Frege-Church line and say that the object of belief is not an ordinary object — nine, the number of planets, etc. — but rather the intension or

---

6. Cf. Hintikka (1967 and 1969).

7. Church (1951).

8. Marcus (1962) and Stine (1976). A substitutional interpretation of quantification allows one to go from "Necessarily, 9 = 9" to "$(\exists x)$ Necessarily, (x = 9)," because on this interpretation all that the latter formula means is that there is at least one substitution instance of "Necessarily, x = 9" which is true.

9. Kaplan (1969).

10. A point continually raised by Quine. cf. (1953b), (1956), (1960).

sense of the words "nine," "number of planets," etc.[11] and we let variables range over these intensions. Then, if we say "$(\exists/x)$(.....)," doesn't this commit us to accepting these entities in our ontology? To be is to be the value of an existentially quantified variable, unless we follow the line of Routley, Parsons and others[12] and introduce quantifiers which do not have this *existential import.*

c. Is belief, knowledge, etc. a relation between an individual and a set of words, or is it a relation between an individual and a non-verbal entity, a proposition? Quine, Kaplan and Carnap choose the former line, but Church has shown that serious problems will inevitably arise if one translates a belief statement like "I believe that snow is white" into something like "I believe that 'snow is white' is true in English."[13] I mention these elements because they will be useful in situating the Buddhist position.

---

11. "Intension" is Carnap's term: "Two designators have the same intension = *def.* they are L-equivalent." Carnap (1956), p. 23. In other words, two words have the same intension if the appropriate equivalence relation (i.e. identity or biconditional, etc.) is necessarily true. Frege's (1892) notion of sense is very similar, although cf. Carnap (1956) sec. 28 for the few differences which there are. Frege's main point is that in opaque contexts words *refer* to their ordinary *sense* rather than to their ordinary reference.

12. Routley (1966), Parsons (1974).

13. Church (1950). The point is as follows: if we say that "*A* believes that 'Snow is white' is true in English" is a translation of, and hence necessarily equivalent with, "*A* believes that snow is white," this necessity could be refuted by pointing out that *A* need not be a speaker of English, but could still believe that snow is white (although he presumably would not believe that the English sentence is true). Church discusses more sophisticated attempts along this line, but the result is always more or less the same: the translation into a belief about a statement presupposes some contingent fact about *A*'s linguistic competence, or about the meaning of a set of words in the language in question. And this fact is not implied by "*A* believes that snow is white."

B. The Problem for a Buddhist Logician

In *Pramāṇavārttika*, k. 40-42 of the *Svārthānumānapariccheda*, Dharmakīrti introduces his theory of "exclusion of the other" (*anyāpoha, gźan sel*), a theory which has a twofold purpose: to counter realism with regard to universals; but also — as the *svavṛtti* makes clear — to defend inference from charges of circularity. It is this latter aspect which joins up with the problem of referential opacity. The problem, in Dharmakīrti's terms, is to avoid the charge that the reason or probans (*hetu, gtan tshigs*) is "a part of the thesis" (*pratijñārthaikadeśa, dam bca'i don gyi phogs gcig*). Here is Mookerjee and Nagasaki's translation of a key passage in the *svavṛtti*:[14]

> One word signifies one difference which cannot be expressed by another word, [for instance impermanent and being a product are inexpressible by one word. They are expressed by different words and appear to be different, though in reality they are identical. In view of the conceptual difference of meanings conveyed by different words] it follows that each and all words cannot express the same meaning and so the charge of the probans being a part of the thesis (i.e. being the same thing as the probandum) does not hold good.
>
> — *svavṛtti* to k. 40-42, in Mookerjee and Nagasaki

Using *rNam 'grel thar lam gsal byed* pp. 74-80, we can reconstruct the potential problem as follows:

5. Product is a valid reason (*rtags yah dag*) for proving that sound is impermanent.

   Product = impermanent (i.e. everything which is a product is impermanent and vice versa).

   Therefore, impermanent is a valid reason for proving that sound is impermanent. (The conclusion seems to follow by the law of substitutivity.)

---

14. Mookerjee and Nagasaki, p. 97. The Sanskrit is: *tasmāt svabhāvābhede 'pi yena yena dharmeṇa nāmnā yo viśeṣo bhedaḥ pratīyate na sa śakyo 'nyena pratyāyayitum iti naikārthāḥ sarvaśabdāḥ* | *tan na pratijñārthaikadeśo hetur iti* |.

Clearly, proving that sound is impermanent because it is impermanent will not do; this would be circularity or *pratijñārthaikadeśahetuḥ*.

The problem can also be formulated in terms of more typical opaque contexts such as ". . . knows that . . . " and ". . doubts that. . . . " As *rtags rigs* and other logic texts make clear with their notion of a "faultless subject of enquiry" (*śes 'dod chose can skyon med*), if a reason is to be valid, the opponent (*phyir rgol*) must be able to doubt that the subject is qualified by the property to be proved (*sādhyadharma, bsgrub bya'i chos*).[15] Otherwise, the inference is pointless and doesn't establish anything which the opponent didn't know before. So a reformulation of (5) would be:

6. The opponent knows that sound is a product, and doubts that sound is impermanent.

   Product = impermanent

   The opponent knows that sound is impermanent.

   (The conclusion seems to follow by substitutivity.)

Whereas a modern logician such as Quine would treat belief contexts as a special troublesome case, Dharmakīrti and rGyal-tshab-rje use the problems in (5) and (6) to come up with a general theory of language. In other words, for the Buddhist, if it is necessary that the words in *opaque contexts* refer to a certain type of intensional entity, then words in *non-opaque* contexts will also have to refer to these type of entities. We might say that they make no clear difference between intensional and

---

15. The definition in *rtags rigs* (p. 2b) is on the basis of the sound-impermanent example: "*x* is taken as the basis of debate for the reason, product, to prove that sound is impermanent; it is possible that someone validly ascertains that *x* is a product but still wishes to know whether or not *x* is impermanent." *khyod byas pa' i rtags kyis sgra mi rtag par sgrub pa' i rtsod gźir bzuṅ ba yaṅ yin | khyod byas par tshad mas ṅes nas | khyod mi rtag pa yin min śes 'dod źugs pa' i gaṅ zag srid pa yaṅ yin pa' i gźi mthun par dmigs pa |.*

extensional contexts.[16] This gives rise to another aspect of the problem, and although the starting-point was referential opacity, we are now faced with a general problem of the relation between language and reality.

In *rNam 'grel thar lam gsal byed* a sceptic argues that if the words "products" and "impermanent" refer to real particulars (*svalakṣaṇa, rah mtshan*), then they must refer to exactly the same thing and the consequences in (5) and (6) are unavoidable. Suppose, however, that they do not refer to *svalakṣaṇa*, but rather to a conceptually created entity (*rtog pas brtags pa tsam*) a *sāmānyalakṣaṇa* (*spyi mtshan*, in our terms we could say an "intension").[17] Then, indeed, we might be able to say that product and impermanent — taken in this way — are not identical. But according to the sceptic, the problem arises that because all *sāmānyalakṣaṇa*s are permanent, it would be impossible to prove a statement like "sound is impermanent." The subject, sound, would not be the impermanent *svalakṣaṇa*, sound, but rather a permanent, mentally created fiction. We could never express anything about *svalakṣaṇa* at all.[18] So let us summarize rGyal-tshab-rje and Dharmakīrti's problem:

a. If words refer to *svalakṣaṇa*, then by application of substitutivity, inferences would become circular or pointless.

b. If words refer to *sāmānyalakṣaṇa*, then the application of substitutivity in (5) and (6) may be avoided, but many inferences become invalid and language cannot describe *svalakṣaṇa*.

---

16. Intensional contexts being those where substitutivity does not seem to hold, and extensional contexts being those where it holds non-problematically.

17. rGyal-tshab-rje, vol. 1, p. 74.

18. Ibid., p. 74. *byas pa mi rtag pa sgrub pa' i gtan tshigs yin na mi rtag pa yin par 'gal bas* | *khyab pa ' gal nas ma grub par 'gyur źiṅ* | *rjes dpag gis lkog gyur gyi don raṅ mtshan go ba mi srid pas phra ba ' i mi rtag pa dah rdul phran la sogs pa tshad mas mi ' grub par 'gyur te . . .*

C. The Attempted Solution

I. REVISING THE NOTION OF IDENTITY

As shown in the quoted passages from *Pramāṇavārttikasvavṛtti*, Dharmakīrti maintains that "one word signifies one difference, which cannot be expressed by another word." *Prima facie*, this is bizarre: each word refers to a different entity! rGyal-tshab-rje and Yoṅs-'dzin Phur-bu-lcog byams-pa rgya-mtsho follow this lead, and introduce a notion of identity (*gcig*) and difference (*tha dad*) such that only entities corresponding to the *same name* can be said to be *gcig*. Otherwise, they are *tha dad*.

Consider Phur-bu-lcog's explanation, which I shall translate in full (remember that "Son of Śuddhodana," etc. are all names for Śākyamuni):[19]

> An opponent says that real entity (*dṅos po*), impermanent (*mi rtag pa*), product (*byas pa*) and composite (*'dus byas*), as they are simply a group of synonyms, are all identical (*gcig*, "one"). Analogously, knowable thing (*śes bya*), existent (*yod pa*), established basis (*gṢi grub*) and discriminable entity (*gṢal bya*) are also identical. Just for example, the Incomparable Son of Śuddhodana, the Omniscient One of Solar Line, and the Omniscient Sugar Cane One [are identical]. [We reply]: This is incorrect because the Son of Śuddhodana, the One of Solar Line and Sugar Cane One are all different (*tha dad*). If [you say that the reason is] not established, then we affirm that it does follow [that the Son of Śuddhodana, etc. are different] because it is possible that one might validly ascertain

19. *yaṅ kha cig | dṅos po | mi rtag pa | byas pa | 'dus byas rnams miṅ gi rnam graṅs tsam las gcig yin ciṅ | de bźin du śes bya | yod pa | gźi grub |gźal bya rnams kyaṅ gcig yin te | dper na | mñam med zas gtsaṅ sras po | kun mkhyen ñi ma' i gñen |kun mkhyen bu ram śiṅ pa rnams bźin no | zer na | de mi 'thad de | zas gtsaṅ sras po daṅ |ñi ma' i gñen | bu ram śiṅ pa rnams tha dad yin pa' i phyir | ma grub na | der thal | zas gtsaṅ sras po źes pa' i sgra gźi gaṅ la ' jug tshad mas hes kyaṅ | ñi ma'i gñen daṅ | bu ram śiṅ pa źes pa' i sgra gźi gaṅ la ' jug tshad mas ma ṅes pa srid pa' i phyir ro || des na zas gtsah sras po | ñi ma' i gñen | bu ram śiṅ pa źes pa' i sgra' jug pa' i' jug gźi gcig yin kyaṅ |de dag gcig ma yin te | gcig yin na sgra don gñis ka nas gcig yin dgos pa' i phyir |.*

> (*tshad mas hes pa*) to which basis one applies (*' jug*) the words "One of Solar Line" and "Sugar Cane One," even though one does not validly ascertain when one applies the words "Son of Śuddhodana." Therefore, although the basis for applying the names "Son of Śuddhodana," "One of Solar Line," "Sugar Cane One" is identical, they [i.e. the Son of Śuddhodana, etc.] are not identical; if they were identical, they would have to be identical both in name (*sgra*) and object (*don*). — *bsdus grwa chuṅ*, p. 12b

Let us reformulate things. The troublesome inference can be reworded as:

7. *A* knows who the One of Solar Line is.

   The Son of Śuddhodana = the One of Solar Line.

   A knows who the Son of Śuddhodana is.

Phur-bu-lcog's reasoning from (7) is:

A knows who the One of Solar Line is.

It is possible that *A* does not know who the Son of Śuddhodana is.

Thus, the Son of Śuddhodana ≠ the One of Solar line.

(Note that here "=" is being used in the Buddhist sense, *gcig*)

Now obviously Dharmakīrti's, and Phur-bu-lcog's notion of *gcig* is tantamount to rejecting Leibniz's law. As the passage shows, substitutivity would only universally apply, when the entities are the same and their name is the same. But only allowing substitution of the symbol Ø for Ø is no substitution at all!

The result is that we seem to be stuck with a plethora of *ultra-intensional* entities, one for each name; it looks as if we've created an oriental version of what Quine would call "Plato's beard."[20] If belief were taken as a relation between a person and a set of words, as in the Quine-Kaplan approach, then there

---

20. Cf. Quine (1953a). "Plato's beard" is the doctrine that all words — even words such as "the unicorn" — must refer to something, even if it only subsists rather than exists. The beard needs trimming, according to Quine, by a sharp Occam's razor.

would be no problem in denying that the name "Son of Śuddhodana," and the name "One of Solar Line" are not identical. (There might, of course, be other types of problems, such as those which Church has pointed out.) But it is clear that the Buddhist would be closer to a Frege-Church approach where belief is a relation with a non-verbal entity. However, whereas Fregean senses (or intensions) are individuated by analyticity, the entities which a Buddhist would postulate are even more intensional than those of Frege. For a Fregean "bachelor" and "unmarried man" would express the same sense (intension). But for a Buddhist, they would have different sense because the names are different. Hence, I will speak of the Buddhist entities as being "ultra-intensional."

rGyal-tshab-rje and also Dharmakīrti — as can be seen from the parenthetical remarks which Mookerjee and Nagasaki add to the above-quoted passage from the *svavṛtti* — ameliorate things a bit by saying that *gcig* and *tha dad* are *sāmānyalakṣaṇa,* and hence mentally created notions.[21] Thus, the distinction between product and impermanence is mentally created, and does not belong to the *svalakṣaṇa*. So if we say that we would only count *svalakṣaṇa* in our ontology, then *sāmānyalakṣaṇa*, such as the difference between product and impermanent, need not imply a bloated catalogue of what exists as real. A Quinean would, of course, reply that all we've done is to reintroduce a distinction between subsistence (a kind of semi-reality) and existence. And for Quine, subsistence is incomprehensible. Imagine a Quinean asking if he could quantify over ultra-intensions![22]

(8) (x)(x = the Son of Śuddhodana & $x \neq$ the One of Solar Line)

---

21. Cf. rGyal-tshab-rje, vol. 1, p. 110. *bsgrub bya sgrub byed sogs tha dad pa' i cha dań de dag gi rań ldog rtog pas btags par ston pa yin gyi . . . . . .*

22. Quine's dislike of intensions, those "creatures of darkness," is well known. cf. Quine (1960), chapter 6.

Unless we reinterpret "(x) (. . .)" to mean simply "for some *x*": rather than "there is an *x*: . . .," we are stuck with ultra-intensions. At any rate, I think such a reinterpretation of quantification would be inescapable; having *sāmānyalakṣaṇa* is not much different from allowing subsistence.

II. HOW CAN WORDS DESCRIBE SVALAKṢAṆA?

Even if rGyal-tshab-rje and Dharmakīrti can live in the ontological slum of *sāmānyalakṣaṇa*, how do they answer the sceptic who says, "Fine, all your words refer to only *sāmānyalakṣaṇa*, and can never describe reality (*svalakṣaṇa*)?" This is a legitimate objection, all the more so because the general thrust of Dharmakīrti's Yogācāra philosophy is, as B.K. Matilal puts it, a "a pan-fictional approach." Let me quote Matilal in full:[23]

> The Buddhist, in fact, would like to put all the objects over which our thoughts and other psychological activities may range at the same level; and this will include not only (a) things which do exist now (i.e. which are assumed to be existent by the common people or by the realist) but also (b) things which do not exist now (i.e. past and future things), (c) things which cannot exist (viz. the rabbit's horn) and also (d) things of which it would be a logical contradiction to say that they exist (viz. the son of a barren women). One point is common to all of these four groups, and this is that we can think about them and our mental activities can be directed toward all of them. In their theory of objects, the Buddhists were not interested in ontology or in the metaphysics of being. If this opens the door to idealism, it may be welcome to the Buddhist (because that would simply prove the Yogācāra point that objects are integral parts of, in fact, indistinguishable from, consciousness). Even without giving in to idealism, the Sautrāntika Buddhist may maintain this theory of objects with due modification while emphasizing that the *real* objects are only momentary point-instants which are beyond the range of ordinary experience.

23. Matilal (1970), p. 103.

As we shall see below, we can give a (somewhat) more precise picture of what these fictions are, at least of what they are in the Tibetan tradition: they turn out to be object-universals (*don spyi*). And Matilal would be correct in saying that all objects, existent, non-existent,[24] even impossible are on the same level. To everything, be it a vase or the barren woman's son, in short, to all items whatsoever, there corresponds an object-universal, and it is this, properly speaking, over which our thoughts and other psychological activities range. Although the item might be inconsistent, the object-universal corresponding to it is not, and this object-universal is always a *sāmānyalakṣaṇa*, a fiction and an ultra-intension.[25]

Phur-bu-lcog byams-pa rgya-mtsho defines the object-universal corresponding to a vase (*bum pa'i don spyi*) as : "a projected entity which appears, to the mind thinking about vases, as like a vase, but which is not in fact a vase."[26] The example (*mtshan* gźi) is: "what appears as non-non-vase to a mind thinking about vases" (*bum 'dzin rtog pa la bum pa ma yin pa las log par snaṅ ba*). A less literal, but perhaps more comprehensible, translation

24. Mimaki (1976) p. 60 shows that Indian authors held that even in cases of non-existent subjects, the words still refer to a "concept." In McDermott's (1969) edition and translation of Ratnakīrti's *Vyatirekātmikā* we find use of the word *ākāra* for this notion of a "concept." *Ākāra* seems very similar to a *don spyi*. cf. also note 32 below.

25. McDermott (1969 and 1970) uses Routley's R* (1966) to formalize Buddhist logic. She interprets the variables as ranging over *possible* objects from vases to rabbits' horns. Impossible items, such as the barren woman's son, lead to a danger of inconsistency and require a great deal of logical ingenuity to handle. cf. Routley, and Parsons (1974) for some attempts. However, if we follow rGyal-tshab-rje's lead, and let the variables range over *don spyi*, there is no problem in handling inconsistent items: although *mo śam gyi bu* (the barren woman's son) is inconsistent, *mo śam gyi bu ma yin pa las log par snaṅ ba* is not.

26. *bsdus grwa chuṅ*, p. 21a: *bum 'dzin rtog pa la bum pa ma yin bźin du bum pa lta bur snaṅ ba' i sgro btags kyi cha.*

would be "the image of non-non-vase appearing to the mind thinking about vases," and this might be an acceptable way of looking at the matter, except that it would have the possible disadvantage of making object-universals look like images in a mentalist theory of meaning; it is not at all clear if object-universals are subjective, mental images along the lines of Hume, or more impersonal, objective, entities, perhaps something like the pictures of the early Wittgenstein's theory of meaning. One piece of information which we do have, however, is that an object-universal is obviously a type of *apoha*, in particular, it is known as a "mental exclusion of the other" (*blo'i gźan sel*).[27]

Now the Buddhist holds that the object of a word (*śabdārtha, sgra don*)[28] — or in other synonymous terms, the direct basis (*dṅos rten*),[29] or the grasped object (*gzuṅ yul*) — is always such an object-universal. In this sense, the sceptic might seem justified in saying that *svalakṣaṇa* could never enter into the picture. rGyal-tshab-rje, interpreting Dharmakīrti, tries to avoid this problem by introducing the notion of an implied object (*brda'i źen yul*),

---

27. Cf. *bsdus grwa che ba*, p. 31b. There, the definition of *blo's gźan sel* is : "an other-exclusion which is a negation with implication (*paryudāsapratiṣedha*) and is projected by conceptualization." *ma yin dgag gi gźan sel kyaṅ yin rtog pas sgro btags kyaṅ yin pa' i gźi mthun pa.* Note that in the interest of readability I am not translating the *bsdus grwa* idiom of "common bases" (*gźi mthun*) literally. Cf. also n. 15. To say that something is a common basis between *A* and *B* simply means that it is both *A* and *B*.

28. Dharmakīrti, in *Pramāṇavārttika* III k. 287, makes the point that a *śabdārtha* is always a conceptual construction (rather than a *svalakṣana*, which is perceived by direct perception (*pratyakṣa*). *śabdārthagrāhī yad yatra taj jñānaṁ tatra kalpanā* I *śes gaṅ gaṅ la sgra don 'dzin / de ni de la rtog pa yin* I. "Wherever a [consciousness] grasps an object of a word, there, that consciousness is conceptual." cf. *lCaṅ skya grub mtha'*, Sautrāntika chapter, for a long discussion of *sgra don* and *rtog pa*.

29. The term is Tsoṅ-kha-pa's. cf. *dBu ma rgyan gyi zin bris*. In this work Tsoṅ-kha-pa reiterates a number of *Pramāṇavārttika* arguments (chapter I), also turning around the theme of referential opacity, to show that what words directly refer to are *don spyi*.

arguing that at least some of the object-universals can indirectly give information about *svalakṣaṇa*.[30] Obviously, the object-universal corresponding to the barren woman's son cannot convey such information, but the one corresponding to vase can. To take the vase example, the implied objects would be vase (*bum pa*) and non-non-vase (*bum pa ma yin pa las log pa*), the latter being termed an "exclusion of the other, which is a *svalakṣaṇa* object" (*don raṅ mtshan gyi gźan sel*).[31] (I might remark in passing that this distinction between two types of *apoha* — e.g. *bum pa ma yin pa las log par snaṅ ba* and *bum pa ma yin pa las log pa* — is extremely important in the Tibetan interpretation of *Pramāṇavārttika*,[32] and seems to get blurred when Western authors simply speak of words as referring to double negations.)[33]

---

30. rGyal-tshab-rje, vol. 1, p. 116.

31. *bsdus grwa che ba's* (p. 31b) definition of *don raṅ mtshan gyi gźan sel is* : "an other-exclusion which is a negation with implication, and which is also able to ultimately perform a function." *ma yin dgag gi gźan sel kyaṅ yin don dam par don byed nus pa yaṅ yin pa' i gźi mthun par dmigs pa.*

32. A-lag-śa Nag-dbaṅ bstan-dar (*Raṅ mtshan spyi mtshan rnam bźag*) and rGyal-tshab-rje argue that what is responsible for the notion of a universal, according to Dharmakīrti, is the *blo'i gźan sel*, the object-universal. In most cases, the *spyi* which exists only conventionally by mental creation (*bsam pa'i dbaṅ gis, abhiprāyavaśāt*, cf. *Svārthānumānapariccheda* k. 70) is, in fact, the *don spyi*. It is often similar for *ldog pa* (*vyāvṛtti*). *Don raṅ mtshan gyi gźan sel*, as its name implies, is a *svalakṣaṇa*, exists ultimately, and shares the properties of *svalakṣana* in being absolutely individual (*ṅo bo ma 'dres pa*), in one place at one time (*yul ma 'dres pa*), and temporally discrete (*dus ma'dres pa*). cf. rGyal-tshab-rje, p. 78. In Tillemans (1982), I have shown how the notion of *don spyi* or image (*ākāra*) is used by Tsoṅ-kha-pa and Kamalaśīla (*Madhyamakāloka*) to explain *Pramāṇavārttika* IV and *Pramāṇasamuccaya*'s "solution" to the problem of *āśrayāsiddha*, a problem which arises when one tries to prove that some would-be entity is, in fact, non-existent.

33. Herzberger (1975) does not make this distinction. While *blo'i gźan sel* does not imply ontological commitment, *don raṅ mtshan gyi gźan sel* (the simple double negation) does.

rGyal-tshab-rje's point is that words refer to *blo'i gźan sel,* and via these ultra-intensional proxies they can give information about *don raṅ mtshan gyi gźan sel.*[34] Naturally, the basic process

34. rGyal-tshab-rje's account begins on page 74, vol. 1, and is long and elaborate. For a more condensed explanation, cf. *lCaṅ skya grub mtha'* p. 113, where he is commenting on *Pramāṇavārttika* I, k. 40, an important *kārikā* in which Dharmakīrti shows that all entities (*bhāva, dṅos po*) are "distinguished from similar and dissimilar entities" (*svabhāvaparabhāvābhyāṁ yasmādyāvṛttibhāginaḥ, mthun dṅos gźan gyi dṅos dag las* ॥ *ldog pa la ni brten pa can* ।) and, hence, are *don raṅ mtshan gyi gźan sel.* lCaṅ-skya writes:

ldog pa de dag gi sgo nas sgra mi rtag pa lta
bu'i raṅ gi mtshan ñid dbyis phyin par rtogs pas
dgag sgrub kyi dṅos rten don dam par ma grub
kyaṅ de la brten nas don dam pa'i gnas lugs legs
par rtogs nus pa 'di ni tha sñad pa' i tshad ma
don dam pa' i gnas lugs rtogs pa'i rgyur 'gyur
tshul sogs lugs 'di dag gi bden gñis kyi rnam
dbye śes pa la med du mi ruṅ ba yin no ।

Cf. also pp. 100 and 104. It is interesting to note that on p. 111 lCaṅ-skya cites a passage from Śāntarakṣita which speaks of *blo'i* and *don raṅ mtshan gyi gźan sel,* a passage which, alas, I have not traced back to Śāntarakṣita, but which would show that these terms are also found in Indian texts.

As a final point, let me explain my use of the word "refer" here to express the Tibetan *brda sbyor ba,* "applying a symbol." It might be tempting to see the relationship between object-universals and *svalakṣaṇa* as being like Frege's sense and reference, rather than reference and indirect description. One might wish to say that words express *sāmānyalakṣaṇa* as their meanings, and via such *sāmānyalakṣaṇa* they refer to *svalakṣaṇa.* This is especially seductive in view of the fact that *artha* (*don*) may mean either "meaning" or "object." However, I think that it would be a misinterpretation, in that the point of Dharmakīrti's philosophy is that although one might think that the object of one's thought is a *svalakṣaṇa,* it in fact is not: *svalakṣaṇa*s are ineffable; the objects of our language and thought are universals, something which *svalakṣaṇa*s can never be. For Frege, by contrast, the objects of language (in non-opaque contexts) are ordinary things such as tables, chairs, planets, etc. and such things are not ineffable.

explaining as to how this occurs is *apoha*, a theory whose broad outlines have been resumed by Matilal as follows:[35]

> A word expresses a concept and a concept being a fiction cannot POSITIVELY qualify or characterize the particular (as a Nyāya realist believes), but it can NEGATIVELY disqualify the particular from being claimed by other fictions or concepts.

In rGyal-tshab-rje's elaboration of this basic idea, the essential points go something like this. (a) Each *svalakṣaṇa, A,* is at the same time a non-non-*A*, a *don raṅ mtshan gyi gźan sel.* (b) The object-universal corresponding to *A*, the *blo'i gźan sel,* is an appearance of non-non-*A*. (c) Thus, the former and the latter are related by a certain homomorphism: the former excludes all non-*A*s, and the latter excludes all *appearances* of non-*A*.[36] (d) This relation between *svalakṣaṇa* and its corresponding *sāmānyalakṣaṇa* is so close that the two are said to be indistinguishable to the user of language. rGyal-tshab-rje and other Tibetan authors use the word "mixed," (*dres pa*), a metaphor which, however, is fairly easily understood: one takes the *sāmānyalakṣaṇa* for the *svalakṣaṇa*, and is unaware that the object, which appears to the mind (*snaṅ yul*) is only an object-universal.[37] In short, there is a subjective indistinguish-ability, but one which is justified by a homomorphism of double negation.

---

35. Matilal (1971) pp. 44-45.

36. I use the word "homomorphism" because although the two have a similar structure with regard to double negation, there are other aspects in which they are not parallel. *bLo'i gźan sel,* for example, can "qualify" many distinct *svalakṣaṇa*s.

37. This is brought out often in rGyal-tshab-rje, and is summarized nicely by Phur-bu-lcog's definition of conceptual thought (*rtog ppa*): "a consciousness which grasps [its] object as fitting to be mixed with a word [that is, as a *śabdārtha* or *don spyi*]." *sgra don 'dres ruṅ tu 'dzin pa'i źen rig* (*blo-rigs* p. 19b). cf. also *lCaṅ skya grub mtha'*, chapter on Sautrāntika.

III. ANOTHER APPROACH TO GCIG AND THA DAD

Given the preceding discussion concerning object-universals, we are now somewhat better equipped to understand *gcig* and *tha dad*. As the example of product and impermanent would illustrate, the relation between *svalakṣaṇa* and corresponding *sāmānyalakṣaṇa* is not a one-to-one correspondence. After all, although the *svalakṣaṇa*, product = the *svalakṣaṇa*, impermanent, it is not so that for all x, x is an object-universal of product (*byas pa'i don spyi*) if, and only if, x is an object-universal of impermanent (*mi rtag pa' i don spyi*). The appearance of non-non-product is the former but *not* the latter. Thus, using the Western notion of identity,[38] we can say that the *svalakṣaṇa*s are identical (=), but the *sāmānyalakṣaṇa*s are different (≠), as are the words "product" and "impermanent." And here, then, may be the easiest way to understand the notions of *gcig* and *tha dad*. One translates them into our own Western notion of identity:

> *A* is *gcig* with *A* because the object-universal referred to by *A* = the object-universal referred to by *A*. *A* is *tha dad* with *B* because the object-universal referred to by *A* the object-universal referred to by *B*.

Appendix: Intensionality in Buddhist Logic

We have seen how a problem similar to that of referential opacity motivated Buddhist logicians to devise a pan-fictional and highly

---

38. The Tibetans *do* have a notion of identity similar to our own: it is termed *don gcig* (*ekārtha*, "same object"). Rationalizing Ṅag-dbaṅ ñi-ma's definition (p. 22) where he speaks of "mutually satisfying eight implications" (*phan tshun khyab pa bryad tshaṅ ba*), we can say:

    F is *don cig* with G = def. (x) (Fx *iff* Gx).

    In the *sKabs daṅ po spyi don* (p. 102b) we find mention of six types of identity and difference: (1) *rdzas gcig*, (2) *don gcig*, (3) *raṅ bźin gcig*, (4) *bdag ñid gcig*, (5) *ṅo bo gcig*, and (6) *ldog pa gcig*. In Tillemans (1981) I discussed (1), (3), (4), and (5). (6) is the notion of identity that Phur-bu-lcog means by *gcig*. Thus, the explanation of all six is finally nearing completion!

intensional theory of language. A side-result of this discussion is that we can now sketch out which types of statements in Buddhist logic (or, at least, Tibetan Buddhist logic) would unavoidably require an intensional interpretation to overcome failures of the law of substitutivity. By "unavoidably" I mean that while there are certainly large segments of Buddhist philosophy which can still be understood when one uses an ordinary extensional semantics, certain Buddhist notions just cannot be taken extensionally. It turns out that any notion which is defined by, or makes reference to, *gcig* or *tha dad*, or to opaque contexts such as ". . . knows that . . . ," or ". . . doubts that . . . , " will be of this sort. And this will include quite a lot. Here are some examples:

a. Logical language involving terms such as "subject" (*dharmin, chos can*), "property to be proved" (*sādhya dharma, bsgrub bya' i chos*), "reasons" (*hetu, gtan tshigs*), "examples" (*dṛṣṭānta, dpe*), etc.

b. The theory of defining marks (*lakṣaṇa, mtshan ñid*) and definienda (*lakṣya, mtshon bya*). In Tibetan logic texts one finds a theory of real, rather than nominal, definition; definitions and definienda are things, rather than just words.

c. The theory of relatedness (*sambandha, 'brel ba*). Although impermanent and product have a one-nature relation (*tādātmya, bdag gcig tu 'brel*), it is impossible to say that product has such a relation with product; the usual Tibetan definitions of relatedness specify that both relata must be *tha dad*.[39]

References

A-lag-śa Ṅag-dbaṅ bstan-dar, *Raṅ mtshan spyi mtshan gyi rnam gźag rtsom 'phro,* pp. 156-208 in volume *ka* of the *Collected gSung 'Bum of bsTan-dar Lha-ram of A-lag-sha.* Delhi: Lama Gurudeva, Delhi, 1971.

---

39. Ṅag-dbaṅ ñi-ma, p. 36.

lCaṅ-skya rol-pa'i rdo-rje, *Grub pa'i mtha' rnam par bźag pa gsal bar bśad pa thub bstan lhun po'i mdzes rgyan*. Sarnath: Pleasure of Elegant Sayings Press, 1970.

Dharmakīrti, *Pramāṇavārttika*, ed. D. Shastri, *Pramāṇavārtika of Ācārya Dharmakīrti*, with the commentary of Ācārya Manorathanandin. Bauddha Bharati Series, Varanasi: 1968. English translation of *kārikā* 1-51 of chapter 1 (*Svārthānumānapariccheda*) by S. Mookerjee and H. Nagasaki, *The Pramāṇavārttikaṁ of Dharmakīrti*, Patna: 1964. Tibetan translation: Peking *bstan 'gyur* 130, 5709 Ce 190a-250b.

Dharmakīrti, *Pramāṇavārttikasvavr̥tti*, Gnoli, Raniero, ed., *The Pramāṇavārttikaṁ of Dharmakīrti*, the first chapter with the auto-commentary. Roma: Instituto Italiano per Il Medio 5d Estremo Oriente, 1960. See also S. Mookerjee and H. Nagasaki (1964). Tibetan: Pek. 130, 5717 Ce 404b-535a.

rGyal-tshab-rje = rGyal-tshab dar-ma rin-chen, *rNam 'grel thar lam gsal byed*. 2 vols. Sarnath: Pleasure of Elegant Sayings Press, 1975.

Herzberger, Hans, "Double Negation in Buddhist Logic." *Journal of Indian Philosophy* 3 (1975) :3-16.

McDermott, A.C.S, *An Eleventh Century Buddhist Logic of "Exists," Ratnakīrti's Kṣaṇabhaṅgasiddhiḥ Vyatirekātmikā*, ed. with tr., introduction and notes. Dordrecht: D. Reidel Publishing Company, 1969.

———, "Empty Subject Terms in Late Buddhist Logic," *Journal of Indian Philosophy* 1 (1970): 22-29.

Matilal, B.K., "Reference and Existence in Nyāya and Buddhist Logic," *Journal of Indian Philosophy* 1 (1970): 83-110.

———, *Epistemology, Logic, and Grammar in Indian Philosophical Analysis*, The Hague: Mouton, 1971.

Mimaki, K., *La Rèfutation bouddhique de la permanence des choses* (*Sthirasiddhidūṣaṇa*) *et la preuve de la momentanéité des choses* (*Kṣaṇabhaṅgasiddhi*), Paris: 1976.

dGe-bśes Ṅag-dbaṅ ñi-ma, *bsDus grwa brjed tho*, Leiden 197? Photocopy in my possession. The text was handwritten by dGe-bśes ñi-ma during his stay at the University of Leiden. It provides a record of a large number of orally passed-on debates, sophism, and definitions used in dGe-lugs-pa monasteries, many of these debates, etc. not appearing in other *bsdus grwa* texts.

Se-ra Chos-kyi rgyal-mtshan, *sKabs daṅ po'i spyi don = bsTan bcos mṅon par rtogs pa'i rgyan 'grel pa daṅ bcas pa'i rnam bśad rnam pa gñis kyi dka' ba' i gnad gsal bar byed pa legs bśad skal bzaṅ klu dbyaṅs gi rol mtsho źes bya ba las skabs daṅ *po'i spyi don.* Blockprint, textbook (*yig cha*) of Se-ra byes monastery, Bylakuppe, Karnataka, India 1977.

Tillemans, Tom, "The 'Neither One nor Many' Argument for *Śūnyatā* and Its Tibetan Interpretations," to appear in the *Proceedings of the Csoma de körös Symposium, Velm,* 1981 in the series *Wiener Studien zur Tibetologie und Buddhismuskunde*, Vienna, 1981.

———, "The 'Neither One nor Many' Argument for *Śūnyatā* and Its Tibetan Interpretations: Background Information and Source Materials," *òtudes de Lettres* no. 3, University of Lausanne, 1982, pp. 103-28.

Tsoṅ-kha-pa, *dBu ma rgyan gyi zin bris.* Sarnath: Pleasure of Elegant Sayings Press, 1976.

Yoṅs-'dzin Phur-bu-lcog byams-pa tshul-khrims rgya-mtsho, *bsdus grwa = Tshad ma'i gźuṅ 'byed pa'i bsdus grwa'i rnam bźag rigs lam 'phrul gyi lde'u mig* (3 vols : *chuṅ, 'briṅ, che ba*). Blockprint, Tashi Jong, H.P., India 1977 ?

———, rtags rigs = *Tshad ma'i gźun don 'byed pa'i bsdus grwa'i rnam par bśad pa rigs lam phrul gyi lde'u mig las rigs lam che ba rtags rigs kyi skor.* Blockprint of Se-ra byes monastery, 1978.

———, blo rigs = *Tshad ma'i gźuṅ don 'byed pa' i bsdus grwa' i rnam bźag rigs lam 'phrul gyi lde'u mig ces bya las rigs lam che ba yul can daṅ blo rigs gi rnam par bśad pa.* Blockprint of Se-ra byes monastery, 1978.

MODERN LOGIC

Carnap, Rudolf, *Meaning and Necessity, A Study in Semantics and Model Logic,* 2nd edn., enl. Chicago: University of Chicago Press, 1956.

Church, Alonzo, "On Carnap's Analysis of Statements of Assertion and Belief," *Analysis* 10, 5 (1950): 97-99. Reprinted in Linsky (1971), pp. 168-70.

———, "A Formulation of the Logic of Sense and Denotation." In *Structure, Method, and Meaning : Essays in Honor of Henry M. Sheffer,* ed. Paul Henle, et al., New York : Liberal Arts Press, 1951, pp. 3-24.

Frege, Gottlob, "Über Sinn und Bedeutung," First published in *Zeitschrift fòr Philosophie und Philosophische Kritik* 100 (1892): 25-50. English translation: "On Sense and Reference," in *Translations from the Philosophical Writings of Gottlob Frege,* P. Geach and M. Black. Oxford: Blackwell, 1960.

Hintikka, J, "Individuals, Possible Worlds, and Epistemic Logic," *Nous* 1 (1967): 33-62.

———, "Semantics for Propositional Attitudes," In *Philosophical Logic,* ed. J.W. Davis, et al., Dordrecht: D. Reidel Publishing Company, 1969. Reprinted in Linsky (1971), pp. 145-67.

Kaplan, David, " Quantifying In," in *Words and Objections: Essays on the Work of W. V. Quine*, ed. D. Davidson and J. Hintikka, Dordrecht: D. Reidel Publishing Company, 1969, pp. 178-214. Reprinted in Linsky (1971), pp. 112-44.

Linsky, Leonard (ed.), *Reference and Modality*, Oxford: Oxford University Press, 1971.

Marcus, R.B, "Interpreting Quantification," *Inquiry* 5 (1962): 252-59.

Parsons, T., "A Prolegomenon to Meinongian Semantics." *Journal of Philosophy* 61, no. 1 (1974): 561-79.

Quine, W.V., "On What There Is," In *From a Logical Point of View*. Cambridge: Harvard University Press, 1953.

———, "Reference and Modality," in *From a Logical Point of View*. Reprinted in Linsky (1971), pp. 17-35.

———, "Quantifiers and Propositional Attitudes," *Journal of Philosophy* 53 (1956). Reprinted in Linsky (1971), pp. 101-11.

———, *Word and Object*, New York: Wiley and Sons, 1960.

Routley, R., "Some Things Do not Exist," *Notre Dame Journal of Formal Logic* 7, no. 3 (1966): 251-76.

Stine, G.C., "Intentional Inexistence," *Journal of Philosophical Logic* 5 (1976): 491-510.

14

Does the Mādhyamika Have a Thesis and Philosophical Position?[1]

D. Seyfort Ruegg

NĀGĀRJUNA is recognized as the founder of the Madhyamaka School of Philosophy, the chief *śāstra* source of which are his *Mūlamadhyamakakārikās*, otherwise known as the *Madhyamakaśāstra* or *Prajñāmūla*.

In a work closely related in its doctrine to these *Madhyamakakārikās* and entitled *Vigrahavyāvartanī* — Rejection of Conflict — Nāgārjuna has made what are, for a philosopher, a series of striking statements that have caused perplexity among his followers, the Mādhyamikas, as well as among modern interpreters of his philosophy. Thus we read in the *Vigrahavyāvartanī* (verse 29): "If I had some *pratijñā* (thesis) [this]

---

1. This paper is a summary of points of philosophical interest to which attention has been called in another article of a more historical and philological nature in *Contributions on Tibetan and Buddhist Religion and Philosophy,* edited by E. Steinkellner and H. Tauscher (Vienna, (1983) pp. 205-41.

   On the literary sources mentioned below see our *Literature of the Madhyamaka School of Philosophy in India History of Indian Literature,* vol. VII/1 (Wiesbaden: Otto Harrassowitz, 1981). And for the chronology see also our article "Towards a Chronology of the Madhyamaka School," in *Indological and Buddhist Studies: Volume in Honor of Professor J.W. de Jong on His Sixtieth Birthday,* ed. L.A. Hercus et al. (Canberra: [Australian National University], Faculty of Asian Studies, 1981), pp. 505-30.

defect [mentioned by an opponent] would as a consequence attach to me, but I have no *pratijñā* so there is no defect for me." This is Nāgārjuna's reply to the objection, set out in verse 4, that the Mādhyamika's statement "All entities (*bhāva*) are empty (*śūnya*) [of self-nature (*svabhāva*)]" is a defective assertion or thesis (*pratijñā*). In addition, as Nāgārjuna's opponent is represented as having argued in verse 1 of the *Vigrahavyāvartanī:* "If [as you maintain] no self-nature (*svabhāva*) exists for all entities (*bhāva*), then your [own] statement (*vacana*) [that all *bhāva*s are empty of self-nature, which is therefore itself] also without self-nature, cannot controvert self-nature [which I maintain]."

Moreover, Nāgārjuna explains, since according to Madhyamaka Philosophy all *bhāva*s are empty of *svabhāva*, any criticism levelled against the Madhyamaka by an opponent will inevitably relate to something not asserted as a thesis in the Madhyamaka (*VV* 59). In his autocommentary on verse 64 Nāgārjuna then points out that the statement "All *bhāva*s are without self-nature (*niḥsvabhāva*)" is not supposed by the Mādhyamika to make *bhāva*s non-substantial and hence empty (*śūnya*); rather, it simply makes known what *bhāva*s really are, namely non-substantial and empty.

Concerning negation (*pratiṣedha*) Nāgārjuna says (*VV* 63): "I negate no thing and there exists no thing to be negated: by saying that I negate [some thing] you therefore make a [false] imputation (*adhilaya*)." And in verse 23 he describes the nature of Madhyamaka negation.

In the final analysis, then, the Madhyamaka theory of *niḥsvabhāvatā* and *śūnyatā*, based on the fact that things arise in dependent conditionship, is not open to criticism and rebuttal (see for example *MMK* iv.8-9 and xxiv.13). This is because the Madhyamaka is not a constructive speculative doctrine made up of a system of propositions that presuppose the existence of entities in the frame of binary conceptualization (*vikalpa*) and the quaternary set of conceivable positions (*catuṣkoṭi*).

Nāgārjuna's disciple Āryadeva mentions in his *Catuḥśataka* the Mādhyamika's disowning of any position with respect to the three extremes of existence, non-existence and both existence and non-existence of a thing, saying (xvi.25): "It is not at all possible to level criticism (*upālambha*) against one who has no position (*pakṣa*) positing [something] existent (*sat*), non-existent (*asat*) and both existent and non-existent (*sadasat*)." And in another passage of his *Catuḥśataka* (viii.20) Āryadeva explains that if, on occasion, the Buddha has spoken in terms of the four positions — viz. the three just mentioned and the "neither . . . nor" position that relates to an undefinable entity— this is simply because he employs them in particular cases as counteragents or remedies against specific misapprehensions.

Āryadeva's statements on this subject are explications of Nāgārjuna's own which are to be found in *MMK* xviii.6 and 8, for example. The *Ratnāvalī* (ii.15) also mentions the Buddha's having eschewed any determination in terms of the *catuṣprakāra* based on the pairs *śānta/ananta* and *dvaya/advaya*. And in the *Acintyastava* (verse 23), a hymn ascribed to Nāgārjuna, the Buddha is praised as having stated that *dharma*s are free from the four conceivable positions of the tetralemma (*catuṣkoṭi-virnirmukta*), unknowable for discursive cognition (*vijñāna*) and not with the scope of words.[2]

The Mādhyamika's rejection of theses, assertions and speculative views about a *bhāva* or a *dharma* possessing a self-nature stems basically from three considerations:

(i) An assertion and proposition — either one stated positively or one that includes negation of the presuppositional and implicative type (*paryudāsapratiṣedha*) — gives rise, in the binary structure of conceptual thinking where the principle of bivalence operates, to a counter-assertion and counter-proposition. (See, e.g.,

2. On the *catuṣkoṭi* or "tetralemma" see our article in *Journal of Indian Philosophy* 5 (1977): 1-71.

MMK xiii.7 on *śūnya* as the counterpart and contraplete of *aśūnya*; *MMK* xviii.6 on *ātman* as opposed to *anātman* [cf. *Ratnāvalī* ii.3], and xviii.8 on the four positions *tathya*, etc.) The idea has been summed up in Nāgārjuna's *Yuktiṣaṣṭikā* (verse 51cd)" How could there be another's [counter-] position for those who have no position," and in the *Ratnāvalī* (ii.4) "What is seen, heard and so forth is said by the Sage [i.e. the Buddha] to be neither true nor false: from a position (*pakṣa*) [holding something to be either true or false] a counter-position (*pratipakṣa* = *mi mthun phyogs*) may proceed, but neither [holds] in fact." (See also *Ratnāvalī* i.72.)

(ii) Any such assertion or proposition tends to involve its proponents in strife (*vivāda*) and vain conflict; and this is not compatible with the ideal of strifelessness and eirenicism set forth in both Sūtras and Śāstras. (See, e.g. *Yuktiṣaṣṭikā* 47 and 51; Āryadeva, *Catuḥśataka* viii.10 [cf. xii.15, and Candrakīrti, *Mādhyamakāvatāra* vi.118].) The Mādhyamika's employment of deconstructive *prasaṅga*-type reasoning (whereby a disputant is brought to understand the impossibility or absurdity of his theses and views) also corresponds to this ideal of strifelessness, for which reason also it is preferable to formal refutation which is, in addition, undesirable since it inevitably gives rise to counter-assertions and counter-refutations as noted under (i) above. (In the case of (i) the issues are essentially logical, ontological and gnoseological, while in (ii) they are ethical as well as psychological and soteriological. It is to be noted that both these points are not exclusive to the Madhyamaka school, and that they have been alluded to, or at least anticipated, in texts of the old canon such as the *Dīghanikāya*, the *Saṁyuttanikāya* and, especially, the *Suttanipāta* of the Pāli canon.)

(iii) On the level of ultimate reality (*paramārtha*) — as distinct from transactional usage (*vyavahāra*) and the surface level of *saṁvṛtti* — the Mādhyamikas (like other Mahāyānists) have recognized that only the silence of the Ārya is in the final analysis appropriate. The absence of a *pratijñā* and a *pakṣa* is thus, in a certain sense, the methodological corollary of this silence.

Now these and many other similar statements by Nāgārjuna and his Mādhyamika followers appear to have given credence to the idea that a true Mādhyamika must disown all theses and philosophical theories without exception, and even that Mādhyamaka philosophy has been developed in a way calculated to make it immune to criticism and refutation. And this could lead to the charge that the Mādhyamikas have adopted an anti-rational and anti-philosophical stance, or one of philosophical indifferentism; and that, in all their extensive philosophical works devoted to explicating the *niḥsvabhāvatā* and *śūnyatā* of *dharma*s because of the principle of dependent conditionship (*pratītyasamutpāda*) — which they indeed consider to be the authentic teaching of the Buddha — the Mādhyāmikas have, at the same time, been inconsistent and unfaithful to their own principle of not entertaining any thesis or philosophical theory.

In the face of such objections against Madhyamaka thought and the Mādhyamika's procedures it will be worthwhile to examine more closely the logical and semantic implications of Nāgārjuna's statement. "I have no *pratijña*," and to enquire in particular whether this statement really implies that the Madhyamaka has no place for a thesis or philosophical theory.

Taken in the context of the objections voiced in the first part of the *Vigrahavyāvartanī* as well as of other statements in this work and elsewhere in the literature of the Madhyamaka, it seems clear that when Nāgārjuna says "I have no *pratijñā*" he means that he asserts no thesis or proposition positing the existence of a *bhāva* (positive, negative, both positive and negative, or indescribable).It does not imply, however, that he has nothing of philosophical significance to say himself, nor that he denies all philosophical content to the Sūtra teachings which he proposes to explicate. And least of all is Nāgārjuna a mere quibbler or sophist trying to escape philosophical problems and difficulties.

That a *pratijñā* "thesis" and a *pakṣa* "position" are not always, and necessarily, avoided and rejected by the true Mādhyamika is shown by Candrakīrti's usage in his commentary on the *Madhyamakakārikās*, the *Prasannapadā*.

Thus, in Candrakīrti's commentary on *MMK* i.1. — "Nowhere are any entities whatever ever produced from self, an other, both and from no cause" — Nāgārjuna's four points are explicitly described as *pratijñās* (p. 13.3). Nāgārjuna's two points in *MMK* viii.1 — "A real agent does not effect a real action, nor does an unreal agent bring about an unreal action" — are also described by Candrakīrti as *pratijñās* (p. 181.1-2). And in commenting on *MMK* xxi.2 — "How indeed without coming into existence (*sambhava*) will there be destruction (*vibhava*), [for then] without birth precisely [there would be] death; there is [then] no destruction without birth" — Candrakīrti identifies a *pratijñā* in addition to a *nigamana* "conclusion" and a *pra-saṅgāpādana "reductio ad absurdum."* Candrakīrti speaks moreover of the position (*pakṣa*) of the Mādhyamikas in the *avataraṇikā* to xxiv.15 (p. 501.10). In none of these cases, of course, is a thesis postulating the existence of any kind of *bhāva* or *dharma* possessing a *svabhāva* being asserted by Nāgārjuna and Candrakīrti.

It thus appears that not only a (Svātantrika) Mādhyamika like Bhāvaviveka (sixth century) — who employs constructive, independent inferences (*svatantrānumāna*) and "syllogisms" (*svatantraprayogavākya*) to establish Madhyamaka doctrine — but also a (Prāsaṅgika) Mādhyamika like Candrakīrti (seventh century) — who has rejected the use of such constructive, independent inferences and "syllogisms" and has confined himself to a kind of deconstructive reasoning that brings a disputant to recognize the impossibility or absurdity of his theses and views (*prasaṅga*) — has allowed a place in Madhyamaka thought to both a *pratijñā* and a *pakṣa* in specific senses of these terms.

What the Mādhyamika has disowned, then, is any thesis, assertion or view (*dṛṣṭi*) that posits the existence of some kind of *bhāva* or *dharma* possessing a *svabhāva,* and not all philosophical statements, doctrines and theories (*darśana*) without distinction.

There does, however, exist a tension between two currents of thought within the Madhyamaka school concerning the question whether a true Mādhyamika may legitimately entertain a thesis and philosophical theory. And since this point has not been fully elucidated in our Indian sources, we have now to turn for a more complete treatment of the problem to the Tibetan sources, where it has been discussed in considerable detail.

Several Tibetan masters — evidently following some Indian teachers who introduced them to Madhyamaka thought — considered that, in the authentic (*prāsaṅgika*) Madhyamaka, there is place neither for a thesis (*dam bca'* = *pratijñā*) nor, more generally, for a philosophical tenet (*khas len* = *abhyupagama*) or theory (*lta ba* = *darśana*). This interpretation of Nāgārjuna's, Āryadeva's and Candrakīrti's writings has, however, been subjected to searching analysis and penetrating criticism by Tsoṅ-kha-pa (1357-1419), in whose *Lam rim chen mo* it is recorded as a *pūrvapakṣa* which is then rejected.

Tsoṅ-kha-pa has, moreover, sought to show in his *Draṅ ṅes legs bšad sñiṅ po* that the Prāsaṅgika-Mādhyamika not only employs a logical reason and inference to negate the substantial self-nature of *bhāvas,* but that he employes them also to establish the non-substantiality and *śūnyatā* of *dharmas*. In fact, for the comprehension of non-substantiality and *śūnyatā,* we require a positive determination (*pariccheda*) of negation (i.e. *niḥsvabhāvatā*) alongside the negative determination (*vyavaccheda*) of the negandum (i.e. *svabhāva*), these two aspects of negation arising inseparably in the conscious stream of the philosopher-exercitant in the process of comprehending reality. Tsoṅ-kha-pa in this way combined Madhyamaka philosophy with the current of logico-epistemological thought descending from Dharmakīrti (in, whose *Hetubindu* the correlation between *pariccheda* and *vyavaccheda* is brought out in the discussion of the *anupalabdhihetu*). Tsoṅ-kha-pa has thus sought to demonstrate that Candrakīrti's Prāsaṅgika-Madhyamaka does not differ from Bhāvaviveka's Svātantrika-Mādhyamaka by not entertaining a *pratijñā,* an *abhyupagama* and a *darśana,* as had been mistakenly supposed by many of his predecessors and contemporaries.

Tsoṅ-kha-pa's disciple mKhas grub dGe legs dpal bzaṅ (po) (1385-1438) has devoted an important section of his *sToṅ thun chen mo* — an exposition of the topics treated in his teacher's *Draṅ hes legs bšad sñiṅ po* — to the problem as to whether the Mādhyamika may legitimately entertain a thesis, a tenet and a philosophical theory. In doing this he has largely followed Tsoṅ-kha-pa's *Lam rim chen mo,* but adding some points of considerable interest drawn from other works by Tsoṅ-kha-pa and from other sources.

According to mKhas grub rje, the Mādhyamika's refraining from asserting a thesis or philosophical tenet is not to be interpreted (i) as a total rejection of all philosophical and ethical praxis, nor of all philosophical positions in surface-level pragmatic usage, (ii) Nor, on the contrary, is this rejection to be understood as a quasi-thesis, which would amount in effect to position IV of the *catuṣkoṭi* where an indeterminate or undefinable entity x is posited and defined as being without the predicates A and $\bar{A}$ (either in a logic which is not two-valued and based on the principle of bivalence, or in some putative "logic of mysticism" postulating an ineffable entity), (iii) The disowning of a thesis, assertion and tenet cannot, moreover, represent the essential philosophical and ethical outlook of the Prāsaṅgika-

Mādhyamika as one who — in contradistinction to the Svātantrika — would entertain no philosophical position of any kind whatever. For, according to mKhas grub rje and his school, whereas the Prāsaṅgika does indeed differ from the Svātantrika by not employing an independent inference let alone a full, independent "syllogism" to establish the theory (*ita ba*) and understanding (*rtogs pa*) of the Madhyamaka, he nevertheless does have a philosophical theory — the *śūnyatādarśana* and *niḥsvabhāvavāda* — which he upholds both by means of philosophical investigation and by *prasaṅga*-type reasoning which deconstructs and dissolves any thesis or assertion positing a *bhāva* of any kind. The difference between the Prāsaṅgika and the Svātantrika cannot, therefore, lie in the latter's having a philosophical position while the former does not, contrary to what had been supposed by several authorities.

For Tsoṅ-kha-pa and his school the question whether the Mādhyamika entertains a *pratijñā,* a tenet and a theory is accordingly not mainly a logical and methodological problem. It has acquired an epistemological — or rather gnoseological — significance which is of fundamental importance for the Mādhyamika.

Given the two distinct uses of the word *pratijñā* identified above in Candrakīrti's *Prasannapadā,* Nāgārjuna's statement "I have no *pratijñā*" may be interpreted in accordance with the more specific meaning "thesis/assertion positing an entity" rather than in accordance with the wider meaning of philosophical thesis (doctrine or position). And it is then possible to understand it as a metaphilosophical statement by which Nāgārjuna stipulated that none of the Madhyamaka doctrines is to be taken as asserting the substantial existence of an entity. The Madhyamaka philosophy is rather a non-speculative and non-constructive discourse relating to non-substantial factors (*dharma*) originating in the structured conditionship of *pratītyasamutpāda.*

Regarding the second question raised above as to whether the notion that the Madhyamaka statements are proof against attack and refutation is anti-rational and anti-philosophical, it is to be observed that the Mādhyamikas have evidently not set out deliberately to develop a theory, and to frame their statements, in a manner calculated to make them immune to objections and refutations. Their unassailability is rather a corollary of the theory of *śūnyatā,* which does not posit *bhāva*s or *dharma*s possessing a *svabhāva* and therefore does not make assertions or propositions referring to such entities, and also of the Mādhyamika's method of deconstructive *prasaṅga*-type reasoning in which assertions and propositions are neutralized ontologically (since they do not refer to substantial entities) and logically (since they do not give rise to counter-assertions and counter-propositions). This particular kind of unfalsifi-ability cannot, then, substantiate the charge that the Mādhyamika avoids rational thinking and takes up a stance of philosophical indifferentism or facile agnosticism.

In sum, the Mādhyamika's approach to the question of the *pratijñā* and *pakṣa* stems from his rejection of epistemic commitment to any proposition — positive or negative — that presupposes the existence of a *bhāva* or *dharma* possessing a *svabhāva* and posits such an entity in terms of the binary structure of *vikalpa* and the quaternary structure of the *catuṣkoṭi.*

Some recent work in semantics, logic and speech-act theory can perhaps help to cast light on our problem. In the second volume of his book *Semantics,* John Lyons has proposed distinguishing the three components in a categorical statement or assertion: (i) the propositional content or phrastic component, (ii) the modal or it-is-so tropic component, and (iii) the performative I-say-so neustic component or sign of subscription, the last two components being classified in speech-act theory as illocutionary. Negation in its turn may then relate to any of these three components, so that the semiotician and logician will take into account (at least) three distinct kinds of negation: (i) propositional, i.e. negation of the phrastic, (ii) modal, i.e. negation of the tropic, and (iii) performative, i.e. negation of the neustic. Here the first kind of negation corresponds to what is termed internal negation, and the last two are kinds of external negation.[3]

Now it seems especially appropriate to consider the statement "I have no *pratijñā*" in the light of the concept of performative negation. Such an interpretation will indeed fit in well with the Madhyamaka school's concern with philosophical pragmatics and transactional usage (*vyavahāra*). This approach to the question is also pertinent to the ethical aspect of the Mādhyamika's eirenic refraining from taking up contentious positions and eschewing vain conflict.

It has, at the same time, to be recognized that in the middle period of its history[4] the Madhyamaka school's concern with the pragmatics of transactional usage became overshadowed by the more specifically logical and epistemological problems into which the Mādhyamika was obliged to enter in the course of his exchanges with other schools of philosophy, and that from the time of Bhāvaviveka (sixth century) in particular Madhyamaka philosophy was deflected from a consideration of pragmatics towards a preoccupation with the proposition and the logical problems arising from the Svātantrika Mādhyamika's

3. See J. Lyons, *Semantics*, vol. 2 (New York: Cambridge University Press, 1977), pp. 749 f., 768 f., and 802 f. In addition to concepts developed by Austin, Searle and others, who have developed speech-act philosophy, Lyons makes use of ideas and terms used by R. M. Hare in his article "Meaning and Speech Acts"in *Philosophical Review* 79 (1970), reprinted in his book *Practical Inferences* (Berkeley: University of California Press, 1972), pp. 74-93, where the tropic is defined as the sign of mood and the neustic as the sign of subscription.

4. For this periodization of the Madhyamaka school, see *Literature of the Madhyamaka School of Philosophy in India*, p. 58 ff.

use of constructive, independent inferences and "syllogisms" in the understanding of reality. And the question of the *pratijñā* and the *pakṣa* then tended to be treated above all in terms of the thesis in an *anumāna* or *prayogavākya,* rather than in the broader context of statements and speech-acts.

The historian of the Madhyamaka — and of Indian and Buddhist philosophy in general — has besides to beware of anachronistically transposing and unsystematically imposing the concepts of modern semantics and philosophy, which have originated in the course of particular historical developments, on modes of thought that evolved in quite different historical circumstances, and which have therefore to be interpreted in the first place in the context of their own concerns and the ideas they themselves developed. Still, in studying Indian and Tibetan thought, the importance of religious and philosophical praxis deserves attention. Recent work in semiology and pragmatics may then provide us if not with precise parallels at least with useful heuristic instruments, and serve as an aid in explicating what the Mādhyamikas have had to say on the *pratijñā* and related topics.

Abbreviations

MMK *Mūla-Madhyamakakārikas* by Nāgārjuna, ed. together with the *Prasannapadā Madhyamakavr̥ttiḥ* by L. de La Vallée Poussin, Bibliotheca Buddhica IV (St. Petersburg, 1903-13); verses alone ed. J.W. de Jong (Adyar, 1977).

VV *Vigrahavyāvartanī* by Nāgārjuna, ed. together with the author's own commentary by E.H. Johnston and A. Kunst, *Melanges chinois et bouddhiqes* 9 (1948-51): 99-152.

15

Bhavya's Critique of Yogācāra in the Madhyamakaratnapradīpa

Christian Lindtner

1. THE purpose of this paper is to draw attention to Bhavya's (*c.* 500-570) critique of Yogācāra, the rival school of Madhyamaka, as it is presented in his (*Madhyamaka-*) *Ratnapradīpa* (*MRP*), chapter IV, entitled *Neyārthatathyasaṁvṛttiprajñā*. I believe that this generally neglected work of one of the most remarkable Buddhist thinkers will prove to be of great interest from a historical as well as philosophical point of view.[1]

---

1. I have argued for the authenticity of *Madhyamakaratnapradīpa* in *Wiener Zeitschrift fòr die Kunde Sòdasiens, 26* (1982):172-84, q.v. A survey of its contents may be found in my paper "On Bhavya's *Madhyamakaratnapradīpa*" to appear in *Indologica Taurinensia,* 12. Recently my esteemed colleague Professor D. Seyfort Ruegg (*The Literature of the Madhyamaka School of Philosophy in India,* Wiesbaden: Otto Harrassowitz, 1981, pp. 66 and 71) has claimed that I should have disregarded the reference to Dharmakīrti given in *MRP*. That, however, is not the case, as Professor Seyfort Ruegg himself has pointed out even more recently in his useful paper "Towards a Chronology of the Madhyamaka School" in L.A. Hercus et al. (eds.), *Indological and Buddhist Studies, Volume in Honour of Professor J.W. de Jong on his Sixtieth Birthday,* Canberra: Faculty of Asian Studies, 1982, p. 530. In this paper Professor D. Seyfort Ruegg (p. 513) seems inclined to ascribe *MRP* to "a second Bhavya who lived later than the middle of the seventh century" on the grounds that "it refers to Vajrayānist ideas and to the *Vidyādharapiṭaka*" (ibid., p. 525, n. 29). But this is no argument against its authenticity because similar features are already to be found in Bhavya's earlier work *Tarkajvālā* (e.g. 199b2 →

Preliminarily, however, I shall briefly have to deal with two decisive circumstances which must be kept in mind when one endeavours to understand this chapter by considering it within the broader framework of his work and thus trace his thought in its genesis, namely its relationship to the Yogācāra chapters in his other extant works and its own position within the *MRP* as a whole.

2. First, then, I shall offer a summary of descriptive analysis of Bhavya's controversy with Yogācāra as found in his other extant major works, viz. *Madhyamakahṛdayakārikā* (*MHK*)[2] (with the auto-commentary *Tarkajvālā* (*TJ*)), *Karatalaratna* (*KTR*) (Zhǎng-zhēn lù n)[3] and *Prajñāpradīpa* (*PP*)[4] (commentary on *Mūlamadhyamakakārikā*), all of which were most likely composed earlier than *MRP* and in the light of which it must be studied to be properly assessed.

I. Yogācāratattvaviniścaya (Mhk, V, 1-113)

I. 1-7: Introduction. The basic tenets of Yogācāra according to Asaṅga, Vasubandhu, etc.: Their idea that *tattva* (*tathatā*, *paramārtha*,

---

→ seq.). To be quite precise *MRP* does not refer to the *Vidyādharapiṭaka* either, but it might in fact have done so as it often refers to Candrakīrti's *Triśaraṇasaptati* in which this *piṭaka* is mentioned (58). Hence I see no reason for *pratijñāhāni*.

2. The Sanskrit text will be published in the near future. Until then one may refer to the Tibetan version (based on *P* and *D*) ed. by S. Yamaguchi, *Bukkyo ni okeru Mu to U no Tairon*, Tōkyō 1941/1964. In the summary of *MHK*, V that follows I have retained Yamaguchi's numbering of the verses though the text actually consists of 114 (not 113) verses. Please refer to our forthcoming edition of *MHK* and *TJ*, V.

3. Only extant in Chinese, see *Taishō daizōdkyō*, XXX, 1578. For a French translation by Louis de La Vallée Poussin and a "retranslation" into Sanskrit by N. Aiyaswami Sastri see the reference in S. Iida, *Reason and Emptiness: A Study in Logic and Mysticism*, (Tōkyō: 1980), p. 18.

4. The Tibetan version of the appendix to *Nirvāṇaparīkṣā* of *PP*, XXV has appeared in the Csoma de Körös Memorial Volume (Budapest: 1984). The English version by Dr. David Eckel in my *Indiske Studier* (Copenhagen: 1985).

etc.) as *grāhyagrāhakābhāva* is a real *viṣaya* of *nirvikalpabuddhi* (1-3). On *ālayavijñāna*, the *svacittadharmatā*, where, by *āśrayaparāvṛtti*, no *ālambana* outside *citta* is perceived (4). This is *vijñaptimātratā* and should be penetrated gradually through *svabhāvatraya* (i.e. *parikalpita-*, *paratantra-*, and *pariniṣpannasvabhāva*) incorporated in the *ālayavijñāna* so as to achieve *sarva-jñātā* (5-7).[5]

II. 8-9: Bhavya's basic orthodox attitude. All the *āgamas* of Tathāgata provide us with valid *pramāṇa*. They should be supported by *yukti* so as to refute the misunderstandings, or misinterpretations, of others, *in casu* Yogācāra (8-9).[6]

III. 10-16: Refutation of the notion of *pariniṣpannasvabhāva* conceived as *dvayābhāvabhāva* (cf. *Madhyāntavibhāga*, I, 13), or as *abhāva* of *parikalpitasvabhāva* in *paratantrasvabhāva* (cf. *Triṁśikā*, 20-21) (10-11), or as *bhāva* not abandoning *dvayābhāva* (12-13), or as an *ālambana* of *nirvi-kalpabuddhi* (14-16). Refutation of various attempts to establish the *pratijñā*, based on the dictum that *traidhā-tuka* is *cittamātra*, in the sense that there is no *bāhyārtha*. Not only is the *pratijñā* in conflict with *abhyupagata* and *prasiddha*, but the *dṛṣṭānta*, viz. *svapnavat*, is also mistaken. Moreover, *viṣayāpavāda* accrues (17-19). Refutation of attempts to maintain that *vijñāna* is *dvyābhāsa* (i.e. appears as itself and as *viṣaya*). The adherents of this branch of Yogācāra (*sākāravāda*) claim that it is like the *svacchasphaṭika* appearing as *nīlādi* (cf. *Saṁdhinirmocanasūtra*, VI, 8-9) (20-22), or like *rūpa* and its *pratibimba* (23), or regard it as *pramāṇa* and its *phala* (cf. *Pramāṇasamuccaya*, I, 8-9) (24-26). Others, misinterpreting the *āgama* (*Daśabhūmikasūtra*, VI), conceive the "external" *artha* as having *cittarūpa*, just because it is *vijñānaviṣaya* (27-28), or because *vijñāna* is supposed to be *arthaśūnya*, which is absurd (29-30). A summary and refutation of the arguments to this effect found in Diṅnāga's *Ālambanaparīkṣā*

---

5. Note that v. 4 is a quotation from *Madhyāntavibhāgakārikā*, I, 6 and that v. 6 is from Asaṅga's *Vikhyāpana* (only Chinese: Xiǎn-yáng-shèng-jiào — lùn). Both quotations are also given in the *PP*, q.v.

6. On these two verses in particular, cf. S. Iida, "Āgama (Scripture) and Yukti (Reason) in Bhavaviveka," in *Kanakura Kinenrodbunshū*, Tōkyō 1966, pp. 79-96.

(31-38).[7] On the assumption that there has never been an external *viṣaya* it is impossible to subdue the *vijñānabīja*, or *grāhyagrāhaka*, and thus achieve a *nirvikalpabuddhi* of *mokṣa* (*advaya-pariniṣpannasvabhāva*) (39-43). Moreover, *cittamātra* cannot be supported by claiming that the *caittas* are not different from *citta* (44). In fact, *citta*, as well as *rūpādi*, must be *adravyasat*. Only in this way its activity can be subdued (45-53).

IV. 54-67: Refutation of *parikalpitasvabhāva* and *lakṣaṇa-niḥsvabhāvatā*. The *rajjusarpadṛṣṭānta* is not valid (54-55), nor does *saṁkleśa*, as claimed, arise from an *artha* based on *nāmasaṁketa* (56). Moreover, the *buddhiviṣaya*, i.e. *rūpādi*, cannot just be discarded as *abhilāpamātra* (57-58), nor can, to criticize Diṅnāga's theory of *anyāpoha*, the *abhidheya* be conceived as something which is merely *sāmānya* (59-68).

V. 68-83: The existence of *paratantrasvabhāva* (cf. *Laṅ-kāvatārasūtra*, II, 191) is only valid *saṁvṛtsitaḥ*, not *tattvataḥ* (68-70). Speaking of *utpattiniḥsvabhāvatā*, this really means that all *dharma*s are *anutpanna*. It is only for a *saṁvṛttibuddhi* that they are *svalakṣaṇa-* and *sāmānya-lakṣaṇaviṣaya* (cf. *Anavataptahradāpa-saṁkramaṇasūtra*, etc.) (69-74). It can in no way be maintained that there is real *utpatti* on the basis of an independently existing *paratantra*, etc. and when the Yogācāra criticizes the Mādhyamika's conception of *utpatti* as *māyā*, "such a stench of hatred's putrid meat" only proves their "undigested conceit" (75-83).

VI. 84-98b: Further refutation of *pariniṣpannasvabhāva* from various angles: *tattva* cannot be a *nirvikalpabhāva* like *ākāśa* (84), nor can *pariniṣpannasvabhāva* be *anabhilāpya* (cf. V, 60) (85), nor is *tattvadarśana* possible in this way (86). Critique of *dharmadhātu* as originally pure from defilement (Cf. V, 46) (87-90b). A *lokottarajñāna* which has *dharmatā* as *ālambana* cannot be *nirvikalpa*, nor can there be a *jñeya* for *svayaṁbhūjñāna* (90c-92); a real *nirvikalpajñāna* can have no object (cf. III, 257 seq.) (93). The absolute is no *sadasadbhāva*

---

7. Cf. most recently P. Tola and C. Dragonetti, "Dignāga's *Ālambanaparīkṣāvṛtti*," in *Journal of Indian Philosophy* 10 (1982): 105-34, which gives references to earlier editions and translations (but not to Bhavya's critique).

but free from both *antas* (94-95). According to *āgama* the Buddha, etc. is also *nirālamba* (cf. *Sarvabuddhaviṣayāvatāra-jñānālokālaṁkāra-sūtra*) (96). Moreover, the notion of a *buddhi* having *tathatā* as *ālambana* proves incompatible with the Yogācāra doctrine of *ālayavijñāna* (97). It is also absurd to claim that *pariniṣpannasvabhāva* and *paratantrasvabhāva* are neither identical nor different (cf. *Triṁśikā*, 22ab) (98b).

VII. 98c-113: The Mādhyamika's conception of *paramārtha- tattva* as *anutpāda*, or *dharmanairātmya*, etc. has already been dealt with fully in *Tattvajñānaiṣaṇā* (III, 257 seq.) (98c-102).[8] Though *tattva* is certainly *tārkikāṇām agocara* (cf. III, 286d) the purpose of *yukti* is to support *āgama* by proof and by refutation of various *vipakṣa*s (103-108). By means of *anumāna vyavahārasatya* is established as *samyak-saṁvṛtti*, and gradually *paramārtha* is obtained. It is, according to Munīndra, not *jñānagocara* (109-111). Conclusion (112-113). So, in the final words of III, 266:

jñeyasya sarvathāsiddher nirvikalpāpi yatra dhīḥ | *notpadyate tad atulyaṁ tattvaṁ tattvavido viduḥ* ||[9]

II. Karatalaratna (Taishō daizōkyō, XXX, 1578)

The purpose of this treatise is to help the student generate *lokottaranirvikalpajñāna* by realizing, through *śrutamayī* and *cintāmayī* the *prajñā*, *śūnyatā* of any kind of *jñeya* maintained by Buddhists and non-Buddhists, be it classified as *saṁskṛta* or *asaṁskṛta*. The text, accordingly, has three main parts dealing respectively with *saṁskṛta*, *asaṁskṛta* and *bhāva-nāmayī prajñā* (based on the two former kinds of *prajñā*). In each of these three main parts Bhavya deals briefly, and rather incidentally, with Yogācāra.

I. First the Yogācāras claim that the Mādhyamika is merely establishing *their* doctrine of *utpattiniḥsvabhāvatā* of *paratantra* when he argues that the *saṁskṛta*s being *pratītyasamutpanna* are

---

8. The Sanskrit text and its Tibetan version are edited by Y. Ejima, *Chūgan-shisō no tenkai: Bhavaviveka kenkyū*, Tōkyō 1980, pp. 268-361.

9. Ibid., p. 334. Also quoted in *MRP*, VI (cf. *Wiener Zeit-schrift fòr die Kunde Sòdasiens, 26* (1982).

not born by themselves. Moreover, referring to the *āgama: yena hi śūnyaṁ tadasadbhāvāt, yac ca śūnyaṁ tatsadbhāvāc chūnyatā yujyate* (cf. *Bodhisattvabhūmi,* p. 32, etc.), the Yogācāra maintains that *parikalpitasvabhāva* does not exist, whereas *paratantrasvabhāva,* in which it is absent, certainly must exist (271a 22 - 272a 10). Bhavya, referring to his *Tattvāmṛtāvatāra* (272a 13) for details, offers a summary critique of these two basic points (272a 10 - 272c 10).

II. Second, speaking of *asaṁskṛta,* the Yogācāra claims that *tathatā,* or *dharmāṇām paramārtha,* is the *ālambana* of *lokottaranirvikalpajñāna* (274b 28 - 274c 3). But, for various reasons, *tathatā* cannot be the object of any kind of *jñāna.* This point has also already been dealt with at length in *Tattvāmṛtāvatāra* (274c 4 - 275a 12).[10]

III. Third, in the final part dealing with *bhāvanā,* or Madhyamaka *yoga,* the Yogācāra's contention that *lokottara- nirvikalpajñāna* is an object free from *grāhyagrāhaka* is shown to be in conflict with *āgama,* and, of course, *yukti* (276c 17 - 277a 5).

PRAJÑĀPRADIPA, APPENDIX TO NIRVĀṆAPARĪKṢĀ

I.1: Introduction. The Yogācāra conception of *svabhāvatraya* and the three kinds of *niḥsvabhāvatā* (cf. *Vikhyāpana,* VII, 1-2) (1).

II. 2: Critique of *parikalpitasvabhāva* and *lakṣaṇaniḥsva-bhāvatā* (2).

III. 3-13: Refutation of *paratantrasvabhāva* as defined by Asaṇga, etc. and as interpreted on the basis of the *āgama: anādikāliko dhātuḥ* . . . , etc. (3-4), or according to the verse: *nāsti vai kalpito bhāvaḥ*. . .(5). The *kleśaṣ* are not *āgantuka* in relation to *dharmadhātu* (6). On the correct interpretation of *utpattiniḥsvabhāvatā* (7). Critique of the Yogācāra's contention of "not reviewing" (*na samanupaśyati*) by not grasping *paratantrasvabhāvanimitta,*everything being claimed, for various reasons, to be *citta-mātra* (8-13).

---

10. Here and above *amṛta* is rendered by *gān-lù,* "sweet dew."

IV. 14-15: Critique of *pariniṣpannasvabhāva* as *dharmāṇām tathatā*, or *advayabhāva* (14). A *nirvikalpajñāna* cannot have any *ālambana* (15).

V. 16: Conclusion. A more detailed critique is given in *Madhyamakahṛdayatattvāvatāra*, (i.e. in the chapter called *Yogācāratattvāvatāra*, thus Avalokitavrata!) and it is shown that according to *āgama*, when critically analysed, there is really no *svabhāvatraya*, etc. (16).[11]

3. After this brief survey of the relevant passages of *MHK* (*TJ*), *KTR* and *PP* we may now draw our attention to the critique of Yogācāra as it emerges in *MRP*, IV (translated infra).[12]

I. Introduction. Though Yogācāras such as Asaṅga, Vasubandhu, Diṅnāga, etc. belong to Mahāyāna they are however, as we shall see, only in possession of a *tathyasaṁvṛttiprajñā* at the level of *neyārtha*, not at that of *nīrtārtha* (cf. *MRP*, V).

II.1: It is true that several *sūtras* of Mahāyāna such as *Ghanavyūha*, *Saṁdhinirmocana*, *Daśabhūmika*, etc. claim that *traidhātuka* is *cittamātra*. Such statements, however, are not to be taken verbatim, but have to be interpreted according to their actual intention, viz. the denial of a *kartṛ* and *bhoktṛ*. They must be classified as conveying *neyārtha*, not *nītārtha* (1).

III. 2-7: There are two groups of Yogācāra, both merely in possession of the said kind of *saṁvṛttiprajñā*. The first, *sākāravāda*, claims that cognition is invested with a true image, the second, *nirākāravāda*, claims that cognition does not represent any real object (2).

The first branch of Yogācāra advances three arguments in support of their basic assumption that everything is *cittamātra:* (i) because cognition is void of real objects such as material form, etc. (ii) because it is only consciousness which *appears* bifurcated as cognitive process and result, and (iii) mind only has itself as objective realm. Consequently, they believe that they can attain the self-cognition of a Buddha by freeing mind from the unreal duality of subject and object (3).

---

11. For further details see reference in n. 4, supra.

12. A critical edition of *MRP* will be published by Mr Per K. Sörensen (Copenhagen 1986).

Bhavya then refutes these arguments one after another: (i) The *pratijñā* cannot be proved by the *hetu* as the *dṛṣṭānta* is not valid, (ii) Diṅnāga's assumption that cognition appears as two is shown to be inconsistent with his own theory that the resulting cognition is self-cognition, i.e. a form of self-evident cognition which, as such, cannot be expressed, (iii) Neither the external nor the internal mind can serve as objective realm of itself as mind (4). Besides, if everything is only mind the existence of *other* minds cannot be established, and, moreover, all appearances would either have to be immaterial like mind, or mind would always have to be inert matter like the appearances, which is, of course, absurd (5). One can only abandon the duality of subject and object by realizing its reality on the level of *saṁvṛtisatya* and its unreality on the level of *paramārtha satya.* The Yogācāras, on the other hand, who claim that even though there has ever been any external object there has always been a duality of subject and object, have no means whatsoever (i.e. *svabhāvatraya-praveśa*) of disposing of it and thus attain a non-dual gnosis (6).

The other branch of Yogācāra, *nirākāravāda,* is, to put it briefly, in hopeless conflict with *yukti* and *āgama* (7).

IV. 8-11: On the Yogācāra's possibility of obtaining *bodhi.* The Yogācāra cannot get the direct self-cognition (*pratisvasaṁvedana*) of a Buddha because the very idea of self-cognition is absurd, or even heterodox (8).

The Yogācāras cannot adduce the celebrated *Prajñāpāramitā* passage extolling *svabhāvatraya* as a means to obtain the ultimate form of cognition, because this passage should not be taken *ad verbum* (9). Finally, they claim that they can, in fact, obtain *bodhi,* namely by "change of basis" (*āśrayaparavṛtti*), etc. and quote various authorities to that effect (10), but Nāgārjuna has already pointed out the absurdity of this idea (II).

V.12: Conclusion. The doctrine of *cittamātra,* as announced in the introduction, is, according to all authorities, not to be understood on the level of *paramārtha satya,* but merely on the *neyārtha* level of *tathyasaṁvṛttiprajñā* (12).

4. We are now in a position to add a few general remarks on

the relationship between *MHK* (*TJ*), *KTR*, *PP* and *MRP* as far as their critique of Yogācāra is concerned.

First of all, it is clear from the above summary that almost all the ideas and arguments given in *KTR*, *PP* and *MRP* are already to be found in *MHK* (*TJ*). (I cannot here, of course, go into philological minutiae, no matter how interesting they may be.) It is, therefore, hardly surprising that not only *KTR* and *PP*, as pointed out, but also *MRP* (in chapter III) refers to *TJ* for further details. Though, when taken as a unit, *KTR*, *PP* and *MRP* are, as a rule, to be seen as a reshuffled summary of *MHK* (*TJ*), adding a new argument here and there, *KTR*, *PP* and *MRP* are, however, clearly supplementary when seen in mutual relation. They hardly ever overlap one another.

In comparison with *MHK* (*TJ*), *KTR* and *PP* we find some particular features characterizing *MRP*. In the earlier works he criticized Yogācāra mainly as a doctrine of *svabhāvatraya*. In *MRP* he hardly dwells on this aspect, but instead introduces the distinction between *sākāra* and *nirākāravāda*. These terms — later to become technical — are not found in his other works, but all the ideas behind them are already present in *MHK* (*TJ*). This shift in approach, then, is perfectly intelligible. The other conspicuous feature in *MRP* — not only in chapter IV, but also in *MRP* as a whole — is that the stress is now more on *āgama* than *yukti*. *MRP* mainly confines itself to summarize old arguments but adds a wealth of new quotations from *āgama*. This is, in fact, only what one would expect the author to do when one recalls the very orthodox attitude towards tradition briefly stated, but hardly developed, e.g. in *MHK*, V, 8-9 and 98c — 113, q.v.[13] As his earlier works were mainly polemical in their scope and thus mainly concerned with *yukti*, it seems fair to assume that he would redress the balance with *āgama* in such a work as *MRP*.

13. Cf. reference in n. 6, supra.

5. Having thus reviewed *MRP*, IV from the point of view of content and form in relation to his critique of Yogācāra in his other works, we may now be permitted to cast a glance upon the position of this chapter within the frames of *MRP* itself.

MRP as a whole may best be summarized in terms of its own colophon: *Sakalaśāsanasārasaṁgrahatattvaprakāśa*. It is a summary of the essentials of all doctrines which is almost tantamount to saying that it gives a summary of *Tarkajvālā*, etc. (see *MRP*, III).

It consists of nine chapters the titles of which may be reconstructed as follows:

I. *Satyadvaya*

II. *Saṁvr̥ti-bhrānta-prajñā-*

III. *Neyārtha-tathyasaṁvr̥tti-prajñā* (1)

IV. *Neyārtha-tathyasaṁvr̥tti-prajñā* (2)

V. *Nātārtha-tathyasaṁvr̥tti-prajñā*

VI. *Paramārtha-prajñā*

VII. *Bhāvanākrama*

VIII. *Ācāryapāda-māhātmya-abhidhāna*

IX. *Anuśaṁsa*

MRP is structured on the basis of Bhavya's philosophical, or even religious, concept of *prajñā* as the foremost *pāramitā*. "Objectively" there are two basic kinds of *prajñā* corresponding respectively to *saṁvr̥tti* and *paramārtha satya* and its subdivisions (I). Now *saṁvr̥ttiprajñā* may, as evidenced by the presence of various non-Buddhist philosophers, either be erroneous (*bhrānta*) (II), or correct (*tathya*) as represented in Buddhist dogma as a whole. There are, however, different kinds of *tathyasaṁvr̥ttiprajñā*, corresponding respectively to the three major trends of Buddhist thought: Śrāvaka and Yogācāra belong to the level of *neyārtha* (III-IV), Mādhyamika to the level of *nītārtha* (v). "Subjectively" *prajñā* moreover, admits of a threefold division: *śrutamayī*, *cintāmayī* and *bhāvanāmayī prajñā*. Chapters I-V deal with *śrutamayī* and *cintāmayī prajñā* whereas, *paramārthaprajñā* (vi) is the result of *bhāvanā* based on personal "Verwirklichung" upon *nītārthatathyasaṁvṛtti* (V) established by the two preliminary kinds of *prajñā* (III-IV). Chapter VII, accordingly, delineates the gradual advancement in *bhāvanā*. Thus I-VI are, in a sense, "theoretical" while VII (and the two final chapters) may be said to be "practical."

The following table illustrates the "*prajñā*-system" in its "objective" aspect.[14]

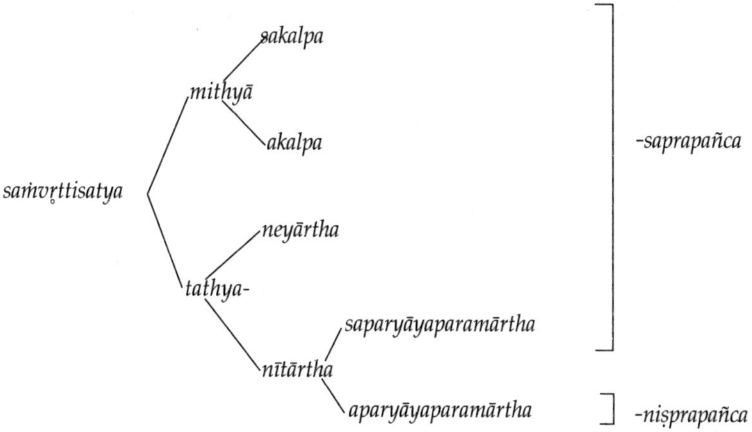

The *śrutamayī* and the *cintāmayī* aspects are only fully developed at the stage of *saparyāya-paramārtha*. With the full development of *bhāvanāmayī prajñā* the level of *aparyāyaparamārtha* is obtained. What parts these two kinds of *paramārtha satya* is only the prevalence of *prapañca*.

MADHYAMAKARATNAPRADĪPA, CHAPTER IV:

Analytical Understanding of the Correct Convention in the Provisional Sense

---

14. The terminology is mainly based on Bhavya's *Madhyamakārthasaṁgraha* as edited by Ejima, op. cit., pp. 18-21. I have given a translation of the text in *Journal of Indian Philosophy* 9 (1981): 200-201, q.v. See also *TJ* ad *MHK*, III, 1-26 for *satyadvaya*, the three forms of *prajñā*, the two kinds of *paramārtha* (one with and one without *abhisaṁskāra*, i.e. *saprapañca* and *niṣprapañca*), etc.

(*Neyārthatathyasaṁvṛttiprajñā*)

Part Two

Though [the Yogācāras] are of Mahāyāna stock.[15] They are, however, shrouded in ignorance (*avidyā*). It is in order to guide such dilettantes (*bāla*) of mediocre intellect

That [the Buddha] has spoken of "mere mind" (*cittamātra*).[16]
The purpose [of this statement] is [only] to deny
The existence of an agent (*kartṛ*) and an enjoyer (*bhoktṛ*).[17]
The Omniscient [Buddha] has stated it in a provisional sense[18]

---

15. Like the Srivakas (*MRP*, III) the Yogācāras (represented by Asaṅga, Vasubandhu, Diṅnāga, etc.), though belonging to Mahāyāna, only possess a *neyārthatathyasaṁvṛttiprajñā*. Though Buddhists do not possess the *nītārthatathyasaṁvṛttiprajñā* specific to a Mādhyamika. Cf. *TJ* ad *MHK*, V, 1: *theg pa chen po pa ñid kyi slob dpon thogs med daṅ, dbyig gñen la sogs pa gźan dag ni de bźin gśegs pas luṅ bstan ciṅ, sa rab tu brñes pa'i 'phags pa klu sgrub kyis yaṅ dag par rtogs pa'i theg pa chen po'i don gyi lugs gźan du 'dren par byed ciṅ ho tsha daṅ khrel med pa don rnam par mi śes pa de bźin du rnam pa śes śiṅ mkhas par ṅa rgyal byed pa dag . . . .*

16. Here *brid pa* probably renders Skt. *upalāpana*. This kind of "persuasive pedagogy" is very common in early Mādhya-mika (reference in my *Nagarjuniana: Studies in the Writings and Philosophy of Nāgārjuna* (Copenhagen: Akademiskforlag, 1982), p. 143 and e.g. *Mūlamadhyamakakārikā*,XVIII, 6 & 8; *Bodhicittavivaraṇa*, 27, op. cit., p. 192. Note also the clearly Buddhist influenced line in *Vākyapadīya*, II, 238ab, ed. W. Rau only!). There are numerous variations on this theme, e.g. *Laṅkāvatāra-Sūtra*, II,205cd (read *prakarṣaṇārtham*, m.c.). The idea of three levels of *buddhi* (*hīna*, *madhya*, *uttama*) already occurs e.g. *Yuktiṣaṣṭikā*, 55 (*Nagarjuniana*, p. 116); *Catuḥśataka*, VII, 14, and often in later sources, e.g. Atiśa's *Bodhipathapradīpa*, 2, q.v.

17. The doctrine of *cittamātra* only denies the existence of *ātman*, not *bāhyaviṣaya*. Hence these *sūtra*s should be read *neyārtha*, cf. infra.

18. The distinction between *sūtra*s conveying *neyārtha* and *nītārtha* is canonical, cf. above all *Akṣayamatinirdeśa-Sūtra* quoted *Prasannapadā*, p. 43 and Nāgārjuna's allusion to this in *Acintyastava*, 56-57 (edited in *Nagarjuniana*, p. 158 where further references are given).

To those who are full of devices, but lack wisdom (*prajña*).[19]

1. The *Ārya-Laṅkāvatārasūtra*[20] abounds in statements such as:

> The content of experience is simply one's own mind, But it appears as if external to mankind. The "objects of experience" are *not* external, Hence an external object (*artha*) does not exist.[21]

In the *Lokottaraparivarta* it is also said: "O, Jinaputras, the triple world (*traidhātuka*) is only mind (*cittamātra*)."[22] Similarly, the statements in such scriptures as the *Ghanavyūha-Sūtra*,[23] the *Ārya-Saṁdhinirmocana-Sūtra*,[24] *Mahadharmādarśa*,[25] etc. that all phenomena

---

19. More precisely, the Yogācāras only have a *saṁvṛttiprajñā* of *neyārtha*, cf. n. 15 supra; n. 29 infra. Possibly the compound *thabs rgyas* (for *mkhas?*) *pa* should be construed with *thams cad mkhyen pas.*

20. It should be noted that this *sūtra* (so often claimed to be a "Yogācāra text") is one of the most authoritative *sūtras* not only for Bhavya (passim) but already (but, of course, not necessarily in the *textus receptus* form) for Nāgārjuna and Āryadeva (cf. *Nagarjuniana, passim,* where numerous allusions to *Laṅkāvatāra-Sūtra* in his works — not vice versa — are pointed out) and all later Mādhyamikas.

21. *Laṅkāvatāra-Sūtra,* X, 442 (ed. Nanjio whose readings are often suspicious) *svaccitaṁ dṛśyasaṁsthānaṁ bahirdhā khyāyate nṛṇām* | *bāhyam na vidyate dṛśyam ato 'py arthaṁna vidyate* || (Cf. X, 101).

22. Cf. the quotation in *Bhāvanākrama,* III, p. 217 (ed. Tucci): . . . *bho jinaputra, cittamātraṁ traidhātukam.* . . . The *Lokottaraparivarta* is old, being already quoted in *Sūtrasamuccaya, Śikṣāsamuccaya,* etc.

23. This *sūtra* is often quoted by Yogācāras as well as Mādhyamikas. Cf. *Siddhi,* pp. 89, 126, 134, 135, 423. A critical edition of this text (Chinese, Tibetan, Sanskrit fragments) is certainly a desideratum.

24. See in particular VIII, 7 [ed. Lamotte, pp. 90-91 (text) and pp. 211-12 (translation)]. Also *Mahāyānasaṁgraha,* II, 7 [ed. Lamotte, p. 27 (text) and pp. 93-96 (translation)], and *Siddhi,* p. 420.

25. Like the *Ghanavyūha,* a *sūtra* requiring further study. A passage referred to in *MRP,* V is found in Skt. in the *Abhidharma-samuccayabhāṣya,* p. 112 (ed. Tatia). Only fragments seem extant.

(*dharma*) only consist of mind (*cittamātra*), do *not* [intend to] deny the external empirical world (*bāhyaviṣaya*) absolutely, but actually devise an adequate means of denying [the existence of] an agent (*kartṛ*) and an enjoyer (*bhoktṛ*). As is stated in the *Ārya-Daśabhūmikasūtra*:

> On the sixth *bodhisattvabhūmi*, a *bodhisattva* considers the natural (*anuloma*) and the reverse (*pratiloma*) aspect of dependent origination (*pratītyasamutpāda*) as follows: Based on the twelve factors, viz. ignorance (*avidyā*), etc. this sheer (*kevala*) mass of suffering (*duḥkha-skandha*) arises without there being an agent (*kāraka*) or an enjoyer (*vedaka*); a tree of suffering (*duḥkhavṛkṣa*) grows into existence.[26]

Convinced of this he exclaims:

> O, Jinaputras, this triple world is only mind, it is moulded by mind, it is schemed by mind. An agent and an enjoyer apart from mind does not exist.[27]

Consequently, the Buddhas and the Bodhisattvas have only advocated "mind-only" (*cīttamātra*) in order to refute the [soul or] agent (*kartṛ*) and enjoyer (*bhoktṛ*) conceived to be different from consciousness (*vijñāna*) by the heretics (*paratīrthika*). It is *not* in order to refute the external empirical world (*bāhyaviṣaya*)! Therefore, these *sūtras* [mentioned above] should only be understood to convey a provisional sense (*neyārtha*).[28]

---

26. This passage of the *Daśabhūmikasūtra* (ed. Rahder, pp. 47 seq.) is also quoted, or rather paraphrased, in the same form in *TJ* ad *MHK*, V, 28, q.v. The reference in the appendix to *PP* (section 9) is closer to the *textus receptus*: . . . *ayaṁ kevalo duḥkhaskandho duḥkhavṛkṣo'bhinirvartate kārakavedakavirahita iti*. . . .

27. Same passage in *TJ* and *PP*, loc. cit., but the *textus receptus* (ed. Rahder, p. 49) only has: . . . *citta-mātram idaṁ yad idaṁ traidhātukam* . . . Again, Bhavya seems to be quoting *ad sensum* rather than *ad verbum*.

28. Cf. n. 17 supra. The brief statement in *Madhyamakāvatāra*, VI, 94-97 q.v. presupposes Bhavya's much more exhaustive critique in *TJ* (not *MRP*).

2. What was said above [in the introductory verse, viz. that the Yogācāras] "lack wisdom" (*prajñā*) was a fine expression. As a matter of fact, the yogic analytical understanding (*prajñā*) *of* "mind only" (*cittamātra*) is only a [superficial] conventional understanding (*saṁvṛttiprajñā*).[29] How is this [to be understood]? Well, in the system [of Yogācāra] two basic tenets are held: One which maintains that cognition (*jñāna*) is [in itself] invested with [a true objective] image (*sākāravāda*), and the other which maintains that cognition (*jñāna*) does not have [a true objective] image (*nirākāravāda*).[30]

3. Now, those claiming that [cognition in itself] is invested with [a true objective] image (*sākāra*) argue as follows:

> (i) The entire triple world and *nirvāṇa* also are all simply mind (*cittamātra*), because [cognition] is void of objects such as material form, etc. (*rūpādyarthaśūnyatvāt*), as, for instance, [cognition in] a dream-state (*svapnāvasthā*).[31]

---

29. For the idea that the *cittamātrayogaprajñā* is only a *saṁvṛttiprajñā* cf. n. 15, supra and n. 49, infra (on the term *yoga*).

30. This, if I am not wrong, is the earliest occurrence of what were later to become technical terms, viz. *sākāra*-and *nirākāravāda* (cf. e.g. M. Hattori, *Dignāga, On Perception,* (Cambridge: Harvard University Press, 1968), p. 98; K. Mimaki, *La réfutation bouddhique de la permanence des choses* (*Sthirasiddhidūṣaṇa*) *et la preuve de la moment anéité des choses* (*Kṣaṇabhaṅgasiddhi*), (Paris: 1976), p. 296 with reference; Y. Kajiyama, "Later Mādhyamikas on Epistemology and Meditation, " in M. Kiyota (ed.), *Mahāyāna Buddhist Meditation: Theory and Practice* (Honolulu: University Press of Hawaii, 1978), pp. 114-43).To Bhavya (as to Bodhibhadra, Mokṣākaragupta, etc.) Diṅnāga represents *sākāravāda* whereas Vasubandhu represents *nirākāravāda,* cf. infra where the arguments are mostly to be found already in *TJ*. It is one of the remarkable features of *MRP* (and *Madhyamakārthasaṁgraha*) that Bhavya here introduces several "technical terms" not found in his (for this reason perhaps also) earlier works. But all the ideas behind the terms are already to be found in *TJ, KTR* and *PP*.

31. Based on *MHK,* V, 30 and *TJ,* cf. n. 35 and 36, infra.

(ii) They also claim that consciousness (*vijñāna*) itself appears as two (*dyābhāsa*), because it is both a means of cognition (*pramāṇa*) and a result (*phala*) [of cognition]. Here [it is to be noted] that a *pramāṇa* is a *pramāṇa* because [cognition] infers [the result] by means of it. Cognitive consciousness (*vijñāna*) appears as itself. The result (*phala*) is its understanding of the "object" (*viṣayaparatyavekṣaṇa*), i.e. cognition (*jñāna*) appearing as "object" (*viṣaya*).[32] The means and the result of cognition appertain to consciousness appearing as object alone.

(iii) And moreover [they claim] that all external and internal phenomena (*dharma*) are [only] mind (*citta*), because they are "objects" (*viṣaya*) [consisting] of mind-only, as, for instance, the immediately preceding condition (*samānāntarapratyaya*).[33]

Therefore, they say that the apprehension (*adhigama*) to be realized is the "nature of things" (*dharmatārūpa*) which can only be understood by the direct self-cognition of a Buddha (*tathāgatapratisvasaṁvedana*), i.e. in the original state of the nature of one's mind (*svacittadharmatā*) when it is free from the impurity of subject and object (*grāhyagrāhakamalarahita*).[34]

4. Now we shall refute these arguments (*yukti*) in due order

(i) As far as the first is concerned the proposition (*pratijñā*) and the logical reason (*hetu*) [cannot be] established as valid (*siddha*) in this case (*?tatra*) [because they are contradictory (*viruddha*)].[35] As far as

---

32. Here Bhavya gives a paraphrase of Diṅnāga's *Pramāṇasamuccaya*, I, 8cd: *savyāpārapratītatvāt pramāṇam phalam eva sat* I. It is explained below (notes 37 and 38) and its inconsistency with Diṅnāga's own theory of *pratyakṣa* is pointed out. See *MHK*, V, 24-26 with *TJ*.

33. *MHK*, V, 27 with *TJ*, cf. infra, n. 42-44. For *samānāntarapratyaya*, see Hattori, op. cit., p. 93; *Siddhi*, pp. 228, 242, 246, 247, 437.

34. For the term *dharmatārūpa*, cf. n. 65. Bhavya's refutation in section 6.

35. The brackets are mine; cf. *TJ* ad *MHK*, V, 30 for the entire passage: *gźan yah –*

rmi lam la yaṅ brtags min pa' i, ṅo bo ñid blos ma ṅes 'gyur zes bya ba ni khams gsum pa ni sems tsam ste, gzugs la sogs pa' i don gyis stoh pa' i phyir, rmi lam la

→

the example (*dṛṣṭānta*) is concerned, viz. like a dream (*svapnavat*), this analogy must in fact [illustrate a cognition] which is *either* void of an object being purely imagined (*kalpitārthaśūnya*) [i.e. unreal], *or* void of an object which is not at all imagined (*akalpitārthaśūnya*) [but really existent]. In the first case cognition (*jñāna*) and the object of that cognition (*jñeya*) cannot [so *ipso*] be established and must be false (*mithyā*). Hence, your basic contention (*siddhānta*) is not valid (*hīna*). If the example [illustrates a cognition] void of a purely imagined object, it cannot exclude that [remaining] part of the object, which is not imagined [but real], and for that reason also [the theory] of *cittamātra* is illogical. The other example (*dṛṣṭānta*) is not established as valid (*siddha*) either, because it is only the dream-cognition (*svapnajñāna*) [not the external object as such] which is false, because it *perceives* real material objects (*dharmatārūpa*) [and believes in their presence]. So it cannot serve as an example.[36]

(ii) With regard to the statement about cognitive con-sciouness (*vijñāna*) appearing as object (*viṣaya*) [Diṅnāga] maintains that cognition (*vijñāna*) does not apprehend (*adhigacchati*) the object (*viṣaya*) as long as it is only arising (*utpadyamāna*). Hence the cognition (*jñāna*) which is still merely arising is [not yet objectified

→ *sogs pa'i rnam par śes pa bźin no — źes bya ba de la di ltar rmi lam la yaṅ brtags pa ma yin pa'i ṅo bo ñid kyi blo'i cha yod pa'i phyir des na ci re źig rmi lam la sogs pa'i r nam pa śes pa bźin no źes bya ba de rmi lam gyi rnam par śes pa brtags pa'i ṅo bo ñid kyi skyes bu la sogs pa'i don gyis stoṅ par 'gyur ram, 'on te gaṅ gi cha la dmigs pa brtags pa ma yin pa'i don gyis mi stoṅ par 'gyur ba'i gtan tshigs ma ṅes pa ñid du 'gyur ro.*

<u>dmigs pa med par mi 'dod de. dpe ni rab tu ma grub ph yir</u> źes bya ba ni brtags pa'i don gyis stoṅ pa'i phyir ro. - źes bya ba'i dpe rmi lam blaṅs pa der yaṅ brtags pa'i don sel bar byed kyi brtags pa ma yin pa'i don gyi cha sel bar mi byed pas des kyaṅ sems tsam ñid du mi 'grub pa'i phyir "dmigs pa med par mi 'dod de,' "dpe bsgrub par bya ba'i phyogs gcig daṅ mi ldan par rab tu ma grub pa'i phyir ro. rmi lam gyi śes pa'i chos ñid kyi don la dmigs pa'i phyir dmigs pa med pa ñid ma yin no. 'di ltar rmi lam ni yaṅ dag pa ma yin pa'i phyir gtan la dbab par na de dpe ñid du mi ruṅ ṅo źes bya bar bsams so.

In view of this the passage within brackets may have to be omitted.

36. For the *svapnadṛṣṭānta* in Yogācāra, see *Mahāyānasaṁgraha*, II, 6.

as *phala*, but is only] as a means of cognition (*pramāṇa*). But when consciousness (*vijñāna*) *has* arisen, the object (*viṣaya*) is perceived [by it] and therefore one's cognition (*jñāna*) is definitely and fully established (*abhinirvartita*). This, therefore, is maintained to be the *pramāṇa* and the *phala* of the very cognition (*jñāna*) which, as a result (*phala*), appears as object (*viṣaya*).[37] It is, by way of illustration, like when you cleave a log with an axe: first you are about to do it, then you hit it, and, *voilà*, you have got two pieces.[38]

To this we reply: [According to your theory of perception] an immediately evident cognition (*pratyakṣajñāna*) perceives the particular character of a thing (*bhāvasvalakṣaṇa*) and it is devoid of the dichotomies of conceptuality and recollection (*kalpanāsmṛtivikalpāpoḍha*).[39] Accordingly [the manifold perceptual objects such as] material form, etc. (*rūpādi*) have blue, etc. (*nīlādi*) as their inexpressible nature (*anirdeśyarūpa* [= *svalakṣaṇa*]).[40] Similarly it [i.e. *pratyakṣajñāna*], in the form of self-awareness (*svasaṁvedanākareṇa*), apprehends [a perceptual object which is] just as inexpressible in its nature.[41] Since, therefore, the *pramāṇa* and the *phala* only belong to one single cognition (*jñāna*) appearing as object (*viṣayābhāsa*), the logical reason (*hetu*), [i.e. because it is both *pramāṇa* and *phala*) is not proved (*asiddha*). Consequently, the assumption that *one* mind (*citta* [= *vijñāna*]) appears as two [i.e. as *pramāṇa* and *phala*], must be erroneous (*vyabhicārin*)!

(iii) The third argument (*yukti*) is also not true. In fact, the assertion (*pratijñā*), the logical reason (*hetu*) and the example (*dṛṣṭānta*)

---

37. Cf. n. 32 supra and Hattori, op. cit., p. 98. For the final passage *TJ* ad *MHK*, V, 26ab: . . . *rnam par śes pa de skyes pa na yul mthoṅ ba'i phyir śes pa des mṅon par grub pa ni 'bras bu yin pas yul du snaṅ ba'i rnam par śes pa ñid la tshad ma daṅ 'bras bu gñis yod par 'dod de. . . .*

38. Same example in *Ślokavārttika*, cf. Hattori, op. cit., p. 99.

39. Cf. *Pramāṇasamuccaya*, I, 3 . . . *pratyakṣaṁ kalpanāpoḍhaṁ*. . . etc.

40. Ibid., I, 5cd: *svasaṁvedyam anirdeśyaṁ rūpaṁ indriyagocaraḥ*

41. *Self-cognition* (*svasaṁvitti, svasaṁvedana*) is also *akalpikā* (Ibid., 6b). Since *svasaṁvittiḥ phalaṁ vātra* (ibid., 9a) and *svasaṁvitti*, as said, is also (*pratyakṣa-*) *pramāṇa*, cognition cannot, of course, be *dvyābhāsa*.

[consist of] a property-locus [i.e. in this case, the external object (*bāhyārtha*)] and a property logically establishing it (*sādhanadharma*) [i.e. in this case, its mental nature (*cittasvabhāva*)].[42] However, your assertion (*pratijñā*) [that all external and internal phenomena (*dharma*) are only mind (*citta*)] is not established for you [by the logical reason (*hetu*):] "because they are objects (*viṣaya*) [consisting] of mind only (*cittasyaiva*)." Now, in this case, mind (*citta*) must *either* be the object (*viṣaya*) when it exists outside, *or* it must be the object (*viṣaya*) when it is located inside [mental phenomena (*caitta*) such as] feeling, etc. (*vedanādi*).[43] But if the external mind (*bāhya-citta*) is object (*viṣaya*), then, when one makes the assertion (*pratijñā*) by maintaining that everything external and internal is only mind (*citta eva*), there cannot possibly be a sensory object (*viṣaya*) and a possessor of the object (*viṣayin*). Nor can the internal mind (*adhyātmacitta*) be the object of mind (*cittaviṣaya*): that is a fallacious argument (*hetvābhāsa*).[44] [Hence *citta* cannot be *viṣaya*, and, consequently your *pratijñā* remains unproved.]

5. But there are also mistakes (*doṣa*) such as this: If everything is only mind (*citta*), then, for instance, when one sees a jar (*ghaṭa*), one would also have to perceive the mental content (*cittasaṁtāna*) of all other living beings (*sarvasattva*). By perceiving this [everybody] in the five destinies (*pañcagati*) would automatically have the intuition (*abhijñā*) cognizing the minds of others (*paracitta*) [which is, of course, quite absurd].[45]

And again, if everything were mind (*citta*), an appearance (*ākāra*) would, like mind (*cittavat*), be immaterial (*arūpin*), or mind

---

42. Cf. *TJ* ad *MHK*, V, 27: . . . *'di la phyi rol gyi don ni chos can no. de sems kyi ho bo ñid yin par bsgrub pa ni de'i chos so. . . .*

43. Cf. *TJ* ad *MHK*, V, 28ab: . . . *re źig rnam par śes pa'i yul yin pa'i phyir de ma thag pa'i rkyen bźin du phyi rol gyi yul yaṅ sems kyi ṅo bo ñid yin par 'gyur ram, 'on te rnam par śes pa'i yul yin pa'i phyir tshor ba la sogs pa sems las byuṅ ba so so dag sems kyi ṅo bo ñid ma yin pa bzin du phyi rol gyi yul yaṅ sems kyi ṅo bo ñid ma yin par 'gyur ba'i gtan tshigs ma hes pa ñid do.* Cf. *Siddhi*, p. 395.

44. Nothing directly corresponding to this in *TJ*.

45. On this problem (not in *TJ*) see *Siddhi*, p. 430.

(*citta*), like the image (*ākāravat*), would be material (*rūpin*). But then mind would also, like the appearance, be inert matter (*jaḍa*), or the appearance would understand and cognize [which is, of course, absurd].[46]

6. Again, *you* cannot possibly attain liberation (*mokṣa*) "by freeing [mind] from the impurity of subject and object (*grāhyagrāhakamala*)."[47] But [a Mādhyamika] who maintains the existence of the external realm (*bāhyaviṣaya*) [on the level of *saṁvṛttisatya*],[48] and apprehends, through *yoga*,[49] the unsubstantial nature of the realm (*viṣayaniḥsvabhāvatā*) [on the level of *paramārtha satya*][50] can certainly generate the transcendental non-discursive cognition (*lokottaranirvikalpajñāna*)[51] by eliminating object-subject (*grāhyagrāhaka*).

According to you [i.e. Diṅnāga] asserting that there is no external realm (*viṣaya*) there has never been any external object (*bāhyārtha*) in the first place (*prathamata eva*).[52] Nevertheless, [you

46. This (not in *TJ*) is not accepted by Yogācāra, cf. *Mahāyānasaṁgraha*, II, 9 quoting *Mahāyānasūtrālaṁkāra*, XI, 24.

47. Cf. n. 34, supra. For the entire paragraph, see *MHK*, V, 39-43 (i.e., in Tibetan).

48. Cf. *MRP*, I (translated in *Journal of Indian Philosophy*, 9 (1981) : 169-177 and V.

49. Bhavya distinguishes between a *sthūlayoga* by which all *dharmas* are seen as empty, and a *sūkṣmayoga* by which they are seen as created by *svacitta* only which is *prabhāsvara* (see *MRP*, VII).

50. Cf. n. 48, supra.

51. The Yogācāra notion of (*lokottara-*)*nirvikalpajñāna* (cf. *Siddhi*, pp. 585-88, 607-10, etc.) is criticized in *TJ* and *KTR* (cf. supra). It is, according to Bhavya, only possible when there is no *jneya* of any kind.

52. This passage follows the critique of Diṅnāga's *Ālambana-parīkṣā* given in *MHK*, V, 31-38 (note that this is *not* repeated in *MRP* but instead given in the appendix to *PP*, section 11, q.v.): . . . *khyed yul med pa* (read with *MRP*: *med par 'dod pa*) *la ni daṅ po nas kyaṅ phyi rol gyi don med la, phyis kyaṅ med pa bźin du gzuṅ ba daṅ 'dzin pa'i ṅo bo* →

claim that one can] penetrate (*praviś-*) its object-subject (*grāhyagrāhakasvabhāva*) later on.[53] But by which counteraction (*hetu*) can one really eliminate it *later on* [when it never was there in the first place]! You have no means whatsoever of getting a transcendental non-discursive cognition (*lokottaranirvikalpajñāna*). So when you say that: "When objective supports (*ālambana*) such as material form, etc. (*rūpādi*) do not appear outside mind (*citta*), then mind (*citta*), definitely located in its own original mental nature (*svacittadharmatā*), is called 'non-dual gnosis (*advaya jñāna*) [and that] truth (*tattva*), reality (*bhūta*), immortality (*amṛta*), the highest level of all Buddhas [constitute the] nature of the triple body (*trikāya*)"[54] — we must be aware that this is based on a misunderstanding!

7. Nor do those, who claim that [cognition] does not have [a real] image (*nirākāravādin*) possess a cognition of the ultimate meaning (*paramārtha-jñāna*).[55] Their basic textbook begins as follows:

> The entire universe is only a mental act,
> Because the "object" which appears is unreal,
> As, for exmaple, when a person suffering from amblyopia sees [unreal things] such as hair or moons.[56]

→ *ñid du 'jug par 'gyur fa de'i phyis rgyu gaṅ gis Idog ciṅ 'jig rten las 'das pa'i ye śes rnam par mi rtog pa skye bar 'gyur ba'i thabs ci yaṅ med do. yul med par smra ba la ni 'jig rten las 'das pa'i lam skye ba'i thabs med pas nus pa daṅ yul gyi ṅo bo ñid kyi rnam par śes pa thog ma med pa'i dus nas 'jug pa de ji Itar Idog pa'i rigs pa brjod par bya dgos so.*

53. For this and the following, cf. n. 52.

54. This passage is glossed *TJ* ad *MHK*, V, 41-42. Cf. *TJ* ad *MHK*, V, 4. *MRP* only adds the term *trikāya* (cf. *Siddhi*, pp. 762-813). The term *advaya* refers to the absence of *grāhya* and *grāhaka*.

55. Tib. *don dam pa'i śes pa* (probably *paramārthajñāna*, cf. *Mahāyānasūtrālaṁkāra*, passim). For the corresponding Mādhyamika term, see n. 15, 19 and 29, supra.

56. Vasubandhu's (cf. n. 30, supra) *Viṁśatikā*, 1: *vijñaptimātram evedam asadarthāvabhāsanāt* | *yadvat taimirikasyāsatkeśacandrādidarśana* || (cf. the variants) (Note that there are also several quotations from *Triṁśikā* in TJ.)

With a whole lot of arguments they try to prove that the appearance as object (*viṣayākāra*) is false, and maintain that ultimately only knowledge (*pratipatti*) and cognition (*jñāna*) exist.[57] But this is not all reasonable. According to logic (*yukti*) as well as tradition (*āgama*), the fact is that when the external image (*bāhyākāra*) is false the subjective cognition is also false, and to the extent cognition is true the image (*ākāra*) must also be true.

8. Moreover, granting your opinion that there is such a thing as "self-cognition" (*svasaṁvedana*), it must be possible to examine it critically.[58] As what kind of entity (*katama*) can it be cognized by you among the three [possibilities]: "cognizable" (*vedya*), "cognizer" (*vedaka*) or "cognition" (*vedana*)? How can the cognizer (*vedaka*) be such an entity! What can a cognition (*saṁvedana*) independent of those two [viz. *vedya* and *vedaka*] cognize so that it is "self-cognition" (*svasaṁvedana*)! Consequently, you have not [got the faintest idea of] the meaning of the term (*padārtha*) "cognition knowing all aspects" (*sarvākārajña jñāna*), so how can you [even dream of] getting the cognition of a Buddha (*buddha-jñāna*)![59] Please point it out without professional jealousy (*mātsarya*) about those things (*artha*) determined by your logic![60]

If you say that [*svasaṁvedana*] cannot be expressed to others because it is a matter of *self-cognition*, then it is not different from the *ātman* maintained by non-Buddhists.[61] But which sensible person can consider taking serious their statements that *ātman* is eternal (*nitya*), one (*eka*), omnipresent (*vyāpin*), incorporeal (*amūrtta*)

---

57. Tib. *śes pa daṅ, ye* (*mi* P) *śes dag* . . .

58. Here Bhavya reverts to refute the notion of *svasaṁvitti/svasaṁvedana* as found in *Pramāṇasamuccaya*, I, cf. n. 40 and 41, supra and n. 60 infra. An earlier critique of this (and known to Bhavya) is to be found in Nāgārjuna's *Bodhicittavivaraṇa*, 36-39 (my *Nagarjuniana*, p. 196).

59. I.e. a *tathāgatapratisvasaṁvedana*, cf. supra.

60. Allusion to *Pramāṇasamuccaya*, I, 9ab: *svasaṁvittiḥ phalaṁ vātra, tadrūpo hy arthaniścayaḥ* . . . The sarcasm is obvious.

and rigmarole (*na kiṁcit*), not even congruous with their own [notion of *ātman*]! The idea about *svasaṁvedana* and that of *ātman* are, in fact, sheer subjective discriminations (*prativikalpamātra*).[62] [The Yogācāras do not understand *pudgalanairātmya*][63] and they do not understand *dharmanairātmya* either, because this is such a tremendous clinging to self (*ahaṁkāra*).

Apart from that there are many more mistakes (*doṣas*), but let this suffice for now.

9. Here [the adherents of] *nirākāravāda* [interrupt and] attempt to refute:

> [Perhaps the adherents of *sākāravāda* do not have it but] we *do* have the understanding of the ultimate sense (*paramārthaprajñā*)![64] In fact, it is said in the *Prajñāpāramitā* which imparts the definite sense (*nītārtha*): "Maitreya, a Bodhisattva, must understand the concept of various types of material form (*rūpaprabhedavijñapti*) from three points of view, viz. the totally fictitious (*parikalpita*) form, the discursive (*vikalpita*) form, and the natural form (*dharmatārūpa*)"[65] — and so on. Therefore, a cognition (*jñāna*) which has the natural form as its object (*dharmatā-rūpaviṣaya*) conveys the understanding of the ultimate sense (*paramārthaprajñā*) !

---

61. Cf. *TJ*, VIII and IX, passim; *KTR*, 275a2 seq.

62. This term seems to be idiosyncratic to the *Laṅkāvatara-Sutra* (see Suzuki's *Index* . . . p. 113).

63. The brackets are justified by the *yaṅ* in Tib.: *chos bdag med pa yaṅ* . . .

64. Cf. n. 55, supra, with reference.

65. This celebrated passage is quoted *in extenso TJ* ad *MHK*, V, 29, q.v. The Sanskrit is edited in *Mélanges d'Indianisme*, Paris, 1968 by E. Conze and S. Iida, "Maitreya's Questions" in the *Prajñāpāramitā*," pp. 237-38 . . . *tribhir, Maitreya, ākārair bodhisattvena . . . rūpapra-bhedaprajñaptir anugantavyā, . . . idaṁ parikalpitaṁ rūpam, idaṁ vikalpitaṁ rūpam, idam dharmatārūpam* . . . Clearly Bhavya takes this as a reference to *svabhāvatraya* (note that he does not discuss these in *MRP*, probably because he had treated them exhaustively in *TJ*, *KTR* and the appendix to *PP* already).

[No!] This has been stated by Bhagavat in a provisional sense (*neyārtha*), so [you Yogācāras] do not get the *paramārthaprajñā*![66]

10. But these mediocre minds interrupt us once again:

What must be established, viz. enlightenment (*bodhi*) is also possible
in our system, for Bhagavat has declared:
In order to abandon the *saṁskāras* totally
[They] should not be said to have own-being (*svabhāva*).
[This] *prajñā* [consists] in self-cognition (*svasaṁvedana*)
In that state one may speak of *tathāgata*.[67]

Therefore [we Yogācāras say]:

By change (*parāvṛtti*) of the basis (*āśraya*)
One gets the transcendental gnosis (*lokottarajñāna*).
This is the pure element (*anāsravo dhātaḥ*):
The great Muni's *dharmakāya*.[68]

When one's consciousness (*vijñāna*) does not any more apprehend
any object (*ālambana*). Then it abides in mind-only (*vijñāptimātra*):
As there is no object it cannot be grasped.

By change (*parāvṛtti*) of the basis (*āśraya*)
One gets the *pañcajñāna* and the *trikāya*.
As long as he is in the world, for the sake of the world,
He [as Bodhisattva] remains in *apratiṣṭhitanirvāṇa*.[69]

---

66. Cf. n. 64 with reference.

67. This seems to be the sense of this verse, though its syntax is not quite clear. I have not traced the *sūtra*.

68. These two verses are adapted from *Triṁśikā*, 28-30: *yadātv ālambanaṁ jñānaṁ naivopalabhate tadā* । *sthitaṁ vijñānamātratve grāhyābhāve tadagrahāṭ* ॥ *acitto 'nupalambho 'sau jñānaṁ lokottaraṁ ca tat* । *āśrayasya parāvṛttir dvidhā dauṣṭhulyahānitaḥ* ॥ *sa evānāsravo dhātur acintyaḥ kuśalo dhruvaḥ* । *sukho vimuktikāyo 'sau dharmākhyo 'yaṁ mahāmuneḥ* ॥ *Cf. Siddhi*, pp. 585 for variants, etc.

69. Seems to be partly based on *Mahāyānasūtrālaṁkāra*, IX, q.v. For *pañcajñāna*, see *Siddhi*, p. 681. On *apratiṣṭhitanirvāṇa*, see Nagao in L.S. Kawamura (ed.), *The Bodhisattva Doctrine in Buddhism* (Waterloo, Ontario: 1981), pp. 61-79.

Here an *āgama* is spoken by Bhagavat:

Impurity (*saṁkleśa*) consists in being imbued (*vāsanā*)
By clinging (*abhiniveśa*) to *parikalpitasvabhāva.*
Purification (*vyavadāna*) consists in not being imbued
By [such] clinging (*abhiniveśa*).[70]
Of these this [viz. *saṁkleśa*] is the impure element (*sāsravadhātu*)
But, when changed, the very same [viz. *saṁkleśa*]
Is the pure element (*anāsravādhātu*).
This is the unsurpassed purification (*anuttaraśuddhi*) ![71]

11. We [Mādhyamikas] must object to this! The statement "by change of the basis (*āśrayaparāvṛtti*)" is not true. The argument for this has been expressed by Ārya-Nāgārjuna:

Since the past does not exist, therefore, the future does not exist either. The present occurrence of the basis changed — In which [period] can it take place?[72]

According to this argument the [notion of] "change of the basis" (*āśrayaparāvṛtti*) cannot be proved. Therefore, the five cognitions (*pañcajñāna*) and the triple body (*trikāya*) cannot be established either. Hence you do not have "what must be established, viz. *bodhi.*"[73]

12. Therefore it is stated in the *Ārya-Laṅkāvatāra-Sūtra:*

Just as a physician ordains [various kinds of] medicine to each of his suffering patients, Thus the Buddha also advocates [the doctrine of] "Mind-only" (*cittamātra*) to [some] living beings.[74]

---

70. This and the following verse are also quoted in L. Schmithausen, *Der Nirvāṇa-Abschnitt in der Viniścayasaṁgrahaṇī der Yogācārabhūmiḥ* (Wien: 1969), p. 44, q.v.

71. Ibid. Read *'di la de ñid* for *'di la de gñis* in *pāda* a.

72. *Bodhicittavivaraṇa,* 31 (my *Nagarjuniana,* p. 194).

73. Cf. supra.

74. *Laṅkāvatāra-Sūtra,* II, 123 (also *Madhyamakāvatāra,* p. 196; *Subhāṣitasaṁgraha,* p. 394): *āture āture yadvad bhiṣag dravyaṁ prayacchati* | *buddhā hi tadvat sattvānāṁ cittamātraṁ vadanti vai* || (see v.1.)

Ārya-Nāgārjuna has also argued:

The teaching of the Muni
That everything is only mind (*cittamātra*)
Is intended to remove the fear of fools,
It is not to be taken as a true statement.[75]

It has also been said:

It has been stated that this manifold world
Is only mind (*vijñānamātra*),
But it is only to a person of dull intellect
That it lacks the distinction between subject and object![76]

End of Part II of [The Chapter Entitled]
Neyārthatathyasamvṛttiprajñā

---

75. *Bodhicittavivaraṇa*, 27: *cittamātram idaṁ sarvam iti yā deśanā muneḥ* ၊ *uttrāsaparihārārthaṁ bāśānāṁ sa na tattvataḥ* ॥

76. This verse along with two others is quoted in *Subhāṣita-saṁgraha*, pp. 388-389: *vijñānamātram evedaṁ citraṁ jagad udāhṛtam* ၊ *grāhyagrāhakabhedena rahitaṁ madhyamedhase* ॥ (Ms. *mandamedhase*). All three verses also occur in Jñānakīrti's *tattvāvatārākhya . . . prakaraṇa* (*TP.* 4532, 46b8-47a2). In *MRP*, VII the third verse (*gandharvanāgarākāram . . .*) is quoted from Mahāsukha (*bde ba chen po*) twice. In Āryadeva's *Caryāmelāyanapradīpa* there are several quotations from this author's *Śrī-Guhya-Sādhana* (or-*siddhi*).

16

The Concept of Reason in Jñānagarbha's Svātantrika Madhyamaka

Malcolm David Eckel

IT would be difficult to read the literature of the Madhyamaka tradition and not be aware of a certain ambivalence in the Madhyamaka encounter with Indian epistemology and logic. On one side the Mādhyamikas were enthusiastic philosophers. From the time of Nāgārjuna, they entered forcefully into dialogue with a host of opposing schools, and they clearly were convinced that in the soundness of their methods and the cogency of their claims they were more than a match for any of their rivals. But there was an aspect of their method that would never fit comfortably in the rigid structures of either Hindu or Buddhist logic. If in some fashion they were to deny the reality of things, as their Emptiness doctrine seemed to entail, they could not make unambiguous use of a logic based on assertions about things. It was not clear, in fact, how they could say anything at all. Nāgārjuna summarized the logical dilemma and left it as a challenge to his followers in a series of verses in the *Vigrahavyāvartanī*:

> [Objection:] If nothing has own-being at all, your statement has no own-being and cannot deny own-being.
>
> [Reply:] If my statement does not exist, either with a combination of causes and conditions or without, Emptiness is proven, since things have no own-being.

> If I had any thesis, I would be at fault. But since I have no thesis, I am not at fault.[1]

It is understandable that Nāgārjuna's arguments are sometimes taken not as attempts to establish the logical validity of a Madhyamaka position, but as an attempt to dissolve logic into mysticism, as if he were a philosopher trying to show the futility of philosophy in the face of direct, mystical awareness.[2] But to take Nāgārjuna or his followers as enemies of logic is to miss both the unity of their thought and the force of common assumptions that tied even their radically sceptical arguments into a common Indian system of philosophical discourse. "Philosophy" (or simply "seeing," *darśana*) was not taken, at least by those who engaged in it, as speculation for its own sake. It was closely linked to the attainment of fundamental human goals. In one system the goal might be heaven, in another liberation (*mokṣa*). But in either case, the practice of philosophy, or the seeking of insight (*darśana*) through reasoned analysis (*nyāya*), was understood as a way to generate the knowledge (*jñāna*) that made such goals possible. Insight was not opposed

---

1. *sarveṣāṁ bhāvānāṁ sarvatra na vidyate svabhāvaś cet* | *tvadvacanam asvabhāvaṁ na nivartayituṁ svabhāvam alam* | *hetupratyayasāmagryāṁ ca pr̥thak cāpi madvaco na yadi* | *nanu śūnyatvaṁ siddhaṁ bhāvānām asvabhāvatvāt* || *yadi kācana pratijñā syān me tata eṣa me bhaved doṣaḥ* /*nāsti ca mama pratijñā tasmān naivāsti me doṣaḥ* || found in E.H. Johnston and A. Kunst, eds., "The Vigrahavyāvartanī of Nāgārjuna with the Author's Commentary," *Mélanges chinois et bouddhiques*, 9 (1948-52): 108, 121, 127.

2. "But for Buddhists reality is something quite different from logic. For a certain class of Buddhists truth consists in the negation of logic. Truth according to the conviction of these men will emerge from the destruction of all logic. The truth is the world of the mystic. It is cognized by the logical Method of Residues, as a residue from the destruction of logic, it is translogical. The school of the Mādhyamikas identified itself with this method." F. Th. Stcherbatsky, *Buddhist Logic*, Bibliotheca Buddhica, 26 (Leningrad: Academy of Sciences of the U.S.S.R., *ca*. 1930; reprint ed., New York: Dover Publications, 1962), I, p. 344.

to logical analysis, it was gained in and through it, and even the most illogical logicians or mystifying philosophers saw their dialectical efforts as part of a pan-Indian soteriological system in which analysis of reality gave insight that could lead to the final goal of human life.

Without some acknowledgement of this aspect of the cultural context, even specialists in Indian philosophy are liable to misrepresent its intentions. Among Nāgārjuna's works, for example, the basic outline of Madhyamaka thought was given the title *Wisdom* (*prajñā*), not because the text was preparatory to a form of direct awareness attained only after the text was understood, but because its contents *were* wisdom. The analysis of categories in the text itself was considered coterminous with the highest insight. The Mādhyamikas' problem was thus much more subtle and difficult than it would have been if their tradition had allowed them to glide happily to an irrational solution. A mystical completion of their analysis was not enough. They had to show how their methods could generate a knowledge of reality with some sense of the rational certainty found in other Hindu or Buddhist philosophical schools.

This is not to say, however, that the drive to articulate a Madhyamaka logical method was no more than a desire to catch up with their counterparts in other philosophical traditions. It is true, Madhyamaka arguments naturally took the shape of a critical response to points others had already made. But there was more to the Madhyamaka method than the need to respond to what others were saying. In the word *madhyama*, from which the school's name is derived, is a reference to the "middleness" of the Buddha's Middle Path (*madhyamā pratipad*). What the Middle Path meant to Buddhists was different in different areas of Buddhist life, but in philosophy it reflected a sense of balance between too great an affirmation of accepted structures of reality and too great a denial. For Mādhyamikas the narrow path between yes (*asti*) and no (*nāsti*) took the form of a balance between ultimate and conventional or between Emptiness and the means by which Emptiness was understood. The concept of Emptiness involved the denial that words, concepts, or things had reality in themselves, but the concept itself could not be expressed without "accepting" or "presupposing" the significance of the words or concepts whose reality it denied.[3] Nāgārjuna expressed the relationship between Emptiness and the conventions it presupposed in a key verse in the *Madhyamakakārikās* — "There is no teaching about the Ultimate that is not based on conventional usage" — and in the process fixed in terms in which Mādhyamikas would work out the balance of the Middle Path.[4] Ultimately (*paramārthena*) all things were empty (*śūnya*), but ultimacy could not even be mentioned without presupposing conventional usage (*vyavahāra*).

Thus, quite apart from any response to other schools, Mādhyamikas had the job of explaining to each other what it

---

3. An example of the balance between affirmation and denial among Nāgārjuna's commentators was the statement "Ultimately the self does not exist." Does this mean that one "accepts" the existence of a self in some prior sense before denying its ultimate existence? Bhāvaviveka thought that it did and took the word "accepted" (*abhyupagata*) to be the equivalent of "established" (*siddha*). (See the analysis of *Madhyamakakārikā* 18.1 in Bhāvaviveka's *Prajñāpradīpa,* translated in Malcolm David Eckel, "A Question of Nihilism: Bhāvaviveka's Response to the Fundamental Problems of Mādhyamika Philosophy," Ph.D. Diss. Harvard University, 1980, pp. 192-200). Candrakīrti used the term *abhyupagata* to refer to the position he takes simply in opposition to his opponent. Since Candrakīrti did not consider his own position to be independently established, David Seyfort Ruegg (On the Thesis and Assertion in the Madhyamaka/dBu ma, unpublished paper, 1982) suggests the translation "presuppose." Candrakīrti's usage is seen most clearly in the criticism of the *svatantra-anumāna* in *Prasannapadā* chapter 1 (Louis de La Vallée Poussin, ed., *Mūlamadhyamakakārikās* [*Mādhyamikasūtras*] *de Nāgārjuna avec la Prasannapadā Commentaire de Candrakīrti,* Bibliotheca Buddhica, 4 [St. Petersburg, 1903-13], p. 19.3-7).

4. *Madhyamakakārikā* 24.10: *vyavahāram anāśritya paramārtho na deśyate* (de La Vallée Poussin, ed., *Prasannapadā*, p. 494).

meant to base one's statements about the ultimate on conventional usage. Did it mean simply to presuppose forms of discourse in a weak sense, as one might "presuppose" some form of error in the process of correcting it? Or did one in some sense "affirm" conventional usage before going on to use it in reference to the ultimate? At stake for Mādhyamikas was the balance between affirmation and denial, or between the extremes of the Middle Path. They had to articulate a method — simply as a matter of dialogue within their own school — that would make positive use of the Indian categories of argument, but not be rigidly bound by the reality they presupposed.

Finally, if more motivation were needed, the Mādhyamikas could turn to their disagreement with other Mahāyāna philosophical schools. Nāgārjuna's philosophical works had been based largely on the system of religious reflection embodied in the *Perfection of Wisdom Sūtras.* In the centuries after Nāgārjuna's work, new scriptural texts appeared to give a radically different interpretation of the central categories of Mahāyāna thought. The Mādhyamikas of the sixth and seventh centuries faced a far more serious interpretive problem than would have been faced three centuries earlier. They accepted all Mahāyāna *sūtras* as authoritative utterances of the Buddha (*buddhavacana*), and they had to devise rational methods to interpret conflicting *sūtra*s in a way that would conform to Madhyamaka views. Bhāvaviveka (*c.* CE 500-570) outlined the Madhyamaka problem, by no accident, in the chapter of his *Tarkajvālā* on the views of his chief Mahāyāna rival, the Yogācāra.

> (5.8) We reply that for us all the statements of the Tathāgatas are authoritative (*pramāṇa*), for it is because a trustworthy person's (*āpta*) teaching is authoritative that the fortunate achieve understanding.
>
> For us all the statements of the Sugatas are authoritative, because who pronounce them see reality (*tattvadarśin*). The fortunate understand them without error.

(5.9) Our opponent is in doubt about other scriptures and is confused. Thus, to make [the opponent] understand, it is necessary to follow a rational (*yuktimat*) method.[5]

This meant, for Bhāvaviveka, that the scriptures had to be investigated rationally before the truth they embodied could be properly understood. His best statement of the relationship between scripture and reason occurs in the analysis of the Yogācāra in chapter 25 of his *Prajñāpradīpa.*

Someone may say that, according to a *sūtra* the ultimate cannot be investigated and is not accessible to logical reasoning, hence it cannot be expressed through inference. But this is wrong. Inference (*anumāna*) in harmony with scripture (*āgama*) negates all concepts and brings about non-conceptual insight. The ultimate is therefore not the object (*viṣaya*) of inference, [inference] none the less has priority, for there is no other way to investigate what is true and false.[6]

---

5. *'dir bshad de bzhin gshegs bka' kun* ‖ *kho bo cag gi tshad ma yin* ‖ *tshad ma yid ches lung yin phyir* ‖ *bzang po dag ni sgrub par byed* ‖ *ces bya ba ni bde bar gshegs pa'i bka' thams cad ni kho bo cag gi tshad ma yin te* | *de dag ni de nyid gzigs pa rnams kyis gsungs pa yin pa'i phyir ro* ‖ *dge legs kyi bsam pa can nyid dag ni de sgrub par byed cing mi mthun par mi byed do* ‖ *lung gzhan dag gi the tshom dang* [‖] *log pa'i blo can gzhan mi byed* ‖ *de phyir de dag sgrub gzhug phyir* ‖ *rigs pa ldan pa'i tshul btsal bya* ‖ (*Peking Tibetan Tripiṭaka*, volume 96, *Dza* 223a/2-4). The Sanskrit of verses 5.8 and 5.9 is quoted by Shotaro Iida, "Agama (Scripture) and Yukti (Reason) in Bhāvaviveka," *Kanakura Festschrift* (Kyoto: Heirakuji Shoten, 1966), pp. 82-83: *atrocyate pramāṇam naḥ sarvan tāthāgataṁ vacaḥ/ āptopadeśaprāmāṇyād bhadro hi pratipadyate* ‖ *nāgamāntarasandigdhaviparyastamatiḥ paraḥ* ‖ *tasmāt tatpratipattyarthaṁ tan mr̥gyo yuktimannayaḥ* ‖

6. *ci ste mdo sde las don dam pa ni brtag mi nus pa dang* | *rtog ge'i spyod pa ma yin pa'i phyir rjes su dpag pas bstan par bya ba ma yin no* ‖ *zhe na* | *lung dang mthun pa'i rjes su dpag pa'i stobs nyid kyis rnam par rtog pa thams cad bkag pa'i rnam par mi rtog pa'i ye shes 'grub pa'i phyir don dam pa ni rjes su dpag pa'i yul ma yin yang de gtso bo ma yin pa ma yin te* ‖ *yang dag pa dang yang dag pa ma yin pa btag pa'i sgrub pa gzhan med pa'i phyir de ni rigs pa ma yin no* ‖ (*Peking Tibetan Tripiṭaka*, volume 95, *Tsha* 311b/1-3). The *sūtra* quoted is virtually identical to the objection given in verse 5.104 of the *Madhyama-*

→

In these passages Bhāvaviveka gives us a glimpse of why logical procedure became such a preoccupation for Mādhyamikas in the later phases of the school's development. There were pressures from outside, from the growing sophistication of the Buddhist and Hindu philosophical schools. There were also pressures from inside to give more sophisticated articulation to the movement from conventional usage to ultimacy. But, above all, there was the presence of an articulate and contrary interpretation of the very Mahāyāna sources on which the Madhyamaka itself was based. Any single challenge might have been enough, but the three together forced the Mādhyamikas in the school's classical period — from Bhāvaviveka to Jñānagarbha, Śāntarakṣita, and Kamalaśīla, and from Candrakīrti to Śāntideva — to explain in ways they had never before been forced to do, what they took reason (*yukti* or *nyāya* = Tibetan *rigs pa*) to be, how it functioned, and on what it was based. Out of the discussion came not only the complex analysis of the two truths that was to dominate certain areas of Tibetan philosophy, but a sophisticated *rapprochement* between Yogācāra and Madhyamaka thought.

Rather than take on the job of tracing the development of the concept of reason through the history of late Madhyamaka — a task that our present, fragmentary knowledge of the late Madhyamaka sources would make extremely difficult — this paper will simply isolate one moment in that complex development for a closer look, in the hope that by examining the argument of a text that comes at a key moment — after Dharmakīrti's expression of Buddhist logic had begun to influence Madhyamaka thought, but before Śāntarakṣita's final synthesis of the Madhyamaka and Yogācāra — we can see a mature Madhyamaka position in the process of being formed.

→ *kahr̥dayakārikās*. Compare *gal te de nyid rtog ge yi* || *spyod yul min phyir rjes dpag pas* || *de mi rtog pa de yi phyir* || *chos rnams chos nyid brtag min na* | (*Peking Tibetan Tripiṭaka*, volume 96, Dza 252a/3-5).

We can also see its evolution, at least in parts, as the struggle of a particular Madhyamaka author to assimilate certain key categories of Buddhist logic and turn them to a distinctly Madhyamaka end.

The text in question is the *Satyadvayavibhaṅga,* "The Distinction between the Two Truths," a work of mixed verse and prose, occupying about thirty folio sides in the Tibetan Tripiṭaka.[7] The Sanskrit original has been lost, but verses quoted in later Madhyamaka works help us fix at least some of the key terminology. For the rest we are dependent on a subcommentary, also in the Tibetan Tripiṭaka, attributed to Śāntarakṣita. Tibetan bibliographies indicate that rGyal-tshab-dar-ma-rin-chen may have written a commentary on the text, but the work seems to be missing from all extant collections of rGyal-tshab's works.[8]

The *Satyadvayavibhaṅga* and its author, Jñānagarbha, occupy an intermediate position between Bhāvaviveka, the source of Svātantrika Madhyamaka, and Śāntarakṣita, who represents the Svātantrika tradition in its classic phase. The Tibetan tradition treats the text, along with Śāntarakṣita's *Madhyamakālaṁkāra* and Kamalaśīla's *Madhyamakāloka,* as one of the three chief works, the so-called *rang-rgyud-shar-gsum,* of Svātantrika Madhyamaka; yet the tradition has not been unanimous about the form of Svātantrika Madhyamaka the text best exemplifies. mKhas-grub, following Tsoṅ-kha-pa, classified Jñānagarbha with Bhāvaviveka

7. The *Satyadvayavibhaṅgakārikā* and its autocommentary are found in the *Derge Tibetan Tripiṭaka* (Tôhoku Nos. 3881 and 3882; Sa lb-3b and 3b-15b). A *pañjikā* attributed to Śāntarakṣita is found in the *Peking Tibetan Tripiṭaka* (Otani No. 5283; Sa l-48b), as well as in the *Derge* (Tôhoku No. 3883; *Sa* 15b-52b).

8. See the reference to *dBu-ma-rang-rgyud-pa'i-slob-dpon-ye-shes-snying-pos-mdzad-pa'i-dbu-ma-bden-gnyis-kyi-ṭikk* in Lokesh Candra, *Materials for a History of Tibetan Literature,* vol. 3 (New Delhi: International Academy of Indian Culture, 1963), p. 619.

as a Sautrāntika-Svātantrika-Mādhyamika.[9] mKhas-grub was led to this position by Jñānagarbha's alleged acceptance, conventionally, of form (*rūpa*) and sound (*śabda*) as external objects different from mind (*citta*).

The historical accounts, however, link Jñānagarbha closely to Śāntarakṣita. Bu-ston associates Jñānagarbha with Śāntarakṣita as a Yogācāra-Mādhyamika.[10] Jñānagarbha is also listed as Śāntarakṣita's immediate predecessor in an ordination lineage recorded in the *Blue Annals.*[11] Śāntarakṣita's alleged authorship of a subcommentary on the *Satyadvaya* has already been mentioned. This and the appearance of quotations from the *Satyadvaya* in Haribhadra's *Abhisamayālaṁkārāloka,* along with other quotations from a commentary on the *Anantamukhanirhāradhāraṇī* also attributed to Jñānagarbha, indicate at the very least that the author of the *Satyadvayavibhaṇga* was closely associated with Śāntarakṣita's circle and was involved, as Śāntarakṣita was, in formulating a response to the challenge of both the Yogācārins Sthiramati and Dharmapāla and the logicians Dharmakīrti and Devendrabuddhi.[12] The historical connections have led modern scholars to place Jñānagarbha's philosophical activity in the early part of the eighth century.[13]

9. F.D. Lessing and A. Wayman, trans., *Mkhas Grub Rje's Fundamentals of the Buddhist Tantras* (The Hague: Mouton, 1968), p. 90.

10. E. Obermiller, trans., *History of Buddhism by Bu-ston,* Part II (Heidelberg: O. Harrassowitz, 1932), p. 135.

11. George N. Roerich, *The Blue Annals* (Calcutta, 1949; rpt. edn. Delhi: Motilal Banarsidass, 1976), p. 34.

12. See Hisao Inagaki, "Haribhadra's Quotations from Jñānagarbha's *Anantamukhanirhāradhāraṇīṭīkā*" in Leslie S. Kawamura and Keith Scott, eds., *Buddhist Thought and Asian Civilization* (Emeryville, Calif.: Dharma Publishing, 1977), pp. 132-44. On Haribhadra's quotations from the *Satyadvaya* see note 26.

13. See, for example, David Seyfort Ruegg, *The Literature of the Madhyamaka School of Philosophy in India* (Wiesbaden: Otto Harrassowitz, 1981), p. 69. Inagaki also reports (Haribhadra's

→

When we move from matters of chronology to the parentage of Jñānagarbha's arguments, the question immediately becomes more complex. This is not to say that the opponents who appear in Jñānagarbha's works are difficult to identify. The subcommentator, whether he be Śāntarakṣita or a pseudonymous substitute, identifies Dharmapāla, Sthiramati, Dharmakīrti, and Devendrabuddhi as their arguments appear in the text. Even the areas in which Jñānagarbha depends, not on specific arguments, but on the general concepts and terminology of the Buddhist logical tradition seem to stand out in sharp relief. The more difficult problem in assessing influence is weighing the importance of these terms. This is true of any philosophical system in which the meaning of a particular argument or concept is determined by its place in the system as a whole. But it is particularly true of the Madhyamaka, in which the very idea of asserting a proposition is so ambiguous and subject to so many qualifications.

A good study still needs to be written about the structure of Madhyamaka thought. The topic is too large to be treated adequately here, but a few words should be said about the patterns in Madhyamaka thought against which Jñānagarbha's individual arguments should be understood. Madhyamaka arguments need to be read constantly with an eye to the way they harmonize and blend with one another. One argument may be particularly negative. Another may be particularly positive. No single argument ever seems to be allowed to stand without some kind of qualification. The reason for this is simply the balance, again, of the Middle Path. Mādhyamikas felt compelled to claim that theirs was a middle (*madhyama*) path between unwarranted reification (*samāropa*) and rejection (*apavāda*). But it is also the element of balance that makes

→ Quotations, p. 143) that this is the opinion of J. Nagasawa, whose book on Jñānagarbha was not available to the author at the time this paper was written.

Madhyamaka so maddeningly elusive. Every assertion seems to be balanced by a denial, and every denial balanced by another assertion, to the point that, to someone without an eye for its inner consistency, the "middleness" of the Madhyamaka seems just another name for philosophical confusion.

What has to be kept in mind is that the Mādhyamikas themselves were convinced there was no confusion. As they saw it, the structure of reason demanded that two perspectives be maintained simultaneously. From one perspective it was impossible to attribute ultimate reality to any of the categories of the conventional order. From another perspective it was quite possible to go about using ordinary categories in a useful way. If one focused on one perspective to the exclusion of the other, one was in danger of falling into one of the extremes that the Middle Path was intended to avoid: one either affirmed too much or denied too much. Yet language itself offers few options other than affirming or denying. Madhyamaka arguments thus naturally led into a pattern in which affirmation was qualified by denial, and denial by affirmation. The effect was sometimes paradoxical; sometimes it merely seemed confusing. But the intention was to maintain two perspectives simultaneously, even when language required at any moment that one option appeared to be favoured over another.

If this pattern in Madhyamaka thought were more widely recognized, it would be possible to avoid many of the common misconceptions in Madhyamaka interpretation. For example, Nāgārjuna's statement (if it is to be called that) *nāsti mama pratijñā* (I have no thesis) is sometimes taken to mean that Mādhyamikas could not make an assertion of any sort.[14] Thus when

14. *Vigrahavyāvartanī* 29: *nāsti ca mama pratijñā tasmān nai-vāsti me doṣah* (quoted from E.H. Johnston and A. Kunst, eds., "The *Vigrahavyāvartanī* of Nāgārjuna with the Author's Commentary," *Mélanges chinois et bouddhiques*, 9 [1948-521: 127). On the interpretation of this phrase see Kamaleswar Bhattacharya, "Mādhyamika et Vaitaṇḍika,"*Journal Asiatique* 263 (1975): 99-102, where Bhattacharya argues that →

Bhāvaviveka claims to hold a thesis, his position is taken as a peculiar anomaly.[15] Yet the pattern of Madhyamaka thought was not to say no absolutely, but no with a qualification. The qualification gave Bhāvaviveka the room he needed to develop the notion of a conventional assertion, and it gave Tsoṅ-kha-pa the opportunity to argue that, even for Candrakīrti, Emptiness constituted a position, albeit a position of a very qualified sort.[16] Greater recognition of this pattern would open up areas of Madhyamaka thought that are generally ignored. Important Madhyamaka works, for example, contain long sections outlining the Madhyamaka view of Buddhahood, how it functions, and how it is attained. If these were viewed not as a perfunctory bow to a tradition that had already been demolished, but as essential elements of the argument itself, they would likely be the focus of more attention.

In Jñānagarbha's case the pattern of movement back and forth between the extremes of denial and affirmation is particularly clear. He sometimes uses categories or arguments from the Buddhist logical tradition, only to turn around moments later and reject them. Sometimes he appears to reject all use of positive categories, only then to reaffirm them. The process would be confusing and the importance of individual

---

→ Mādhyamikas are not guilty of *vitaṇḍā*, which is defined as the failure to maintain a position (*sa pratipakṣa-sthāpanā-hīno vitaṇḍā: Nyāya-Sūtra* 1.2.3.), because they have no position to maintain.

15. See particularly Edward Conze's now well-known remark: "We still have no clear idea of Bhāvaviveka's Svātantrika system, which can be studied only in Tibetan translations, and which seems to have upheld the well-nigh incredible thesis that in Mādhyamika logic valid positive statements can be made." Edward Conze, *Buddhist Thought in India* (Ann Arbor: University of Michigan Press, 1967), pp. 238-39.

16. See Robert A.F. Thurman's translation of the *Legs-bshad-snying-po, Tsoṅg Kha pa's Speech of Gold in the Essence of True Eloquence* (Princeton: Princeton University Press, 1984).

elements would be impossible to evaluate, if one did not recognize that Jñānagarbha proceeds by deliberately shifting his perspective. Sometimes he considers a category from the point of view of ultimate reality, or rather from the point of view of a cognition seeking (and not finding) an ultimately real. At other times he considers a category purely from the point of view of conventional usage. The results of the two types of investigation are quite different, but Jñānagarbha does not consider them contradictory. They are merely the result of applying two different perspectives, both of which need to be recognized to understand the "middleness" of the Middle Path. Jñānagarbha himself says as much in his response to an objector who argues that the Madhyamaka view of two truths is contradictory.

> When examined by reason [a thing] is not real;
> otherwise [i.e. conventionally] it is real.
> Why is it contradictory, then, for the same
> thing to be both real and unreal?[17]

To see how the conception of reason developed, partly in reaction to Dharmakīrti, and partly by incorporating his logical categories in a distinctively Madhyamaka form, the first step is to set out the structure of Jñānagarbha's text.

The argument of the *Satyadvayavibhaṅga* can be divided into four sections. The text begins with a discussion of ultimate truth (*paramārtha satya*), with particular emphasis on the Madhyamaka critique of the Yogācāra conception of self-cognition (*svasaṁvedana*). It then moves on, in the second section, to the definition of conventional truth (*saṁvṛttisatya*). Here Jñānagarbha

---

17. *Antaraśloka* 6 following *kārikā* 15: *rigs pas brtags na bden ma yin* | *de las gzhan du bden pa yin* || *des na gcig la bden nyid dang* || *mi bden par ni ji ltar 'gal* || The objector is identified in the subcommentary as Dharmapāla, as is confirmed by Yuichi Kajiyama in "Bhāvaviveka, Sthiramati, and Dharmapāla," *Wiener Zeitschrift fȍr die Kunde Sud-und Ostasiens* 13 (1969): 201.

makes direct use of Dharmakīrti's concept of useful action (*arthakriyā*) as a criterion for the validity of conventional cognition, but he also uses this section, in a more sceptical way, as an occasion to elaborate the Madhyamaka critique of real causality. In the third section, he takes up the Yogācāra claim that without ultimate reality as a basis there can be no conventional reality. The work then closes with a section of ten verses, or approximately a quarter of the text, devoted to an explanation of how *karma*, Buddhahood, and enlightenment can function meaningfully in a Madhyamaka system.

The Yogācārins, Dharmapāla and Sthiramati, appear at crucial points throughout the text — along with Dharmakīrti and Devendrabuddhi — as critics to provide the occasion for certain key arguments. So it is no accident that we find, behind the first three of the text's four sections, the three basic categories of Yogācāra ontology: absolute, dependent, and imagined nature, or *parinispanna-*, *paratantra-*, and *parikalpitasvabhāva*. In the first section, Jñānagarbha gives his own definition of the ultimate by criticizing the Yogācāra conception of absolute nature, particularly as it is embodied in the concept of pure consciousness, aware only of itself. The second section takes up causality, both in a positive sense, as the ground for valid conventional cognition, and in a negative sense, as the object of well-known Madhyamaka arguments against ultimate causation. Clearly, in the background of this second section, is the Yogācāra concept of *paratantrasvabhāva* or dependent nature.

The correspondence between Jñānagarbha's argument and the three natures of the Yogācāra is least obvious, perhaps, in the case of *parikalpitasvabhāva* or imagined nature. Jñānagarbha's third section begins in verse 23 with what seems simply to be an extension of the argument against *paratantrasvabhāva*. The objector, Sthiramati, argues that if *paratantra* is unreal, then conventional usage (*vyavahāra*) can have no real basis (*āśraya*). Behind Sthiramati's claim lies the Yogācāra notion of ultimate reality as a real substratum over which the imagined distinctions of conventional reality are laid. Jñānagarbha's reply is typically Madhyamaka: he simply asks why conventional reality cannot have an equally conventional basis. The real point of the argument however, begins to emerge in verse 24. Here Jñānagarbha simply turns around and accuses the Yogācāra notion of having an inadequate concept of conventional reality. If conventions require no real basis, as Mādhyamikas claim, then it is the Yogācāra denial of conventional reality (that is, of *parikalpitasvabhāva* or imagined nature) that falls into the extreme of nihilism (*nāstikatva*). Jñānagarbha says:

> According to you [Yogācārins],
>
> 24ab. Imagined nature does not depend on anything.
>
> That is, [you say that] it does not depend [on anything] because it does not exist. But this contradicts perception. Subject and object are of imagined nature, and it is generally accepted (*'grags pa*) that both are perceptible (*mngon sum kho nar*).[18]

The Yogācārins hope to guarantee the "middleness" of the Middle Path by affirming the reality of an absolute nature (*pariniṣpannasvabhāva*) beneath the imagined distinctions of the conventional order, while at the same time, denying the reality of the imagined distinctions themselves. Jñānagarbha, like Bhāvaviveka, turns the Yogācāra system upside down and claims that ultimately there can be no reality, but conventionally all things, including the duality of subject and object that in the Yogācāra characterize imagined nature, must be real. Thus, from the Madhyamaka perspective, the Yogācāra denial that there even is

---

18. *khyod kyi ltar na yang | 'di ltar brtags pa'i ngo bo nyid || ci la'ang mi ltos kho na yin || gal te med pa'i phyir mi ltos so zhe na | mngon sum dang 'gal ba kun tu spyod de | gzung ba dang 'dzin pa ni brtags pa'i ngo bo nyid yin la | de gnyis kyang mngon sum kho nar grags pa de dag yin no ||* (*Derge Tibetan Tripiṭaka Sa* 10b/7-11/1).

imagined nature (*parikalpita-svabhāva*) conventionally is the extreme of nihilism (*ñāstikatva*) that the Middle Path is meant to avoid.[19]

So, on one level Jñānagarbha's argument simply mirrors the Yogācāra position it is meant to defeat. It begins with the conception of ultimate reality, proceeds through an analysis of causation, then ends with a defence of his own conception of conventional reality against the charge of nihilism. The fourth section, in which Jñānagarbha elaborates the concepts of *karma* and Buddhahood, only needs to be read as a footnote to the question of conventional reality in section three. But while Yogācāra categories give the argument its form, the overall pattern still remains characteristically Madhyamaka. The first two sections can be read as expressions of the Madhyamaka denial that anything has ultimate reality. The last two sections then set about rebuilding a conception of conventional reality that will withstand Yogācāra objections. The negations of the first two parts are balanced by the affirmations of the last.

If we are careful, we can find the same sense of balance coming into play when we look at Jñānagarbha's specific development of the concept of reason (*nyāya*). The concept appears to be appropriated in its most positive form in the definition of ultimate truth at the beginning of section one. In the *Pramāṇavārttika*, Dharmakīrti had defined ultimate reality (*paramārtha-sat*) as what is "capable of producing useful action" (*arthakriyā-samartha*), and he identified "useful action" with

---

19. A student of the Tibetan tradition would recognize this argument as the key to distinguishing the subdivisions of the Madhyamaka school. In rejecting the Yogācāra conception of *parikalpita-svabhāva* as overly nihilistic, Jñānagarbha indicates precisely what he thinks is real conventionally. The conception of conventional reality can then be used to distinguish Jñānagarbha, not only from other Svātantrikas, but from Candrakīrti and other members of the Prāsaṅgika wing of the school. The classic presentation of this argument is found in the 25th chapter of Bhāvaviveka's *Prajñāpradīpa*. See Eckel Dissertation cited above.

particulars (*svalakṣaṇa*), rather than with universals (*sāmānya*).[20] Jñānagarbha's definition goes in quite a different direction and puts much more stress on the positive role of reason.

> Ultimate truth (*paramārtha-satya*) is the ultimate's truth. That is, it is the truth of that [cognition] which conforms to reason (*nyāya*). For,
>
> 4ab. Reason (*nyāya*) is ultimate (*paramārtha*), inasmuch as it is free from contradiction (*avisaṁvādin*).
>
> To determine an object by force of reason is to be free from contradiction. A cognition produced by a threefold logical mark (*liṅga*) is ultimate (*paramārtha*) because it is both ultimate (*parama*) and the meaning (*artha*). The object (*artha*) determined by the [cognition] is also the ultimate (*paramārtha*).[21]

Christian Lindtner has pointed out that the definition of truth as that which is free from contradiction (*avisaṁvādin*) is at least as old as Nāgārjuna.[22] But Jñānagarbha's equation of the ultimate (*paramārtha*) with a cognition that conforms to reason (*nyāya*) is quite unexpected. Jñānagarbha's predecessor Bhāvaviveka was committed to the priority of reason in the interpretation of scripture, but the concept of reason is absent from his definition of ultimate truth. Here Jñānagarbha brings the concept into the centre of his system.

---

20. *Pramāṇavārttika* 2.3: *arthakriyāsamarthaṁ yat tad atra paramārthasat* । *anyat saṁvṛttisat proktam te svasāmānya-lakṣaṇe* ॥ (quoted from Swami Dwarikadas Shastri, ed., *Pramāṇa-vārttika of Ācārya Dharmakīrti* [Varanasi: Bauddha Bharati, 1968], p. 100).

21. *dom dam par bden pa ni don dam pa'i bden pa ste* । *de ni rigs pa' i rjes su 'gro ba can gyi bden pa nyid ces bya ba'i tha tshig go* ॥ *gang gi phyir* । *slu ba med pas rigs pa ni don dam yin te* । *rigs pa'i stobs kyis don la nges pa ni slu bar mi 'gyur te* । *de'i phyir tshul gsum pa'i rtags kyis bskyed pa'i rtogs pa gang yin pa de ni dam pa yang yin la* । *don yang yin pas don dam pa'o* ॥ *des gtan la phab pa' i don kyang don dam pa ste* । (*Derge Tibetan Tripiṭaka Sa* 4a/4-5).

22. See *Ratnāvalī* 2.35a quoted by Chr. Lindtner, "Atīśa's Introduction to the Two Truths, and Its Sources," *Journal of Indian Philosophy* 9 (1981): 203.

Should we take the apparently central role of *nyāya* as the indication of a new dependence on Diṅnāga and Dharmakīrti, the great proponents of *bauddha nyāya?* Certainly, Jñānagarbha shows a respect for the logical process that seems to exceed even that of his master. But to say that such a formula indicates direct dependence on Diṅnāga and Dharmakīrti is to overstate the case. Too much was already present to Jñānagarbha in the Madhyamaka tradition itself, both in Bhāvaviveka's own reverence for the interpretive function of reason and in Nāgārjuna's identification of truth as *avisaṁvāda*. But the more important reason for questioning direct influence is that Diṅnāga and Dharmakīrti would both have been uncomfortable with Jñānagarbha's formulation. In the system of the Buddhist logicians, *nyāya* would be considered *anumāna* or inference. With universals (*sāmānya*) as its object, *anumāna* would be a conventional (*saṁvṛtti*) rather than an ultimate (*paramārtha*) truth. From the logicians' point of view, Jñānagarbha has turned reasoning on its head, making ultimate what should only be conventional. Jñānagarbha shared the logicians' reverence for logical reasoning, as did Bhāvaviveka before him, but he used it in a very different way.

The seemingly excessive reverence for rational thought should warn the reader to look for another perspective — a qualification that will move the balance again back to the centre. There actually is no need to read very far. The fourth *pāda* of verse 4 defines conventional truth (*saṁvṛttisatya*) briefly as "the way things appear" (*yathādarśana*). Jñānagarbha then uses verse 5 to distinguish the ultimate from the conventional:

> 5. [The ultimate] cannot exist as it appears, [because] it does not appear at all to one who is omniscient.
>
> The ultimate does not exist as it appears, because it does not appear to the cognition of one who is omniscient. Therefore the *sūtra* says: "Not to see anything is to see the truth."[23]

23. *ji ltar snang ba'i dngos por ni* ॥ *rnam par gnas par mi rung ste* ॥ *shes pa'i dngos po thams cad la* ॥ *ji lta bur yang snang mi 'gyur* ॥ *don dam pa ni ji ltar snang ba* →

The contrast between verses 4 and 5 is deliberate and consistent with a Madhyamaka position at least as old as Bhāvaviveka. As the subcommentator explains, verse 4 gives a definition of *saparyāya-paramārtha,* the ultimate that can be translated or expressed. Verse 5 then gives a definition of *aparyāya-paramārtha,* the inexpressible ultimate.[24] All that can be said of the latter is that it cannot be identified with any concept or image we have of it.[25]

We therefore, have a picture in which *nyāya* is not *the* ultimate, but simply one aspect of ultimacy that may still need to be transcended. But how can Jñānagarbha claim that ultimacy is both conceptual (or identical to reason) and non-conceptual? This seems only to compound the problem by stratifying the ultimate. Not only is there a question of how to go from conventional to ultimate, but now there is the added problem of explaining the transition from the conceptual ultimate to the non-conceptual. To find a reply we have to look ahead to verses 17, 18, and 19, where Jñānagarbha reverses the process of differentiation and explains how, when viewed in the proper way, the distinctions between the two truths disappear. At this point in the argument, Jñānagarbha has finished the critique of real causation and has begun to attack the notion that there can be any real distinctions between things.

> 17. He [the Buddha] considers the very suchness of convention (*saṁvṛtti*) to be [the suchness] of the ultimate (*paramārtha*), because they are not different. For reason also exists as it appears (*yathādarśana*).

→ *bzhin du rnam par gnas pa med de* | *thams cad mkhyen pa'i mkhyen pa nyid la yang mi snang ba'i phyir ro* || *de nyid kyi phyir mdo sde las 'ga' yang mthong ba med pa ni de kho na mthong ba zhes gsungs so* || (*Derge Tibetan Tripiṭaka Sa* 4a/7-4b/1).

24. *Derge Tibetan Tripiṭaka Sa* 18b/3-4.

25. For a comparable distinction in the *Tarkajvālā* see Shotaro Iida, *Reason and Emptiness: A Study in Logic and Mysticism* (Tokyo: The Hokuseido Press, 1980), p. 87.

18. An item appears to the cognition of both parties, and only on this basis are the *dharma, dharmin,* and so forth, constructed.

19. When this is the case, there is an inference. Otherwise [if an item is not accepted by both parties], there is no [inference]. If logicians state such [an inference], who can refute them?[26]

The point here is that reason, or the ultimate, when considered from the point of view of reason — that is, when someone asks how it actually comes into existence — is not different from ordinary, conventional reality. The ultimate, when viewed ultimately, is only conventional. So to say that the ultimate and the conventional are indistinguishable does not mean, as one might suspect, that they share some ultimate substance. It means simply that when they are examined, they are both *conventional* realities. Reason, which is itself the ultimate, is based only on appearance, and appearance is precisely what is conventional.

With the argument of verses 17-19 in mind, we can go back to verse 4 and see it in a different light. Reason is the ultimate, but only from a certain point of view. Reason itself is based only on appearances. So, as long as one stands on appearances, the ultimate is expressible and truly ultimate. Once one probes behind them, what was expressed is no longer seen as ultimate. It is simply conventional. The apparent contradiction between verses 4 and 5 is therefore due to a shifting of perspective. From one perspective, reason is ultimate; from another, there is no ultimate that can be expressed. The argument can be reduced to the paradoxical but, to Svātantrikas, comprehensible statement

26. (17) *kun rdzob de bzhin nyid gang yin* ‖ *de nyid dam pa'i don gyis bzhed* ‖ *tha dad min phyir rigs de yang* ‖ *ji ltar snang ba bzhin du gnas* ‖ *(18) rgol ba gnyi ga'i shes pa la* ‖ *ji tsam snang ba'i cha yod pa* ‖ *de tsam de la brten nas ni* ‖ *chos can chos la sogs par rtog* ‖ (19) *de tshe rjes su dpag pa 'byung* ‖ *gang gi tshe na gzhan na min* ‖ *de bas rigs pa smra ba rnams* ‖ *de skad smra la su zhig 'gog* ‖ (*Derge Tibetan Tripiṭaka Sa* 9b). Verse 17 also appears in Haribhadra's *Abhisamayālaṁkārāloka,* ed. Wogihara (Tokyo: The Toyo Bunko, 1932-35), p. 407: *saṁvṛtes tathatā yaiva paramārthasya sā matā* | *abhedāt so 'pi hi nyāyo yathādarśanam āsthitaḥ* ‖.

that conventionally reason is ultimate, but ultimately reason is only conventional.

To speak of a direct, positive impact of the Buddhist logicians on Jñānagarbha's conception of reason would seem to do clear injustice to the complex balance of Jñānagarbha's position. But there is still no reason to be so paralyzed by the complexity as to overlook the obvious convergences. The role of reason itself is certainly central for Jñānagarbha, as it was for the logicians, and there seems little question that the importance of reason grew rather than diminished for Jñānagarbha, as a sign both of the development of the Svātantrika tradition and of the continuing impact of Diṅnāga and Dharmakīrti. But it is also clear that he held the concept of *nyāya* in a distinctly Madhyamaka balance. It was ultimate, but only as long as it was spared too many embarrassing questions.

A second important area in which Jñānagarbha's concept of reason converges with Dharmakīrti's is in the definition of the second of the two truths. Jñānagarbha gives two formal definitions of conventional truth, then expands the definitions in important ways in his subsequent discussion. The two definitions appear in verses 8 and 12.

> 8. A thing in itself (*vastumātra*), free of any imagined object and arising dependently, is known as correct convention (*tathya-saṁvṛtti*), It is precisely what is imagined that is incorrect.
>
> 12. Though they may be similar in appearance, correct and incorrect convention are distinguished by the ability or inability to produce useful action (*arthakriyā*).[27]

An important further qualification is added in verse 21.

---

27. (8) *brtags pa'i don gyis dben gyur pa* || *dngos tsam brten nas gang skyes te* || *yang dag kun rdzob shes par bya* || *yang dag min ni kun brtags yin* || (12) *snang du 'dra yang don byed dag* || *nus pa'i phyir dang mi nus phyir* || *yang dag yang dag ma yin pas* || *kun rdzob kyi ni dbye ba byas* || (*Derge Tibetan Tripiṭaka Sa* 5b and 6b).

21. [Convention] is the way things appear (*yathādarśana*), *so* analysis (*vicāra*) does not apply to it. An item is contradicted if when analysed it becomes something else.[28]

The three verses together give at least the terms from which Jñānagarbha constructed the concept of conventional truth. First, convention (*saṁvṛtti*) is distinguished from the ultimate (*paramārtha*) by having to do with appearances (*yathādarśana*). These appearances are then further subdivided into two categories: the correct and the incorrect (*tathya* and *mithyā*). Correct convention is defined as a thing in itself (*vastumātra*), arising dependently, not shaped by false conceptions, and capable of producing useful action.

Of the different terms in the definition, the concept of useful action (*arthakriyā*) plays the key role. It is the concept that allows Jñānagarbha to talk about a conventional cognition's empirical validity, in spite of the fact that all convention, including correct convention, is ultimately empty. The commentary on verse 12 indicates how Jñānagarbha thought someone could use "useful action" to test a cognition's validity.

Though the cognitions [i.e. correct and incorrect conventional cognitions] may be similar in the appearance or form they manifest, the world knows that such things as water and a mirage are [respectively] correct and incorrect by determining whether the way they appear is true or false with regard to useful action. In reality (*vastutaḥ*) both are equally empty. But they are distinguished with respect to their appearances. To be true or false with regard to useful action is simply a matter of common consent (*yathāprasiddha*), because that [useful action] also is empty.[29]

---

28. (21) *ji ltar snang bzhin ngo bo'i phyir* ॥ *'di la dpyad pa mi 'jug go* ॥ *rnam par dpyod pa byed na don* ॥ *gzhan du song has gnod par 'gyur* ॥ (*Derge Tibetan Tripiṭaka Sa* 10a).

29. *shes pa gsal ba'i rnam pa snang ba can du 'dra yang* । *ji ltar snang ba bzhin du don byed pa la slu dang mi slu ba yin par nges par byas nas chu la sogs pa dang smig rgyu la sogs pa dag 'jig rten gyis yang dag pa dang yang dag pa ma yin par* →

Jñānagarbha's explanation intersects directly with Dharmakīrti's. In what must be one of the best-known verses of the *Pramāṇavārttika,* Dharmakīrti also ties his conception of valid cognition to the concept of useful action.

> A valid means of knowledge (*pramāṇa*) is a cognition that is free from contradiction. Being free from contradiction means being consistent with useful action (*arthakriyā*).[30]

For both Jñānagarbha and Dharmakīrti, cognitions of the conventional order are grounded in the sense of useful action, which means simply that if they are right they will turn up water and not a mirage.

The similarity with Dharmakīrti is close enough to draw even Jñānagarbha's comment in verse 13. He introduces the verse through an opponent, who points out that their positions seem to be identical:

> [Objection:] Both of us agree that a thing in itself arises dependently and performs useful action. Then is there any difference between us?
>
> [Reply:] No.
>
> 13. If you also think that the way things appear is unreasonable, we agree. But if [you think] it is reasonable, everything is upset.[31]

Jñānagarbha, in effect, concedes that there is no difference in their reliance on useful action, conventionally. But he

---

→ *rtogs so* ॥ *dngos su na gnyis ni ngo bo nyid med pa nyid du ngo bo nyid mtshungs pa kho na'o* ॥ *ji ltar snang ba bzhin du ni rnam par gnas so* ॥ *don byed pa la slu ba dang mi slu ba yang ji ltar grags pa kho na bzhin te* । *de yang ngo bo nyid med pa'i phyir ro* ॥ (*Derge Tibetan Tripiṭaka Sa* 6b/5-7).

30. *pramāṇam avisaṁvādi jñānam arthakriyāsthitiḥ* । *avisaṁvādanaṁ* (*Pramāṇavārttika* 1.3). Translation by Masatoshi Nagatomi.

31. *kho bo dang khyod kyis kyang khas blangs te* । *de la 'u bu cag bye brag ci zhig yod pa ma yin nam* । *bden te* । *gal te khyod kyang rigs min par//ji ltar snang bzhin 'dod na ni* ॥ *'u bu cag la de mtshungs nyid* ॥ *rigs par na ni thams cad 'khrugs* ॥ (*Derge Tibetan Tripiṭaka Sa* 6b/7-7a/1).

immediately moves the discussion to analysis by reason. From that perspective Jñānagarbha accepts no real causation, and his concept of useful action is far from identical to that of the Buddhist logician.

There is no point here in going into Jñānagarbha's arguments against real causation in any detail. It would be interesting only to note in passing, perhaps, as a sign of his reshaping of Madhyamaka arguments in epistemological form, that Jñānagarbha's first line of attack is not against ultimate causation itself, but against the notion that one can have certain knowledge of a causal relationship. But the arguments themselves are of more interest to someone tracing the evolution of Madhyamaka ontology than to someone concerned with Jñānagarbha's conception of reason. It is sufficient simply to say that Jñānagarbha ends where Nāgārjuna did in the first chapter of the *Madhyamakakārikās* : with the notion that nothing can truly arise or cease.

Does this mean, then, that Dharmakīrti's conception of useful action is simply a conventional truth that must be rejected ultimately? In a sense, yes. Jñānagarbha says as much in a verse that is well known in the Tibetan tradition.

> What is ultimate for one is conventional for another, just as one person's mother is considered another person's wife.[32]

But the question is more complicated than simply one of assigning different realities to different categories, as if the categories could be clearly separated. When the two truths are clearly analysed, there is no difference between the ultimate and the conventional. Mādhyamikas speak of two truths and often subdivide them in a way that suggests a clear delineation of levels. But ultimately Mādhyamikas take the prosaic position that truth is one.

---

32. *gzhan gyi don dam byas gang yin || de ni gzhan gyi kun rdzob ste || gzhan gyi mar 'dod gang yin de || gzhan gyi chung mar 'dod pa bzhin ||* (*Derge Tibetan Tripiṭaka Sa* 10a/3-4).

Jñānagarbha takes quite seriously the arguments attributed to Devendrabuddhi and Dharmapāla that the Madhyamaka conception of two truths leads to the attribution of contradictory qualities to the same object. In the form of an objection attributed to Devendrabuddhi, Jñānagarbha says:

> If convention (*saṁvṛtti*) [means that] there is nothing, yet also [means that] things arise, then in the same thing at the same time there is both capability and the lack of capability.[33]

Dharmapāla is credited by the subcommentator with a similar argument in which he claims that it is contradictory to think of the same thing at the same time as both ultimately real and conventionally unreal.[34] The arguments are not easily brushed aside. If Jñānagarbha intends the conventional and the ultimate to be two real and distinct categories, then the fact that they yield contradictory images of the same thing must surely be a contradiction. Jñānagarbha again has to dissolve the real difference between the two perspectives and yet leave them sufficiently distinctive to give different views of the same object.

The first part of his reply does not need to be repeated. He argues, as before, that the difference between ultimate and conventional disappears when they are considered ultimately. So it is too simple to say that Jñānagarbha appropriates the notion of useful action in the conventional realm, rather than in the ultimate. Ultimately, the distinction between the two disappears, and the ultimate is as conventional as the conventional. The more interesting question is to ask how, once the distinctions have been dissolved, Jñānagarbha can again appropriate conventional reality. How can he know that things are empty and still be able to discern an object's useful action? The answer

---

33. *kun rdzob dngos po med yin na* ‖ *skye ba dngos po yin pa'i phyir* ‖ *de tshe dngos po gcig de la* ‖ *nus dang mi nus cig car 'gyur* ‖ (*Derge Tibetan Tripiṭaka Sa* 9a/5-7).

34. *Derge Tibetan Tripiṭaka Sa* 36a/1.

to this question, for Jñānagarbha, comes from a close look at the kinds of questions that push a person over the line from what might be called a form of conventional investigation to the investigation of an object's ultimate reality. The key passage starts with an objection in the first half of verse 20.

> 20ab. According to reason, there is no arising even conventionally.
>
> If neither a *sākāra* cognition nor the opposite can specify [an object], then, as explained earlier, there is no determination of cause and effect. [Cause and effect] are [also] impossible for reasons given earlier in such statements as "many do not produce one," and so forth.[35]

"According to reason" is the key phrase. What Jñānagarbha is arguing is that whenever someone asks whether an object has come into being in and of itself, the discussion passes to a level of analysis on which there can be no satisfactory conclusion. It is a form of "ultimate" analysis, and ultimately nothing can arise. This is just the analysis that would collapse the two truths into one.

By turning the point around Jñānagarbha can then argue that by abstaining from this kind of analysis (*vicāra*) a person can see convention functioning simply on the basis of appearance. If analysis by reason dissolves the conventional into Emptiness, then conventions can only function in the absence of such analysis. Jñānagarbha makes this point in verse 21.

> 21ab. [Convention] is the way things appear, so analysis (*vicāra*) does not apply to it.
>
> If convention is the way things appear, the analysis just mentioned [i.e. is cause and effect cognized by *sākāra* or *nirākāra* cognition, or does many produce one, and so forth] does not apply to it. For,

35. *gal te rigs pa'i stobs kyis na* ‖ *kun rdzob tu yang mi skye dang* ‖ *ci ste kun rdzob tu yang snang ba dang ldan pa dang* | *shes pa cig shos kyis yongs gcod par mi rung ba'i phyir snga ma bzhin du rgyu dang 'bras bu nyid nges pa med pa kho na'o* ‖ *du mas dngos po gcig mi byed* | *ces bya ba la sogs pa gtan tshigs snga ma kho na'i phyir yang de ni rigs pa ma yin no zhes bya bar 'dod na* | (*Derge Tibetan Tripiṭaka Sa* 10a/4-5).

21cd. An item is contradicted if when analysed it becomes something else.

We [Mādhyamikas] do not analyse [convention].
Instead we deny such analysis. If something is
impossible when analysed, it is simply impossible.[36]

A crucial criterion of correct conventional truth is therefore that it not be subjected to a form of causal analysis. It is proper and entirely permissible to ask whether a vision of water is water or a mirage, but the distinction between water and a mirage disappears when someone asks whether either *actually* arises. The qualifier "actually" (or *vastutaḥ*) invokes the analysis of the causal process, in which Mādhyamikas contend no real entity can be found.

The addition of "no analysis" (*avicāra*) to the definition of correct conventional truth completes a list of criteria that became common in late Svātantrika literature. In the *Madhyamakālaṁkāra*, for example, Śāntarakṣita defines correct conventional truth:

A phenomenon (*dharma*) which arises and is destroyed; which only satisfies when it is not analysed (*avicāraramaṇīya*), and is capable of efficiency (*arthakriyāsāmarthyavāt*) — is maintained to be the genuine relative truth (*tathya-sṁvr̥tti*).[37]

The same formula also appears in the *Madhyamakaratnapradīpa*, a text that has been attributed to Bhāvaviveka, but which may just

36. *ji ltar snang bzhin ngo bo'i phyir* ‖ *'di la dpyad pa mi 'jug go* ‖ *ci ste kun rdzob ni ji ltar snang ba bzhin yin te* | *de la ni ji skad bshad pa'i dpyad pa'i gnas med pa nyid do* ‖ *'di ltar* | *rnam par dpyod pa byed na don* ‖ *gzhan du song bas gnod par 'gyur* ‖ *kho bo cag ni 'di la dpyod par mi byed kyi* | *dpyod par byed pa la ni 'gog par byed do* ‖ (*Derge Tibetan Tripiṭaka Sa* 10a/7-10b/1).

37. *Madhyamakālaṁkāra* 64: *ma brtags gcig pu'i nyams dga' zhing* ‖ *skye dang 'jig pa'i chos can pa* ‖ *don byed pa dag nus rnams kyis* ‖ *rang bzhin kun rdzob pa yin rtogs* ‖ (*Derge Tibetan Tripiṭaka Sa* 70b/6-7). This verse is also quoted in Atiśa's *Satyadvayāvatāra*. See Chr. Lindtner, "Atiśa's Introduction to the Two Truths, and Its Sources," *Journal of Indian Philosophy* 9 (1981): 193. The translation is Lindtner's.

as well date from a later period.[38] The notion that convention cannot be subjected to analysis without ceasing to be convention also plays an important role in Candrakīrti's account of the way Madhyamaka language acquires its meaning.[39] Where the notion originated is still uncertain, but its importance in the classical Madhyamaka accounts of conventional truth would be hard to overestimate.

How then does Jñānagarbha finally account for the appearance of conventional causality? He asks himself the question and, with a simplicity worthy of Dōgen, gives his own answer.

> 22ab. Tell us why one thing appears to be caused by another.
>
> 22cd. It is just that one thing appears to be caused by another. What more is there to say?[40]

To say that correct conventional truth is produced from causes, capable of useful action, and not subject to analysis, for Jñānagarbha, is sufficient to ground the causal process. No other ultimate ground is necessary.

With Jñānagarbha's account of the two truths before our eyes, it takes a certain fondness for ambiguity finally to summarize his concept of reason. The first thing to say is simply that for him reason is of central importance. From the idea of

38. See Lindtner's translation of portions of this work in "Atiśa's Introduction," pp. 169ff.

39. See for example Candrakīrti's statement in the first chapter of the *Prasannapadā* "Such analysis is not carried out in common, conventional usage, and it is without [such] analysis that common categories exist." *laukike vyavahāra itthāmvicārāpravṛtter avicārataś ca laukikapadārthānām astitvāt* (Sanskrit quoted from L. de La Vallée Poussin, ed., *Mūlamadhyamakakārikās (Mādhyamikasūtras) de Nāgārjuna avec la Prasannapadā Commentaire de Candrakīrti*, Bibliotheca Buddhica, 4 (St. Petersburg, 1903-13), pp. 67.

40. (22) *ci yi phyir na rgyu 'di las* ॥ *der snang ba 'di smra bar byos* ॥ *'di 'dra 'di ni rgyu 'di las* ॥ *snang ste ci zhig smra bar bya* ॥ (*Derge Tibetan Tripiṭaka Sa* 10b).

useful action (*arthakriyā*), or the empirical justification for correct conventional judgements, to the identification of reason with the conceptual ultimate, Jñānagarbha makes strong and consistent use of epistemological categories central to Dharmakīrti and the Buddhist logical tradition. The impression, from one point of view, is of a system in which there is a cognitive ascent from correct conventional truths, based on useful action, through reason (or the conceptual ultimate), again based on appearance, to the cessation of all concepts, identified with the non-conceptual ultimate. But we also see that the use of reason in the curious intermediate category of the conceptual ultimate blurs the distinctions between strata, so that from the point of view of reasoned analysis, what appeared to be levels are seen simply as different aspects of the same thing (or no thing). Viewed conventionally the ultimate is ultimate. Viewed ultimately the ultimate is only conventional. What from one perspective seems to be a cognitive ascent, seems from another to be more of a circle, with reason leading to a questioning of conventional categories, while at the same time leading to the understanding that the questioning itself is only conventional.

The image of a straight line that bends on itself to form a circle is a common image of enlightenment in the Mahāyāna tradition. What is missing from our picture, however, but is strongly stressed in the accounts of Emptiness in the Ch'an or Zen traditions, is the soteriological significance of the passage around the circle. In the dissolving of conventional categories, followed by their reappropriation in a new spirit, the Mādhyamikas see an image of Buddhahood. If this is so, it should give us new eyes for the fourth section of Jñānagarbha's work. The last quarter of the text has to do with Buddhahood and might seem no more than a perfunctory addition to the central argument against the Yogācāra unless one understands that the point, or *artha*, of such an argument is to reappropriate the category of Buddhahood and outline the cognitive transformation that can help achieve it.

In an important article on *arthakriyā,* Masatoshi Nagatomi has pointed out that for Dharmakīrti the meaning of *artha* in *arthakriyā* is not exhausted by the object — like the water in Jñānagarbha's example — that is capable of producing a recognizable effect.[41] *Artha* also refers to the *puruṣārtha,* the goal of human life. The empirical verification, if it is still to be called that, of Jñānagarbha's argument is therefore more than the conventional agreement about appearances out of which reason grows. It is also the final goal of life, whether conceived as the cessation of suffering or as Buddhahood, to which the philosopher's practice of rational argument is meant to lead.[42]

41. Masatoshi Nagatomi, "Arthakriyā," *Dr. V. Raghavan Felicitation Volume, Adyar Library Bulletin* 31-32 (1967-68): 52-72, and "The Framework of the *Pramāṇavārttika,* Book I," *Journal of the American Oriental Society* 79 (1959): 263-66.

42. The author's translation of Jñānagarbha's *Satyadvayavibhaṅgakārikā* and *vṛtti* with introduction and explanatory notes is forthcoming from the State University of New york Press.

17

Ratnakīrti on Apoha[1]

Gopikamohan Bhattacharya

THE theory of *apoha* (i.e. differentiation theory of meaning) has perplexed Indian philosophers of different ages. It has a long history from Diṅnāga to Ratnakīrti and we notice three different stages in the evolution of the Buddhist *apoha* theory of meaning of an expression. At the outset, it needs to be mentioned that to the Buddhist words have their origin in a concept (*vikalpa*) and they refer to a concept. Words and their meanings or what we understand by a word are both fictions of our imagination. An expression cannot directly refer to a unique particular (*svalakṣaṇa*) which alone is real. As a unique particular is alone real and since what we understand from a word are thought-constructs, the so-called word-meaning relation cannot be logically asserted. Such a relation works between a word-universal and a corresponding object-universal, which are also produced in the mind through thought-construction.

Communication is possible only through universals — the unreal fictions — and, as the unique particular is alone real, it would be a natural corollary to define meaning in the terms of double negation (*anyāpoha*). To be explicit: when I utter the word "cow" the hearer understands, so a Naiyāyika would think, a

1. This paper is a slightly revised version of the one read at the conference on Buddhist Studies at Oxford University in August 1982. I wish to thank my friend Professor J.T. O'Connell for suggesting some stylistic improvements.

positive individual cow. But the fact is otherwise. On hearing the word "cow" I understand its meaning — it is not necessary that the real cow must be present before me. Thus the word's relation with the particular (*svalakṣaṇa*) cannot be established. The word expresses its meaning without the particular; so the meaning is a logical construct. But without a particular our behaviour would not be possible, because when one is asked to bring or tie a cow his activity refers to a particular. So we have to establish some connection between the uttered word and the particular with which we deal. That connection is established through double negation. The word presents a concept (*vikalpa*) which is not the universal cowness, but an exclusion of all non-cows which finally determines the particular. When I utter the word "cow," at once all non-cow possibilities are rejected. What remains is the particular, which is qualified by this exclusion of non-cow possibilities. In the case of the word "cow," its utterance also excludes the possibilities of all utterances of non-cow words. In perceptual awareness the particular shines in its own glory as such; in verbal awareness of words the same particular is determined by the exclusion of all contrary possibilities. As Matilal puts it: "The only way a name can identify, or refer to, a particular is through negation and elimination of other concepts."[2]

An analysis of the text of *Apohasiddhi*[3] (*AS*) of Ratnakīrti shows that it is a very brief reworking of his teacher Jñānaśrī's *Apohaprakaraṇam*[4] (*AP*). Ratnakīrti has rejected almost the same

2. B.K. Matilal, *Epistemology, Logic and Grammar in Indian Philosophical Analysis* (The Hague: Mouton, 1971), 41.

3. A. Thakur (ed.), *Ratnakīrtinibandhāvalī of Ratnakīrti*, Tibetan Sanskrit Works Series, vol. 3 (Patna: K.P. Jayaswal Research Institute, 1959). [*AS*]

4. A. Thakur (ed.), *Jñānaśrīmitranibāndhāvalī of Jñānaśrī*, Tibetan Sanskrit Works Series, vol. 5 (Patna: K.P. Jayaswal Research Institute, 1959). [INM]. The following table shows Ratnakīrti's indebtedness to Jñānaśrī:

→

non-apoha arguments as his teacher. Where Jñānaśrī has not referred to his opponents by name, Ratnakīrti has specifically

---

→ *AS*	*AP*
cf. pp. 53, 4	p. 202, 12-14
53, 8-18	201, 15-202, 4
53, 19-22	202, 7-11
54, 3-6	206, 15-16
54, 9-12	203, 19-21
54, 12-14	205, 12-16
54, 14-15	206, 13-14
54, 16-24	206, 25-207, 5
54, 25-28	203, 22-204, 2
55, 5	206, 1
55, 6-9	206, 6-9
55, 16-56, 1	208, 11-209, 3
55, 3-6	210, 3-5
56, 7	219, 3
56, 11-16	211, 7-13
56, 18-21	212, 18-21
56, 23-25	213, 3-5
56, 25-26	213, 7
57, 1-5	213, 11-14
57, 6-8	213, 15-17
57, 16-19	215, 3-5
57, 23-24	215, 8-9
58, 1-4	220, 2-5
58, 10	221, 11
58, 10-12	221, 11-14
58, 14-17	221, 20-24
58, 18-23	222, 3-8
58, 24-25	222, 10-11

named them. He took up for criticism the arguments of Kumārila, Nyāyabhūṣaṇakāra, Trilocana, Jayanta and Vācaspati. Both have cited the same Buddhist authors.

Ratnakīrti has first outlined three possible construals of the *apoha* doctrine. These may be understood in the following way:

> (i) *Apoha* might mean the external object. In that case it will have a cognition as "This is excluded from others" (*idam anyasmāt apohyate*).
>
> (ii) Or *apoha* might refer to the representation cognition. In that case we will have a cognition of the form: "From this others are excluded" (*asmād vā any ad apoyate*).
>
> (iii) Or it may refer to the exclusion itself. In that case we will have a cognition of the form: "In this way others are excluded" (*asmin vā anyad apohyate*). To be explicit: *apoha* is expressed as "A excludes B." Now in this we can give primacy either to "A" or to "B" or to "exclusion" itself.

Next, Ratnakīrti says that alternatives (i) and (ii) are excluded, because *apoha* refers to a particular and not simply to the exclusion of the opposite. Alternative (iii) does not stand up either, because it is contradicted by our experience. When I hear the expression "There is fire on the mountain" I understand existence of a particular fire and not merely the negation of non-fire. Ultimately, Ratnakīrti accepts that *apoha* means the external object itself as determined by the exclusion of others.[5]

→	59, 6-8		222, 23-25
	59, 9-11	→	223, 15-18
	59, 12-13		224, 6-7
	59, 14-16		224, 9-11
	59, 20-60, 3		225, 1-9
	60, 10-11		229, 3-4
	60, 12-13		229, 14-15

5. *anyāpohaviśiṣṭavidhiḥ śabdānām arthaḥ*. *AS*, p. 54, 2.

Then Ratnakīrti presents an opposing view or *pūrvapakṣa* which seeks to suggest that when something is known to be excluded, the exclusion from the contrary is known through implication. The other *pūrvapakṣa* presented is that the exclusion (*nivṛtti*) of the contrary is presented as a qualifier (*viśeṣaṇatayā*) of the thing denoted.

Diṅnāga's theory of *apoha* is influenced by his theory of inference.[6] In his opinion both inference and the cognition from a word involve the same process, i.e. the exclusion of the contrary. As a logical mark (*liṅga*) proves that which is to be inferred (*sādhya*) through the exclusion of others (*anyāpoha*), likewise a word tells us about what it means by excluding it from what it is not. Let us take an example. When I infer fire from smoke on the mountain, the logical mark "smoke" does not prove a particular fire, but fire-as-such. But fire-as-such is a concept, a mental construct. Then how does one reach to the particular fire? Diṅnāga would say that through the process of exclusion of non-fire we get to the notion of fire. Similarly, a word does not denote its object directly, but "captures" the object by excluding it from what it is not. Diṅnāga argues that to denote a tree we can use any one of the terms, "existent" (*sat*), "tree" (*vṛkṣa*), "substance" (*dravya*), "earthly substance" (*pārthiva*), etc. But if a word is said to point to a real entity, all these terms would be synonymous, because they all refer to the self-same object. The other possibility would be to say that all these words characterize the different aspects of the tree — a position not

6. M. Hattori (1980) cites the following verse of *Pramāṇasamuccaya*, chapter 5 quoted in *Tattvasaṁgrahapañjikā* (Varanasi: Bauddha Bharati Series, 1968), 539,17-18: *na pramānāntaraṁ śābdam anumānāt tathā hi tat* | *kṛtakatvādivatsvārtham anyāpohena bhāsate* || (Word is not an independent means of cognition different from inference, because the meaning of it [word] is expressed through the exclusion of others, [in the same way] as [in inference the logical mark] effecthood, etc. [proves the inferable property] through the exclusion of what it is not.)

logically tenable because the self-same object cannot have in it different realities. Hence, in fact a word does not denote a real object, but it functions only to exclude (*vyavaccheda*) an infinite number of other possibilities. So, the word, "existent" tells only about the exclusion of non-existent possibilities, the word "substance" tells only about the exclusion of non-substance possibilities, and so on.[7]

The above discussion was introduced to show that according to Diṅnāga the meaning of a word consists solely in the exclusion of the contrary possibilities — a theory which met with vehement objections at the hands of Realists such as Kumārila and Uddyotakara. They have interpreted Diṅnāga's theory as a negative theory of meaning and have argued against his theory by bringing the charge of infinite regress. If the meaning of *A* is ascertained solely in terms of the exclusion of its contrary, i.e. "not non-*A*," then the meaning of "not non-*A*" would be understood through the exclusion of its contrary, i.e. "not non-(not non-*A*)" and so on.

The charges levelled against the *apoha* theory served as an impetus for Śāntarakṣita to give a new turn to the theory. He admits that a word denotes a positive meaning. What is denoted by a word is the image of a thing (*artha-pratibimba*), but he also argued that the negative aspect of the meaning cannot be totally ignored. He says that a word first denotes a positive meaning, the image, and thereafter by implication (*sāmarthyena*) the negative

7. Diṅnāga sets forth this theory in the following verse: *bahutve py abhidheyasya na śabdāt sarvathā gatiḥ* । *svasambandhānurūpyāt tu vyavacchedārthakāry asau* ॥ (Although the thing to be denoted has many [aspects], a word cannot denote [all of them]. It functions as an instrument of exclusion in accordance with its relation [with that particular aspect of the thing.) See E. Frauwallner, "Dignaga, sein Werk und seine Entwicklung," *Wiener Zeitschrift fòr die Kunde Sud-und Ostasiens* 3 (1959); cf. also M. Hattori, "Apoha and Pratibhā," in *Sanskrit and Indian Studies*, edited by M. Nagatomi et al. (Dordrecht: D. Reidel Publishing Co., 1980), p. 70.

aspect, i.e. the exclusion from the contrary, is ascertained. Obviously, Śāntarakṣita wants to attach to the word two aspects of meaning, primary and secondary, and the exclusion from the contrary comes under the scope of the latter.

Ratnakīrti records another view of the negativists, who hold that the primary meaning of an expression consists in the exclusion and that we get the positive meaning by logical construction (*vikalpa*). Ratnakīrti rejects all these theories as untenable. He holds that there are two shades of meaning, primary and secondary. But the meaning of an expression is the positive thing, say "cow" individual, qualified by the exclusion of the other, i.e. what is not "non-cow." He differs from Śāntarakṣita when he says that we do not find any successive stages of grasping (*pratipattikrama*) of affirmative and then negative meaning. Nor is the converse true, i.e. we do not understand a positive meaning *after* having ascertained the negative meaning. But the positive and negative meanings are the different aspects of the same meaning complex. The grasping of the positive meaning and exclusion of other meanings (*anyāpoha*) occur simultaneously — the latter qualifying the former — i.e. the meaning of the expression "cow" is understood as "cow-excluded-from-non-cow." Whenever we understand something we understand it as qualified by the exclusion of others. All our actions are directed to an individual thing, but at the same time that desired thing is understood in terms of exclusion of the undesired things. As already stated, when one is asked to tie a "cow" he is at the same time directed to avoid tying "horse," etc. This act of selecting a particular type of individual proves that these two acts of understanding occur simultaneously in the same way as when we see a "blue lotus." The "blue" colour and the "lotus" are cognized in one sweep: there is no time sequence in grasping the positive and the negative meaning. Suppose we use the word *indīvara* to denote a blue lotus. The word *indīvara* does not contain any reference to blue. But nevertheless, the utterance of the word *indīvara* conveys the impression of blue and lotus simultaneously. Similarly the word "cow" may not contain any direct reference to the exclusion of non-cows, but nevertheless, as soon as the word "cow" is uttered, we understand the particular as distinguished by non-cows in one sweep.[8]

In his attempt to reject the exclusively positive and exclusively negative theories of meaning Ratnakīrti depends upon Diṅnāga, who says: "A word conveys a positive meaning qualified, by the exclusion of the other things."[9] Here also Ratnakīrti drew upon Dharmakīrti. Dharmakīrti says:

> It cannot be said that a word has two types of denotation — one serving exclusion of the contrary and the other conveying its own meaning — because as soon as the meaning is conveyed the exclusion of what is different from it is understood, because the referent here is unique which excludes everything but itself. That which does not present itself cannot exclude anything.[10]

It is a case of mutual implication — one is the logical counterpart of the other.

The basic thesis of *apoha* can be ascertained, as Ratnakīrti puts it, from the consideration of redundancy. To the *non-apoha*

---

8. *yathā nīlotpale niveśitād indīvaraśabdān nīlotpalapratītau tatkāle eva nīlimasphūraṇam anivāryaṁ tathā gośabdād api agavāpoḍhe niveśitād gopratītau tulyakālam eva viśeṣaṇatvāt ago 'pohasphuraṇam anivāryam. AS*, p. 54,9-12; cf. *AP* (JNM, p. 203, 19-21).

9. *śabdo 'rthāntaranivṛttiviśiṣṭān eva bhāvān āha.* Quoted in *Pramāṇavārttika-Svavṛtti* (ed. R. Gnoli, Roma: ISMEO, 1960), 62-63; *Tattvasaṁgrahapañjikā* (ed. Varanasi, 1968), 408; cf. also E. Frauwallner, "Beiträge zur Apohalehre," in *Frauwallner Kleine Shcriften*, ed. G. Oberhammer and E. Steinkellner (Wiesbaden: Franz Steiner Verlag GMBH, 1982), p. 413.

10. *Pramāṇavārttika-Svavṛtti* (ed. R. Sankrityayan): *ata eva śabde tadanyavyāvṛttiḥ svārthābhidhānaṁ ca na vyāpāradvayaṁ, svārthasyābhidhānad eva tadanyavyāvṛttigatiḥ, svārthasya bhedarūpatvāt na hy anvaya avyāvṛttimataḥ, nāpy ananvayino vyāvṛttiḥ.*

theorists a word has always a reference to an actual object. Ratnakīrti says:

> If by a word we understand in its entirety the particular to which it refers, then such expressions or sentences, conveying affirmation and negation, would be redundant. For example, if we understand by the expression "cow" the cow-particular in its entirety, it would be redundant to use such sentences as "the cow exists" or "the cow does not exist."[11]

For whatever is conveyed by the predicate expression should already be included in our knowledge of the particular. Hence the predicate expression would be redundant. But ordinarily we do use such expressions as "the cow exists," "the cow stands there" or "the cow does not exist" and in all such cases we do not treat them to be redundant expressions. Thus the non-*apoha* theorists would run counter to such common sense.

Ratnakīrti finally concludes that the word refers to a positive entity. That positive entity may be an external object like the cow or it may be the representation of the cow in our cognition (*buddhyākāra*).[12] Now a problem arises when we say something about that reference, i.e. either affirm something of it or negate something about it. For the representation of the cow in our cognition is amenable to neither negation nor affirmation because the cow-form is revealed in our self-awareness (*svasaṁvedana*) by itself. Also the external object is amenable to neither affirmation nor negation, for it is not presented in the cognition derived from the word. And if it is not represented in cognition by a word we cannot affirm or negate anything by using a word with regard to it. But this leads to the great problem in explaining our ordinary verbal usages where we do affirm or

---

11. *svalakṣaṇātmaṇi vastūni vācye sarvātmanā pratipatteḥ vidhiniṣedayor ayogaḥ.* *AS*, p. 56, 6-7 - *AP* (JNM), p. 219, 3.

12. *tad evaṁ vidhir eva śabdārthaḥ. sa ca bāhyo 'rtho buddhyākāraś ca vivakṣitaḥ.* *AS*, p. 60, 5.

negate things with regard to something else. Therefore the final solution is this: the external object itself becomes amenable to both affirmation and denial at the conventional level (*saṃvṛtti*), but it becomes so only by being an external object. Here Ratnakīrti quotes Jñānaśrī, who says that at the ultimate level neither the external object nor its representation is amenable to affirmation, but rather it is either the external object at the conventional level or its representation that becomes amenable to affirmation.[13]

13. *nākārasya na bāhyasya tattvato vidhisādhanam* | *bahir eva hi saṁvṛttyā saṃvṛttyāpi tu nākṛteḥ*. *AS*, p. 60,10-11 = *AP* (JNM), p. 229,3-4.

Index